Stress Management in
Law Enforcement

Stress Management in Law Enforcement

Edited by

Leonard Territo

and

James D. Sewell

CAROLINA ACADEMIC PRESS
Durham, North Carolina

Library of Congress Cataloging-in-Publication Division

Stress management in law enforcement / edited by Leonard Territo,
James D. Sewell.
    p.   cm.
    Includes bibliographical references.
    ISBN 0-89089-956-8
    1. Police—job stress. 2. Police—Mental health services.
3. Stress management. I. Territo, Leonard. II. Sewell, James D.,
1950–   .
HV7936.J63S77   1998
363.2'01'9—dc21   98-40730
                                                                    CIP

Carolina Academic Press
700 Kent Street
Durham, North Carolina 27701
Telephone (919) 489-7486
Fax (919) 493-5668
E-mail: cap@cap-press.com
www.cap-press.com

Printed in the United States of America.

*Dedicated to all law enforcement officers and their families
as well as to our good friend, colleague and mentor, Hal Vetter.*

Contents

30   Gil Watson (1986) "Thoughts on Preventive Counseling
     for Police Officers," in J.T. Reese and H.A. Goldstein
     (eds.), *Psychological Services for Law Enforcement*. U.S.
     Government Printing Office, Washington, DC   341

31   Rory Gilbert (1986) "A Coordinated Approach to
     Alcoholism Treatment," in J.T. Reese and H.A. Goldstein
     (eds.), *Psychological Services for Law Enforcement*. U.S.
     Government Printing Office, Washington, DC   349

Part Eight — Management Issues in Dealing with Police Stress   359

32   James D. Sewell (1986) "Administrative Concerns in Law
     Enforcement Stress Management," *Police Studies*, 9(3),
     153–159 (This journal is now *Policing: An International
     Journal of Police Strategies and Management*)   361

33   Peter Finn (1997) "Reducing Stress: An Organization-
     Centered Approach," *FBI Law Enforcement Bulletin*,
     66(8), 20–26   373

34   Ellen M. Scrivner (1994) *Controlling Police Use of Excessive
     Force: The Role of the Police Psychologist*. National Institute
     of Justice Research in Brief   383

35   Bill Rehm (1996) "Retirement: A New Chapter, Not the End
     of the Story," *FBI Law Enforcement Bulletin*. 65(9), 6–11   393

About the Editors

Dr. Leonard Territo is Professor of Criminology at the University of South Florida, Tampa. Prior to joining the faculty at the University of South Florida, he served first as a Major and then as Chief Deputy (Undersheriff) with the Leon County Sheriff's Department, Tallahassee, Florida. He also served for almost nine years with the Tampa Police Department and had assignments as a patrol officer, motorcycle officer, homicide, rape, and robbery detective, internal affairs detective, and member of the police academy training staff. Dr. Territo is the former Chairperson of the Department of Police Administration and Director of the Florida Institute for Law Enforcement at St. Petersburg Junior College.

Dr. Territo has co-authored some of the leading books in the law enforcement including *Police Civil Liability: Police Administration* (in its 4th edition), *Criminal Investigation* (in its 6th edition), *Crime and Justice in America* (in its 5th edition), *The Police Personnel Selection Process*, *Stress and Police Personnel, Hospital and College Security Liability*, and *College Crime Prevention and Personal Safety Awareness*. His books are used in over 1000 colleges and universities nationwide and he has had numerous articles published in nationally-recognized law enforcement and legal journals.

Among his professional distinctions, Dr. Territo was selected as Florida's Outstanding Criminal Justice Educator by the Florida Criminal Justice Educators Association, was cited for ten years of Meritorious Service to the Florida Police Chiefs Association, was given the Outstanding Teacher Award by the College of Social and Behavioral Sciences, University of South Florida, Tampa, and was cited for 25 years of teaching and meritorious service to the Florida Policy Academy, Tampa.

Dr. Territo has served as a lecturer throughout the United States and has instructed a wide variety of police subjects to thousands of law enforcement officials.

Dr. James D. Sewell is the Regional Director of the Tampa Bay Regional Operations Center. He was appointed Regional Director of the Tampa Bay Regional Operations Center within The Florida Department of Law Enforcement (FDLE) on November 1, 1996, after serving for over two years as Director of its Division of Criminal Justice Information Systems and over three years as Director of the Florida Criminal Justice

Executive Institute. Before the latter appointment, Dr. Sewell served as Chief of Police for the City of Gulfport, Florida, from March 1986 to August 1990, and, for nine months, also served as Acting City Manager.

From December 1982 to February 1986, he served as Director of the Office of Management and Planning Services with the Florida Department of Highway Safety and Motor Vehicles. During an earlier tenure with the Florida Department of Law Enforcement, Dr. Sewell held a variety of positions including Deputy Director of the Division of Criminal Justice Information Systems, Deputy Director of the Division of Local Law Enforcement Assistance, and Chief of the Criminal Intelligence Bureau. Prior to joining FDLE in 1980, he was a Lieutenant with The Florida State University Department of Public Safety and supervised the Support Services Section, including the Crime Prevention Unit.

Dr. Sewell hold a B.S., M.S., and Ph.D. in Criminology from The Florida State University. His primary area of dissertation research was in law enforcement stress. He has published over forty articles, principally on law enforcement management and law enforcement stress issues, in academic and professional journals and is a graduate of the Florida Criminal Justice Executive Institute Chief Executive Seminar (Eighth Class) and F.B.I. National Academy (114th Session).

Acknowledgments

We wish to express our thanks and indebtedness to the many distinguished authors for allowing us to use the results of their hard earned labors. Without their dedicated efforts this book would never have come to fruition. We also wish to thank the many publishers who have allowed us to use the materials from their books and journals: Chapter 1, Lennart Levi, "Stress As a Cause of Disease," reprinted from *Stress: Sources, Management, and Prevention* by Lennart Levi, M.D.; with the permission of Liveright Publishing Corporation. Copyright © 1967 by Liveright Publishing Corporation; Chapter 2, James C. Coleman, "Life Stress and Maladaptive Behavior," reprinted with the permission of the American Occupational Therapy Association, Inc. Copyright © 1973, *The American Journal of Occupational Therapy*, vol. no. 27, Issue no. 4, pp. 169–180; Chapter 4, Thomas E. Malloy and G. Larry Hayes, "The Police Stress Hypothesis: A Critical Evaluation," reprinted by permission of Sage Publications, Inc., Copyright © 1988; Chapter 27, Robert P. Delprino and Charles Bahn, "National Survey of the Extent and Nature of Psychological Services in Police Departments," reprinted by permission of the American Psychological Assoc. Copyright © 1988; and Chapter 28, Laurence Miller, "Tough Guys: Psychotherapeutic Strategies with Law Enforcement and Emergency Services Personnel," reprinted with the permission of the Division of Psychotherapy (29) of the American Psychological Association. Copyright © 1995. In Chapter 32, James D. Sewell, "Administrative Concerns in Law Enforcement Stress Management," the journal, formerly titled *Police Studies*, is now *Policing: An International Journal of Police Strategies and Management*.

We also wish to thank our publisher, Keith R. Sipe, for sharing our conviction that this book will make a significant contribution to the law enforcement profession.

Typing and numerous other clerical services were provided by a number of people who collectively made innumerable contributions. Most especially we want to thank Carole Rennick and Marianne Bell for the long hours they devoted to typing the manuscript and Brian Stephens for his superb computer and editorial expertise.

Preface

This book has been designed for three different audiences: first, academicians who have a scholarly interest in police stress and who may also teach the subject; second, police administrators who must deal with the negative effects of stress on their officers on a daily basis; and third, police officers who work on the streets and are regularly exposed to violence, cruelty, and aggression.

This book has been divided into the following eight sections.

Part One — Understanding Stress provides the reader with an orientation and introduction to the topic of stress and some of its principal psychological, physiological, and social consequences. It acquaints the reader with some basic concepts and terminology relating to stress.

Part Two — Stress and the Police Officer examines some of the coping behaviors engaged in by police officers to deal with stress, the events police officers view as most stressful, certain health problems associated with police work (i.e., coronary risk), and the insidious and costly nature of police cynicism.

Part Three — Police Suicide discusses one of the most destructive manifestations of stress in police work—namely, suicide. The selected articles will assist the reader in understanding why police suicides occur and the ways in which they can be prevented.

Part Four — Stress and the Police Family examines the toll exacted from spouses, children and relatives of police personnel as a result of the stressful aspects of police work. The alarmingly high rate of marital discord which too often includes violence in the police family and divorce is only one of the most visible consequences of job-related stress. Other effects on the police family include chronic family bickering and strife; the disruption of family-centered activities due to irregular work schedules; and incidents of delinquency and promiscuity, and school and adjustment problems among their children.

Part Five — The Trauma of Law Enforcement focuses on those features of police work that often expose officers to crisis or disaster situations with people violently killed or injured. This regular and consistent contact may—and often does—result in vicarious traumatization as well as post-traumatic stress.

Part Six — Coping with Stress looks at the ways in which some police departments deal with death in the line of duty and the means by which departments assist family members to cope with the death and its devastating impact. Some of the articles in this section also address critical incident debriefing and the concept of peer counseling.

Part Seven—Psychological Services for Law Enforcement Personnel examines the extent and nature of psychological services in police departments as well as some of the techniques and external programs determined to be useful in police psychological services. Issues of alcoholism and confidentiality are also discussed.

Part Eight—Management Issues Dealing with Police Stress examines the role of the psychologist in assisting police officers in controlling the use of force and the ways in which the organization itself can reduce stress. This section also deals with the difficulties encountered by police officers who have reached the end of their careers and are going into retirement.

Stress Management in
Law Enforcement

Part One

Understanding Stress

Over the last several years, society in general and a number of professional fields in particular have shown increasing concern over the concept and visible manifestations of the phenomenon referred to as *stress*. Broadly defined by Hans Selye, the recognized "father of stress," as the "body's nonspecific response to any demand placed upon it," its effects have been linked to hypertension, coronary heart disease, alcohol and drug abuse, and a deterioration in normal interpersonal relations. In the business world, "stress has moved from the nether world of 'emotional problems' and 'personality problems' to the corporate balance sheet...stress is now seen as not only troublesome, but expensive" (Slobogin, 48).

But exactly what is this phenomenon of stress which has caught the concentrated attention of the professional and academic communities? Selye has amplified the parameters of his definition, saying that:

> ...stress is essentially reflected by the rate of all the wear and tear caused by life.... Although we cannot avoid stress as long as we live, we can learn a great deal about how to keep its damaging side-effects, "distress," to a minimum (Selye, xvi)

It was as a result of his research into the effects of stress on the body's homeostatic tendencies that Selye hypothesized the existence of the General Adaptation Syndrome (G.A.S.). Defined basically as the manifestations of the body's adaptive reactions to stress, the G.A.S., or stress syndrome, "...evolves in time through three stages...(1) The alarm reaction, (2) The stage of resistance, and (3) The stage of exhaustion" (Selye, 38).

Selye pinpointed a number of indices of stress which he felt were indicative of an acute impact on the stressed individual, including (Selye, 174-8):

- General irritability, hyperexcitation, or depression
- Impulsive behavior or emotional instability
- Emotional tenseness and alertness
- Hypermotility
- Pain in the neck or lower back
- Insomnia
- Increased smoking
- Alcohol addiction

- Psychoses
- Free-floating anxiety

Holding that it is an individual's "ability to cope with the demands made by the events in our lives, not the quality or intensity of the events, that counts" (Selye, 178), Selye attributed a number of physical and psychological ailments to inappropriate or excessive bodily adaptations to stress. Among these "diseases of adaptation" were cardiovascular illness and heart attack, renal disease, hypertension, inflammatory or allergic diseases, sexual difficulties, digestive disturbances, metabolic problems and nervous/mental disorders.

It is within the parameters first suggested by Selye that the authors in Part One provide their contributions. Their discussions are critical in establishing the framework for understanding stress, especially as we will later apply it to policing.

In his work from the early days of stress studies, Levi examines the ways in which the body reacts to stress. He provides a discussion of the autonomic nervous system as well as an overview of the role played by the endocrine glands within the hypothalamus. To assure a full understanding of "the stress process", Levi discusses in considerable detail the three phases of the now classic General Adaptation Syndrome (GAS) and the mustering of the body's physiological and psychological defenses against stress.

Acknowledging that "there is an increasing body of research pointing to the role of life stress in the occurrence of seriously maladaptive behavior," Coleman addresses four questions key to the understanding of the effects of stress on individuals. What is meant by the term *stress* and its severity? How does one attempt to cope with stress and what are the outcomes of such coping efforts? What are some of the specific findings concerning the effects of stress on physical and mental disorders? What are the effects of rapid social change on stress patterns and on resulting physical and mental disorders?

References

Selye, H. (1967). *The Stress of Life* (Revised Edition). New York, NY: McGraw-Hill.

Slobogin, K. (1977). "Stress." *New York Times Magazine,* November 20, 48-55.

1

Stress as a Cause of Disease

Lennart Levi

As we have seen, it appears that the various parts of our body are influenced by and themselves influence brain impulses that are associated in some unknown way with our psychological processes. But how does this influence act? Most likely it occurs *partly* through the autonomic nervous system, *partly* through the endocrine glands, with the *hypothalamus* serving as a connecting link between the two.

The following presentation will certainly be clearer if we first take a brief look at these important links in the psychosomatic chain of events.

The Autonomic Nervous System

The nerves in our body do not all perform the same tasks and functions. Some transmit sensory impressions from the skin; others direct voluntary impulses to the muscles. Both these cases involve what are generally conscious phenomena — we are usually aware that we have pricked ourselves with a pin or that we want to move an arm.

There is, however, another important group of nerves, over which we do *not* exercise conscious control. These are the nerves which regulate our internal organs—the heart, intestines, glands, etc. This group—the autonomic (independent) or vegetative nervous system—has its most important centers in the part of the brain known as the *hypothalamus*.

Anatomically, the autonomic nerves can in turn be classified into a sympathetic and a parasympathetic system, each with a somewhat different set of functions. Thus, the *sympathetic* system accelerates the activity of the heart and the lungs but inhibits the digestive organs, while the *parasympathetic* nerves inhibit the heart and the lungs but stimulate the digestive system. These two parts of the autonomic nervous system are constantly interacting to maintain a state of dynamic *equilibrium*. In this way the body can adjust to the demands of life by increasing or decreasing the relative preponderance of one of the two systems. In battle, for instance during an attack, the sympathetic activities dominate: heart, lungs,

---

* The figures appearing in the original article have been omitted.

and muscles are rapidly brought into "alarm readiness," and work more rapidly, powerfully, and untiringly than usual. On the other hand, during a quiet nap on the sofa, it is the parasympathetic system that generally dominates, to the "benefit" of, for instance, the digestive system while lungs and muscles simply "tick over."

The Endocrine Glands

The autonomic nervous system functions in close association with the *endocrine glands* in helping the body to adjust to the demands of the environment. These glands produce the *hormones*, which are distributed with the blood to all parts of the body, and serve to regulate its many different functions.

The hormone-producing glands are the adrenals, thyroid, parathyroid, pancreas, ovaries, testicles, and pituitary (*hypophysis*). The last organ, barely the size of a cherry, is located at the base of the brain, approximately in the middle of the skull, and is a center for the regulation of hormones. Despite its unassuming appearance, the hypophysis influences the activity of nearly all endocrine glands. It does this chemically, by discharging into the blood stream small amounts of biologically potent substances, which then regulate the other endocrine glands. These substances include the adrenocorticotropic hormone (ACTH), which acts upon the adrenal gland; the gonadotropic hormones, which affect activity in the genital glands; and the thyreotropic hormones, which regulate the thyroid gland.

Then there is a pair of *adrenal glands*, situated on the upper poles of the kidneys. Each of these important but insignificant-looking organs (in man they weigh only about one-third of an ounce) consists of two anatomically and functionally different parts, the medulla and the cortex. The *cortex* secretes a number of very important hormones, referred to collectively as the *corticosteroids*. One group, the glucocorticosteroids (e.g. cortisol), regulates the carbohydrate metabolism, blood pressure, and body temperature. Another group, the mineral corticosteroids, regulates the balance of water and salts between the cells and the body fluids.

The hormones of the adrenal medulla are called *adrenaline* and *noradrenaline*. These regulate the blood supply to the different organs, stimulate the heart, mobilize fuel for the muscles and heart, and counteract fatigue. They are jointly instrumental in heightening the body's state of readiness, rousing it to fight or flight, and stepping up its performance in a critical situation. The medulla is closely associated with the sympathetic nervous system, which is also capable of producing noradrenaline.

As already mentioned, there is close collaboration between the endocrine glands and the autonomic nervous system. This is achieved in part by coordination between their respective centers in the hypophysis and the hypothalamus.

What Is a Stressor?

We have now learned about some of the regulators with which our body can adjust to the dangers and strains it may encounter.

What are these dangers? We can mention a few of the most common ones. Bacteria and viruses attack the body. Heat and cold in various forms can threaten life. Accidents are becoming increasingly frequent in the age of automobile and other machines. Hunger, while it may be of little importance in some countries, is a terrible reality for about one third of the world's population. A further danger, about which we can only theorize at present, was added with the arrival of nuclear power and radioactivity. The senseless desire by human beings for destruction has time and again released increasingly effective means of annihilation—poison gas, incendiary bombs, high explosives, and now hydrogen bombs.

All these brutal dangers and external forces, as well as the slighter strains of influences to which we are exposed daily, tend to upset our body's balance. They can be referred to collectively as *stressors*. What they all represent is an excess or a deficiency of influences to which the body is normally exposed (such as oxygen, nutrition, warmth, air pressure, irradiation) or else the introduction of something new and foreign (such as certain bacteria and viruses, poisons, accidents).

The above stressors are all *physical*. They can damage or destroy the body irrespective of how we experience them psychologically. But human nature is such that people react not only to the actual existence of dangers, but also to threats and symbols of danger experienced in the past. People want to be prepared to meet a new situation the moment it appears. This creates a situation in which organ function is adjusted not only to the needs of the organism in prevailing conditions but to anticipated needs as well. Irrespective of whether this preparedness is adequate or not, it may affect the adaptive-protective mechanism of the living organism. The organism's pattern of response—the *common* denominators of which may be called *"stress"*—involves endocrine as well as psychic processes.

Mental stressors may also present themselves in the psychological and social dangers in our lives, for instance, financial insecurity, poor social contracts, an unhappy marriage and strained working conditions, which may bring on persistent discontent and various forms of anxiety. Besides, different people experience the same situation in different ways. To some, a creaking sound in the middle of the night simply means that the floorboards are dry; to others, there is a burglar in the house. There are people who see danger lurking everywhere, either because they suffer from general anxiety of a hereditary nature or because of a previous frightening experience. The lives of such individuals abound in psychological stressors. *A difficult mother-in-law, a strict and demanding employer, or heartlessly joking companions may cause stress or even disease in many individuals as effectively as bacteria, poor nutrition, or persistently cold weather.*

Stress and the Adaptation Syndrome

Now it so happens that for *all* these potential forms of attack, the body generally speaking reacts with *one and the same defense plan,* in which the most important weapons are the endocrine glands and the autonomic nervous system. This "plan of defense," consisting of three phases of stress reactions, has been termed the *General Adaptation Syndrome* (GAS) by prominent Canadian scientist, Dr. Hans Selye. Adaptation means adjustment, while "syndrome" indicates that the different forces are coordinated in their efforts to adjust to the environmental changes; the adjective "general" emphasizes the extensive nature of the defensive reaction.

The three essential phases in the war between the stressors and the body can be described schematically as follows.

1. The Alarm Reaction

When the body is attacked, the initial reaction is the alarm, which consists of two phases. Phase one comprises a series of somatic disturbances, indicating that the body is faltering under the assault. However, the body's defenses are also rapidly mobilized to meet the assault. A report is immediately transmitted to the headquarters of the defense centers, the hypothalamus and the pituitary. From these headquarters, via the autonomic nervous system and the endocrine glands, respectively, such changes are transmitted in the body functions as may neutralize the damaging effects of the attack. This is the second or defensive phase of the alarm reaction.

2. Resisting the Invasion

In fortunate cases the assault is of short duration and the defense rapid and emphatic. In others the assault may be so powerful that the organism succumbs before the defense can intervene. When both opponents are of approximately equal strength, however, the struggle develops into the second stage of the adaptation syndrome, *the stage of resistance.*

The defense now tries to make good the damage caused in the first phase of the alarm reaction; meantime the fight continues on a more defensive level. The most important "weapon" at this stage are the hormones of the adrenal cortex, the corticosteroids; their production is stepped up on the order of the pituitary gland. During this stage there is some *adjustment* to the stressor.

3. Exhaustion

If the assault nevertheless persists, the body's defenses give way and the adjustment to changes resulting from the assault is also lost. This is *the stage of exhaustion*. The attacker (the stressor) again inflicts the same damage on the organism as during the first phase of the alarm reaction. The defense is no longer able to sustain the process of adjustment, and the organism succumbs.

How Does the Defense Function?

To simplify matters, the body's defense against stressors has been described above in military terms. Now, a more physiological presentation is in order.

The initial and swiftest reaction against stressors is generated by the two parts of the *autonomic nervous system*, the sympathetic and the parasympathetic. Together these attempt to adjust the various body functions to meet the stressor. The next move is an increased production of adrenaline by the adrenal glands, stimulated via the sympathetic nervous system. This increased production of adrenaline coupled with impulses from the hypothalamus, brings the pituitary and its hormones into battle. These hormones, in turn, influence the other endocrine glands and their hormones, thereby regulating the somatic defenses and adaptation. Probably most important is the ACTH of the pituitary, stimulating as it does the adrenal cortex to produce its hormones, including cortisol.

In the case of *mental stressors* the course of events is thought to be as follows: Impulses are transmitted from the cerebral context to the hypothalamus, which regulates not only the autonomic nervous system but also the pituitary—its posterior lobe directly via nerve endings, its anterior lobe by a secretion from the hypothalamus which flows through direct vascular connections to the pituitary. The increased production of adrenaline, which is a result of the increased sympathetic stimulation, also activates the pituitary (directly or through the hypothalamus). This produces a radical adjustment of the body's processes, an adjustment that—strangely enough and sometimes unfortunately—is of approximately the same nature as when the stressors are physical.

Adaptation Diseases — Tactical
Errors by the Defense

During a war the High Command sometimes makes mistakes. Thus, the artillery fire ordered to counter an attack may be *too weak*, and fail to stop the enemy. Or the barrage may be *too strong* and pulverize one's own previous fortifications, which cannot then be used when they have been retaken from the enemy. Or, again, a heavily armored tank may be sent into unsuitable terrain; in other words, the means of defense have been *wrongly chosen*.

· These same three possibilities are also present in the defense of the human body. The reaction of the endocrine glands and the autonomic nervous system may be too weak, too strong or wrongly chosen. In the first case the defense will be insufficient. In both the other cases, physical changes may develop of such a nature and extent that they harm the organism much more than the stressor itself would have done. Instead of reconquering its own fortifications, the body is destroyed by its own weapons.

Here, too, the body attempts to adjust to the stressors. But its attempt fails; either directly or through side effects, damage is caused and produces disease, termed by Dr. Selye the "diseases of adaptation."

Summary

To sum up. The reaction to stressors is initiated from the autonomic nervous system, then from this system in collaboration with the adrenaline-producing adrenal medulla, and finally from the pituitary with its influence on the adrenal cortex. The pituitary may also be influenced through *higher cerebral centers* via the hypothalamus and by the adrenaline of the adrenal medulla. As a result the adaptation syndrome is activated even by mental stressors. The defense put up by the pituitary and the adrenal glands causes profound changes in the body functions in an attempt to adapt to the new stress-producing conditions. These changes are basically the work of two groups of corticosteroid hormones which in some respects are antagonistic to each other.

Extensive animal experiments have shown that prolonged *disturbance of the balance* between these two groups of hormones can lead to injuries closely resembling certain diseases in man. For this reason Dr. Selye holds that there must be a similar mechanism behind these "adaptation diseases" in humans. This theory has been considerably criticized. Thus it is argued that the adaptation syndrome in humans is elicited only by out-and-out stressors, that the organism adjusts in another manner to everyday influences, and that there are other adaptation syndromes in addition to the one mentioned by Dr. Selye. In reply, Dr. Selye has referred to a vast number of experiments, and made out a good case against his critics. It remains to be seen which of his theories will be confirmed by further research.

Finally, something should be said about the danger of regarding all "stress" as something unpleasant, dangerous, and unhealthy. This is by no means the case. The training undertaken by an athlete to improve his strength, speed, and skill is in itself a form of stressor. A shy, hesitant salesman who gradually overcomes his uncertainty when facing the general public by deliberately seeking out customers is also inducing in his/her organism stress. But in both cases the stressors and the stress come in doses, within the individual's capacity and in moderate amounts that are only gradually increased. Dosed in this way, stress can be a positive factor.

2

Life Stress and Maladaptive Behavior

James C. Coleman

There is an increasing body of research pointing to the role of life stress in the occurrence of seriously maladaptive behavior. Available findings, however, are fragmented, often contradictory, and in many instances raise more questions than they answer. It will be our task to construct a coherent picture out of these research findings. The relation of stress to maladaptive behavior, whether referring to physical or mental disorders, is a new and emerging frontier of man's knowledge which is relevant to individuals and to society as a whole. It is useful to proceed in terms of four basic questions that will help to structure the discussion. What is meant by the terms *stress* and *severity of stress*? How does one attempt to cope with stress and what are the outcomes? What are some of the specific findings concerning the effects of stress on physical and mental disorders? What are the effects of rapid social change on stress patterns and on physical and mental disorders?

Stress and Severity of Stress

Essentially stress refers to the adjustive demands made upon the individual—to the problems in living with which he must cope if he is to meet his needs. Typically one thinks in terms of three types of stress—frustration, conflict, and pressure. *Frustration* occurs when the ability to achieve a desired goal is impeded or blocked as in the case of physical handicaps which severely restrict our life activities and satisfactions. *Conflict* occurs not from a single obstacle but when a choice must be made between two or more goals. A particularly important form of conflict is referred to as approach-avoidant, for example, when an emotionally disturbed young woman wants to establish a warm interpersonal relationship with her therapist but at the same time wants to avoid such a relationship fearing that she will ultimately be rejected. *Pressure* involves demands that force one to speed up or intensify efforts and often stems from ones own aspirations, standards, and values. Admittedly the increasing tempo of change in this so-called manic world is increasing the pressure on most of us. Adjustive demands, such as frustration, conflicts, and pressures, are closely interrelated and form part of the total stress pattern which every individual faces.

It is apparent that stress may occur primarily on physiological or psychological levels. For example, pneumonia viruses would represent stress primarily on a physiological level since the immunological defenses of the body are involved in dealing with it; while a hurtful divorce would represent stress primarily on a psychological level since the stress situation requires psychological adjustment. Weiss has developed techniques for separating physiological and psychological sources of stress—at least for rats.[1] For example, he found that psychological factors were the main cause for stomach ulcers and similar disorders among rats. On the human level it is often difficult to make a clear-cut distinction between physiological and psychological stress, since the two interact and the organism responds as a total unit rather than segmentally. Dunbar concluded that it is often "more important to know what kind of patient has the disease than what kind of disease the patient has."[2] And more recently Somers has arrived at essentially the same conclusion, "Indeed, most of the nation's major health problems—including automobile accidents, all forms of drug addiction, alcoholism, venereal disease, obesity, many cancers, most heart disease, and most infant mortality—are primarily attributable not to shortcomings on the part of the providers but to the living conditions, ignorance, or irresponsibility of the patient."[3]

Severity of stress refers to the degree of disruption in the system that will occur if the individual fails to cope with the adjustive demand. The severity of stress is, in turn, determined primarily by three factors: the characteristics of the adjustive demand, the characteristics of the individual, and the external resources and supports available to him.

The importance, duration, and multiplicity of demands are some of the key characteristics of the stress situation that determine its severity. Bereavement is a more important and severe source of stress than the loss of a small sum of money. The longer a stress operates the more severe it is likely to become. Similarly a number of stresses operating at the same time or in a sequence that keeps the individual off balance are more stressful than if these events occurred separately. In general systems theory this is called "overloading" and the behavioral capabilities of the organism tend to drop dramatically with even a mild degree of overloading.[4][5]

In their study of midtown Manhattan, Langner and Michael found that the number of stresses, rather than any particular stress, best predicted the mental health of their subjects;[6] and in a more recent replication of the midtown Manhattan study, Berkman arrived at essentially the same conclusion.[7] Other characteristics of the adjustive demand that tend to make it more stressful, for example—the more unfamiliar and less anticipated, and the pyramiding effect, that is, the gradual building up of relatively insignificant events over a period of time—may add up to a greater stress than a single traumatic event.[8] [9] The latter phenomenon is, of course, not uncommon in marriage.

The second factor determining the severity of stress, the characteristics of the individual, is also of key importance. Particularly relevant here are the individual's stress tolerance and the way he perceives or evaluates the stress situation. Stress tolerance refers to the degree of stress the individual can tolerate without undergoing disorganization or decompensation. In general, it appears that females evidence more stress tolerance than do males.[10] There is of course a great deal of overlapping, and for either males or females with low stress tolerances (who are marginally adjusted either physically or psychologically) mild adjustive demands may prove highly stressful. A physical demand that would be relatively easy for a healthy person to meet might prove lethal for a patient suffering from severe emphysema. Similarly, a patient recovering from schizophrenia may have his psychosis reactivated when subjected to relatively mild sleep depravation, a stress that would not be nearly as disruptive for more effectively adjusted persons.[11] [12] Stress tolerance also includes "weak spots," that is, high susceptibility to specific types of stress. All individuals have such weak spots or Achilles heels often as a consequence of past illnesses, traumatic experiences, and learning which leave one vulnerable to specific types of physical or psychological stress. Closely related to such special vulnerabilities is the way the individual perceives or evaluates the stress situation. What one person views as highly stressful may be only mildly stressful to another person. An objective observer might not see the stresses in a patient's life situation that led to that persons acute schizophrenic break, but from the standpoint of the patient, the situation may be intolerable. In general, the degree of threat which the individual perceives in the stress situation (its potential for harming him) is of key importance in determining its severity regardless of the objective characteristics of the stress situation.[13] [14] The personality makeup of the individual comes within this realm, particularly their frame of reference involving assumptions about reality, value, and possibility.

Without minimizing the importance of personality factors, which have been shown to be of crucial importance in withstanding particular types of stress, there is a substantial body of evidence to suggest that in the face of extreme and prolonged stress, constitutional and personality factors may do no more than determine how long the individual can withstand the stress; the outcome being temporary or permanent disorganization or decompensation.[15]

The external resources and supports available to the individual make up the third factor determining the severity of stress. Lack of resources, either interpersonal or material, ordinarily make a given stress situation more severe and reduce an individual's capacity for coping with it. Following a severe stroke, for example, a patient who can look forward to returning to a loving spouse and reasonable financial support is likely to have a more favorable prognosis than if that person were faced with returning to an unfavorable life situation replete with financial problems. Environmental supports, especially interpersonal ones, are complex, and behavior by one's spouse or loved ones that is intended to provide support may actually increase the severity of stress. Mechanic, for example, found that, among married graduate students facing crucial examinations, spouses who expressed the viewpoint "I am sure you will pass" often added to the stress since they were in a sense demanding that their spouse do so; while those who simply stated "Do the best you can" were most helpful.[16] Similarly, well-meaning family members or friends who hold out hope that some new medical miracle will restore the vision of a recently blinded person are apt to do more harm than good.

In general, both the characteristics of the individual and the external resources and supports available determine the level of stress tolerance.

In dealing with the nature and severity of stress the terms crisis, trauma, and strain are also commonly encountered. Lazarus has defined crisis as "a limited period in which an individual or group is exposed to threats and demands which are at or near the limits of their resources to cope."[13] Trauma has been variously defined but refers in general to some highly aversive event in the individual's life which requires a readjustment.

Strain is a term borrowed from engineering and refers to the distortion caused in an object by stress. When the stress is severe, the strain is correspondingly great as when a bridge might sag or buckle under heavy weight. In speaking of organisms, strain is usually thought of as occurring only under conditions of severe stress, since the individual can cope with mild stress which causes little or no strain. However, difficult adjustive demands may place a severe strain on the individual's adjustive resources and lead to some disorganization or even breakdown of integrated functioning. In essence, psychological crises and trauma, which may be defined as events that require a major readjustment on the part of the individual, can be assessed in terms of type, incidence, and severity; and this assessment can be quantified by means of rating scales that measure such readjustments or life change units.

Finally, in reviewing the nature and severity of stress, we are concerned with the practical problem of measuring the severity of life stress. The severity of a given stress or combination of stresses can be assessed by a variety of physiological and psychological measures including autonomic and cortical changes, level of muscle tension, rating scales, and introspective reports. Usually, such measurements are made in relation to the ability of persons to perform given tasks under certain types and degrees of stress. Grether, for example, has reported on the effects of combined stress in operational flying in the military.[18] In general, such studies have reported an inverted-U curve with respect to the effects of stress on performance.[19] This paper is less concerned with the effects upon performance of specific and immediate situations than with the effects, over a long period of time, of life crises and prior stress on the occurrence of physical and mental disorders.

Perhaps the most widely used instrument in research studies dealing with the long term effects of stress is the Social Readjustment Rating Questionnaire (SRRQ) developed by Holmes and Rahe.[20] This is a self-rating-questionnaire consisting of 43 life events to which the patient may have been exposed and is designed to give an estimate of the occurrence of life-change events or the amount of stress in the patient's life over a given period, usually weeks or months, prior to the onset of ones physical or mental disorder. Interestingly enough there appears to be general agreement concerning the severity of stress occasioned by the various life change events covered by the SRRQ. The first six events arranged in rank order of severity of stress for adult patients are: death of spouse, divorce, marital separation, jail term, death of a close family member, and major personal injury or illness. Adolescents come up with comparable severity ratings with death of spouse, marriage, divorce, and death of a close family member heading the list followed by change in financial status and pregnancy.

Results have also been found to be concordant with respect to the severity ratings among various segments of the population as well as between Americans and peoples of other cultures.[21] In general, the SRRQ appears to have a high degree of reliability and validity with respect to the life events that it covers, although some question could be raised as to the adequacy of the coverage itself in terms of other stressful life events that might have been included.

Various other assessment procedures have been used. One approach is to utilize ratings by family members or other informed persons rather than by patients themselves, particularly, when the patient is severely depressed, suffering from a stroke, or subject to other conditions that make a self-rating inappropriate. Unfortunately, self-ratings and ratings by informants do not always show close correspondence.[22] Still other procedures utilize word sorts, adjective check lists, and critical incidents for measuring the severity of prior life events.[23 24 25]

How We Cope with Stress and the Outcomes

It is useful to note the concept of three levels of resources for coping with stress. On a biological level, damage repair mechanisms and immunological defenses against disease are present; on a psychological level built-in defensive and damage repair mechanisms as well as learned coping patterns including self or ego defense mechanisms exist; and on a sociocultural level there are interpersonal resources such as marital partners and friends as well as group resources such as labor unions and professional organizations.

The first of three types of psychological coping patterns are built-in defensive and damage repair mechanisms. The term built-in is used here, since such reactions appear to operate with minimal learning. Included here would be such specific reactions as fainting in the face of a very traumatic situation or repetitive talking about the situation after it has occurred. Raker, Wallace and Raymer have delineated a *disaster syndrome* which includes a shock stage, a suggestible stage, and a recovery stage in which repetitively telling about the catastrophic event appears to have a marked therapeutic effect.[26] Following Bowlby's study of children's reactions to separation experiences involving hospitalization, we now have a substantial body of evidence concerning what happens in these circumstances.[27] [28] Most, but not all, children show an initial response of acute distress and crying (the period of protest), followed by a phase of misery and apathy (the phase of despair), and finally a stage when the child loses interest in his parents (detachment) and appears relatively contented.

Several other reaction patterns of this type are of immediate interest. Cholden delineated the typical psychological reaction sequence of newly blinded persons as involving three stages: (1) a period of shock; (2) a period of depression involving self-pity and feelings of hopelessness, which he considered to be one of mourning in which the person dies as a sighted person to be reborn as a blind one; and (3) a period of readjustment involving changes in life plans and the utilization of remaining resources in order to salvage what he can from the wreckage.[29] Parkes studied reactions to both amputations and bereavement and again pointed to a three-stage process which he found to be typical.[30] The first stage was characterized by feelings of shock and numbness accompanied by a strong tendency to deny or screen out reality. This first phase was followed by a phase of anxiety and distress, the so-called pangs-of-grief period. Finally, came stage three in which the individuals gave us hope of getting back what they had lost and made the necessary readjustment. Interestingly, amputees tended to experience a sense of mutilation while bereaved women mourned for something "out there" which had been lost. Many amputees also went through a period of mourning and many widows experienced feelings of mutilation. Parkes noted the phantom limb phenomenon experienced by every one of the amputees during the first weeks following their loss and the phantom husband involving a strong sense of the dead husband being near at hand, occurring in 73 percent of the widows.

Kubler-Ross findings involved patients reacting to a diagnosis of terminal cancer.[31] Again, there is an initial shock period progressing into stages of denial, anxiety, depression, and eventually acceptance of life termination. Not all patients go through the phases and reactions of denial, anxiety, depression, withdrawal, exaggerated dependency, and resentment, and may or may not involve eventual acceptance.[32]

Similarly, there are studies dealing with severe kidney disease and hemodialysis, with the reactions of children who have serious physical handicaps that prevent them from attending regular school, and with the typical phases involved in the development of combat exhaustion or adjusting to life as a P.O.W.[33] [34] [35] [36] [37] [38] [39]

A second type of psychological coping pattern consists of what may be termed learned task-oriented reactions.[40] [41] Such reactions may take the form of approach, withdrawal, or compromise reactions and typically involve problem-solving and decision-making that tend to be rational and constructive. As Hammond and Summers have pointed out, such cognitive processes and resulting behaviors involve two distinct processes: the acquisition of essential knowledge and cognitive or inner control over such knowledge.[42]

For example, in their studies of parachutists, Fenz and Epstein found that while all were anxious and showed raised autonomic activity, for trained parachutists the peak occurred prior to the jump, while for the untrained parachutists the intense anxiety continued right up to the jump and interfered with performance.[43] Capel, Youngblood and Stewart made comparable findings with trained astronauts and concluded that they had learned some method for controlling anxiety during stressful situations even to the extent that it was below that of the population at large; while after the stressful situation was terminated, their anxiety levels returned to levels that approximate those of the general population.[44]

Finally, a third type of psychological coping pattern consists of defense-oriented reactions; the so-called self or ego defense mechanisms, such as denial, rationalization, and emotional insulation. These reactions, with the possible exception of denial, are largely or entirely based on learning and tend to defend the individual against stress that might otherwise lead to intense and disabling anxiety or self-devaluation. Thus, such reactions may be highly useful in alleviating anxiety and dealing with other life stresses, although these may also exact a high price for their defensive value. For example, Katz and his associates made an intensive study of the ego defenses of 30 hospitalized women awaiting the outcome of breast tumor biopsy.[45] It was found that denial and rationalization, particularly, in combination, were highly effective in coping with anxiety. However, many of the women who used these defenses to allay their anxiety had failed to seek early medical assistance and so impaired their chances for survival.

In general, of course, our coping efforts involve a combination of task and defense-oriented responses as well as the more or less automatic operation of our built-in defense and damage repair mechanisms. The outcome of such coping efforts can be evaluated in terms of adaptive and maladaptive behavior. The term behavior is used to include physiological as well as psychological reactions and responses. Attempts to define adaptive and maladaptive behavior have led to considerable disagreement and controversy. Often the answer can apparently be found in the form of answers to several more specific questions. Does the action meet the demands of the stress situation? Does the action meet the needs of the individual? Is the action economical in terms of cost in adaptive resources or is it wasteful? Is the action compatible with group welfare?

For our immediate purposes, suppose we simplify the matter and tentatively accept the answer advanced by Coleman that adaptive behavior is behavior which contributes to the well-being of the individual and ultimately to that of the group; while maladaptive behavior is detrimental to the well-being of the individual or the group.[40] [41] Of course, this answer hinges on what we mean by well-being and perhaps it should be noted that certain types of behavior—the excessive use of alcohol, incest, and racial prejudice—have been shown to be detrimental to the individual or the group. As the biological and social sciences increasingly delineate those conditions that foster or impede the health and fulfillment of human potentialities, we shall have an increasingly sound foundation for delineating adaptive and maladaptive behaviors.

The biologist Herrick in his book, *The Evolution of Human Nature*, has pointed out that the laws of man's nature are self-executing and carry their own punishment.[46] If we drink alcohol excessively, we damage our health; if we lie, deceive, and cheat in our interpersonal relationships, we deny ourselves satisfactions and the full experience of being and self-fulfillment. No prosecuting attorney is involved, no judge is involved, no jury is needed to render a verdict. And ignorance of the law excuses no man.

Findings Concerning the Effects of Stress on Physical and Mental Disorders

First, the point must be emphasized that adaptation to severe stress is expensive. Stress exacts its toll in several ways. Under severe stress there is a lowering of adaptive efficiency—a narrowing of the perceptual field and an increased rigidity of cognitive process so that it becomes difficult for the individual to reevaluate the situation or perceive more effective coping responses than the ones being used. Second is a reduction in resistance to other stresses, for example, soldiers who develop resistance to combat conditions may show a lowered tolerance to other stresses such as bad news from home. Third is wear and tear on the system. Selye has shown that under severe and sustained stress there is irreversible wear and tear on the system, which he refers to as aging and which cannot be completely repaired by rest.[47] [48] Fourth are the sequelae of stress on the organism which may take such forms as hyperirritability, sleep disturbances, and disturbed interpersonal relationships as well as a wide range of somatic and psychological patterns detrimental to the individual.[49] [50] [15] [51] [52] [53] [54] [55] [56]

Prisoners of war and concentration camp survivors subjected to extreme and inhuman conditions typically showed organic as well as psychological damage with a lowering of tolerance to stress of any kind. In an intensive study of large numbers of men who survived P.O.W. camps in World War II, Chambers emphasized the following: fatigability, inability to withstand frustration, abuse of alcohol and sedative drugs, low resistance to physical illness, varying degrees of emotional instability, and various somatic complaints such as edema of the ankles and feet.[53] Similarly, Hafner has delineated what he considered to be a typical clinical picture of sequelae following the systematic terror and cruelty experienced in concentration camps during World War II.[55] This syndrome included anxiety, insomnia, nightmare, headaches, irritability, depression, social withdrawal, and loss of sexual potency. The syndrome varied somewhat in severity, of course, depending upon the degree of stress suffered as well as the prior makeup of the individual.

Similarly, in a study of veterans returned home from the war in Vietnam, Strange and Brown reported more conflicts in interpersonal relationships, more drug abuse, and a higher incidence of depression and somatization for a combat group than for a noncombat group.[51] The combat group also manifested more aggressive and suicidal threats although they did not ordinarily carry out such threats. More recently, Lifton has referred to the detrimental effects on combat soldiers of what he terms the Gook Syndrome and *numbed warfare*.[57]

A fifth factor concerning the cost of stress relates to the pattern of decompensation which takes place under excessive stress. For example, we can point to combat exhaustion occurring in the face of prolonged combat experience, to P.O.W. camps where men sometimes simply gave up and died; and to the downfall of societies such as the Roman Empire.

In all fairness it should be emphasized that surviving and adapting to extreme stress may increase the adjustive resources of the individual. Examples are when it leads to increased competence, self-confidence, and to needed changes in goals, expectations, and values. However, the long-range effects of extreme and sustained stress appear more likely to result in maladaptive rather than constructive results. At the same time, it is useful to bear in mind Admiral Halsey's statement that "There are no great men, there are only ordinary men forced by circumstances to face great challenges." And often we do see stronger and more mature persons forged by such challenges.

In any event, the stresses we face and the outcomes of our coping efforts play a key role in the satisfactions and fulfillment we achieve in living. When persons over 50 years of age were asked to summarize their lives, the answers were found by Charlotte Buhler to fall into three categories roughly described as follows: "All in all it was a good life." "There were so many disappointments." "It all came to nothing."[58] Perhaps there is a lesson to be learned here.

Specific Findings Concerning the Effects of Stress on Physical and Mental Disorders

Over the past decade a considerable volume of research has accumulated with respect to physical and mental disorders and the stresses in a person's life situation. While in the main these studies have dealt with the role of stress in peptic ulcers and other so-called psychosomatic disorders, they have also dealt with a considerable range of other disorders as well.

In a report published by the U.S. Department of Health, Education, and Welfare it was found that: "The great majority of patients hospitalized for physical illness...had experienced a psychological disturbance shortly before they got sick. Most commonly this had not been anxiety, fear, or anger, the emotions generally considered to be associated with illness, but with an attitude of helplessness or hopelessness usually described by the investigators as giving up. 'It was just too much,' a patient would report. Or, 'I couldn't take it any more.' Or, 'I didn't know what to do.' Or, 'I threw up my hands.'"[59]

These investigators also reported that throughout a person's lifetime there is a close relationship between the timing of physical illness and life stress. Comparable findings have been made by other investigators, but deserving of special mention is the pioneering work of Rahe and his colleagues which we shall also examine shortly.[60][61][62][63][64][65][66]

Studies of illness rates in the United States Navy have also revealed some interesting findings. Rubin, Gunderson, and Arthur studied life stress and illness patterns among approximately one-third of enlisted crew members aboard an attack carrier during a six-month deployment to Vietnam.[67] Using the Schedule of Recent Experience (SRE) designed to document significant recent life changes, they found significantly higher illness rates among men who had undergone a high incidence of SRE's as contrasted with those whose SRE scores were relatively low. In their study of illness rates aboard three cruisers, utilizing a similar research procedure, Rahe, Mahan, Arthur, Ransom, and Gunderson found illness rates to be significantly higher when crew members were under stress and among crew members who had experienced many recent life changes.[68] Similar findings were reported for battleship crews by Rubin, Gunderson, and Arthur.[69] [70] Both overall illness and most categories of individual illness were elevated during combat periods compared with in-port periods. Illness rates were also significantly higher for men who worked in hostile environments or performed hazardous tasks, and for younger, unmarried, inexperienced crew members.

Now, let us briefly note some of the findings with respect to specific physical and mental disorders, starting with psychosomatic disorders that have received a good deal of research attention. For our immediate purposes, let us briefly view the role of stress in peptic ulcers, migraine headaches, and hypertension, which will serve as representative examples of these disorders.

In a now classic experiment, Wolf and Wolff utilized a subject who had, as a consequence of an operation, a window over his stomach that permitted direct observation of his gastric functioning.[71] When this subject was given stress interviews designed to elicit strong resentment, hostility, and anxiety, changes occurred in digestive functioning, including a marked increase in acid production, comparable to those that occur when the stomach is full of food. More recent studies have shown this to be the basic mechanism in peptic ulcer production, but only in cases where persons evidenced sustained emotional tension and the excessive secretion of digestive acids eats into the gastric lining and causes ulceration.[72] Although the epidemiology of peptic ulcers will not be gone into it is interesting that our society appears conducive to the occurrence of this psychosomatic disorder, and an estimated one in every ten Americans will at some time in his life develop a peptic ulcer.[73] [74] The incidence is about two to three times higher among men than women. However, it may be noted that the incidence of peptic ulcers appears to vary markedly among occupational groups and to be practically unheard of among the Navajo Indians of Arizona.[75] In a slightly broader perspective it may also be noted that an increased incidence of peptic ulcers has been reported among civilian populations following heavy air raids and among populations undergoing severe stresses such as rapid social change.[76] [77]

Some 15 million Americans suffer from tension headaches, the great majority of which are related to emotional stress. In the case of migraine, it has been shown that the onset of the headache is accompanied by progressive dilation of the cranial arteries. Individuals with unilateral headaches show dilation of the cranial artery only on the side where the pain occurs. A variety of experimentally induced stresses, for example excessive work demands, threatening interviews, and frustrations result in dilation of the cranial arteries among migraine sufferers but not among other persons.[78]

Hypertension may result from a variety of organic conditions as well as emotional stress. However, an estimated 10 to 25 million persons in the U.S. suffer from essential hypertension presumably associated with psychological stress.[79] [80] Davies studied a group of 128 middle-aged factory workers and found that some were prone to develop high blood pressure when subjected to sustained emotional stress for which they were unable to find an acceptable outlet in terms of verbal or fantasy expression.[81]

In general, psychosomatic disorders appear to involve: (1) sustained emotional arousal in response to stress; the degree and duration of arousal depending both on the nature of the stress and the individual's perception of it; (2) response stereotype in which the damaging effects of chronic emotional arousal are concentrated in a specific organ system, presumably one that is more vulnerable than others as a result of heredity, illness, and conditioning; and (3) the overall role of sociocultural factors in relation to the stresses characteristic of a given society and the patterns of psychosomatic disorders most likely to occur. It may also be noted that in some cases, such as obesity associated with stress factors, there appears to be a somewhat different pattern in which the individual attempts to compensate for frustration and tension by eating. Menzies found that high sugar carbohydrate foods were so prominent in reducing anxiety and tension produced by life stress that he called them the "pleasure foods."[82] Crisp has used the term "reactive obesity" to refer to overeating during or following severely stressful periods.[83]

Recently, cardiac heart disease has been included in the category of psychophysiologic or psychosomatic disorders.[84] For our immediate purposes, however, we shall consider it separately. In a study of sudden cardiac death, Rahe and Lind gathered life change data on 39 subjects over the last three years of their lives.[65] For both subjects with and without prior histories of coronary heart disease, there was a significant increase in the number and intensity of life-change units during the final 6 months of their lives compared to identical time periods two and three years prior to death. The life-change event increase was threefold in magnitude.

In a review of available research studies concerning five categories of coronary disease. Jenkins reported that patients differed markedly from healthy controls in terms of job difficulties. It was concluded that job dissatisfactions and frustrations are predisposing factors to myocardial infarctions.[85] This is reminiscent of an old saying to the effect that to destroy a man, it is only necessary to make his work seem useless.

In this context it is also interesting to note that McQuade in a review of available research findings, concluded that there is a coronary-prone personality type who is aggressive, competitive, ambitious, and restless.[86] Of 257 patients who developed coronary heart disease, 70 percent evidenced these personality characteristics; while a control group of subjects characterized as easygoing, patient, and less concerned with achievement seemed to be immune to coronary heart disease. Finally, in a study of widowers, Parkes, Benjamin, and Fitzgerald reported that the death rate during the six month period following the death of their wives was 40 percent above their expected death rate.[87] The incidence of cardiac deaths was so high that they referred to this finding as the "broken heart syndrome."

A few additional findings may give some idea of the range of physical disorders that have come under research scrutiny in relation to stress. In a study of subarachnoid hemorrhage, Penrose found that for the type he studied, bleeding from a ruptured cerebral artery aneurysm (the fourth most common variety of strokes), stressful life events and crises in the weeks immediately beforehand occurred significantly more often than would be expected in the general population.[88] In a study of life stress and respiratory illness, Jacobs, Spiken, Norman, and Anderson found that college students who developed respiratory illnesses and sought medical care were much more likely than normals to perceive the preceding year prior to their illness as characterized by disappointments and failures. Also the more severe the illness, the more frequent and intense were the reports of such aversive events and affects.[89]

In a group of 450 cancer patients, LeShan found 72 percent had suffered severe emotional trauma in early life; this contrasted with an incidence of only ten percent in the noncancerous control group.[90] And typically the cancer occurred from six months to eight years following a second crisis in later life. In a study of emotional factors in juvenile diabetes mellitus, Stein and Charles found that diabetics had a significantly higher incidence of parental loss and severe family disturbances in early life than did a matched control group of normal adolescents.[91] Roark found the life situations of patients suffering from mononucleosis to be so stressed that he referred to it as "the stress disease."[92] Similarly, Heisel has demonstrated that children who develop juvenile rheumatoid arthritis, which afflicts some 175,000 children annually, have recently experienced a cluster of life changes significantly higher in amount and intensity that were characteristic for the average child.[93] Finally, in a study of hyperthyroidism, Voth, Holzman, and Wallerstein found that thyroid "hot spots" activated by specific crises can progress to nodular and diffuse hyperthyroidism under conditions of severe and prolonged personal strain.[94]

In discussing the relation of stress to mental disorders, it is useful to think in terms of a continuum with disorders that appear primarily associated with organic pathology—cancer or coronary artery disease, at one extreme and disorders such as neuroses, where no organic pathology appears directly involved, at the other extreme of the continuum. Between these two extremes there is a wide range of disorders from psychosomatic to psychoses, drug dependence, suicide, delinquency and crime, mental retardation, acute and chronic brain syndromes, combat exhaustion, transient emotional disturbances among both children and adults including reactions to civilian catastrophe, and acute situational maladjustment, for example, the case of P.O.W.'s, concentration camp inmates, and even disappointing and frustrating marriages where there seems to be no way out.[104] Increasingly too, the role of psychological complications or overt mental disorders associated with childbirth, hysterectomy, abortions, and various other forms of surgery including open heart surgery and organ transplants are coming under scrutiny. In essence, the role of stress in physical and mental disorders covers the entire gamut of human behavior. Following are some selected research findings that appear representative as well as relevant; first, being the role of stress in two major types of psychoses, schizophrenia and depression.

Brown and Birley found a marked increase in life change events just prior to onset in cases of acute schizophrenia and over a longer period prior to the onset in cases of depression.[95] And in a later study, Brown utilized both a control group and a refinement in the assessment of life change units.[96] This refinement involved measuring the degree of severity of life change events rather than simply the total number in terms of marked, moderate, little, or none, with regard to the threatening implications of the event as perceived by the patient. Utilizing this approach he found that forty-two percent of depressed women had experienced at least one markedly threatening event in the nine months before onset compared with nine percent in the community or control sample. In general, the severity of stress appeared to be greatest during the ten-week period before the onset of acute schizophrenia and during the two-year period prior to the onset of depression.

Similar findings with respect to the role of stress in schizophrenia and depression have been made by a number of other investigators. Prominent here are the studies of Paykel et al., who found a general excess of aversive life events prior to the onset of depression in a sample of 185 depressed patients as compared with a matched control group.[97] Stresses focused around marital difficulties, personal illness, and death of loved ones. Similarly, King and Pittman reported a number of cases of young patients in which difficulties in school or love relationships were contiguous with the onset of depression.[98] Beck studied the dreams of several hundred depressed patients and found the central themes involved themselves as victims of aversive experiences involving frustrations and losses;

he concluded that these dreams depicted the depressed patient's picture of himself as a loser.[99] Gadoret, et al. found a significantly higher incidence of real or threatened losses preceding the onset of depression, particularly, for patients under 40 years of age.[100] Comparable findings have been reported for schizophrenia and need not be reviewed here. Suffice to note the conclusion of R.D. Laing that "The experience and behavior…labeled schizophrenia are a special sort of strategy that a person invents in order to live in an unlivable world."[101]

Closely related to depression is the problem of suicide. Of course, not all persons who attempted suicide are depressed, nor are all depressed persons suicidal. However, Motto has estimated that 75 to 80 percent of suicides are associated with severe depression.[102] Suicide is a very complex behavior, and the role of stress has not been fully delineated. Nevertheless, there is considerable research evidence pointing to the role of bereavement, interpersonal crises, failure and self-devaluation, and loss of meaning and hope.[103][72] Often the suicidal attempt is a cry for help in which the person attempts to communicate his distress and need for assistance to significant others. The role of one type of extreme stress in suicide is dramatically depicted by Abram, Moore, and Westervelt who found that the incidence rate of suicide among chronic dialysis patients is 400 times that of the general population. These investigators concluded that the hemodialysis patient who kills himself does so as a result of a combination of serious emotional conflicts often centering around the decision to die rather than live their lives on terms they find unacceptable. In this context, they quote from a letter written by Ernest Hemingway to a friend, "Hotch, if I can't exist on my own terms, then existence is impossible. Do you understand? This is how I've lived and that is how I must live or not live."[105] This letter was written shortly before Ernest Hemingway took his own life after receiving a diagnosis of a terminal illness.

Similarly, we could examine the role of stress in alcoholism, delinquent and criminal behavior, and other maladaptive patterns. Jones has studied the personality correlates and antecedents of drinking patterns in adult females and males, and concluded that certain personality traits make the individual more prone to alcoholism when subjected to severe stress.[106][107] Similarly, Szyrynski has reported that serious criminal offenses are often associated with periods of crisis.[108] Simon has pointed to the role of physical and sociopsychological stress in the mental disorders of the aged;[109] and Pavenstedt and Bernard have pointed to the role of family crises in childhood behavior disorders.[110] Other studies have shown the relation of stress to nightmare behavior and pavor nocturnus or night terrors of children.[111]

It is hoped that the preceding discussion has sufficed to point up the important role stress often plays in the etiology of physical and mental disorders. This role may involve three facets by no means mutually exclusive: (1) the stress may precipitate a given maladaptive pattern as in acute schizophrenia or suicide; (2) the stress may be a primary causal agent as in peptic ulcers or coronary heart disease; and/or (3) the stress may exacerbate an existing disorder as in cases of cancer and a wide range of other disorders. Often, of course, a vicious circle occurs, coronary heart disease resulting primarily from severe stress may in turn intensify the overall stress situation with which the individual is confronted.

Effects of Rapid Social Change on Patterns of Stress

The stresses to which individuals are exposed and the disorders, both physical and mental, are determined in no small part by when and where they live. In the emerging or developing nations of the world, children under five years of age account for more than 60 percent of the deaths, although they represent only 20 percent of the population. And, among those who do survive, two-thirds will be restricted in physical and mental development as a consequence of malnutrition.[112] At present over four-fifths of the world's population exist in the so-called have-not nations and the gap between the have and have-not nations is widening. The implications appear anything but constructive in relation to the incidence of physical and mental disorders in the lives of so many of our fellow astronauts on the planet earth. Certainly, we are a long way from the goal of comprehensive health advanced by the World Health Organization of "a sound mind, in a sound body, in a sound society."[113]

In any event, our world is undergoing rapid and profound change and few are the places in the world today where sons and daughters follow as a matter of course the customs and values of their parents and elders. In fact, Margaret Mead has pointed out that in New Guinea some youths whose parents were cannibals are studying in our modern medical schools.[114] Thus, the generation gap that we see in our own society is often magnified in the developing countries.

Rapid and accelerating social change, change that appears to be associated with shifting patterns of maladaptive behavior can be seen in our own country. Included in such patterns are: (1) the marked increase in crimes of violence with violent crimes increasing much more rapidly than the population; (2) the marked increase in suicide among our young people, with suicide now ranking third behind cancer and accidents as the leading cause of death among teenagers and youth under 19 years of age; (3) the marked increase in alcoholism and drug abuse, with the number of alcoholics in our society now being estimated at between nine and twelve million with the gap between the number of male and female alcoholics rapidly closing; (4) the emergence of coronary heart disease as a leading cause of death in our society as well as the disproportionate and continuing increase in the number of other "diseases of adaption"; and (5) the emergence of new patterns of psychopathology such as that characterized by alienation, aimlessness, and apathy which appear to be largely replacing neurasthenia and other traditional forms of neuroses with which we are familiar.

Crucial to the phenomenon of uncontrolled technological and social change is the question of whether we are either physiologically or psychologically equipped to cope with the accelerating rate of change in our manic society. Almost three decades ago, Kenniston made this definitive statement: "The human capacity to assimilate such innovation is limited. Man can, of course, adjust to rapid change, that is make an accommodation to it and go on living, but truly to assimilate it involves retaining some sense of connection with the past, understanding the relationship of one's position to one's origins and one's destinations, maintaining a sense of control over one's own life in a comprehensible universe undergoing intelligible transformations. This assimilation becomes increasingly difficult in a time like our own."[115]

Toffler has proposed the term "future shock" to describe the result of social change that has become too rapid for people to assimilate without undergoing serious decompensation, in essence, the future will have arrived too soon.[116] The consequences of future shock have been variously depicted as involving the fracturing of family and other interpersonal relations, alienation, depersonalization, aimlessness, apathy, and various forms of irrational behavior including senseless violence. In essence, as Ford has pointed out, accelerating technological and social change are confronting us with new sources and levels of stress that result not only in physical disease, disability, and death, but also in alienation and other maladaptive behaviors.[117]

From the few studies dealing with the nature and effects of rapid social change, it would appear that social change is likely to be particularly stressful when certain conditions are present: "When the tempo is accelerating and especially when major dimensions of change occur within the life span of a single generation; When change involves pervasive reorientation about basic values and assumptions; When change is experienced at the onset of a cycle when few guides and models exist; When there has been little formal training and preparation in the skills and techniques necessary to accomplish the new tasks; If there are serious ambiguities about what the change is leading to; If change involves new roles or values that are imperfectly integrated into or incompatible with the rest of the sociocultural system; If change involves expectations that are prone to be frustrated given the preexisting pattern of life; If change involves expansion rather than substitution and creates a sense of overloading."[118]

In concluding this discussion of technological and social change, stress, and maladaptive behavior, it is appropriate to point out that society is confronted with three Herculean tasks: (1) unfinished business relating to such problems as poverty and racial discrimination which still afflict a sizable segment of our population; (2) current business relating to many new problems including ecological violations and uncontrolled technological and social change; and (3) new business relating to building a good future for man.

Whether or not we wish to buy in on the type of utopia depicted by Skinner in his *Beyond Freedom and Dignity* the fact remains that we now have the capability of shaping our own future world as well as the type of persons we wish to inhabit it.[119] And, depending on the type of future we choose, we shall be faced with differing forms of stress and maladaptive behavior.

As mental health personnel, we all face the challenge not only of being aware of the nature of existing social problems and trends, but of participating as actively and effectively as we can in helping to build a good future for man and one which we may characterize as a participatory and anticipatory democracy in which our people are directly involved in establishing priorities and guiding social change—a society in which each individual has maximal opportunities for fulfilling his potentialities and living a meaningful and fulfilling life in a society in which human freedom and dignity are truly established.

References

1. Weiss, J. M.: Psychological factors in stress and disease. Sci. Am.: 104-113, Aug. 22, 1972.
2. Dunbar, F.: Psychosomatic Diagnosis, New York, Harper, 1943.
3. Somers, A. R.: The nation's health: issues for the future. Ann. Am. Acad. Political Soc. Sci. 399: 160-174, 1972.
4. Miller, J. G.: Information input overload and psychopathology. Am. J. Psychiatry 116: 695-704, 1960.
5. Gottschalk, L.A., Haer J.L., Bates D.E.: Effect of sensory overload on psychological state. Arch. Gen. Psychiatry 27: 4561-456, 1972.
6. Langner, T.S., Michael, S.T.: Life Stress and Mental Health, Vol. 20, New York, Free Press, 1963.
7. Berkman, P.L.: Life stress and psychological well-being: a replication of Langer's analysis in the midtown Manhattan study. J. Health Soc. Behav. 12(1): 35-45, 1971.

8.   Birley, J.: Stress and disease. J. Psychosom. Res. 16: 235-240. Aug 1972.
9.   Coddington, R.D.: The significance of life events as etiologic factors in the diseases of children II: a study of normal population. J. Psychosom. Res. 16: 205-213, June 1972.
10. Marks, D.: Is the "weaker" sex better able to cope with stress? Los Angeles Times, Section K, Nov. 5, 1972, pp. 6-7.
11. Bliss, E.L., Clark, L.D., West, C.D.: Studies of sleep deprivation: relationship to schizophrenia. Arch. Neurol. Psychiatry 81: 348-359, 1959.
12. Koranyi, E.D., Lehmann, H.E.: Experimental sleep deprivation in schizophrenic patients, Arch. Gen. Psychiatry 2: 534-544, 1960.
13. Lazarus, R.S.: Psychological Stress and the Coping Process, New York, McGraw-Hill, 1966.
14. Coleman, J.C.: Abnormal Psychology and Modern Life (4th ed.), Glenview, Illinois. Scott Foresman and Co., 1972.
15. Hocking, F.: Extreme environmental stress and its significance for psychopathology. Am. J. Psychother. 24(1): 4-26, 1970.
16. Mechanic, D.: Students under Stress, New York, Free Press, 1962.
17. Bieber, I.: Homosexual dynamics in psychiatric crisis. Am. J. Psychiatry 128(10): 88-92, 1972.
18. Grether, W.F.: Effects on human performance of combined environmental stresses. USAF AMRL Technical Report, 1970 (Sept), No 70-68, 15 pp.
19. Martens, R., Landers, D.: Motor performance under stress; a test of the inverted-U-hypothesis. J. Pers. Soc. Psychol. 16: 29-37, 1970.
20. Holmes, T.H., Rahe, R.H.: The social readjustment rating scale. J. Psychosom. Res. 11: 213, 1967.
21. Holmes, T.S., Holmes, T.H.: Short-term intrusions into the life style routine. J. Psychosom. Res. 14(2): 121-132, 1970.
22. Hudgens, R., Robins, E., Delong, W.: The reporting of recent stress in the lives of psychiatric patients: a study of 80 hospitalized patients and 103 informants reporting the presence or absence of specified types of stress. Br. J. Psychiatry 117(541): 635-643, 1970.
23. Smith, R.: Affect adjunctive check lists and the assessment of psychological effects of stress: a study of response bias. Proceedings of the Annual Convention of the American Psychological Association 6(1): 123-124, 1971.
24. Parisen, M.P., Rich, R., Jackson, C.: Suitability of the subjective stress scale for hospitalized subjects. Nurs. Res. 19(6): 529-533, 1969.
25. Prunkl, P.R., Boyles, W.R.: A preliminary application of the critical incident technique to combat performance of Army aviators. HumRRO Professional Paper 24-68: 11, 1968.

26. Raker, J., Wallace, A., Raymer, J.: Emergency medical care in disasters, Disaster Study No. 6 National Acad. of Sciences, Natl. Res. Coun. Publ. 457, Washington, D.C., 1956.
27. Bowlby, J.: Separation anxiety, Int. J. Psychoanal. 41: 89-93, 1960.
28. Rutter, M.: Maternal deprivation reconsidered. J. Psychosom. Res. 16(4): 241-250, 1972.
29. Cholden, L. : Some psychiatric problems in the rehabilitation of the blind. Bull. Menninger Clin. 18: 107-112, 1954.
30. Parkes, C.M.: Components of the reaction to loss of limb, spouse, or home. J. Psychosom. Res. 16(5): 343-349, 1972.
31. Kubler, R.E.: On Death and Dying, New York, Macmillian, 1969.
32. Bronner-Huszar, J.: The psychological aspects of cancer in man. Psychosomatic 12(2): 133-138, 1971.
33. Minde, K.K., Hackett J.D., Killous, P., et al.: How they grew up: 41 physically handicapped children and their families. Am. J. Psychiatry 128(12): 104-110, 1972.
34. Cummings, J.W.: Hemodialysis: feelings, facts, fantasies: the pressures and how patients respond. Am. J. Nurs. 70(1): 70-76, 1970.
35. Sobel, R.: Anxiety-depressive reactions after prolonged combat experience, the old sergeant syndrome. Bull. US Army Med. Dept., Combat Psychiatry Suppl. 137-146, 1949.
36. Glass, A.J.: Observations upon epidemiology of mental illness during warfare. In Symposium on Stress. Washington, D.C., National Research Council and Walter Reed Army Medical Center, 1953, p. 185.
37. Block, J.: Parents of schizophrenic, neurotic, asthmatic, and congenitally ill children. Arch. Gen. Psychiatry 20: 659-674, 1969.
38. Nardini, J.E.: Survival factors in American prisoners of war of the Japanese. Am. J. Psychiatry 109: 241-248, 1952.
39. Strassman, H.D., Thaler, B., Schein, E.H.: A prisoner of war syndrome: apathy as a reaction to severe stress. Am. J. Psychiatry 112: 998-1003, 1956.
40. Coleman, J.C.: Psychology and Effective Behavior, Glenview, Illinois, Scott Foresman and Co., 1969.
41. Coleman, J.C.: Abnormal Psychology and Modern Life, (4th ed.) Glenview, Illinois, Scott Foresman and Co., 1972.
42. Hammond, R., Summers, D.A.: Cognitive control. Psychol. Rev. 79 (1): 58-67, 1972.
43. Fenz, W.D., Epstein, S.: Gradients of physiological arousal in parachutists as a function of an approaching jump. Psychosom. Med. 29: 33, 1967.

44. Capel, W.C., Youngblood, D., Stewart, G.: Note on stress, anxiety, and related defenses in a controlled situation. Psychol. Rep. 27(2): 351-355, 1970.
45. Katz, A., et al.: Stress, disease, and ego defenses. Arch. Gen. Psychiatry 23: 131-142, 1970.
40. Coleman, J.C.: Psychology and Effective Behavior, Glenview, Illinois, Scott Foresman and Co., 1969.
41. Coleman, J.C.: Abnormal Psychology and Modern Life, (4th ed.) Glenview, Illinois, Scott Foresman and Co., 1972.
46. Herrick, D.J.: The Evolution of Human Nature, Austin, University of Texas Press, 1956.
47. Selye, H.: The Stress of Life, New York, McGraw-Hill, 1956.
48. Selye, H.: Stress. Psychol. Today 3(4): 24-26, 1969.
49. Horowitz, M.J., Becker, S., Moskowitz, M.L.: Intrusive and repetitive thought after stress: a replication study. Psychol. Rep. 29(3 Pt. 1): 763-766, 1971.
50. Braverman, M., Hacker, F.J.: Posttraumatic hyperirritability. Psychoanal. Rev. 55(4): 601-614, 1968-9.
51. Strange, R.E., Brown, D.: Home from the war: a study of psychiatric probems in Vietnam returnees. Am. J. Psychiatry 127(4): 488–492, 1970.
52. Hersen, M.: Nightmare behavior: a review. Psychol. Bull. 78(1): 37-48, 1972.
53. Chambers, R.E.: Discussion of "survival factors..." Am. J. Psychiatry 109: 247-248, 1952.
54. Eitinger, L.: Psychosomatic problems in concentration camp survivors. J. Psychosom. Res. 13: 183-190, 1969.
55. Hafner, H.: Psychological disturbances following prolonged persecution. Soc. Psychiatry 3(3): 80-88, 1968.
56. Foy, A.: Dreams of patients and staff. Am. J. Nurs. 70(1): 80-82, 1970.
57. Lifton, R.J.: The "Gook Syndrome" and "numbed warfare." Saturday Review Dec. 1972, pp 66-72.
58. Buhler, C.: The course of human life as a psychological problem. Hum. Dev. 11(3): 184-200, 1968.
59. Engel, G. L.: Adler, R.: Psychological factors in organic disease. Ment. Health Prog. Rep. 1: 1-23, 1967. Washington, D.C., Dept. HEW, U.S. Government Printing Office.
60. Rahe, R.H., Holmes, T.H.: Life crisis and major health change. Psychosom. Med. 28: 774, 1966.
61. Rahe, R.H.: Life change measurement as a predictor of illness. Proc. Res. Soc. Med. 61: 1124, 1968.

62. Rahe, R.H.: Life crisis and health changes. In Psychotropic Drug Responses: Advances in Prediction (May, P., Wittenborn, J., Eds.), Springfield, Illinois, Charles C. Thomas, 1969.

63. Theorell, T., Rahe, R.H.: Psychosocial factors and myocardial infarction I: an inpatient study in Sweden. J. Psychosom. Res. 15(1): 25-31, 1971.

64. Rahe, R.H., Mahan, J. I., Arthur, R.: Prediction of near-future health change from subjects preceding life changes. J. Psychosom. Res.14(4): 401-405, 1970.

65. Rahe, R.H., Lind, E.: Psychosocial factors and sudden cardiac death: a pilot study. J. Psychosom. Res. 15(1): 19-24, 1971.

66. Rahe, R.H., Paasikivi, J.: Psychosocial factors and myocardial infarction II: an outpatient study in Sweden. J. Psychosom. Res. 15(1): 19-24, 1971.

67. Rubin, R.T., Gunderson, E.K., Arthur, R.J.: Life stress and illness patterns in the US Navy: Part III prior life change and illness onset in an attack carrier's crew. Arch. Environ. Health 19: 753-757, 1969.

68. Rahe, R.H., Mahan, J.I., Arthur, R. J., et al: The epidemiology of illness in naval environments: Part I illness types, distribution, severities, and relationship to life change. Milit. Med. 135(6): 443-453, 1970.

69. Rubin, R.T., Gunderson, E.K., Arthur, R.J.: Life stress and illness patterns in the US Navy: Part V prior life change and illness onset in a battleship's crew. J. Psychosom. Res. 15(1): 89-94, 1971.

70. Rubin, R.T., Gunderson, E.K., Arthur, R.J.: Life stress and illness patterns in the US Navy: Part IV environmental and demographic variables in relation to illness onset in a battleship's crew. J. Psychosom. Res. 15(3): 277-288, 1971.

71. Wolf, S., Wolff, H.G.: Human Gastric Functions, New York, Oxford University Press, 1947.

72. Coleman, J.C.: Abnormal Psychology and Modern Life, (4th ed) Glenview, Illinois, Scott Foresman and Co., 1972.

73. Necheles, H.: A blood factor in peptic ulcers. The Sciences 10(9): 15-16, 1970.

74. Schwab, J.J., McGinnis, N.H., Norris, L.B., et al.: Psychosomatic medicine and the contemporary social scene. Am. J. Psychiatry 126(11): 108-118, 1970.

75. Stein, J.: Neurosis in Contemporary Society: Process and Treatment, Belmont, California, Brooks Cole Publishing Co., 1970.

76. Birley, J.L.: Stress and disease. J. Psychosom. Res. 16(4): 235-240, 1972.

77. Senay, E.C., Redlich, F.C.: Cultural and social factors in neuroses and psychosomatic illnesses. Soc. Psychiatry 3(3): 89-97, 1968.

78. Alvarez, W.C.: Chocolate "candy" for X rays, a clue to migraines, an antisenility drug. Look, Sept. 22: 13-14, 1970.
79. Finnerty, F.A.: Hypertension among black women. Sci. News 99(7): 116, 1971.
80. Stamler, J.: In Getze, G. (ed): High blood pressure, the unknown killer. Los Angeles Times, Nov. 12: 1, 5, 1971.
81. Davies, M.: Blood pressure and personality. J. Psychosom. Res. 14(1): 89-104, 1970.
82. Menzies, E.: Psychosocial aspects of eating. J. Psychosom. Res. 14(3): 223-227, 1970.
83. Crisp, A.H.: Premorbid factors in adult disorders of weight, with particular reference to primary anorexia nervosa (weight phobia): a literature review. J. Psychosom. Res. 14(1): 1-22, 1970.
84. Eastwood, M.R., Trevelyan, H.: Stress and coronary heart disease. J. Psychosom. Res. 15(3): 289-292, 1971.
85. Jenkins, C.: Psychologic and social precursors of coronary disease II. N. Engl. J. Med. 284(6): 307-317, 1971.
86. McQuade, W.: What stress can do to you. Fortune 85(1): 102-107, 134, 136, 141, 1972.
87. Parkes, C.M., Benjamin, B., Fitzgerald, R.: Broken heart: a statistical study of increased mortality among widowers. Br. Med. J. (1): 740, 1969.
88. Penrose, R.J.: Life events before subarachnoid hemorrhage. J. Psychosom. Res. 16(5): 329-333, 1972.
89. Jacobs, M.S., Spiken, A.Z., Norman, M.M., et al.: Patterns of maladaptation and respiratory illness. J. Psychosom. Res. 15(1): 63-72, 1971.
90. Le Shan, L.: An emotional life history pattern associated with neoplastic disease. Ann. N.Y. Acad. Sci. 125: 780-793, 196.
91. Stein, S.P., Charles, E.: Emotional factors in juvenile diabetes mellitus: a study of early life experience of adolescent diabetics. Am. J. Psychiatry 128(6): 700-704, 1971.
92. Roark, G.E.: The stress disease. Hum. Behav. 1(3): 29-30, 1972.
93. Heisel, J.S.: Life changes as etiologic factors in juvenile rheumatoid arthritis. J. Psychosom. Res. 16(6): 411-420, 1972.
94. Voth, H., Holzman, P., Katz J., et al.: Thyroid "hot spots": their relationship to life stress. Psychosom. Med. 32(6): 561-568, 1970.
95. Brown, G.W., Birley, J.: Crisis and life changes at the onset of schizophrenia. J. Health Soc. Behav. 9: 203, 1968.
96. Brown, G.W.: Life events and psychiatric illness: some thoughts on methodology and causality. J. Psychosom. Res. 16(5): 311-320, 1972.
97. Paykel, E.S., Myers, J., Dienelt, M., et al: Life events and depression. Arch. Gen. Psychiatry 21: 753-760, 1969.

98. King, L., Pittman, G.: Six-year follow-up of affect disorders in adolescents traced. Roche Report 7(5): 3, 1970.
99. Beck, A.T.: The meaning of depression. Sci. News 96(24): 554, 1969.
100. Cadoret, R.J., Winokur, G., Dorzab, J., et al.: Depressive disease: life events and onset of illness. Arch. Gen. Psychiatry 26(2): 133-136, 1972.
101. Laing, R.D.: Schizophrenic split. Time, Feb. 3, 1967, p. 56.
102. Motto, J.A.: Langley Porter receives grant to study depression and suicide. University of California, University Bulletin 17(36): 180, 1969.
103. Bunch, J.: Recent bereavement in relation to suicide. J. Psychosom. Res. 16(5): 361-366.
104. Abram, H.S., Moore, G.L., Westervelt, F.B., Jr.: Suicidal behavior in chronic dialysis patients. Am. J. Psychiatry 127: 1199–1204, 1971.
105. Hotchner, A.E.: Papa Hemingway, New York, Random House, 1966.
106. Jones, M.C.: Personality correlates and antecedents of drinking patterns in adult males. J. Consult. Clin. Psychol. 32(1): 2-12, 1968.
107. Jones, M.C.: Personality correlates and antecedents of drinking patterns in women. J. Consult. Clin. Psychol. 36 (1): 61-69, 1971.
108. Szyrynski, V.: Crisis theory and criminology. Can. J. Corrections 10(2): 1-13, 1968.
109. Simon, A.: Physical and sociopsychological stress in the geriatric mentally ill. Compr. Psychiatry 11(3): 242-247, 1970.
110. Pavenstedt, E., Bernard, V.W.: Crises of Family Disorganization: Programs to Soften Their Impact on Children, Del. Mar., Behavioral Publications, 1971.
111. Hersen, M.: Nightmare behavior: a review. Psychol. Bull. 78 (1): 37-48, 1972.
112. Birch, H.G.: Malnutrition, learning, and intelligence. Mental Health Digest 4(10): 27-32, 1972.
113. Economics Unit US News and World Report: "Havenot" nations lag while The "haves" get richer. US News and World Report, Oct. 16: 53-54, 1972.
114. Mead, M.: Family future. Trans-action 8(1): 50-53, 1971.
115. Kenniston, K.: Social change and youth in America. In Erikson, E.H. (ed.): Youth: Change and Challenge, New York, Basic Books, 1963.
116. Toffler, A.: Future Shock, New York, Random House, 1970.
117. Ford, A.: Casualties of our time. Sci. 167: 256-263, 1916.
118. Murphy, J.M.: Social science concepts and cross-cultural methods for psychiatric research. In Murphy, Leighton (eds): Approaches to Cross-Cultural Psychiatry, New York, Cornell University Press, 1965, pp. 251-284.
119. Skinner, B.F.: Beyond Freedom and Dignity, New York, Knopf, 1971.

Part Two

Stress and the Police Officer

The readings in Part One clearly support the position that this phenomenon called *stress* is indeed a bodily reaction to specific sociocultural and environmental events. Selye included crowding, sensory deprivation, and urbanization as some of these key factors and identified a number of occupations as particularly susceptible to stress:

- Accountants
- Industrial occupations
- Physicians and dentists
- Lawyers
- Members of the armed forces
- Air traffic controllers
- Police officers

It is the impact on the latter that is, of course, the subject of this book. To these editors and to numerous law enforcement administrators and academicians, it is apparent that the manifestations and effects of police stress can be dangerous to the individual officer, his or her family and department, and the community at large. As Burgin has summarized:

> From the perspective of the individual officer, stress manifests itself in physiological problems, such as heart disease, alcoholism, and other stress related disorders. Psychological disorders and emotional instability are also outcomes of stress, as are broken marriages, overt verbal and/or physical hostility toward the public, and in the extreme, suicide by the police officer. From the perspective of the police organization, stress takes its toll through (a) losses of police officer efficiency, (b) complaints from the public, (c) lawsuits resulting from police malpractice, (d) workmen's compensation claims, (e) disability retirements, and (f) from burned-out personnel in supervisory and management positions who create still more stress in their subordinates, peers and commanding officers (Burgin, 53-54).

So what is police stress? The authors in Part Two provide a comprehensive overview of the subject, its general impact on officers, and the research agenda which has been used and which must still be pursued to fully understand the phenomenon.

During the 1960's, as previously discussed by Coleman, Holmes and Rahe were able to identify 43 life events with major stressful impact on large segments of the population; attach a numerical weight to each event; and relate the cumulative effect of each stressor to the onset of disease. In an early attempt to quantify police stress, Sewell identified 144 critical events in the working life of a police officer and, using a survey instrument, was able to give each a numerical value. These events ranged from the most stressful (violent death of a partner in the line of duty) to the least stressful (completion of a routine report).

Malloy and Mays provide a critical commentary on the issue of job related stress in law enforcement. They suggest that the basic assumptions underlying police stress have been ignored or accepted without empirical verification. Consequently, they attempt to identify the assumptions underlying the concept of police stress; review the empirical evidence related to these assumptions; and offer an alternative paradigm designed to guide future research on police stress.

Currently a faculty member at the FBI National Academy, Band, along with his co-author, examined the performance of 60 police officers in relation to their measured levels of self-esteem, self-perception of ability to cope with stress and self-appraisal of competence. Their results indicate that, in general, these officers had substantial levels of self-esteem, perceived themselves as able to cope effectively with stressful police situations, and appraised their job performance as quite good. Supervisors of these officers generally concurred with their assessments and gave them fairly high performance ratings. Most significantly, their finding that perception of self-coping ability is most related to effective performance is important quantitative support for qualitative findings of other researchers.

Recognizing that "the most deadly enemy stalking police officers may be...coronary heart disease," Quire and Blount discuss the concerns and efforts by one major police department over a period of four years to assist its 475 sworn officers in lowering their risk of the disease's debilitating and deadly effects. The agency's efforts included recommendations for improving diets, a physical fitness program and mandatory annual comprehensive medical examinations. Their empirical results after several years support the impact of such an organized program.

Graves defines and discusses the development of the various stages of police cynicism and its adverse side effects, including diminished productivity, lower morale and poor community relations. He also examines the prevention of cynicism and the critical leadership role of police administrators in preventing its occurrence.

In their overview of the status of research into police stress, Sewell and his colleagues suggest that five major questions must be addressed in order to accurately assess the impact of the stress concerns on the administration of law enforcement agencies: First, what is the best method to define and measure individual and collective stress within a police organization? Second, how many police agencies have implemented stress management programs? Third, what type and size of agency are most likely to implement stress management programs? Fourth, what do existing stress management programs encompass? Finally, what are the practical implications of any existing research data and what critical stress research issues must still be addressed?

References

Burgin, A.L. (1978). "The Management of Stress in Policing." *Police Chief*, 45(4), 53-54.

Selye, H. (1967). *The Stress of Life* (Revised Edition). New York, NY: McGraw Hill

3

The Development of a Critical Life Events Scale for Law Enforcement

James D. Sewell

Over the last several years, society in general and a number of professional fields in particular have shown an increasing concern over the concept and visible manifestations of stress, especially those arising from one's occupation. Among the professions where stress has been a special concern is law enforcement. As Burgin (1978, pp. 53–4) has summarized:

> ...From the perspective of the individual officers, stress manifests itself in physiological problems, such as heart disease, alcoholism, and other stress-related disorders. Psychological disorders and emotional instability are also outcomes of stress, as are broken marriages, overt verbal and or physical hostility toward the public, and, in the extreme, suicide by the police officer.
>
> From the perspective of the police organization, stress takes its toll through: (a) losses of police officer efficiency, (b) complaints from the public, (c) lawsuits resulting from police malpractice, (d) workmen's compensation claims, (e) disability retirements, and (f) from burned-out personnel in supervisory and management positions who create still more stress in their subordinates, peers and commanding officers.

Inventories of Stressful Life Events

Since the effects of police stress pose such a serious problem for the law enforcement profession and particularly its administrators, there should be a means to gauge the magnitude of specific stressors. Yet, research on police stress thus far shows more effort devoted to discussions of the existence and nature of the stress than to an evaluation of its magnitude (Eisenberg 1975; Kroes 1976; Ellison and Genz 1978; Stratton 1978). In medical and psychological research into stress as it affects the general population, however, one can find scales designed to measure the degree of stress and subsequent readjustment caused by specific life stressors.

As a result of previous research into stress-precipitated illnesses. Holmes and Rahe (1967. p. 213) held that "a cluster of social events requiring changes in ongoing life adjustment is significantly associated with the time of illness onset." Efforts by Holmes and Rahe (1974) and other colleagues have indicated a common denominator relating each of these events.

> The occurrence of each event usually evoked, or was associated with, some adaptive or coping behavior on the part of the involved individual. Thus, each item was constructed to certain life events whose advent is either indicative of, or requires a significant change in, the ongoing life pattern of the individual. The emphasis is on change from the existing steady state and not on psychological meaning, emotion, or social desirability.

Because prior studies had only produced the number and types of events formulating this cluster, these researchers attempted to develop a scale judging the magnitude of these events. Using the Social Readjustment Rating Questionnaire (SRRQ) made up of 43 life events requiring adaptive behavior and arbitrarily assigning 1 (marriage) a score of 50, Holmes and Rahe utilized a sample of 394 subjects to rate the events on their relative degree of necessary readjustment. The mean value of the life events was subsequently formulated into the Social Readjustment Rating Scale.

In subsequent research, Holmes and Rahe were able to further utilize this scale to accomplish a more detailed understanding of the effects of stress on individuals. As Pilowsky (1974, p. 128) summarized their work:

> The scale was then used to obtain a quantitative assessment of changes in the course of life and to investigate their relationship to illness. A "life-crisis" was defined as any clustering of life-changing events whose individual values added up to 150 or more "life change units" in a single year.... Further work established a linear relationship between the magnitude of the life-crisis and the risk of changes in health. It was also shown that the greater the life-change score, the more severe the illness which ensued. This sort of finding confirms the oft made clinical observation that illnesses, whether predominantly physical or psychological, occur in clusters, usually following a series of changes in life.

Since its development, the Social Readjustment Rating Scale of Holmes and Rahe has been applied to a variety of populations including Japanese (Masuda and Holmes 1967), black, Mexican, and white Americans (Komaroff, Masuda, and Holmes 1968); Danes (Rahe 1969); Western Europeans (Harmon, Masuda, and Holmes 1970); Swedes (Rahe, Lundberg, Bennett, and Theorell 1971); medical students (Mendels and Weinstein 1972); and New Zealanders (Isherwood and Adam 1976). In most of these studies, the researchers found that, when compared with the original Holmes-Rahe sample, their research "indicated essential similarities in their attitude towards life events, but with some interesting differences which reflect cultural variation" (Masuda and Holmes 1967, p. 236). In criticism of the original study, however, several researchers noted that its major limitation "is its failure to discriminate between positive and negative events" (Mendels and Weinstein 1972, p. 531).

The relationship between illness onset and significant stressful events has been further documented by the research of Antonovsky and Kats (1967), who found a significant relationship between the crisis score of patients and the onset of multiple sclerosis; by Brown and Birley (1968, pp. 203–14), who contended that "both first and subsequent acute schizophrenic attacks were at times produced by clear-cut crises and life changes which most commonly occurred in the 3 weeks before the attack;" and by Cline (1978), who found a significant relationship between the quality and magnitude of stressful daily events encountered in the training of officers in the armed forces and daily changes in health, attitude, affect, body biochemistry, and on-the-job performance. As a result of their study, Brown and Birley further suggested that the additive effects of stress events may be of particular concern in emotional disturbances and onset of illness.

Based on these research efforts, the development of a professional stressful life event scale can be hypothesized to be useful in dealing with stress in the law enforcement profession for two primary reasons. First, it should allow administrators and researchers to analyze and assess the stressful events faced by a law enforcement officer. Second, in its refined state, it should allow for better prediction and control of crisis points in an officer's life: those occasions where a buildup of stressful life events will adversely affect his ability to fulfill his occupational role.

Development of the Survey Instrument

The procedures utilized by Holmes and Rahe, that is, the compilation of a list of critical events, the assignment of stress values to these events by a study group, and the ranking of these events as a result of their mean values, would appear to be a logical approach to the development of a professional life events scale in law enforcement. Where Holmes and Rahe drew on their experience in psychiatry to develop the initial list of critical events, this research employed another method as being more empirically sound.

Early in the research process and in response to the criticism that the Holmes-Rahe Scale was not comprehensive enough, it was recognized that a large group of law enforcement officers, drawing from their diverse professional backgrounds, educational levels, and personal skills, could better provide a listing of stressful events than could a single researcher relying on limited experience and research. Thus, an open-ended questionnaire was designed and distributed to an initial survey group. The first part of that instrument gathered basic demographic information from each respondent; the second part asked the respondent to "list specific occupational events...that you see as the most positively and/or negatively stressful upon today's law enforcement officer." It was further emphasized in the instructions that the respondent need not have experienced any of the events which were listed.

This questionnaire was administered to 3 distinct groups of law enforcement officers: 250 officers attending a session of the FBI National Academy; 37 officers of a university public safety agency; and 49 members of a predominantly rural sheriff's department. Although each group may be viewed as a sample of convenience, specific reasons existed for the choice of each.

The FBI National Academy can be viewed as a logical selection for the administration of the initial questionnaire for several reasons. First, it houses under one roof, and within relatively easy access, a large number of potential respondents (250 officers per session). Second, the officers at each 11-week session are at least 5-year veterans who, from either personal experience or observation, should have a reasonably strong understanding of the specific problems which confront a contemporary police officer. Third, because attendees are selected from federal, state, and local agencies throughout the county, the sample offers a broad spectrum of the law enforcement profession in terms of age, race, education, size and types of department, professional expertise, and time in service and, consequently, should allow for the development of a more inclusive list of professional life events.

Yet the strong points of the FBI National Academy also foster its weaknesses. It is a highly selective school, both from the perspective of the agency nominating a candidate for its training and of the Federal Bureau of Investigation in its procedures for final selection of attendees. The criteria used for selection of attendees may, therefore, bias the list of stressful life events. This research assumed, however, that the size of the sample and the broad experiential level of the officers in attendance would reduce the effects of the academy's selectivity and allow for an adequate list of critical life events in the working world of a police officer: as a result, it closely parallels the approach used in an experience survey described by Selltiz (1959, pp. 55–9).

The university public safety department and sheriff's department were chosen for several reasons. First, both were easily accessible to the researcher. Second, the use of both allowed further input from the members of two specialized agencies on specific areas of stress they experienced.

Third, the use of these agencies allowed some comparison and contrast with the responses from the more elite group of officers attending the FBI National Academy. Finally, particularly in the case of the university agency, a high return rate and a significant amount of quantifiable information were expected.

Of the preliminary questionnaires distributed, 281 (83.6 percent) were returned and utilized. As a result of the specific stressors identified by respondents on the initial questionnaire, and based in some measure on the researcher's experience as a law enforcement officer, a list of 130 items was developed for inclusion in the list of Critical Professional Life Events. Subsequent to the development of this listing of events, a variety of academic and professional law enforcement personnel reviewed the questionnaire for its content validity. With the input provided by this informal panel of judges, the listing was expanded to 144 events and prepared in full questionnaire form for distribution. To overcome another major criticism of the Holmes-Rahe instrument, the items of this scale were placed in order by the use of a table of random numbers, hopefully reducing the clustering of serious events at the beginning of the questionnaire.

Final Survey Instrument and Sample Selection

The final survey instrument included both a request for demographic information and the list of 144 Critical Professional Life Events. Respondents were instructed to rate each event from 1 to 100 in terms of professional stress readjustment in comparison with a designated constant event ("changing work shifts") with an assigned value of 50. For the purpose of this study, and based on the wording of the Holmes-Rahe instrument instructions, stress readjustment in one's profession was defined as "the amount and duration of change in one's accustomed pattern of work resulting from various job-related events...it measures the intensity and length of time necessary to adjust to an event within one's professional life, regardless of the desirability of the event." Respondents were asked to carefully read through the entire list, then assign a value to each event based on the proportionate length and intensity of readjustment required when comparing that event to the designated constant. As an additional study variable, respondents were further asked to designate those events which they had personally experienced.

For the same reasons discussed earlier, the FBI National Academy was again chosen as the site for administration of the final questionnaire. With the cooperation of the staff of that facility, 2 sessions of the FBI National Academy, each containing 250 officers, were designated as the study sample. The final instrument was administered by staff of the Academy's

Behavioral Sciences Unit. To provide an additional group for analysis and comparison, a Virginia county police department (N=270) was also selected as a study sample, and the final instrument was disseminated through its Research and Development Section.

In developing their stress scale, Holmes and Rahe turned to the field of psychophysics for the best method of estimating the intensity of stress readjustment. That particular method, magnitude estimation, "has been used to gauge the consensus concerning the intensity or degree for such variable or strength of expressed attitudes, pleasantness, seriousness of crimes, and other subjective dimensions" (Stevens 1966, p. 330). Following a detailed review of the use of magnitude estimation in social sciences. Holmes and Rahe recognized the geometric mean to be the statistic of choice as the measure of central tendency. Similarly in this research, the geometric mean of each professional life event in the law enforcement scale was calculated, and the scores were ranked in descending order of magnitude. Standard deviations were also obtained for each event in order to evaluate the variability of scores within the events comprising the scale. Based on these geometric mean values, a Law Enforcement Critical Life Events Scale was ultimately developed.

Respondent Profile

Of a total of 770 questionnaires distributed, 378 (49.1 percent) were returned and used in the study. The typical respondent from the total sample was a married, Caucasian male, between 30 and 39 years of age, and having at least some college education. In addition, the majority of respondents (73.3 percent) indicated they had not previously married (that is, were single or currently married to their only spouse): 22.8 percent had been married once, and 4.0 percent two or more times.

Although extensive comparison data are not readily available, the personal profile developed here would appear to parallel law enforcement officers in this country. Contemporary American law enforcement is, as a whole, still a predominantly Caucasian male occupation, with college graduates a significant although increasing minority and with the majority of its occupational population under the age of 40.

Surprisingly, in this sample the percentage of officers (26.7 percent) who were divorced at least once was significantly below that found by other research into the police divorce rate in Tacoma (82 percent) and Seattle (60 percent), Washington; and San Jose, California (60 percent). It was more similar to that discovered in Baltimore, Maryland (17 percent): Los Angeles (21 percent) and Santa Ana (27 percent), California: and Chicago, Illinois (33.3 percent) (DePue 1979, p. 9). This particular statistic of police stress may have been scaled downward by the use of the FBI National Academy to provide the major portion of the study population. Most agencies would, in the opinion of this researcher, choose their most stable, productive officers for nomination to the FBI National Academy; such a selection process, which would reward the successful police officer with this benchmark in his career, might necessarily reduce the number of divorced officers in this program because, as DePue has explained:

> ...most experts would agree that a stable family relationship is a signifi-
> cant contributing factor to a successful law enforcement career: an unsta-
> ble relationship would most likely have the opposite result (1979, p. 9).

Additionally, the typical respondent in the total sample had been in law enforcement between 6 and 15 years; was primarily in middle management (sergeant, lieutenant, or captain); was assigned to either patrol, investigations, or administrative functions; and was a member of an agency best respondent-defined as "city" and lacking a stress management program. Again, due to the selection process of the FBI National Academy, the percentage of officers assigned to patrol (29.6 percent), those with less than 5 years service (2.1 percent), and those with less than 5 years service (2.1 percent), and those at entry-level rank (6.4 percent) are probably significantly under represented. Similarly, those with over 15 years "on-the-job" (35.7 percent), performing administrative functions (27.8 percent), or in supervisory and middle-level management positions (sergeant, lieutenant, and captain) (59.4 percent) are probably exaggerated.

From a stress-related illness standpoint, over half (52.1 percent) of the respondents indicated that they had experienced at least one of eight stress-related illnesses; the most commonly reported were digestive disturbances (25.4 percent) and increased alcohol use (22.8 percent). This data were strikingly similar to that developed during the preliminary questionnaire, in which 52.0 percent indicated that they had experienced at least one physical indicator of stress; 26.1 percent reported digestive disturbances; and 19.9 percent reported increased alcohol use. Such information indicates a commonality of stress-related diseases between two distinct samples of police officers (total N=658) and implies the validity of contemporary concerns about such manifestations of stress. The percentages indicating that they had experienced two particular manifestations — coronary heart disease (1.3 percent) and increase alcohol use (22.8 percent) — were lower than expected. The former was in all probability due to the physical requirements for FBI National Academy admission. The latter may be due in part, again, to the selection process of the academy and in part to the reluctance of many persons, not just police officers, to accurately respond to such a question.

Analysis of the Critical Life Events Scale

In its final form, the values of the Critical Life Events Scale (Table 1) run from a high of 88 for the most stressful event, "violent death of a partner in the line of duty," to a low of 13 for the least stressful, "completion of a routine report." The rounding of geometric mean scores resulted in the assignment of the same whole-number value to many events.

As table 1 indicates, the events reflecting over 60 points on the scale, and consequently requiring the greatest amount of readjustment, were concerned with violence or threatened violence, personnel matters, or ethical concerns. Included in these events were also "police-related civil suit" and "criminal indictment of a fellow officer," events which would seem to precipitate high stress. One other event—"assignment away from family for a long period of time"—ranked higher (14) than expected possibly because the majority of respondents, those attending the FBI National Academy, were away from home for 11 weeks, the duration of the FBI National Academy session. A relatively high ranking (31) of that event by the county police subgroup indicates, however, that such a family separation is still a significant stressor, regardless of the current situation of the officers.

The events receiving 35 points or less, that is, those requiring the least amount of readjustment after the event, can also be broadly classified as involving community relations, or legal/judicial, administrative, and operational concerns. Each of these events, such as duty assignments, overtime duty and court appearances, can be defined as "routine" and, with two exceptions, "award from a citizen's group" and "assignment to decoy duty," had been experienced by a minimum of 65 percent of each subgroup within the total sample. It is highly likely that the regular occurrence of these common events reduces the perceived magnitude of the stress which they cause: it seems apparent, then, that repeated experiences lessens much of the fear and frustration which fosters the stressfulness of life events.

An analysis of the rankings by subgroup indicated that the Virginia county police department ranked its most stressful events, "dismissal" and "violent death of a partner in the line of duty," with higher values than the values assigned to *any* event by either of the FBI National Academy sessions. More Arlington County police officers (7.9 percent and 27.0 percent respectively) had also experienced these two stressors than had officers of the other two groups. It is this researcher's opinion that much of this perception of the magnitude of these stressors may be due to the particularly heavy emphasis placed upon both the "job" and one's partner by line officers, for whom the risk and fear of losing either is often perceived as more real and potentially imminent than by personnel who are currently in investigative, supervisory, and administrative positions.

Table 1
Law Enforcement Critical Life Events Scale

Event	Value	Event	Value
1. Violent death of a partner in the line of duty	88	34. Failure on a promotional examination	60
2. Dismissal	85	35. Suicide of an officer	60
3. Taking a life in the line of duty	84	36. Criminal indictment of a fellow officer	60
4. Shooting someone in the line of duty	81	37. Improperly conducted corruption investigation of another officer	60
5. Suicide of an officer who is a close friend	80	38. Shooting incident involving another officer	59
6. Violent death of another officer in the line of duty	79	39. Failing grade in police training program	59
7. Murder committed by a police officer	78	40. Response to a "felony-in-progress" call	58
8. Duty-related violent injury (shooting)	76	41. Answering a call to a sexual battery/abuse scene involving a child victim	58
9. Violent job-related injury to another officer	75	42. Oral promotional review	57
10. Suspension	72	43. Conflict with a supervisor	57
11. Passed over for promotion	71	44. Change in departments	56
12. Pursuit of an armed suspect	71	45. Personal criticism by the press	56
13. Answering a call to a scene involving violent non-accidental death of a child	70	46. Investigation of a political/highly publicized case	56
14. Assignment away from family for a long period	70	47. Taking severe disciplinary action against another officer	56
15. Personal involvement in a shooting incident	70	48. Assignment to conduct an internal affairs investigation on another officer	56
16. Reduction in pay	70	49. Interference by political officials in a case	55
17. Observing an act of police corruption	68	50. Written promotional examination	55
18. Accepting a bribe	68	51. Department misconduct hearing	55
19. Participating in an act of police corruption	56	52. Wrecking a departmental vehicle	55
20. Hostage situation resulting from aborted criminal action	68	53. Personal use of illicit drugs	54
21. Response to a scene involving the accidental death of a child	68	54. Use of drugs by another officer	54
22. Promotion of inexperienced/incompetent officer over you	68	55. Participating in a police strike	53
23. Internal affairs investigation against self	66	56. Undercover assignment	53
24. Barricaded suspect	66	57. Physical assault on an officer	52
25. Hostage situation resulting from a domestic disturbance	65	58. Disciplinary action against partner	52
26. Response to "officer needs assistance" call	65	59. Death notification	51
27. Duty under a poor supervisor	64	60. Press criticism of an officer's actions	51
28. Duty-related violent injury (non-shooting)	63	61. Polygraph examination	51
29. Observing an act of police brutality	62	62. Sexual advancement toward you by another officer	51
30. Response to "person with a gun" call	62	63. Duty-related accidental injury	51
31. Unsatisfactory personnel evaluation	62	64. Changing work shifts	50
32. Police-related civil suit	61	65. Written reprimand by a supervisor	50
33. Riot/crowd control situation	61	66. Inability to solve a major crime	48
		67. Emergency run to "unknown trouble"	48
		68. Personal use of alcohol while on duty	48
		69. Inquiry into another officer's misconduct	47
		70. Participation in a narcotics raid	47
		71. Verbal reprimand by a supervisor	47

Table 1 (continued)
Law Enforcement Critical Life Events Scale

Event	Value	Event	Value
72. Handling of a mentally/emotionally disturbed person	47	106. Unfair plea bargain by a prosecutor	37
73. Citizen complaint against an officer	47	107. Assignment to a specialized training program	37
74. Press criticism of departmental actions/practices	47	108. Assignment to stakeout duty	37
75. Answering a call to a sexual battery/abuse scene involving an adult victim	46	109. Release of an offender on appeal	37
76. Reassignment/transfer	46	110. Harassment by an attorney in court	37
77. Unfair administrative policy	46	111. Administrative recognition (award/commendation)	36
78. Preparation for retirement in the near future	46	112. Court appearance (felony)	36
79. Pursuit of a traffic violator	46	113. Annual evaluation	35
80. Severe disciplinary action to another officer	46	114. Assignment to decoy duty	35
81. Promotion with assignment to another unit	45	115. Assignment as partner with officer of the opposite sex	35
82. Personal abuse of prescription drugs	45	116. Assignment to evening shift	35
83. Offer of a bribe	45	117. Assignment of new partner	34
84. Personally striking a prisoner or suspect	45	118. Successful clearance of a case	34
85. Physical arrest of a suspect	45	119. Interrogation session with a suspect	33
86. Promotion within existing assignment	44	120. Departmental budget cut	33
87. Handling a domestic disturbance	44	121. Release of an offender by a jury	33
88. Answering a call to a scene involving the violent non-accidental death of an adult	44	122. Overtime duty	29
89. Change in supervisors	44	123. Letter of recognition from the public	29
90. Abuse of alcohol by another officer	44	124. Delay in a trial	28
91. Response to a silent alarm	44	125. Response to a "sick or injured person" call	28
92. Chance in the chief administrators of the dept.	43	126. Award from a citizens group	27
93. Answering a call to a scene involving the accidental death of an adult	43	127. Assignment to day shift	26
94. Move to a new duty station	43	128. Work on a holiday	26
95. Fugitive arrest	43	129. Making a routine arrest	26
96. Reduction in job responsibilities	43	130. Assignment to a two-man car	25
97. Release of an offender by the prosecutor	41	131. Call involving juveniles	25
98. Job-related illness	41	132. Routine patrol stop	25
99. Transfer of partner	40	133. Assignment to a single-man car	25
100. Assignment to night shift duty	40	134. Call involving the arrest of a female	24
101. Recall to duty on day off	39	135. Court appearance (misdemeanor)	24
102. Labor negotiations	39	136. Working a traffic accident	23
103. Verbal abuse from a traffic violator	39	137. Dealing with a drunk	23
104. Change in administrative policy/procedure	38	138. Pay raise	23
105. Sexual advancement toward you by a citizen	37	139. Overtime pay	22
		140. Making a routine traffic stop	22
		141. Vacation	20
		142. Issuing a traffic citation	20
		143. Court appearance (traffic)	19
		144. Completion of a routine report	13

During the course of developing the scale, the percentage of respondents within the total sample and each sub-sample who had experienced a given event was determined. From the total sample, these percentages ranged from lows of 2.9 percent for "accepting a bribe" and 3.7 percent for "personal use of illicit drugs," to 59.8 percent for the standard, "changing work shifts," to a high of 96.0 percent for both "work on a holiday" and "making a routine arrest."

The standard deviation of geometric mean values ranged from a low 1.0947 ("passed over for promotion") to a high of 4.4861 ("vacation"). A significant number of events (130) relected a standard deviation between 1.1 and 2.5; in only three cases ("pay raise," "overtime pay," and "vacation") did the standard deviation exceed 3.0. With the elimination of extreme values through the use of the geometric mean, this scale becomes more reflective than the arithmetic mean as a measure of social consensus and, therefore, a more reliable analytic tool.

Implication

The successful development of a scale such as this has a number of practical implications for the field of law enforcement. First, in a more refined state, it should allow police administrators and personnel managers to analyze the stress of their officers, predict times of high potential for negative manifestations of stress within individual officers, and take appropriate measures to control that stress. Second, it should allow for the development of more comprehensive and improved programs of stress recognition and management within law enforcement agencies. Third, it can be used as an instrument to better educate police families, public officials, and the general public about the concerns, frustrations, and pressures of the officers who protect them.

Perhaps more significantly, this research has several implications for future research. First, continued administration of the final questionnaire to groups of police officers in their home departments or in larger educational/training situations such as the FBI National Academy or the Southern Police Institute should allow for refinement of the scale values. Additional review of the list of events by other officers, particularly those in specialized enforcement units, can assure the inclusion of the maximum number of critical events, reduce the number of events with identical scale scores, and increase the applicability of the scale to a greater number of officers and agencies. Such continued research should produce a more accurate assessment of the stress experienced in law enforcement as evaluated by its participants.

Second, significant differences noted in the mean values of the responses of the county police department from the responses of the two

FBI National Academy sessions would indicate the need for further study. Such research should examine the stress magnitudes perceived by officers of differing ages, sex, race, educational background, agency of employment, type of assignment, and time in service. Hopefully, such efforts would allow for better understanding of personal and departmental factors underlying the phenomenon of police stress.

Third, the interpolation of this scale with the Social Readjustment Rating Scale of Holmes and Rahe could allow for a more detailed analysis of overall life stress experienced by a law enforcement officer. Such a comprehensive scale would take into account personal and job-related stressors which contribute to physical and psychological upset and could produce a more complete understanding of the interaction of occupational and home-life stress.

Finally, this research will allow subsequent researchers to retrospectively examine the relationship between specific stressors and physical or psychological manifestations in a manner similar to the efforts of Holmes and Rahe, Antonovsky and Kats, and Brown and Birley. To that end, a close examination of the work history of officers who have shown diseases of adaptation may pinpoint specific levels of stress which contributed to the onset of the disease. Such research would allow for an increased understanding of the cumulative efforts of stress and its impact on persons in law enforcement.

References

Antonovsky, A., and Kats, R. 1967. Life crisis history as a tool in epidemiological research. *J. Health & Soc. Beh.* 8 (1): 15–21.

Brown, George W., and Birley, J.L.T. 1968. Crises and life changes and the onset of schizophrenia. *J. Health & Soc. Beh. 9 (3): 203–14.*

Burgin, A. Lad. 1978. The management of stress in policing. *Police Chief* 45 (4): 53–4.

Cline, David W. 1978. A stress-value scale for officer candidates. *J. Psych. Res.* 22 (1): 47–55.

DePue, Roger L. 1979. Turning inward: the police officer counselor. *FBI L.E. Bul.* 48(2): 9.

Eisenberg, Terry. 1975. Labor-management relations and psychological stress—View from the bottom. *Police Chief* 42(11): 54–8.

Ellison, Katherine W., and Genz, John L. (1978). The police officer as burned-out samaritan. *FBI L.E. Bul.* 47(3): 1–7.

Harmon, David K.: Masuda, Minoru: and Holmes, Thomas H. 1970. The social readjustment rating scale: A cross-cultural study of Western Europeans and Americans. *J. Psych. Res.* 14 (4): 391–400.

Holmes, Thomas H., and Masuda, Minoru. 1974. Life change and illness susceptibility. In *Stressful life events: Their nature and effects.* by

Barbara Snell Dohrenwend and Bruce P. Dohrenwend. New York: John Wiley and sons.

Holmes, Thomas H., and Rahe, Richard H. 1967. The social readjustment rating scale *J. Psych. Res.* 11:213.

Isherwood, Janette, and Adam, Kenneth S. 1976. The social readjustment rating scale: A cross-cultural study of New Zealanders and Americans. *J. Psych. Res.* 20 (3): 211–14.

Komaroff, Anthony L.; Masuda, Minoru; and Holmes, Thomas H. 1968. The social readjustment rating scale: A comparative study of Negro, Mexican, and white Americans. *J. Psych. Res.* 13 (2): 191–5.

Kroes, William M. 1976. *Society's victim—The policeman.* Springfield, IL: Charles C. Thomas.

Masuda, Minoru, and Holmes, Thomas H. 1967. The social readjustment rating scale: A cross-cultural study of Japanese and Americans. *J. Psych. Res.* 11 (2): 227–37.

Mendels, J., and Weinstein, N. 1972. The schedule of recent experiences: A reliability study. *Psych. Med.* 34 (6): 527–531.

Pilowsky, I. 1974. Psychiatric aspects of stress. In *Man under stress.* by A.T. Welford. New York: John Wiley and Sons.

Rahe, Richard H. 1969. Multi-cultural correlations of life change scaling: America, Japan, Denmark, and Sweden. *J. Psych. Res.* 13 (2): 191–5.

Rahe, Richard H.: Lundberg, Ulf; Bennett, Linda; and Theorell, Tores. 1971. The social readjustment rating scale: A comparative study of Swedes and Americans. *J. Psych. Res.* 15 (3): 241–9.

Selltiz, Claire; Jahoda, Maria; Deutsch, Morton; and Cook, Stuart W. 1959. *Research methods in social relations.* New York: Holt, Rinehart, and Winston.

Stevens, S.S. 1966. A metric for the social consensus. *Science* 15 (3710): 330.

Stratton, John. 1978. Police stress: An overview. *Police Chief* 45 (4): 58–62.

4

The Police Stress Hypothesis: A Critical Evaluation

Thomas E. Malloy
G. Larry Mays

The law enforcement literature of the last decade has been character-ized by numerous papers concerned with police stress and a vast array of psychobiosocial concomitants. Indeed, psychological stress stemming from work in law enforcement has been linked to family disturbance (Nordlicht, 1979; Maslach & Jackson, 1981), substance abuse (Van Raalte, 1981), suicide (Heiman, 1977), premature natural death (Fell, Richard & Wallace, 1980), and a perceived need for counseling (Levitov & Thompson, 1980). In response to the hypothesized high levels of stress experienced by police officers, many law enforcement agencies have initi-ated stress reduction programs designed to reduce stress-related life dis-turbance (Dunne, 1973; Eisenberg, 1975; Kroes & Hurrell, 1975; Dishlacoff, 1976; Stratton & Wroe, 1979).

It appears, however, that a number of basic questions that underlie the police stress hypothesis have been neglected. In particular, what are the sources of police stress and are they unique to law enforcement? Does the literature provide empirical evidence demonstrating that law enforcement is inherently more stressful than other occupations? Does evidence exist that demonstrates a causal relationship between the occupational stress of law enforcement and psychobiosocial dysfunction? These questions repre-sent the starting point of this study.

In a recent paper, Fennell (1981) labeled stress a "cop killer" and but-tressed his argument with the statement that police work is "the most dangerous job in the world emotionally" (p. 170). While Fennell is but one author presenting this position, review of the police science literature suggests that similar ideas have been promulgated by numerous writers. In fact, review of this literature reveals the following two assertions that represent our conception of the traditional police stress hypothesis.

(1) Law enforcement professionals, as a result of the nature of their occupational role, experience a significantly greater degree of stress than members of other occupational groups (Kroes & Hurrell, 1975;

Lewis, 1973; Reiser, 1974; Stratton, 1978b; Fennell, 1981; Kroes, 1976; Margolis & Hurrell, 1974; Fell, Richard, & Wallace, 1980).

(2) The high stress associated with the law enforcement role precipitates a disproportionately high incidence of *family disruption* (Cain, 1981; Maslach & Jackson, 1981; Hageman, 1978; Reiser, 1978; Stratton, 1976; Durner, Kroeker, Miller & Reynolds, 1975; James & Nelson, 1975), *suicide* (Fennell, 1981; Fell, Richard & Wallace, 1980; Heiman, 1975b, 1977; Nelson & Smith, 1970) *psychophysiological disorders* (Fennell, 1981; Maslach & Jackson, 1981; Van Raalte, 1981; Stratton & Wroe, 1979; Unkovic & Brown, 1978; Dishlacoff, 1976; Dunne, 1973; Hitz, 1973), and a host of other medical disturbances such as *coronary heart disease* and *diabetes mellitus* to name but a few (Jacobi, 1975; Terry, 1981).

The Stress of Police Work

In an article in *The Police Chief* (Somodevilla, 1978), the following clinical inference was offered: "It is an accepted fact that a police officer is under stress and pressure unequaled by any other profession" (p.21).

There are really two points inherent in this statement. First, it is suggested that law enforcement is *the* most stressful of all professions, and second, it is asserted that this is an accepted fact. A review of the police science literature does indeed show that the police stress hypothesis has been generally accepted as an established fact. Only rarely has the validity of this hypothesis been examined (for example, Terry, 1981; Webb & Smith, 1980; Smith & Webb, 1980) or critically scrutinized (Ford, Alexander, & Lester, 1971; Lester & Mink, 1979; Lester & Gallagher, 1980). What follows is a presentation of evidence (empirical, theoretical, and anecdotal) germane to the police stress hypothesis.

Evidence Related to the Police Stress Hypothesis

An early and often cited study of occupational stress among police officers was conducted by Kroes, Margolis, and Hurrell (1974). This study involved a semistructured individual interview of 100 male policemen from the Cincinnati Police Force. These men ranged in age from 21 and 53 years, with a mean age of 28 years. All but 4 of the 100 subjects of the investigations were Caucasian.

In this study, data were gathered on the basis of responses to four standardized questions. Responses were then assigned to nominal categories and then either the number or percentage of responses falling in each category were tabulated in summary form.

Data from the Kroes, Margolis, and Hurrell (1974) study suggested that the following sources of stress were perceived by officers as paramount:

(1) Court leniency with criminals and a lack of consideration when scheduling court appearances emerged as a major stressor among the sample.

(2) The second major source of stress centered on administrative policies (for example, work assignments, procedures) and lack of support from higher administration.

(3) The third major stressor was equipment. The three major concerns regarding equipment were poor condition, lack of air conditioning (data were collected in the summer), and lack of equipment.

(4) Community relations was the fourth major source of stress, with public apathy and the policeman's negative image being consistently cited as stressors.

(5) Changing shift routine was the fifth most often cited stressor. Shift work was stressful because of the impact on eating habits, family life, and the sleep cycle.

These results indicated that the perceived sources of stress among this sample were largely organizational or bureaucratic in nature. These results stand in direct contrast to clinical observations (for example, Somodevilla, 1978) that posit a strong relationship between the potential for physical injury in this occupation and police officer stress.

Reiser (1974) has presented the argument that traditional police organizations are by nature "authoritarian" and breed alienation among the line officer and management. As a result, the officer is in an essentially helpless position (Selgiman, 1975) within the organizational system—little that he or she does impacts the management level. Reiser maintained that the organizational structure of police departments represents a significant sources of stress for the individual officer. This thesis appears to be supported, in part, by the Kroes, Margolis, and Hurrell (1974) data. Recall that the self-reported sources of stress apparent in this study were largely beyond the control of the line officer.

A major methodological weakness of the Kroes, Margolis, and Hurrell (1974) study stems from the absence of an adequate control group. While their results are intriguing, there is no way of knowing if the sources of police stress they discerned differ markedly from the stressors experienced in other occupational groups. However, a study by Fell, Richard, and Wallace (1980) attempted to bridge this gap. This study involved an epidemiological investigation of recorded death certificates, community mental health center records, and admission data from general medical centers in the State of Tennessee during the years 1972–1974. A major strength of this study was the comparison it permitted of death rates, mental health problems, and medical health records for police officers relative to 130 other occupational groups.

Results from analysis of death certificates suggested that police (N = 48) had a significantly high rate of premature death (between the ages of 18 and 64) relative to what might be expected due to chance. "Police ranked twenty-four among 130 occupations in rate of premature death" (p. 141). A further analysis (chi-squared) of the causes of death for the 130 reference occupations and for police revealed no significant differences. Thus, while these data suggested that police have a higher rate of premature death than the sample of reference occupations, the cause of police officer deaths (both premature and non-premature) was not significantly different from that other occupational groups.

This study also showed that police (N = 5) ranked third among the 130 occupations in rate of suicide, behind laborers and house painters. Unfortunately, the authors failed to report a frequency analysis to ascertain if the observed rate of police suicide was significantly greater than which might be expected by chance.

The rate of admission of police officers (N = 26) to community mental health centers was not significantly greater than that which might be observed due to chance: "Police ranked 70th of the 130 occupations in their rate of admission" (p. 142). Chi-squared analysis further revealed that there was no significant difference in the frequency of any particular diagnosis rendered for police officers relative to the reference occupations.

Finally, this study revealed that police officers (N = 66) were admitted to medical hospitals at a rate significantly greater than that which might be expected due to chance. However, further analysis of the diagnoses rendered showed that no particular diagnosis was significantly more frequent among the police patients relative to the patients from 130 other occupational groups.

These results suggested that police officers may have a significantly higher incidence of premature death and hospital admissions than other occupational groups. However, they do not differ significantly from other occupational groups on cause of death or on the specific diseases requiring hospitalization. Further, they do not differ significantly on admissions to mental health treatment. When officers do seek medical health treatment, the diagnoses rendered are not significantly different from those made for other occupational groups. These data must be cautiously interpreted because of potential hidden sources of artifact. For example, the results may be biased because of the relatively small number of police officers that were compared to the much larger reference samples and may be an artifact of sampling bias. Also, since sampling was not random in this study, the results may not be reliable. Other confounds may exist as well. For example, greater frequency of admission to general hospitals may be due to the availability of health insurance plans with greater benefits that lead police officers to utilize health services at a greater rate than individuals in other occupations. Thus, there appear to be alternative explanations of these data that are not necessarily congruent with a police stress interpretation. Two studies (Lester & Mink, 1979; Lester & Gallagher, 1980) represent the only controlled attempts we have encountered that compare police officers and other occupational groups on stress indices. Lester and Mink, for example, compared policemen and office workers from a semi-rural town on adjective checklist ratings of their work. Results indicated that "the policemen rated their jobs significantly more often as satisfying, good, respected, useful, and providing a sense of accomplishment and less often as routine, boring, frustrating, simple, and endless" (p. 554). Results did show, however, that policemen reported that "job-related stress affected them outside of work" significantly more often than the office workers.

However, the results of the Lester and Mink (1979) study may have been confounded by sex or age differences across the two occupational groups. In a subsequent study, Lester and Gallagher (1980) compared the frequency of self-reported stress symptoms by police officers and division managers at a department store. Subjects in each group did not differ on age, education, marital status, or whether they worked shifts. Results indicated that the two groups did not differ in the frequency of headaches, irritation, satisfaction, anger, fulfillment, tiredness, indigestion, relief, frustration, and happiness. The store managers disagreed more strongly that "the stress from my work is carried over after I have left work, and affects my life at home," (p. 882). Lester and Gallagher concluded that these data did not support the hypothesis that law enforcement involves more stress than other occupations.

In a related study, Ford, Alexander, and Lester (1971) demonstrated that self-reported fear of death was not greater among police officers in comparison to a control group of mail carriers and college students. This result is significant in light of the popular inference in the literature that the impending danger of physical harm and death represents a major stressor for police officers.

A recent study by Levitov and Thompson (1981) was designed to assess the self-perceived stress of police officers (N= 143) from a major metropolitan area and its relationship to their perceptions of counseling. Results indicated that 59% of the officers indicated that they "definitely or probably" would seek counseling if available. The results also showed that 29% of the officers reported "high or above average" levels of stress. Twenty percent of the officers reported "no stress or below average amounts" of stress. Unfortunately, no control group was employed in this study, making a more general interpretation of these data difficult.

Sewell (1981) has developed the Law Enforcement Critical Life Events Scale (LECLES) for the measurement of police stress, an instrument modeled after the Social Readjustment Rating Scale of Holmes and Rahe (1967) for the study of psychophysiological illness. The LECLES is composed of two sections. The first section represents the 25 most stressful events in law enforcement, ranging from the violent death of a partner in the line of duty to a "hostage situation resulting from a domestic disturbance." The other scale represents the 25 least stressful events of this work, ranging from a "departmental budget cut" to the "completion of a routine report." At present, the utility of this instrument is largely undetermined and awaits empirical validation. Yet, given research experience with the Social Readjustment Rating Scale, studies that attempt to link the LECLES with psychobiosocial dysfunction will probably not significantly work in this area.

This rather pessimistic appraisal is based upon the accumulated data from research on human psychophysiological disorders. For example, although many studies (for example, Dohrenwend & Dohrenwend, 1974) suggest a significant relationship between stressful life events and future illness, there are at least two points to consider. First, correlation coefficients computed on measures of stressful life suggests the relative independence (in practical rather than statistical terms) of these two dimensions. Second, as Kobasa (1979) demonstrated, there are apparently many individuals who lead quite stressful lives yet do not succumb to illness. In fact, Kobasa, Maddi, and Kahn (1982) have recently suggested that "by now it seems likely that any blanket conclusion about the debilitating effects of stressful life events is an overgeneralization" (p. 168).

Anlaysis of the Evidence

At present, the major focus in "stress and illness" research has been on organismic and environmental variables that lead to differential susceptibility to stress-related illness. For example, investigators have recently highlighted the capacity of "resistance resources" (Antonovsky, 1979) to counter the deleterious effects of stressful life events. Other researchers have demonstrated that stress-neutralizing effects of psychological "hardiness" (Kobasa, 1979; Kobasa, Maddi, & Kahn, 1982), social support (Katz & Kahn, 1978), and physiological strategies such as paced respiration (McCaul, Solomon, & Holmes, 1979) designed to mediate stressful situations.

In short, it is probably an oversimplification to suggest that stress precipitates illness or that occupational experiences of the police officer necessarily lead to psychobiosocial dysfunction. Rather, the true state of affairs is surely more complex. The data indicate that the development of illness following exposure to the various stressors associated with normal living, and presumably with occupation, are mediated by a number of intervening variables (for example, hardiness, social support, genetic factors, health practices, and personality dispositions). For these reasons, it seems unlikely that a summary of law enforcement stressors will predict the development of illness or other states of distress. In many ways, the stress research methodology has been shaped by the logic of the interactionist strategy for the study of personality and social behavior and thus requires consideration of both personal and environmental variables (see Magnusson & Endler, 1977; Cantor & Khilstrom, 1980; Bowers, 1973; Funder & Ozer, 1983; Snyder & Ickes, in press).

The police stress literature reviewed above raises interesting questions. Why do studies that compare police officers and other occupational groups generally fail to show significantly higher stress levels among the officers? Also, why does the fear of death and personal harm fail to emerge as a significant source of stress for police officer? These questions take on added significance when they are considered in light of the multitude of clinical and/or anecdotal reports that describe the significant levels of stress experienced by law enforcement personnel (for example, Henderson, 1981; Somodevilla, 1978; Leonard & Tully, 1980; Farmer & Monahan, 1980; Stratton, 1978; Reiser, 1978; Leyden, 1977; Lewis, 1973; Kroes & Hurrell, 1975). Perhaps the apparent contradiction between clinical observation and empirical data stems, in part, from the manner in which the police stress phenomenon has been conceptualized and scrutinized.

Police Stress and Its Concomitants: The Available Evidence

Although the police stress hypothesis has strong intuitive appeal, it has very little sound empirical support. The bulk of the work on this topic has been done by law enforcement professionals, while behavioral scientists have rarely ventured into this area. This is unfortunate because a body of well-controlled stress research is available and could serve as a guide for controlled studies of police stress. Even more unfortunate is the gap that exists between the police stress literature and the general experimental literature on stress. As a result, the police stress literature fails to reflect the conceptual shifts regarding stress that have been made as a result of accumulated experimental evidence. In the following paragraphs, a number of the salient and presently outstanding questions regarding the police stress hypothesis will be raised.

Is Police Work Stressful?

The answer to this question is quite likely yes; however, there is a growing awareness that all occupations are stressful (Margolis, Kroes, & Quinn, 1974). A major problem with the police stress hypothesis stems from a priori assumptions regarding the stressors inherent in police work. The anecdotal literature suggests that the impeding threat of physical harm or death and participation in violence are the major police stressors. However, in studies of police officers, these activities fail to emerge as major stressors (Kroes, Margolis, & Hurrell, 1974; Sparger & Giacopassi, 1982). While law enforcement is likely a stressful occupation, it is probably stressful for reasons quite different from those typically presented in the literature. Judging from the strongest research in this area, it seems that helplessness and feelings of uncontrollability in the work environment may be a major source of stress for police officers. Beyond this, little can be safely concluded. Quite clearly, studies are needed that differentiate those stressors peculiar to police work from those of other occupations.

Is Police Work More Stressful Than Other Occupations?

Judging from the most well-controlled studies available (and even these have potentially significant methodological confounds), the answer is no, yet this present conclusion remains very tentative. For example, the Fell, Richard, and Wallace (1980) research suggested that police officers had a significantly higher rate of premature death and hospital admissions, however, they did not manifest a significantly greater incidence of mental health treatment, unique causes of death, or unique mental and physical health diagnoses relative to other occupational groups. Similarly, the controlled studies by Lester and Mink (1979), Lester and Gallagher (1980), and Ford, Alexander, and Lester (1971) suggested that police officers responding to adjective checklists do not report significantly more job dissatisfaction or fear of death than workers in the control occupations. Moreover, other research (Disken, Goldstein, & Grencik, 1977) has suggested that, as a group, police officers may be less anxious than random samples drawn from the general population. There is, however, some evidence that job stress carries into the officer's personal life (Lester & Mink, 1979) and further that some officers perceive a personal need for counseling (Levitov & Thompson, 1981).

There are data that particular occupations are highly stressful and precipitate secondary stress-related illness. For example, Cobb and Rose (1973) reported higher rates of peptic ulcer, diabetes mellitus, and hypertension among air traffic controllers relative to a control sample of pilots.

McCord (1948) has suggested a similar phenomena among railway dispatchers. However, comparable data on police officers does not presently exist. Given the available data, there is little scientific support for the hypothesis that police work is more stressful than other occupations. Clearly, well-controlled studies making inter-occupational comparisons of stress levels are essential if this Gordian knot is ever to be unraveled.

The Stress-Illness Relationship

The earliest assumption in the psychophysiological literature was that high stress levels precipitate physiological dysfunction (Selye, 1956). More recently, this model has been modified to include variables that mediate psychophysiological responses to stress. Data indicate that the impact of stress on an organism is mediated by the predictability of the stressor's occurrence (for example, Seligman, 1968; Weiss, 1971a, 1971b, 1971c; Mezinskis, Gliner, & Shember, 1971; Price, 1972), the ability to control the stress (for example, Weiss, 1968, 1971a, 1971b, 1971c; 1977; Gliner, 1972; Moot, Cebulla, & Crabtree, 1970; Hokanson & Burgess, 1962; Hokanson, Burgess, & Cohen, 1963; Hokanson, Willers, & Koropsak, 1968; Stone & Hokanson, 1969; Hokanson, DeGood, Forrest, & Brittain, 1971; Thompson, 1981), the genetic makeup-predisposing factors of the organism (for example, Engel & Bickford, 1961; Shapiro, 1961; Hodapp, Weyer, & Becker, 1975; Sines, 1963; Mirsky, 1958; Weiner, Thaler, Reiser, & Mirsky, 1957), individual differences in personality (for example, Bandura, 1982; Kobasa, 1979; Kobasa, Maddi, & Kahn, 1982; Antonovsky, 1979), and social support (Katz & Kahn, 1978) to list but a few of these variables.

Thus, it is probably an oversimplification to assume that (a) law enforcement is highly stressful for *all* police officers, and (b) the majority of police officers suffer as a result of occupational stress. Rather, there may be significant variation among individuals who work in law enforcement on the many variables that mediate psychobiosocial dysfunction in response to stress. Future research on police stress should focus not only on intergroup (that is, police-non-police) comparisons but on intragroup (that is, among police officers) which make them more or less susceptible to the deleterious effects of stress.

Theoretical Assumptions and Methodological Concerns in Police-Stress Research

Analysis of existing literature suggest that future research in this area must be undertaken with past methodological flaws in mind. Researchers may wish to conduct controlled inter-occupational studies (that is, police-non-police) to ascertain the relative stress of police work and the nature of the stressors peculiar to this occupation. Studies of this sort will demonstrate the particular and unique stressors experienced by police officers if, in fact, they do exist. However, we believe that well-controlled studies will fail to find significant differences in stress due simply to occupational category. Rather, we suspect the most fruitful strategy will involve studies concerned with variability on relevant mediating dimensions within this occupational group that make one more or less susceptible to the disruptive effects of stress. Second, sampling procedures must be improved in this research area if results are to be taken seriously. Most police stress studies fail to include control groups, fail to sample randomly, have too few subjects and heavily biased samples. Also, almost all of this literature is concerned with the Caucasian male police officer while little attention has been directed at the female, ethnic, or racial minority officer. Third, this literature is characterized by inferences that go well beyond the data. It appears that some authors have a strong emotional investment in a particular position and perceive almost any data as supportive. Fourth, studies in this area are almost entirely uncontrolled or correlational, designs that do not permit inferences regarding causality (Campbell & Stanley, 1963). Experimental and longitudinal studies are essential if research in this area is to progress to a more sophisticated level. And, finally, those interested in police stress are encouraged to abandon the hypothesis that all police officers are highly stressed and that this stress causes an unusually high incidence of alcoholism, drug abuse, psycho physiological disorders, cardiovascular disease, suicide, or family disruption. In its place, we propose an alternative model that does not assume that police work is the most stressful occupation in America. Rather, this model assumes that all occupations are stressful to varying degrees while acknowledging that some occupations may be inherently more stressful than others and that stress may vary as a function of a specific role within an occupational category. It also assumes that occupational stress represents just one source of stress among the many associated with life in a complex modern society. Thus, even if different occupations are differentially stressful, it is essential to consider the various sources of stress different individuals experience in their social-psychological system and their capacity to respond adaptively.

An Alternative Theoretical Paradigm

In the following pages, two theoretical models are presented. The proximity-control hypothesis is offered as a guide for research concerned with person-situation interactions that result in stress among police officers. The stress-diathesis model is offered as a guide for research concerned with adaptive and maladaptive human responses to stress and the mediational link between stress and psychobiosocial consequences.

The Proximity-Control Hypothesis

The greatest heuristic value of the stress-diatheses model lies in its ability to predict differential responses to the stress of police work. However, it fails to address differential levels of stress that appear to be a function of an officer's particular occupational role—such as Cynicism (Niederhoffer, 1967) and Task Related Stressors (Terry, 1981). For example, consider the following duty assignments:

(1) A white police officer assigned to patrol duty in Harlem.
(2) A black police officer assigned to patrol duty in Marin County, California.
(3) A police officer assigned as a computer programmer.
(4) A deputy sheriff in a sleepy Southern town.
(5) A state trooper assigned to radar duty on an interstate highway.

These examples highlight the strong possibility that police stress may vary significantly as a function of the particular occupational role of the officer. To account for this role effect, we propose the proximity-control hypothesis that predicts that police stress (that is, physiological arousal, negative psychological state) is functionally related to the physical and psychological proximity of the officer to society necessitated by the occupational role and the degree to which this interaction requires the social control of others. The proximity-control hypothesis is really a specific organizing principle that falls within the structure of a more general metatheory of social impact (Latané & Nida, 1980). Social impact theory provides a social engineering model that accounts for the impact of individuals on each other, groups on each other, individuals on groups, and groups on individuals. Latane predicts that the social impact (in this case stress) of sources (in this case society) on a target (a police officer) is a multiplicative function of the strength (S), immediacy (I), and the number (N) of sources present during the social encounter. As stated by Latane and Nida (1980):

> When it comes to social impact, the theory suggests that the amount of impact experienced by the target should also be a multiplicative function of the strength (S), the immediacy (I), and the number (N) of sources present. In this case by strength we mean the salience, power, importance, or intensity of a given source to the target – usually determined by such things as the source's status, age, socio-economic status, prior relationship with

the target, or future power over the target. By immediacy we mean close-ness in space or time and absence of intervening barriers or filters. By num-ber we mean how many people there are. Putting this first principle in the form of an equation, we can say that Impact is a function of the Strength times the Immediacy times the Number of sources: I = f(SIN). (p. 7)

The theory further suggests that the impact of the group is not a direct linear function of the size of the group. Rather, as the size of the group increases, the impact of each new additional member is less than the impact of the last member added to the group. This "marginal impact" of each new member of the group is similar to S.S. Stevens's (1957) basic law of psychophysics. This law, concerned with differences between objective physical reality and subjective psychological reality, suggests that as the objective physical inten-sity of a stimulus increases, the subjective psychological perception of stimu-lus intensity is proportional to the objective stimulus intensity raised to a characteristic root. Formally stated, Stevens's law of psychophysics is

$$\Psi = K\phi^{\beta}$$

where Ψ is the psychological perception of stimulus intensity and ϕ is the objective intensity of the physical stimulus. β is the characteristic root (ex-ponent) by which the organism transforms the physical stimulus and K is a scaling constant. It should be recalled that the value β is thought to be a constant value for any particular stimulus dimension (for example, light, weight, pressure).

In a parallel fashion, Latane provides a psychosocial law that is concep-tually similar to Stevens's law of psychophysics. Formally stated:

$$I = SN^{t}$$

where I is the social impact upon the organism. S is scaling constant re-flecting the nature of a particular social encounter, N is the number of sources, and t is the characteristic root of the number of sources. Because of the marginal impact principle, the exponent t will always have a value that is less than unity.

Thus, it can be seen that the Proximity-Control Hypothesis operational-ized by the metatheory of social impact makes specific predictions about what types of situations should engender police stress and at what levels. The stress-diathesis model, on the other hand, makes specific predications regarding probable responses to police stress and resultant consequences.

As stated earlier, the proximity-control hypothesis is but a personifica-tion of social impact theory within the realm of police stress. Thus, the empirical validity of both the former hypothesis and latter theory are of great importance. The proximity-control hypothesis remains untested while social impact theory has a developing data base (for example,

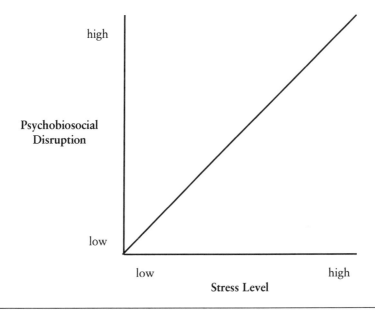

Figure 1: The Traditional Police Stress Model

Latané & Harkins, 1976; Latané & Cappell, 1972; Latané & Darley, 1970; Latané & Nida, 1980; Latané & Dabbs, 1975; Latané, 1981). A review of this literature, however, is beyond the scope of the present article and interested readers should consult the references cited above.

The Stress-Diathesis Model

In Figures 1 and 2 on the following page, the traditional police stress model and an alternative conceptual paradigm are presented. It can be seen from Figure 1 (the traditional police stress model) that a monotonic linear relationship is predicted between police stress and psychobiosocial disruption (for example, alcoholism, drug abuse, suicide, family disruption).

The traditional stress model assumes that police officers are more highly stressed than other occupational groups and suffer a higher incidence of pathological outcomes. In essence, there is a hypothesized one-to-one relationship between the stress engendered by law enforcement and a vast array of psychobiosocial concomitants. However, a major issue this model neglects is the process whereby general high stress levels lead to a particular disturbance from among a vast array of possibilities.

An alternative stress model makes no a priori assumption regarding differential occupational stress levels and recognizes that stress originates

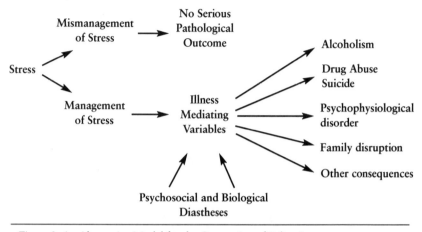

Figure 2: An Alternative Model for the Conception of Police Stress

from many sources. The alternative conception is presented schematically in Figure 2.

This model is built on the assumption that all individuals experience stress (regardless of occupation) that must be managed. While some occupations may be more or less stressful, it does not necessarily follow that "high stress occupations" precipitate physical, psychological, or social disruption among all, or even most, of its members. Rather, it is hypothesized that psychobiosocial distress results from (a) an inability to manage the stress levels experienced, and (b) a complex interaction of genetic and social-psychological illness mediating variables. A similar model has been presented by Davidson and Neale (1982) and termed the Diathesis-Stress Paradigm. They described the model as follows:

> Termed the *diathesis-stress* approach, it considers the often subtle inter-
> actions between a *predisposition* toward disease — the diathesis — and
> environmental, or life, events disturbing people — the stress. Diathesis
> refers most precisely to a constitutional predisposition toward illness, but
> the term may be extended to any tendency or inclination a person may
> have to respond in a particular way to an environmental stress. The cog-
> nitive set already mentioned, the chronic feeling of helplessness sometimes
> found in the depressed, may be considered a diathesis for depression. It is
> a fact that some people break down in certain ways when exposed to cer-
> tain stressors, whereas, others come through even more terrible trauma
> apparently unscathed. (Davidson & Neale, 1982, p. 64)

From a Diathesis-Stress perspective, future research on police stress should focus on those physical and social-psychological variables that significantly affect the management of stress that all police officers are assumed to experience to varying degrees. Also, this model suggests that those physical and social-psychological variables that mediate development of a *particular* psychobiosocial concomitant of stress should be a prime target of future research.

An example of the type of research necessary in the future is exemplified in an experiment on the coping patterns of law enforcement officers exposed to a psychological stressor in the laboratory. In this study (Diskin, Goldstein, & Grencik, 1977), 135 male deputies were randomly selected from the Los Angeles County Sheriff's Department. In the study, the researchers assessed the level of anxiety (high or low) and characteristic personality defense mechanisms (avoidance, nonspecific defense, or sensitivization-coping) and randomly assigned subjects to one of three stressful experimental conditions. In Condition I, subjects were exposed to a relaxing travel film, then given a cognitive rehearsal preparing them for a stress-inducing film. In Condition II, subjects were given a 10-minute relaxation interval, then given a cognitive rehearsal preparing them for the film. In Condition III, subjects were simply presented the film. Psychophysiological measures of skin conductance and self-report measures of reactivity served as indices of arousal in response to presentation of the stressor.

A number of significant results emerged from this experiment. As the authors stated,

> A central outcome of this study is the confirmation of the influences of prior expectational set and level of informational content in the stimulus environment upon psychophysiological reactivity to stress. (p. 70)

This result with police officers was analogous to stress research with animals—the predictability of a stressor mediates the impact on the organism. In the case of police officers, cognitive rehearsal coupled with relaxation significantly reduced arousal to a stress-inducing film in comparison to the condition where police officers were given no preparatory cues. The authors concluded,

> This difference appears attributable to the presence of information: When danger is preceded by some form of preparation, a marked reduction in skin conductance results when the stressor is actually confronted. (p. 65)

Results also revealed the presence of interactions among anxiety level, coping style, and the experimental conditions. The primary significance of these interactions stems from the empirical support they provide for a central theme of this article—there is likely significant within-group variance among police officers on salient dimensions that determine their individual responses to stress.

A final outcome of this experiment involved an analysis of officer performance ratings made by supervisors along the dimensions of coping style and anxiety. The results revealed significant differences on performance ratings due to anxiety level (low anxious officers had highest performance ratings) and an interaction between coping style and anxiety. The authors noted,

> The least amount of reactivity was exhibited by the same groups who earned the highest performance evaluations; it should be noted that low scores on the psychophysiological scale correspond to high scores on the job effectiveness scale. (p. 68)

This study provides an excellent example of research on discrete personality dimensions that affect a police officer's response to stress. Particularly significant is the parallel nature of stress response and performance evaluation data. Perhaps studies on the response to stress by police officers may also aid in the understanding of police officer performance.

Conclusions

Presently, it is difficult to say how much stress is associated with law enforcement or to define the direct consequences of this stress. While most writers have assumed a priori that police work precipitates high stress levels, there has been a growing awareness that many past assumptions may not be valid (see Terry, 1981).

Associated with the issue of stress levels has been a concern over the psychophysiological consequences of stress. As Terry concluded, previous studies on this topic are not definitive and often contradictory. However, if one accepts uncritically the conventional wisdom on police occupational stress, it follows that one should accept all the implications of the traditional police stress paradigm.

In attempting to evaluate the police stress hypothesis, the following factors must be taken into account. First, police work is stressful in the same sense that any occupation is stressful. However, whether police work is more or less stressful than other occupations remains an empirical question. In fact, it may be conceptually disadvantageous to organize this phenomena under the rubric of "police stress." This organizing principle suggests a homogeneity within this occupational category that fails to consider (a) variance on stress due to differences in occupational role, and (b) individual differences on stress response capacities. In short, the traditional police stress theory requires homogeneity assumptions that appear invalid. We encourage a greater appreciation for within-group heterogeneity on significant relevant dimensions.

Second, some attempt has been made to identify the environmental stressors associated with police work. Again, however, because of the limited number and scope of carefully controlled studies, the stressors unique to law enforcement (assuming they exist) have not been clearly identified. Yet, it does appear that the organizational structure and the feelings of uncontrollability they may engender are perhaps major (and readily adjusted) sources of stress for officers. A major outstanding question is concerned with the impact of the potential for physical harm and the effect of participation in violence. The theory of social impact is an appropriate paradigm for the investigation of these issues.

Third, research has failed to adequately address the issues of differential response to environmental stressors. If police work is a highly stressful occupation, what coping mechanisms exist that allow officers to successfully respond to the stressors? The stress-diathesis model is appropriate for the study of these issues.

Finally, future research on police stress may be most productive if it focuses on the nature of stressors peculiar to law enforcement, individual differences in response to stress, and stress inoculation strategies that promote an adaptive response to stress. Until well-controlled, empirically based studies of police stress are completed, we are doomed to espousing the conventional wisdom associated with the police stress hypothesis, or to lamenting the scant data base currently available. Neither of these choices seems acceptable to most social scientists.

References

Antonovosky, A. (1979). *Health, stress and coping.* San Francisco: Jossey-Bass.

Bandura, A. (1982). Self-efficacy mechanisms in human agency. *American Psychologicalist*, 37, 122–147.

Bowers, K.S. (1973). Situations in psychology: An analysis and critique. *Psychological Review*, 80, 307–336.

Cain, M.E. (1981). Interdependence with family — marital integration and domestic life. In G. Henderson (Ed.), *Police human relations.* Springfield, IL: Charles C. Thomas.

Campbell, D.T. & Stanley, J.C. (1963). *Experimental and quasi-experimental designs for research.* Chicago: Rand McNally.

Cantor, N. & Khilstrom, J.F. (Eds.) (1981). *Personality, cognition, and social interaction.* Hillsdale, NJ: Lawrence Erlbaum.

Cobb, S. & Rose, R.M. (1973). Hypertension, peptic ulcer, and diabetes in air traffic controllers. *Journal of the American Medical Association*, 224, 489–493.

Davidson, G.C. & Neale, J.M. (1982). *Abnormal Psychology: An experimental clinical approach.* New York: John Wiley.

Diskin, S.D., Goldstein, M.J. & Grencik, J. M. (1977). Coping patterns of law enforcement officers in simulated and naturalistic stress. *American Journal of Community Psychology, 5,* 59–73.

Dishlacoff, L. (1976). The drinking cop. *The Police Chief,* 43, 32, 34, 36, 39.

Dohrenwend, B.S. & Dohrenwend, B.P. (Eds.) (1974). *Stressful life events.* New York: John Wiley.

Dunn, J. A. (1973). Counseling alcoholic employees in a municipal police department. *Quarterly Journal of Studies on Alcohol,* 34, 423–434.

Durner, J.A., Krocker, M.A., Miller, C.R., & Reynolds, W.R. (1975). Divorce — another occupational hazard. *The Police Chief,* 42, 48–53.

Eisenberg, T. (1975). Job stress and the police officer: Identifying stress reduction techniques. In W.H. Kroes & J.J. Hurrell (Eds.). *Job stress and the police officer: Identifying stress reduction techniques* (HEW Publication No. (NIOSH) 76–187). Washington, DC: U.S. Government Printing Office.

Engel, B.T. & Bickford, A.F. (1961). Response specificity: Stimulus response and individual response specificity in essential hypertension. *Archives of General Psychiatry, 5,* 487–489.

Farmer, R.E. & Monahan, L.H. (1980). The prevention model for stress reduction: A concept paper. *Journal of Police Science and Administration, 8,* 54–60.

Fell, R.D., Richard, W.C. & Wallace, W.L. (1980). Psychological job stress and the police officer. *Journal of Police Science and Administration, 8,* 139–143.

Fennell, J.T. (1981). Psychological stress and the peace officer, or stress — a cop killer. In G. Henderson (Ed.), *Police human relations.* Springfield, IL: Charles C. Thomas.

Ford, R.E., Alexander, M., & Lester, D. (1971). Fear of death of those in a high stress occupation. *Psychological Reports,* 29, 502.

Funder, D.C. & Ozer, D.J. (1983). Behavior as a function of the situation. *Journal of Personality and Social Psychology,* 44, 107–112.

Gliner, J.A. (1972) Predictable versus unpredictable shock: Preference behavior and stomach ulceration. *Physiology and Behavior,* 9, 693–698.

Hageman, M.J.C. (1978). Occupational stress and marital relationships. *Journal of Police Science and Administration,* 6, 402–412.

Heiman, M. (1975). Police suicides revisited. *Suicide,* 5, 3–21.(a)

Heiman, M. (1975). The police suicide. *Journal of Police Science and Administration,* 3, 267–273.

Heiman, M.G. (1977). Suicide among police. *American Journal of Psychiatry,* 134, 1286–1290.

Hitz, D. (1973). Drunken sailors and others: Drinking problems in specific occupations. *Quarterly Journal of Studies on Alcohol*, 34, 496–505.

Hodapp, V., Weyer, G., & Becker, J. (1975). Situational stereotypy in essential hypertension patients. *Journal of Psychosomatic Research*, 19, 113–121.

Hokanson, J.E. & Burgess, M. (1962). The effects of three types of aggression on vascular processes. *Journal of Abnormal and Social Psychology*, 65, 446–449.

Hokanson, J.E., Burgess, M., & Cohen, F.F. (1963). Effects of displaced aggression on systolic blood pressure. *Journal of Abnormal and Social Psychology*, 67, 214–218.

Hokanson, J.E., DeGood, D.E., Forrest, M.S., & Brittain, T. M. (1971). Availability of avoidance behaviors for modulating vascular-stress responses. *Journal of Personality and Social Psychology*, 19, 60–68.

Hokanson, J.E., Willers, K.R., & Koropsak, E. (1968). Modification of autonomic responses during aggressive interchange. *Journal of Personality*, 36, 386–404.

Holmes, T.H. & Rahe, R.E. (1967). The social readjustment rating scale. *Journal of Psychosomatic Research*, 11, 213–218.

Jacobi, J.H. (1975). Reducing police stress: A psychiatrist point of view. In W.H. Kroes & J.J. Hurrell (Eds.). *Job stress and the police officer: identifying stress reduction techniques* (HEW Publication No. (NIOSH) 76–187). Washington, DC: U.S. Government Printing Office.

James, P. & Nelson, M. (1975). The police family. *FBI Law Enforcement Bulletin*, 44, 12–15.

Katz, D. Kahn, R.L. (1978). *The social psychology of organizations*. New York: John Wiley.

Kroes, W.H. & Hurrell, J.J. (Eds.). (1975). *Job stress and the police officer: Identifying stress reduction techniques* (HEW Publication No. (NIOSH) 76–187). Washington, DC: U.S. Government Printing Office.

Kroes, W.H., Margolis, B.L. & Hurrell, J.J. (1974). Job stress in policemen. *Journal of Police Science and Administration*, 2, 145–155.

Kobasa, S.C. (1979). Stressful life events, personality, and health: An inquiry into hardiness. *Journal of Personality and Social Psychology*, 37, 1–11.

Kobasa, S.C., Maddi, S.R. & Kahn, S. (1982). Hardiness and health: A prospective study. *Journal of Personality and Social Psychology*, 42, 168–177.

Latané, B. (1981). The psychology of social impact. *American Psychologist*, 36, 343–356.

Latané, B. & Cappell, H. (1972). The effects of togetherness on heart rate in rats. *Psychonomic Science*, 29, 177–179.

Latané, B. & Dabbs, J. (1975). Sex, group size, and helping in three cities. *Sociometry*, 38, 180–194.

Latané, B. & Darley, J. M. (1970). *The unresponsive bystander: Why doesn't he help?* New York: Appleton-Century-Crofts.

Latané, B. & Harkins, S. (1976). Cross-modality matches suggest anticipated stage fright a multiplicative power function of audience size and status. *Perception and Psychophysics, 20,* 482–488.

Latané, B. & Nida, S. (1980). Social impact theory and group influence: A social engineering perspective. In P.B. Paulus (Ed.). *Psychology of group influence.* Hillsdale, NJ: Lawrence Erlbaum.

Leonard, J.A. & Tully, G.P. (1980). Occupational stress and compensation in law enforcement. *FBI Law Enforcement Bulletin, 49,* 22–26.

Lester, D. & Gallagher, J. (1980). Stress in police officer and department store managers. *Psychological Reports, 46,* 882.

Lester, D. & Mink, S.R. (1979). Is stress higher in police officers? An exploratory study. *Psychological Reports, 45,* 554.

Levitov, J.E. & Thompson, B. (1981). Stress and counseling needs of police officers. *Counselor Education and Supervision, 21,* 163–168.

Lewis, R.W. (1973). Toward an understanding of police anomie. *Journal of Police Science and Administration, 1,* 484–490.

Leyden, J.P. (1977). Police stress: A possible approach. *FBI Law Enforcement Bulletin, 46,* 25–29.

Magnusson, D. & Endler, N.S. (Eds.). (1977). *Personality at the crossroads: Current issues in interactional psychology.* Hillsdale, NJ: Lawrence Erlbaum.

Margolis, B.L., Kroes, W.H., & Quinn, R.P. (1974). Job stress: An unlisted occupational hazard. *Journal of Occupational Medicine, 16,* 659–661.

Maslach, C., & Jackson, S.E. (1981). Burned-out cops and their families. In G. Henderson (Ed.) *Police human relations.* Springfield, IL: Charles C. Thomas.

McCaul, K.D., Solomon, S., & Homes, D.S. (1979). Effects of paced respiration and expectations on physiological and psychological responses to threat. *Journal of Personality and Social Psychology, 37,* 564–571.

McCord, C.P. (1948). Life and death by the minute. *Industrial Medicine, 17,* 377–382.

Mezinskis, J., Gliner, J., & Shember, K. (1971). Somatic response as a function of no signal, random signal, or signaled shock with variable or constant durations of shock. *Psychonomic Science, 25,* 271–272.

Mirsky, I.A. (1958). Physiologic, psychologic, and social determinants in the etiology of duodenal ulcer. *American Journal of Digestive Diseases, 3,* 285–314.

Moot, S.A., Cebulla, R.P., & Crabtree, J.M. (1970). Instrumental control and ulceration in rats. *Journal of Comparative and Physiological Psychology, 71,* 405–410.

Nelson, T. & Smith, W. (1970). The law enforcement profession: An incident of high suicide. *Omega,* 1, 293–299.

Niederhoffer, A. *Behind the shield.* (1967). Garden City, NY: Doubleday.

Nordlicht, S. (1979). Effects of stress on the police officer and family. *New York State Journal of Medicine,* 79, 400–401.

Price, K.P. (1972). Predictable and unpredictable shock: Their pathological effects on restrained and unrestrained rats. *Psychological Reports,* 30, 419–426.

Reiser, M. (1974). Some organizational stresses on policemen. *Journal of Police Science and Administration,* 2, 156–159.

Reiser, M. (1976). Stress, distress, and adaption in police work. *The Police Chief,* 43, 24–27.

Seligman, M.E.P. (1968). Chronic fear produced by unpredictable shock. *Journal of Comparative and Physiological Psychology,* 66, 402–411.

Seligman, M.E.P. (1975). *Helplessness.* San Francisco: W.N. Freeman.

Selye, H. (1956). *The stress of life.* New York: McGraw-Hill.

Sewell, J.D. (1981). Police stress. *FBI Law Enforcement Bulletin,* 50, 7–11.

Shapiro, A.P. (1961). An experimental study of comparative responses of blood pressure to different noxious stimuli. *Journal of Chronic Diseases,* 13, 293–311.

Sines, J.O. (1963). Physiological and behavioral characteristics of rats selectively bred for susceptibility to stomach ulcer development. *Journal of Neuropsychiatry,* 4, 396–396.

Smith, K.L. & Webb, S.D. (1980). Police and stress: research strategies for the future, *Southern Journal of Criminal Justice,* 5, 45–52.

Snyder, M. & Ickes, W. (in press). Personality and social behavior. In G. Lindzey & E. Aronson (Eds.), *Handbook of social psychology.* Reading, MA: Addison-Wesley.

Somodevilla, S.A. (1978). The psychologist's role in the police department. *The Police Chief,* 45, 21–23.

Sparger, J.R. & Giacopassi, D.J. (1982). *Copping out: Why police leave the force.* Paper presented at the annual meeting of the Academy of Criminal Justice Sciences, Louisville, KY, March 23–27.

Stevens, S.S. (1957). On the psychophysical law. *Psychological Review,* 64, 153–181.

Stone, L.J. & Hokanson, J.E. (1969). Arousal reduction via self-punitive behavior. *Journal of Personality and Social Psychology,* 12, 72–79.

Stratton, J. (1976). The law enforcement family: Programs for spouses. *FBI Law Enforcement Bulletin,* 45, 16–22.

Stratton, J.G. (1978). Police stress-part II. Considerations and suggestions. *The Police Chief,* 45, 73–78.

Stratton, J.B. & Wroe, B. (1979). Alcoholism and the policemen. *FBI Law Enforcement Bulletin,* 48, 20–23.

Terry, W.C. (1981). Police stress: The empirical evidence. *Journal of Police Science and Administration, 9*, 61–75.

Thompson, S.C. (1981). Will it hurt less if I can control it? A complex answer to a simple question. *Psychological Bulletin, 90*, 89–101.

Unkovic, C., & Brown, W.R. (1978). The drunken cop. *The Police Chief, 45* 18–20.

Van Raalte, R.C. (1981). Alcohol as a problem among officers. In G. Henderson (Ed.), *Police human relations*. Springfield, IL: Charles C. Thomas.

Webb, S.D. & Smith, D.L. (1980). Police stress: A conceptual overview. *Journal of Criminal Justice, 8*, 251–257.

Weiner, H., Thaler, M., Reiser, M.F., & Mirsky, I.A. (1957). Etiology of duodenal ulcer: Relation of specific psychological characteristics to rate of gastric secretion. *Psychosomatic Medicine, 17*, 1–10.

Weiss, J.M. (1968). Effects of coping responses on stress. *Journal of Comparative and Physiological Psychology, 65*, 251–260.

Weiss, J.M. (1971). Effects of coping behavior in different warning-signal conditions on stress pathology in rats. *Journal of Comparative and Physiological Psychology, 77*, 1–13(a).

Weiss, J.M. (1971). Effects of punishing the coping response (conflict) on stress pathology in rats. *Journal of Comparative and Physiological Psychology, 77*, 14–21(b).

Weiss, J.M. (1971). Effects of coping behavior with and without a feedback signal on stress pathology in rats. *Journal of Comparative and Physiological Psychology, 77*, 22–30. (c)

Weiss, J.M. (1977). Psychological and behavioral influences on gastrointestinal lesions in animal models. In J.D. Maser & M.E.P. Seligman (Eds.), *Psychopatholgy: Experimental models*. San Francisco: W.H. Freeman.

5

Stress and Police Officer Performance: An Examination of Effective Coping Behavior

Stephen R. Band
Caroline A. Manuele

Research studies consistently describe the stress associated with police work as unique and relatively violent in comparison to the stresses encountered in the general population.

Ellison and Genz (1978) identified two main types of stress endemic to police work: (1) acute or situational stress; and (2) chronic stress. The first type of stress (acute stress) results from work with cases involving such situations as child victimization or an accidental death. It also results from being exposed to situations which are physically and emotionally dangerous (Roberts, 1977; Wambaugh, 1975). The second type of stress (chronic stress) arises from frustration with department processes and related work functions. Hillgren, Bond, and Jones (1976) identify these chronic stressors as role conflicts between administration and the individual officer's conception of the police role; problems with a lenient court system; officer peer group influence and internal department investigations.

Police officers also face unique stressors associated with other aspects of their work. Kelling and Pate (1975) identify the stressful effects of being alienated from the client groups they serve when larger numbers of people react to them with fear, suspicion, prejudice, and open hostility. Alienation also occurs as a result of conflicts which tend to mismatch expectations between the police, the community, and fellow officers.

Studies of police work-related stress have identified a variety of problems that result from exposure to these types of stressors. Among these problems are burnout, a syndrome characterized by emotional and physical depletion, negative self-esteem and negative attitudes toward people, life, and work (Ellison and Genz, 1978; Kafrey, 1981); personal difficulties including alcohol abuse, family problems, divorce, and suicide (Baxter, 1975; Blackmore, 1978, Richard, 1975; Roberts, 1977); and physical disorders such as coronary heart disease, ulcers, and hypertension (Jacobi, 1975). The prevention of these stress-related problems is associated with how well officers are able to engage in adaptive coping behavior.

Coping under stress involves an active, adaptive process in which an individual employs strategies to manage a specific environment. Coping can be viewed behaviorally as the level of competence an individual exhibits in response to a stressful situation, i.e., actual job performance. In managing stress, however, there is a psychological component which involves the emotional adaptability a person has to recover from the personal cost of impact incurred by responding to a stressful situation (Goldfried and D'Zubilla, 1969; Zeitlin, 1980). This type of coping has been identified as "self-coping efficacy" by researchers and it involves the degree to which individuals perceive themselves as being able to effectively implement a coping behavior that allows them to tolerate stress. Self-coping efficacy includes the type of positive statements individuals make to themselves about their ability to cope; their feelings of confidence about performing specific tasks and their expectation of how effective they will be as they actively try to cope with a task (Bandura, 1980; Mischel, 1981).

Personality differences also account for a person's ability to employ coping mechanisms in the context of stressful situations. Perhaps the most significant of these differences involves levels of self-esteem. People with high levels of self-esteem seem to be immune to some of the stresses that affect people with low self-esteem. They have more confidence in their ability to solve problems, tend to approach problem-solving tasks more directly, and have less need to protect their self-esteem. They, therefore, tend to cope with problems in an active, direct way with less withdrawal needs than the person with lower self-esteem (Stotland and Canon, 1972).

Individual efforts to cope with stress have also been found to operate on a continuum of adaptive to maladaptive behavior. Adaptive coping facilitates solutions to problems whereas maladaptive coping involves strategies which may provide immediate relief from the stress of the moment but generate increased stress over time (Zeitlin, 1980). An example of maladaptive coping behavior would be using alcohol or drugs to mask the effects of anxiety associated with having to perform competently in a highly stressful environment.

If competence, self-coping efficacy and levels of self-esteem are related to coping effectively with stress in the general populations, it seems likely that these traits would also be related to how well police officers cope with the stress of police work. To date, however, there have been no attempts to examine how these variables influence police officer performance (Bandura et al, 1980; Schalon, 1968; Rosenberg, 1965).

Research on coping with stress suggests that police officers who are competent in their actual work performance should manifest less stress since effective performance generally produces a sense of emotional well being while ineffective performance may result in negative emotional responses like apathy, anxiety, and depression. Effective performance or competence may not, however, be the only indication of how well officers are coping with stress. Performing effectively may, as noted above, be done at some cost to the individual if there is not a concomitant psychological experience of being able to cope. Competent performance without a sense of self-efficacy or self-esteem may result in coping behaviors over time that are more maladaptive than adaptive.

The purpose of this study, then, was to identify levels of competence, self-coping efficacy and self-esteem in police officers and to examine the relationship between these variables and actual field performance with police patrol tasks. Another purpose of this study was to examine how this relationship is affected by length of police service, since research also shows that the effects of police stress may, over time, change personality and behavior.

Changes identified with longer police service include greater cynicism, more alienation, emotional uninvolement and increased aggressive acting out (Berberich and Stotland, 1979; Garmire, 1977; Hageman, 1977; Jirsk, 1975).

It was hypothesized that police officers who exhibited higher levels of perceived competence, self-coping efficacy and self-esteem would exhibit more adaptive coping behavior which would be demonstrated in more effective police performance. It was also hypothesized that maladaptive coping behavior and length of police service would negatively affect police officer coping behavior and have a significant influence on work- related performance.

Method

Sample. Sixty male uniformed police patrol officers from an urban-city police department volunteered to participate in this study. They included 30 officers with more than one but less than three years of mobile patrol services and 30 officers with four or more years of experience. Ninety-five percent of the group were White and five percent were Hispanic. Their ages ranged from 22 to 43 years, with a mean age of 31.45. The majority of the sample had attended some college (46%). Twenty-eight percent graduated from college and 23% were high school graduates. One officer (2%) had a Masters degree. The sample's marital status included 60% married, 27% single, and 13% either divorced or separated.

Measures

Self Esteem. Operationally self-esteem was defined by and measured with the Tennessee Self-Concept Scale (Coppersmith, 1967). This self-report scale asks subjects to select a number from one to six indicating how truthful 100 self-descriptive statements are of them as individuals. The responses reflect the extent to which individuals hold positive attitudes toward themselves. This measure was designed to assess self-concepts and self-esteem as a relatively stable personality trait.

Validity studies of this scale report evidence of its content, predictive and construct validity with a reported test-retest reliability estimate of .92 (Robinson and Shaver, 1965).

Self-Coping Efficacy. The Self-Coping Inventory (Zeitlin, 1980) was used in this study to assess how individuals perceived themselves in terms of their ability to cope with a variety of situations related to police officer performance. The Inventory includes 24 Likert-type items with scales from 1 to 5 where 1 signifies the most negative perception of performance. Inventory sub-scores assess the extent to which an individual's coping behavior is adaptive in the sense that it is productive, active and flexible.

The initial reliability and validity data reported for the Coping Inventory involved the use of an observational rather than self-report form. Observed coping behavior was rated by judges and resulted in an inter-rater reliability coefficient for rating pairs significant beyond the .001 level. Content validity was established by expert judges rating of each item (Zeitlin, 1980).

Self-Appraisal of Competence. Goldfried and D'Zubilla (1969) define competence as the adequacy with which an individual responds to various problematic situations which confront him or her. In this study, competence was assessed in two ways. The first was related to how competent the individual rated himself in responding to actual police situations and the second was how competent supervisors rated the individual officer's performance. Operationally, self-appraisal of competence was measured by modified version of the Police Supervisors' Performance Rating Scale which is described below. The modified version asked subjects to rate on a 1-9 Likert scale how competent they though their performance was in 12 areas of police work. These 12 areas included crime prevention, using force appropriately, traffic maintenance and control, public safety and first aid, investigations, detecting and following up on criminal activity, report writing, integrity and professional ethics, dealing with the public, handling domestic disputes, commitment, dedication and conscientiousness, teamwork, and overall job performance.

Police Performance. Supervisor's ratings of police performance were used to assess subject's levels of competence with respect to field-work performance. Two supervisors rated each subject's performance on the Police Supervisor's Field Performance Rating Scale developed by Dunnette and Motowidlo (1976). On this scale, supervisors assign ratings from 1 to 9, indicating at the low end of the scale reservations about their subordinates' competence to the high end indicating superior to outstanding performance. The 12 areas of police performance are the same as described above under the Self-Appraisal of Competence measure. Content validity for this measure was established using police officer supervisors as judges regarding the validity of the content and criteria. Inter-rater reliability for the measure was reported at .71 by Dunnette and Motowidlo (1976).

Maladaptive Coping. Maladaptive coping was assessed by a specially designed questionnaire for this study. Officers were asked to indicate the number of times per month they engaged in various forms of maladaptive coping behavior identified in the literature. These include (1) feeling down or blue (2) having difficulty sleeping (3) calling in sick (4) being unproductive on patrol (5) arguing with friends or family (6) drinking (7) gambling (8) losing temper (9) having destructive thoughts.

Stress Interviews. Structured interviews were conducted to obtain information about officers perception of the most stressful aspects of police work and to ascertain how they cope with this stress. Seventeen open-ended questions were asked which covered such topics as response to danger, expression of personal needs to others, facility in handling new situations, dealing with frustration, family relationships, anger, gambling and drinking, causes of stress and methods and handling stress.

Procedures

Volunteers for the study were recruited by letter from all police personnel employed in an urban municipal police department. They were asked to complete a personal data questionnaire and sign a form giving permission to obtain performance ratings from their supervisors. From the 200 questionnaires completed, 60 subjects, including more and less experienced officers, were selected for participation in the study. Subjects were tested over a period of 3 days and in groups of 20 each. Three supervisors were contacted individually and requested to complete performance evaluation forms on the officers in the study. Each officer was rated by at least two supervisors. Following this, 10 officers were randomly selected for interviewing to obtain additional data on perceived stress and coping strategies.

Table 1
Descriptive Statistics for Self-Esteem, Self-Coping Efficacy (SC), Self-Appraisal of Competence and Maladaptive Coping Scores (MACLP)

Variable	Possible Range	Actual Range	Mean	S.D.
Self-Esteem	100–600	251–406	346.77	33.79
Self-Coping Efficacy	24–120		89.80	10.96
SC—Productive	12–60	27–57	46.25	6.27
SC—Active	6–30	14–29	21.50	3.48
SC—Flexible	6–30	13–29	22.05	3.13
Self-Appraisal of Competence	12–108	43–103	89.20	10.91
Supervisory Performance Rating (b)	12–108	52.0-99.5	77.77	8.90
Supervisor 1	——	46–92	75.10	10.45
Supervisor 2	——	61–98	81.68	8.59
Supervisor 3	——	43–106	76.53	14.50
Maladaptive Coping (MALCP)	0+(a)		13.72	8.96
Depressed			2.23	1.81
Difficulty Sleeping			2.15	1.98
Off Sick			.67	.91
Not Productive			1.90	1.60
Argue			1.63	1.56
Drink			2.27	1.93
Gamble			.5	1.17
Lose Temper			1.78	1.58
Self-Destructive Thoughts			.58	1.33

(a) Open-ended scoring, the number of times behavior engaged in per month.
(b) Averaged ratings by three supervisors.

Results

Descriptive Statistics on Coping and Field Performance Measures. Means and standard deviations of scores obtained on all the measures used in the study are presented in Table 1. A mean score of 346.77 on the Tennessee Self-Concept Scale indicated that officers levels of self-esteem were similar to those of normative groups representing the National population (Fitts, 1965). An examination of the scores officers achieved on the Self-Coping Efficacy Inventory shows that the mean scores SC-Productive 46.25, SC-Active 21.50, and SC-Flexible 22.05 tend toward the favorable end of the scales indicating that officers perceive themselves as fairly capable when it comes to applying task-oriented skills, mobilizing personal resources and adaptively changing strategies in stressful situ-

Table 2
Pearson Correlations between Officers' Self-Esteem, Self-Appraisal, Self-Coping Efficacy, Maladaptive Coping and Supervisory Ratings of Field Performance

	Supervisor 1	Supervisor 2	Supervisor 3
Self-Esteem (SE)	.02	.01	-.15
Self-Coping Efficacy (SC)	.32*	.30*	-.02
SC Productive	.38**	.29*	
SC Active	.18	.19	
SC Flexible	.19	.28*	
Self-Appraisal of Competence (SAC)	.23	.15	.10
Maladaptive Coping (MALCP)	-.25	-.12	.21

* p < .05
** p. < .02

ations. Self-Appraisal of Competence scores calculated by summing officer's self-ratings, on scales of 1-9, across 12 Task Performance categories, ranged from 43-103 with a mean score of 89.2. On the average then, officers in the study rated their own performance in the superior to outstanding category. However, the range of scores and the s.d. of 10.91 indicates that there were officers who rated themselves below average in performance.

The effectiveness of each officer's performance in the field was evaluated with the Police Supervisor's Field Performance Rating Form. The mean ratings of each supervisor are presented in Table 1 with 77.77 the average rating assigned by all 3 supervisors representing a satisfactory to slightly superior rating of actual performance. A comparison of mean scores of the officer's own perception of their performance effectiveness (X=89.20) with their supervisor's ratings (X=77.77) indicates that the officer's perception of their own effectiveness is higher than that awarded them by their supervisors.

With respect to maladaptive coping behavior, the average number of episodes reported by all 60 officers was 13.72 with depression, sleeping difficulties and drinking reported as occurring most frequently. The average frequency was two times per month. Among the least reported forms of behavior were absence due to sickness, gambling and self-destructive thoughts.

Self-Esteem, Self-Efficacy, Competence, Maladaptive Coping and Field Performance. To test the hypothesis that self-esteem, self-efficacy and self-appraisal of competence were related to effective police performance, Pearson Product Moment Correlations were performed between scores on all these measures and individual supervisor's ratings of field performance. Table 2 indicates that supervisor 1's ratings of field performance

Table 3
Matrix of Pearson Correlations Among Self-Esteem, Self-Coping, Self-Appraisal of Competence, and Maladaptive Coping Scores (N = 60)

Variable	SE	SC	SAC	MALCP
Self-Esteem (SE)		.52*	.41*	-.55*
Self-Coping (SC)			.50*	-.52*
Self-Appraisal of Competence (SAC)				-.36*
Maladaptive Coping (MALCP)				

* ≤ .01

were significantly related to the Self Coping Efficacy measure (=.32, p≤.05) and its subscale Productive Self-Coping (r=.38, p≤.01). The rating of Supervisor 1 did not correlate significantly with any of the other variables. Supervisor 2's ratings of field performance were also significantly correlated with the total Self-Coping Efficacy measure (r=.29, p.05) and with another subscale Flexible Self-coping (r=.28, p≤.05). Supervisor 3's ratings are not significantly related to any of the measures. Ratings of Field Performance and Maladaptive Coping, while not significantly related, are in an expected negative direction for Supervisor 1 and Supervisor 2. Self-coping efficacy then emerges as the variable with the strongest relationship to effective police performance.

Adaptive and Maladaptive Coping Behavior. To examine the relationship between adaptive and maladaptive coping behavior, Pearson Product Moment Correlations were also computed between Self-Esteem, Self-Coping Efficacy, Self-Appraisal of Competence and Maladaptive Coping Behavior. Table 3 indicates that overall maladaptive coping behavior is negatively related to these three variables (1) Self-Esteem (r=.55, pœ.01); (2) Self-coping Efficacy (r-.52, pœ.01); (3) Self-Appraisal or competence (r=.36, pœ.01).

In this study, those who had lower levels of self-esteem, self-coping efficacy and self-appraisal of competence tended to engage more frequently in the type of behaviors that have been associated with a "maladaptive" approach to dealing with experienced stress. Table 3 also shows some significant positive relationships among the three adaptive coping variables. The coefficients in the 40's and 50's suggest that there is a strong relationship between these characteristics so that if one has high levels of self-esteem they would also have high levels of self-efficacy yet the correlations are low enough to suggest that the measures are assessing different traits.

Length of Experience, Coping Behaviors and Field Performance. Many studies have reported evidence that links time involved in police work to greater degrees of cynicism, alienation, and maladaptive coping behavior (Jirsk, 1975; Garmire, 1977; Bouza, 1978). It was hypothesized then that more experienced officers, feeling the effects of stress over time, would evidence more maladaptive coping behaviors which, in turn, would negatively influence their work-related performance. Subjects in the study were divided into 2 groups of less experienced, defined as under 4 years in mobile patrol and more experienced defined as 4 or more years in mobile patrol. Independent t tests were used to compare the two groups on both personality variables and field performance evaluations. With respect to personality variables, the results of the t test indicated that there were no significant differences between the two groups in self-esteem, self-coping efficacy, self-appraisal of competence and maladaptive coping behavior. With respect to Field Performance Evaluations, the t test indicated there were no significant differences between the two groups except for one job task category *Teamwork*. (Less experienced officers X=7.17, s.d. 1.02; more experienced officers X=7.65, s.d..63 t - 2.25, pœ.05).

Stress Interviews. In order to obtain additional information about how officers coped with the stress related to police work, 10 officers were randomly selected to participate in structures interviews. Responses to the 17 questions were content analyzed to determine the sources of stress they experienced, how they responded to this stress and the methods they used to cope with it.

Contrary to expectations, officers stated that they experienced the most stress from problems with the internal bureaucracy of the police department. Specific comments focused on feelings of not being supported by the department, problems with incompetent supervisors and lack of recognition for their work. Examples of their comments included following:

> "Bosses don't like aggressive cops, they want the job done but they don't want to back you."
>
> "The administration is insensitive to individual officer's needs."
>
> "I feel like I'm taking directions from supervisors who don't know the job themselves."

Other sources of stress were identified as problems with the Court system, inadequate pay, and lack of recognition for a college education:

> "Courts and judges undo everything we try to do."
>
> "The court system is frustrating, judges just don't seem to understand the victims."
>
> "The department doesn't care if you have an education - in any other job, a college degree might mean something, here you don't get any credit for it."

In discussing their responses to stress, officers said that they engaged in some patterns of maladaptive coping with stress. Four officers mentioned that they tended to internalize their frustration with the job resulting in angry outbursts at home. Three officers mentioned chronic use of alcohol, another stated that he observed widespread alcohol abuse and another believed that his drinking indicated an "unconscious death wish."

In describing the methods they employed to cope with stress, several officers felt that their ability to do their jobs very well helped them cope. Many also mentioned their need to get away from work, to get distance from the job, to be able to talk to your partner about job problems and knowing people outside the department with whom you could talk about the job.

Educational Level and Stress. As noted above, some officers commented on the fact that they experienced some stress from the fact that their education was not considered in decisions by supervisors about assignments and promotions. This finding stimulated another research question about the effects of educational level on officers' ability to cope with stress. To assess the relationships between levels of education and the variables of self-esteem, self-coping efficacy, self-appraisal of competence and maladaptive coping a series of one-way analyses of variance were performed. One significant finding occurred. There was a significant difference due to educational level on the self-coping efficacy variables (F-2,57) = 3.54, p≤.04). To determine which educational level contributed to the significant difference Duncan's multiple range test was calculated which showed that police officers who were college graduates had higher mean scores (X=95.33) on self-coping efficacy than officers who had some college completed (X=87.04). There were no significant differences in self-coping efficacy between officers who were college graduates and those who had no college experience (X=88.14). Officers who had some college perceived themselves as being less able to cope than those in the other two groups.

Discussion

This study examined the performance of 60 police officers in relation to their measured levels of self-esteem, perception of ability to cope with stress and their self-appraisal of competence. The results indicated that in general these officers had substantial levels of self-esteem, perceived themselves as able to cope effectively with stressful police situations and appraised their job performance as quite good. Their supervisors generally concurred with their assessment and gave them fairly high performance ratings. They did, however, acknowledge some episodes of maladaptive coping behaviors, the most frequent of which were drinking, depression and sleep disorders.

The variable that emerged in this study as most related to effective police performance was self-coping efficacy, a variable which measures how much officers perceive themselves as being able to employ effective coping behaviors in stressful police situations. The finding that perceptions of self-efficacy was most related to effective performance agrees with several researchers' definitions of what stress is and what causes stress. According to Violanti (1983) and others stress is a perceived imbalance between social demands and perceived response capacity; under conditions where failure to meet demands has important consequences. Officers in this study then were perhaps not victims of stress because they believed they were capable of meeting the demands of police work and according to their supervisors ratings these beliefs were realistic ones.

Levels of self-esteem and officers appraisal of their own competence or work performance were not found to be related to their performance as rated by their supervisors. These findings to some extent both agree with and disagree with previous research findings. The results of several studies (Coppersmith, 1967; Rosenberg, 1965; Stotland and Canon, 1972; Wells and Marwell, 1976) indicate that self-esteem plays a major role in (1) effective police performance and (2) ability to cope with stress in the general population. These findings were not replicated here. It is possible that this sample included officers with fairly high levels of self-esteem to begin with. The lack of variability in scores would then affect the significance of the relationships obtained. The finding that there was no relationship between self-esteem and performance may also mean that people perform well regardless of level of self-esteem. According to Somers and Lefkowitz's (1983) self-enhancement theory, efforts to perform well are the means by which people maintain or increase their self-esteem so that people with high or low levels of self-esteem could perform equally well.

While officers rated their own performance as high and supervisors rated the officers performance high, there were no significant correlations between these ratings. The lack of variability in both these sets of data may have been influenced by subjects using a socially desirable response set (Borg and Gall, 1979) and by supervisors who also were invested in maintaining the appearance of having a competent set of officers under their command. There was also some disagreement between the three supervisors on how they rated the same officers, as indicated by the different correlations between the performance ratings of each of the supervisors and the study's other variables. This may have been due to some confusion or disagreement between supervisors as to what the performance categories being rated meant or they may actually have had different views about the competency of the officers they were rating. Future research using the Police Supervisors Field Performance Rating should include specific training for raters regarding the meaning and the value of the tasks they are rating.

This study's finding that there was a negative correlation between maladaptive coping behavior and high levels of self-coping efficacy and competence lends support to the results of other studies (House and Jackman, 1979; Stotland and Cannon, 1972) which found that lower levels of self-destructive behaviors were related to higher levels of self-esteem. This study did not, however, demonstrate a relationship between maladaptive coping and poor police performance.

Contrary to expectation, there were basically no difference between officers who were more or less experienced on any of the measures except that more experienced officers had higher ratings on teamwork. This suggests that officers may over time continue to perform effectively and learn how to handle stress. One response to greater stress over time may be to become more affiliated with fellow officers and perhaps more detached from the outside world (Hageman, 1977).

The interview findings in this study suggest that the stressors most troublesome were ones which have been identified as "Chronic stressors" by other researchers, e.g., police administration, the court system, problems with assignment and promotion (Ellison and Genz, 1978; Stratton, 1978; Wallace, 1978). Symptoms of maladaptive coping such as alcohol abuse, angry outbursts at home and depression were cited by officers as resulting from the stress, impotence and anger they experienced from these situations. Acute stressors, arising from being in physically dangerous situations were not identified as problems for officers in this study. Intervention efforts aimed at alleviating this type of stress may include helping officers acquire more skills for coping with the bureaucracy, giving them more of a role to play in policy-making, rewarding officers who do obtain higher education and training police administrators in better communication techniques.

Further research will be needed to determine whether or not officers adaptive coping ability and performance are related to the personality variables included in this study. The demonstration of such relationships would be beneficial because the results could be used as criteria for identifying candidates who would be best suited for the rigors of police work. Efforts to explore these relationships would include methods for dealing with some of the methodological problems in this study. These include the need for obtaining additional data, beyond self-report data; the need for independent ratings (other than supervisors) of performance and training of raters in how to use rating measures. Future research should also include more direct measures of actual stress experienced by officers and other studies need to be designed to determine whether or not perception of competence is, as was found in this study, the most important correlate of effective police performance.

References

Bandura, A. (1980). "Gauging the relationship between self efficacy, judgement, and action." *Cognitive Therapy and Research, 4,* 263-268.

Bandura, A., & Adams, N. (1977). "Analysis of self-efficacy theory of behavioral change." *Cognitive Therapy and Research,* 1, 287-310.

Baxter, D. (1978). *Coping with police stress.* Trooper, 3, 68.

Berberich, J. & Stotland, E. (1979). "The psychology of the police." In H. Toch (Ed.), *Psychology of crime and criminal justice.* New York: Holt, Rinehart and Winston.

Blackmore, J. (1978). "Are police allowed to have problems of their own?" *Police Magazine,* 1, 47-55.

Borg, W.R., & Gall, M.D. (1979) *Educational research: An Introduction.* (3rd ed.). New York: Longman, Inc.

Bouza, A. (1978). *Police administration organization and performance.* New York: Pergamon Press, Inc.

Coppersmith, S. (1967) *The antecedents of self-esteem.* San Francisco: W.H. Freeman.

Dunnette, M.D., & Motowidlo, S.J. (1976) *Police selection and career assessment.* Washington, D.C.: U.S. Government Printing Office.

Ellison, K.W. & Genz, J.S. (1978). "Police officer as burned-out samaritan." *FBI Law Enforcement Bulletin,* 47(3), 1-7.

Fitts, W. (1972). *Self concept and performance.* Nashville, Tennessee: Counselor Recordings and Tests.

Garmire, B.L. (Ed.) (1977) *Local government police management.* Washington, D.C.: International City Management Association.

Goldfried, M.R. & D'Zurilla, T.J. (1969). "Behavioral-analytical model for assessing competence." In C. Spielberger (Ed.), *Current topics in clinical and community psychology.* (vol. 1). New York: Academic Press.

Hageman, M.J.C. (1977). *Occupational stress of law enforcement officers and marital and familial relations.* Unpublished doctoral dissertation, Washington State University.

Hamburg, D.A., & Adams, J.E. (1967). "A perspective on coping behavior." *Archives of General Psychiatry,* 17, 277-284.

Hillgren, J.S.; Bond, R.B., & Jones, S. (1976). "Primary stressors in police administration and law enforcement." *Journal of Police Science and Administration,* 4, 445-449.

House, J.S. & Jackman, J.F. (1979). "Occupational stress and health." In P. Ahmed (Ed.), *Toward a new definition of health.* New York: Plenum Press.

Jacobi, J.H. (1979). "Reducing police stress: A psychiatrist's point of view." In W.H. Kroes & J.J. Hurrell (Eds.), *Job stress and the police officer: Identifying stress reduction techniques.* Washington, D.C.: U.S. Government Printing Office.

Jirsk, M. (1975). "Absenteeism among members of the New York City police department on Staten Island." *Journal of Police Science and Administration, 3,* 149-161.

Kelling, G. & Pate, M. (1975). "Person role fit in policing: The current knowledge and future research." In W.H. Kroes and J.J. Hurrell (Eds.), *Job stress and the police officer: Identifying stress reduction techniques.*

Mischel, W. (1973). "Toward a cognitive social learning reconceptualization of personality." *Psychological Review,* 80, 252-283.

Pines, A.; Aronson, E., and Kafry, D. (1981) *Burnout: From tedium to personal growth,* New York: The Free Press.

Richard, W.C. & Fell, R.D. (1985) "Health factors in police stress." In W.H. Kroes and J.J. Hurrell (eds.) *Job stress in the police officer: Identifying stress reduction techniques.* Washington, D.C.: U.S. Government Printing Office.

Robinson, J.P., & Shaver, P.R. (1965). *Social psychological attitudes* (3rd ed.) Ann Arbor, Michigan: The University of Michigan, Institute for Social Research.

Rosenberg, M. (1965) *Society and the adolescent self-image.* Princeton: Princeton University Press.

Schalon, C. (1968). "Effect of self-esteem upon performance following failure stress." *Journal of Consulting and Clinical Psychology, 32,* 297.

Somers, M.J. & Lefkowitz, J. (1983). "Self-esteem, need gratification and work satisfaction: A test of competing explanations from consistency theory and self-enhancement theory." *Journal of Vocational Behavior, 22,* 303-311.

Stotland, E., & Canon, L. (1972). *Social psychology: A cognitive approach.* Philadelphia: Saunders.

Stratton, J.D. (1978). "Police stress, part 1: An overview." *Police Chief,* 45 (4), 58-62.

Violanti, J.M. (1983). "Stress patterns in police work: A longitudinal study." *Journal of Police Science and Administration,* 11, 211-216.

Wallace, L. (1978). "Stress and its impact on the law enforcement officer." *Campus Law Enforcement Journal,* 8 (4), 36-40.

Wambaugh, J. (1975). *The choirboys.* New York: Dell.

Wells, L.E. & Marwell, G. (1976). *Self-esteem: Its conceptualization and measurement.* New York: Sage Publishing, Inc.

Zeitlin, S. (1980). *Coping inventory research edition: A measure of adaptive coping.,* Montclair, New Jersey: Innovative Educational Materials, Inc.

6

A Coronary Risk Profile Study of Male Police Officers: Focus On Cholesterol

Donald S. Quire
William R. Blount

The most deadly enemy stalking police officers may be one that is unseen and silent: coronary heart disease. In the Travelers Insurance Company's film, *Silent Killer: A Call to Fitness* (1977) the narrative indicates that a study of insurance actuarial statistics identified heart attacks as the leading cause of death or retirement among police officers. Studies (Velde, Gettman, and Kent 1978) identified a similar trend. A major component of this study was a national survey that dealt with loss of personnel. The single greatest cause of early retirement and the second greatest cause of limited duty assignments were found to be heart disease. The Federal Bureau of Investigation has recently confirmed that federal law enforcement agencies are also not immune to the impact of coronary heart disease on their agents. Beccaccio, Cooper, and Prentice (1982) reported coronary heart disease to be the leading cause of death among FBI agents. Of the 322 active agents who have died since 1947, 38 percent died of heart disease.

That heart disease is a problem for law enforcement is not surprising, given that heart disease is a monumental problem for society in general. The American Heart Association (AHA) reported that in 1981 heart attacks were the leading cause of death, responsible for 599,000 deaths in the United States. The National Heart, Lung, and Blood Institute and the National Institutes of Health, Office of Medical Applications of Research, Consensus Development Conference ("Lowering Blood Cholesterol," 1985) reported that heart disease was responsible for more deaths each year than all forms of cancer, and that the costs associated with the disease were in excess of $60 billion.

According to the Florida Department of Health and Rehabilitative Services, Office of Vital Statistics, the leading cause of death in Florida in 1984 ("Florida Heart Facts," 1985) was heart and blood vessel diseases, which proportionally accounted for 48 percent (53,849/112,969) of the total deaths.

A Focus on Cholesterol

Numerous studies have examined the factors that contribute to the process of coronary atherosclerosis. Population studies, such as the Framingham study (Kannel 1966; Dawber 1973; Kannel, McGee, and Gordon 1976) and others (Cooper, Pollock, Martin, White, Linnerud, and Jackson 1976) have shown not only that the manifestation of coronary heart disease is influenced by a certain risk factors, but also that the probability is significantly higher with added numbers of risk factors.

Cooper (1982) along with the AHA (1980) has identified ten coronary risk factors: (1) hypertension; (2) cigarette smoking; (3) cholesterol/triglycerides; (4) stress/personality behavior patterns; (5) glucose/diabetes; (6) family history; (7) inactivity/sedentary life styles; (8) obesity; (9) abnormal resting ECG; and (10) oral contraceptives. Of these, hypertension (high blood pressure or arterial hypertension), cigarette smoking, and cholesterol have generally been recognized as the three major risk factors.

Most recently, evidence has accumulated which shows that cholesterol may be the most significant predictor of coronary heart disease. The Consensus Development Conference (CDC) reported (1985):

> Elevation of blood cholesterol levels is a major cause of coronary heart disease. It has been established beyond a reasonable doubt that lowering definitely elevated blood cholesterol levels (specifically, blood levels of low density lipoprotein (LDL) cholesterol) will reduce the risk of heart attacks caused by coronary heart disease. This has been demonstrated conclusively in men with elevated blood cholesterol levels, but much evidence justifies the conclusion that similar protection will be afforded to women with elevated levels. ("Lowering Blood Cholesterol," p. 2080)

Cooper (1982) reported that circulation problems can often be traced to atherosclerosis, which involves a build-up in the blood vessels of fatty cholesterol deposits. Cholesterol is a waxy, fatty substance in body tissues and the blood which is essential to many physical functions, including efficient functioning of the brain. While cholesterol is important to certain bodily functions, an excess in cholesterol levels can lead to complications.

The problem comes from the imbalance of cholesterol in the body that can contribute directly to heart disease. The AHA (1980) has established that there are two classifications of cholesterol: high-density lipoproteins (HDLs) and low-density lipoproteins (LDLs). The HDLs are believed to serve two important functions: (1) they line the inside of the artery walls with a protective layer or coating that prevents fatty deposits from building up: and (2) they serve as a cleansing mechanism to actually help dissolve fatty deposits when they do occur. LDLs, on the other hand, can form hazardous deposits on the walls of blood vessels and are the primary source of clogged arteries and atherosclerosis.

Cooper (1982) specified that the ratio of total cholesterol to HDL is probably the best predictor of future coronary heart disease. Cooper suggested "The basic rule of balance for your blood is that it's necessary to have a relatively high amount of HDLs in your body, in relation to your total amount of cholesterol" (p. 83).

Several studies (Gordon, Kannel, and McGee 1974; American Heart Association 1980; Cooper 1982) indicated that, for men, the ratio of total cholesterol (HDLs plus LDLs expressed in mgm% to HDL should always be less than 5.0, and preferably less than 4.5. For example, if total cholesterol is 200, then HDLs should be at least 40, and preferably 45 or above. For women, the ratio should be lower, a recommended standard of under 4.0 and preferably under 3.5.

The CDC ("Lowering Blood Cholesterol," 1985) recommended treatment of individuals with blood cholesterol levels above the 75th percentile. The conference further recommended that individuals with high-risk blood cholesterol levels (values above the 90th percentile) should be treated intensively by dietary means under the guidance of a physician, dietitian, or other health professional. If response to diet is inadequate, appropriate drugs should be added to the regimen.

Methodology

Subjects

The significance of the debilitating and deadly effects of coronary heart disease has been recognized by the St. Petersburg, Florida, Police Department. Thus, in 1981 the department's Research and Development Section proposed a physical fitness program for the department's 475 sworn personnel. A major component of the program was a mandatory, comprehensive medical examination to be administered by physicians of the St. Petersburg Suncoast Medical Clinic. The medical examination included a stress ECG (Balke protocol), as well as coronary risk profiles (using AHA and Cooper Clinic standards). These examinations (initially performed on selected officers) were eventually performed on all officers, and once given were repeated every two years.

The present study examined a 100 percent sample of those officers who received coronary risk profiles from 1981 to 1985, resulting in a total of 584 coronary risk profiles for 380 sworn officers (24 female officers and 356 male officers) who received examinations during this time period.

The 584 coronary risk profiles included 35 female profiles and 549 profiles from males. Since there were only 35 female officer profiles (6 percent of the total), insufficient frequencies existed when the data were cast into the 20 age/year divisions established by Cooper (1977, 1982). Twelve of the female cells were empty altogether, and of the remaining eight only one had a frequency greater than seven. Given this circumstance, the female profiles were excluded from the analyses.

The demographic variable of race was also not examined, as this information was not captured on the risk profile charts. Race, therefore, operates as a possible confounding variable in these analyses. The department's racial characteristics included 9.71 percent black, 87.35 percent white, 1.13 percent Hispanic, and 1.8 percent other nationalities. How this balance was reflected in the age, sex, and year group is unknown.

In addition, some officers were examined more than once. It was not possible to cast the data so that each officer appeared only once, or that only officers who were retested in later years were used. It is known that 71.5 percent (418) were examined once, 22.26 percent (130) twice, and 6.16 percent (36) three times, with no officers being examined more than three times.

A final limitation concerned the risk profile charts employed. The two charts used in the present study were based on coronary risk profile standards established by the AHA (1980) and Dr. Kenneth Cooper's Institute of Aerobics Research (Cooper 1977; 1982). While the two charts are basically identical, a few differences exist as a function of the emergence of more sophisticated measures. Cooper's first coronary risk profile chart (1977) used 15 variables to determine an individual's total coronary risk profile. Each of these variables had scaled values and coronary risk profile scores assigned to them. In 1982 Cooper revised his coronary risk profile chart by eliminating some of the earlier risk variables and adding others. He also revised the coronary risk factor scores given to the variables. The total coronary risk scores were also revised.

Thus, the data for this study for 1981 and 1982 were taken from Cooper's 1977 coronary risk profile charts, and data for 1983, 1984, and 1985 were taken from the charts Cooper revised in 1982.

Of particular significance to the present study is the way cholesterol risk is measured on the two charts. Cooper's earlier research (1977) indicated that the measure of total cholesterol was considered to be the best determinant of cholesterol risk. However, Cooper's later research (1982) indicated that a more precise measurement of cholesterol risk was the ratio of total cholesterol to HDL levels. Consequently, the coronary risk profile charts used to collect the data for 1981 and 1982 were limited to

Table 1
Frequency of Male Coronary Risk Profiles;
Age Groups and Collapsed Year Divisions

Age group	1981/1982	1984/1985	Total	
	(N)	(N)	(N)	%
< 30	19	78	97	32.21
30-39	106	36	142	33.97
40-49	72	75	147	35.16
50-59	19	13	32	7.66
Total	216	202	418	100.00

* Includes the single "over 60" profile.

total cholesterol and cholesterol risk scores, while the data for 1983, 1984, and 1985 contained total cholesterol, HDL level, total cholesterol/HDL ratio, and a cholesterol risk factor score.

This change in the availability of specific data elements provided guidance when it became obvious that our sample sizes were too small in some of the age/year cells. Five of these 25 cells (5 age groups for each of the 5 years) had frequencies less than 9, and nine were empty. To complicate matters, 129 of the 131 profiles taken in 1983 were from the 30-39 age group, but no profiles were available for this age group at all for 1985.

Therefore, to best preserve the integrity of the longitudinal design and to acknowledge the limitations imposed both by changing measurement scales and the availability of risk profiles. the analyses are presented by collapsed year divisions. The 1981/1982 cholesterol analyses were done on the variables of total cholesterol and cholesterol risk factor score, while the analyses for 1984/1985 examined the variables of total cholesterol, HDL level, total cholesterol/HDL ratio, and coronary risk factor score. An analysis using total cholesterol was also performed, but only for the 30-39 age group. This analysis used the four years of 1981 (n=36), 1982 (n=43), 1983 (n=129), and 1984 (n=36). Other frequencies are presented in table 1.

Results

Total Cholesterol

Since total cholesterol level was common to both year groups, a 2 by 4 analysis of variance (ANOVA) was performed. Table 2 shows significant

Table 2
Analysis of Total Cholesterol, Year and Age

Source of Variation	df	Mean Squares	F	p
Year	1	44202.233	18.689	0.001
Age	3	17293.288	7.312	0.002
Age/Year	3	4160.260	1.759	ns
Error	406	2365.097		
Total	413			

Year	N	Mean	SD	Age	N	Mean	SD
81/82	215	215.405	56.770	< 30	94	174.170	35.226
84/85	199	186.342	41.286	30-39	141	205.099	50.674
Total	414	201.435	51.947	40-49	147	211.905	56.338
				50-59	32	217.281	50.881
				Total	414	201.435	51.947

effects for year, $F(1, 406) = 18.689$, $p = .001$, and age group, $F(3, 406) = 7.312$, $p = .002$. The significant effect for year revealed that the officers generally had significantly lower total cholesterol levels in 1984/85 than in 1981/82, a substantial improvement. The age group effect indicated that while the total cholesterol levels generally increased with age, a finding consistent with research dealing with the general population, the under-30 age group was found to have a significantly lower average total cholesterol level (174.170 mgm%) than the other three age groups. Other age differences were not significant.

When the average total cholesterol levels were compared to the general population standards of the CDC ("Lowering Blood Cholesterol" 1985), it is meaningful to note that all of the age groups were found to have low coronary risk. The under-30 age group, with an average of 174.170 mgm% was not at risk when compared to the standard for moderate risk of 200 mgm%. This was also true for the 30-39 group, who with an average of 205.099 mgm%, were not at risk when compared to the standard of 220 mgm%. The 40-49 and 50-59 age groups were both less than the 240 mgm% moderate risk standard established by the conference. These results in themselves are important as they document at least one police department with a consistently low risk of heart disease. It is interesting to note that the age group which achieved the greatest deviation from risk were those persons 40-49 years of age.

Other Measures

Becasue of the change in the way cholesterol was measured in 1981/1982 as opposed to 1984/1985, separate analyses were required for HDL cholesterol, total cholesterol/HDL ratio, and cholesterol risk factor score. Since only the latter measure was available for both 1981/1982 and 1984/1985, it will be presented first. The reader is advised that although the two analyses cover the same topic (cholesterol risk factor score), the method by which those scores were calculated changed for 1984/1985.

Cholesterol risk factor score. While no significant differences were found in the 1981/1982 ANOVA analysis of cholesterol risk factor score by age group $F (3, 204) = .745$, $p =$ ns, a significant difference was found in the 1984/1985 analysis, $F (3, 193) = 4.684$, $p = .004$. The under-30 age group (2.895) was found not to be different than the 30-39 group (3.944), but did have a significantly lower average risk factor score than the 40-49 group (4.444) and the 50-59 group (5.462), indicating that older officers had significantly higher risk factor scores.

HDL cholesterol (1984/1985). Cooper (1982) suggested that higher levels of HDLs were desirable and beneficial in the reduction of coronary risk. Available in the present sample for only 1984 and 1985, this measure indicated no statistically significant difference between age groups $F (3, 191) = 1.070$, $p =$ ns; the overall average HDL level being 31.682 mgm %.

Total cholesterol/HDL ratio (1984/1985). The most precise measurement of determining overall cholesterol risk is the total cholesterol/HDL ratio (Cooper 1982). This measure was also only available for 1984 and 1985. Significant differences in this analysis were found $F (3, 193) = 3.370$, $p = .019$, and demonstrated the same pattern as shown for total cholesterol risk for 1984/1985. The under-30 age group (5.584) was found not significantly different from the 30-39 group (6.569), but did have a significantly lower average total cholesterol/HDL ratio than the 40-49 group (6.772) and the 50-59 group (7.061).

30-39 age group across years. To further assess longitudinal trends, an analysis was done on total cholesterol (the only common measure for all years) for the 30-39 age group (the only age group with sufficient numbers for each of four of the five years, 1981, 1982, 1983, and 1984). Significant differences were found across years $F (3, 266) = 15.444$, $p = .001$. Profiles for 1982 (241.954 mgm%), 1983 (200.798 mgm%), or 1984 (187.1339 mgm%).

When the 30-39 age group was compared to the standards of CDC, it was alarming to note that in 1982 the average total cholesterol level (241.954 mgm%) was in the high risk range of 240 mgm%, but showed no risk in the other years (each year being well below the 220 mgm% risk line).

The "out of pattern" performance by the 30-39 age group in 1982 was possibly the result of an effort made in 1982 to target particularly high risk officers in this age group, or perhaps the result of self selection on the part of some at-risk officers concerned about their health. Both explanations are possible, but the latter is more plausible. No indications were found of a special effort to target high risk officers of any age by those administering the physical examinations in 1982. It seems quite likely, however, that the 1982 results had a significant impact on those being selected for testing in 1983. Only two officers tested in 1983 were not between 30 and 39.

Further, these usually high risk scores had an effect on the other analyses by inflating the 81/82 average as well as the 30-39 age group average (see table 2). Omitting 1982 data, those in the 30-39 group are more like their under-30 peers than they are like those over 40, a pattern consistent with the general population.

Summary and Conclusions

While analyses of cholesterol levels indicated that older officers were at greater risk of coronary heart disease than younger officers, it is important to note that based on the CDC standards, St. Petersburg police officers are at very low risk level over the past five years. This is a singularly impressive finding within an occupation reported to have one of the highest rates of heart disease.

While it is possible that such a dramatic risk reduction would have occurred naturally, the argument is unpersuasive. It is much more likely that this is the result of a concentrated effort on the part of the department to make its officers aware of steps they can take to reduce their risk of heart disease, to make them aware in such a fashion that is entirely personal and virtually impossible to ignore (the individual, complete physical examinations which contained the cholesterol screen and the resultant discussion of their individual risk profiles), and the means to control/reduce their risk (the fitness program which contained exercise and diet recommendations).

While it was not our intent to evaluate the effectiveness of that program, it seems apparent that it is impossible to accept an explanation for the present long-term reduction in overall risk without acknowledging its existence and contribution.

Based on these data, law enforcement agencies would be well advised to implement programs that provide for routine medical examinations which include a comprehensive cholesterol level profile. Such a profile and the recommendations it generates concerning personal health and well-being and diet and exercise, could well be the difference between high and low rates of heart disease.

References

American Heart Association. 1980. *Risk factors and coronary disease: A statement for phsyicians.* Steering Committee for medical and community program of the American Heart Association. Dallas, TX: Author.

American Heart Association. 1981. *Risk: A heart hazard appraisal.* Dallas, TX: Author.

Beccaccio, L.A.; Cooper, K; and Prentice, M. 1982. Police physical fitness [summary]. Proceedings of the 88th annual conference of the International Association of Chiefs of Police, *Police Chief* 49(1): 159-166.

Cooper, K.H. 1977. *The aerobics way.* New York: Evans.

———1982. *The aerobics program for total well being.* New York: Evans.

Cooper, K.H.; Pollack, M.L.; Martin, R.P.; White, S.R.; Linnerud, A.C.; and Jackson, A. 1976. Physical fitness levels vs. selected coronary risk factors. *Journal of the American Medical Association* 236: 166-169.

Consensus Development Conference. 1985. Lowering blood cholesterol to prevent heart disease. *Journal of the American Medical Associaiton* 253: 2080-2086.

Dawber, T.R. 1973. Risk factors in young adults. The lessons from epidemiologic studies of cardiovascular disease - Framingham, Tecumseu, and Evans County. *Journal of American College Health Association.* 22: 81-95.

Florida heart facts. 1985. Office of Vital Statistics: Florida Department of Health and Rehabilitative Services.

Gordon, J.; Kannel, W.B.; and McGee, G. 1974. Death and coronary attacks in men after giving up cigarette smoking. *Lancet* 2: 1348-1356.

Kannel, W.B. 1966. *The Framingham heart study: Habits and coronary heart disease* (Public Health Service Publication No. 1515). Washington, D.C.: U.S. Government Printing Office.

Pollock, M.L.; Gettman, L.R.; and Meyer, B.V. 1978. Analysis of physical fitness and coronary heart disease risk of Dallas area police officers. *Journal of Occupational Medicine* 20: 393-398.

Price, C.S.; Pollock, M.L.; Gettman, L.R.; and Kent, D.A. 1978. *Physical fitness programs for law enforcement officers: A manual for police administrators.* National Institute of Law Enforcement and Criminal Justice. Washington, D.C.: U.S. Government Printing Office.

Travelers Insurance Company (Producer), and French, W. (Director), 1977. *Silent killer: A call to fitness* (film). Hartford, CT: Travelers Insurance Company.

Velde, R.N.; Gettman, L.R.; and Pollock, M.L. 1977. Police physical fitness. *Police Yearbook.* 85-98.

7

Police Cynicism:
Causes and Cures

Wallace Graves

What makes a junkyard dog so mean and a cop so cynical? In the case of the dog, it is a matter of conditioning. The police officer undergoes a similar, but much more complex process. Unfortunately, the public sometimes perceives the results to be the same.

Cynicism often adversely affects officers' productivity, impacts the morale of their colleagues and chills community relations. It also tends to breed a poor quality of life for officers and their families. In some cases, cynicism can be a precursor to emotional problems, misconduct, brutality, and even corruption.

Cynical, distrustful officers hinder a department's efforts to forge collaborative relationships with members of the community. Therefore, police leaders must build a culture of policing that prevents cynicism and promotes a healthy, positive environment. This article examines police cynicism—what it is, what causes it, and how to prevent it.

What Is Cynicism?

Cynicism is an attitude of "contemptuous distrust of human nature and motives"[1] A cynic expects nothing but the worst in human behavior. In short, cynicism is the antithesis of idealism, truth, and justice—the very virtues that law enforcement officers swear to uphold.

Most research on police cynicism took place in the late 1960s and mid-1970s. Using test groups, researchers conducted studies that revealed cynicism to be more prevalent in large urban police departments and in the lower ranks, especially among college-educated officers. The degree of cynicism among officers studied generally increased during their first 10 years of service, then declined slightly, and finally leveled off. Notably, of-

---

1. Kenneth R. Behrend, "Police Cynicism: A Cancer in Law Enforcement?" *FBI Law Enforcement Bulletin*, August 1980. I.

ficers in the studies who received meritorious awards experienced lower levels of cynicism.[2]

Recent research has focused on burnout and stress, two emotional conditions related to cynicism and caused largely by the excessive demands of the police profession. As with cynicism, burnout and stress can result in reduced performance, alienation, and the use of defense mechanisms. Burnout, stress, and cynicism produce two main unhealthy responses from police officers: Withdrawal from society and antipathy to idealism.

Withdrawal from Society

The sordid reality of the streets, particularly in large cities that have higher crime rates and more anonymity, often shocks officers fresh from the academy. As a result, many of the situations they experience cause them to lose faith in others and develop an us-versus-them view in the process. They soon begin to trust only other police officers, the only people whom they believe understand how the world really is. Unfortunately, senior partners oftentimes reinforce such views.

As a consequence, officers socialize with fewer and fewer people outside of the law enforcement circle and might even gradually withdraw from their families and friends. If carried too far, this phenomenon courts domestic disaster. It can even lead to suicide.

As officers withdraw further and further from society, they lose their social safety net—the norms and values that help them make sense of the world—and fall deeper into a state of confusion, alienation, apathy, and frustration. This social estrangement is compounded as officers eventually lose respect for the law. Almost simultaneously, they learn to manipulate the law in their everyday dealings with what they believe to be a dysfunctional judicial system.[3]

Antipathy to Idealism

One of the main reasons young people go into law enforcement is to serve society.[4] When confronted with an unexpectedly hostile or indifferent public, or with a justice system that allows criminals to go free, idealistic officers feel betrayed and victimized by such injustice. They soon

---

2. Arthur Neiderhoffer, *Behind the Shield: The Police in Urban Society.* (Garden City: NY: Doubleday Anchor. 1969); and Robert Regoli, *Police in America* (Washington, DC: R.F. Publishing, Inc., 1977).

3. Ibid.

4. John Stratton, *Police Passages* (Manhattan Beach, CA: Glennon, 1984), 32.

learn that the idealism of the academy and the Law Enforcement Code of Ethics does not reflect reality.

As they lose respect for law and society, these officers might lose their self-respect as well. Embittered, they cannot attack the public they have sworn to protect; so, they nurse their hatreds and become victims of cynicism.

Cynical officers no longer show concern for the values that led them to police service in the first place. Instead, they often view those values with contempt. Unlike employees in other occupations, police officers usually will not leave for another job because they are disillusioned with more than just the job. Like many combat veterans returning from war, they believe that their world has changed forever, no matter what job they hold.

What Causes Cynicism?

In addition to the conditions on the streets and the officers' ensuing loss of respect for the law, occupational stagnation also contributes to police cynicism.[5] This specialization often restricts patrol officers' opportunities for new and enriching experiences. For those officers who cannot be promoted, which happens to be the majority, the job provides few incentives and little built-in satisfaction. Instead, it may become tedious, especially for officers with a college education and high expectations. In a society that defines success in materialistic terms, the lack of promotability causes further frustration, disappointment, and a decrease in self-esteem.

Two concepts introduced here merit further exploration—the need for work to be rewarding and the effects of an excessively materialistic society on police officers. Some researchers postulate that work itself must yield feelings of achievement, responsibility, personal growth, and recognition to satisfy the worker's ego and self-actualization needs.[6] According to police cynicism studies, present methods of policing necessarily do not meet this need for the patrol officer.[7]

The second issue involves the effects of the high value placed on material success in American society. Many researchers over the years have

---

5. Supra note 2.

6. Bert Scanlon and J. Bernard Keys. *Management and Organizational Behavior* (New York: John Wiley & Sons, 1979), 223 and 229. Herzberg discussed the need for achievement, which complements Maslow's works on the fulfillment of needs. Maslow theorized that all motivation was based on satisfying a hierarchy of needs, progressing from basic physiological and safety needs to social and ego needs, and ultimately to self-actualization, a sense of reaching one's fullest potential.

7. Supra note 2.

identified the American dream of material success as a significant factor contributing to the soaring crime rate.[8] Such ambition promotes deviant behavior as individuals trade ethical values for personal gain, thus creating a culture of crime. Police officers not only see this phenomenon in the streets, where everyone is out for themselves, but they also might see it demonstrated by their own political and law enforcement leaders.

Some believe that cynicism has become an ingrained part of everyday life in this country. People adopt a cynical attitude as a reaction to and a defense against dashed hopes—hopes that have been culturally induced and socially reinforced.[9] As members of society, police officers fall victim to the same types of social forces that befall everyone else.

How Can Cynicism Be Prevented?

Just as some of the causes of police cynicism correspond to the causes of burnout and distress among other types of employees, some methods of prevention and cure that help them also work for law enforcement. Leadership plays a significant part.

Competent, principle-centered, people-oriented leadership, as espoused by some current writers[10] on the topic, is required if the law enforcement profession is to develop an ethos based on universally acknowledged ethics, principles, and values. This ethos must accommodate and encourage personal ambition, but not excluded other values and goals.

Leadership

Police leaders must demonstrate their commitment to the ideals of honesty, fairness, justice, courage, integrity, loyalty, and compassion. Leaders who fail to prove themselves trustworthy help spread the seeds of cynicism.

Police leaders must exhibit appropriate conduct by example, not just by words. They also must nurture their employees by working to expose officers to the many good people and good deeds in their communities so they see more than just the bad.

By explaining the intent of rules of evidence and providing comprehensive and continuous training on the subject, leaders can help officers feel

---

8. See, for example, Steven Messner and Richard Rosenfeld, *Crime and the American Dream* (Belmont, CA: International Thompson, 1993)

9. Donald L. Kanter and Philip H. Mirvis. *The Cynical Americans* (San Francisco: Jossey-Bass, 1989).

10. See, for example, Steven Covey, *Principle Centered Leadership* (NY: Simon & Schuster. 1991).

confident and empowered in the legal arena. Such confidence can help officers respect the judicial system rather than feel manipulated by it. Most important, leaders need to build a culture of integrity within their agencies, so that officers have something to believe in when all else seems to fail.

Research on cynicism suggests that principle-centered, compassionate leadership inspires employees and therefore decreases cynicism. To be effective, however, such leadership must be consistent over a long period of time. Role models and mentors also have a positive effect. Employee-oriented leadership and team building provide essential elements of a positive, "upbeat company.'[11]

The research further recommends other ways to help prevent employees from becoming cynical, including job enrichment programs, participatory management styles where employees share responsibility and have a say in workplace policies and practices, and reward systems in which employees have a voice.[12] In policing, as in society in general, an increased emphasis must be placed on sharing power and rewards with employees at all levels.

Every element of effective leadership, from setting an example to listening actively to employees, affects cynicism. As leaders promote esprit de corps, they directly help build esteem and self-worth among employees. Establishing standards, providing the training to reach those standards, and continuously offering refresher training builds officers' competence, which in turn builds their confidence. Following up with positive recognition or guidance when necessary creates and maintains good morale.

Those who write about motivation nearly always discuss the power of positive recognition. In *A Passion for Excellence*. Tom Peters recommends using any excuse to celebrate employee success.[13] Police managers have an obligation to their employees and their agencies to use this and all leadership tools to combat the debilitating disease of cynicism.

Recruiting

Experts routinely recommend that employees become involved in something larger than themselves to combat burnout and cynicism. An organizational culture committed to a quality product, the community, and/or the environment can accomplish this. Caution must be exercised here, however, because thwarted idealism might have made the public

---

11. Supra note 9.
12. Ibid.
13. Tom Peters and N. Austin, *A Passion for Excellence* (New York: Time Warner, 1986).

servant cynical in the first place. Their idealistic visions of public service did not match the realities, which caused them to lose faith and become cynical.

To prevent a repeat of this scenario, some researchers recommend providing a realistic job preview to potential applicants.[14] Recruits should know the exact realities of policing from the outset. At present, some departments offer limited orientation for families of officers, but few, if any, offer a realistic preview to officers. College police science courses also could address such issues.

Training

In addition to a realistic job preview, recruit and ongoing roll call training should be provided on the subjects of cynicism, burnout, and stress management. While many departments offer psychological services to employees once symptoms develop, few offer preventative training.

Police officers must be taught the early warning signs of stress and burnout, as well as the difference between healthy suspicion and insidious cynicism. Once they know how to identify these problems, officers should be taught productive coping techniques and stress management methods. Left to their own devices, too many officers choose counterproductive methods, such as alcohol abuse and withdrawal. In addition, officers' families should receive similar training so that they can provide first-line detection and long-term support to their loved ones.[15]

Mentors and Peer Counselors

Because distraught officers often feel most comfortable talking to their colleagues, peer counseling provides another method for treating cynicism once symptoms appear. A more pro-active measure, however, would be to recruit peer counselors as mentors for new officers.

Mentors provide instruction and help officers manage their expectations early in their assimilation into the police culture. By establishing realistic expectations, officers are less likely to become disillusioned by actual police work.

Community Policing

Community policing offers police departments a unique opportunity to combat cynicism. Involving the police and the public in collaborative

---

14. Supra note 9.

15. James T. Reese, *Behavioral Science in Law Enforcement* (Quantico, VA: FBI National Center for the Analysis of Violent Crime, 1987).

problem solving has the positive side effect of reducing officers' alienation and withdrawal.

In community policing, management empowers employees, and trust is given and ultimately received. When officers feel that they can trust management and that management trusts them, cynicism declines. In such a relationship, two-way accountability ensures that tasks get completed.

The empowerment aspect of community policing enables leaders to help employees develop their potential through creative and innovative problem solving. This leads to a better quality of service to the community achieved with greater efficiency and effectiveness. Particularly at the patrol level where studies have shown the levels of cynicism to be the highest, community policing can provide an outlet for accomplishment that builds employees' self-esteem and fulfills their needs for growth.

Conclusion

Police leaders must take a moment to reflect on cynicism, acknowledge its harmful effects, and use the tools available to prevent it. These tools—employee- and principle-centered leadership, realistic job previews, training, positive recognition, and empowerment—will serve to develop an organizational culture where personal ambition becomes second to the good of the organization and the good of the community.

Police cynicism is insidious and costly. It can attack officers of all ranks in departments of all sizes. Its cumulative effects sneak up on its victims, crushing their idealism and enthusiasm before they even realize what has happened.

Cynicism robs the profession of the very values needed to accomplish its goals. Each time it creates a negative contact with a citizen or impinges on professionalism and productivity among the ranks, cynicism impacts on police officers everywhere.

The demands of policing in the next century require that police leaders examine this disease and take action against it. Cynicism does not have to be a natural part of policing. With realistic expectations, strong and compassionate leadership, and continuous training, officers can avoid the conditions that lead to the pitfalls of cynicism and maintain their ideals and values.

8

Stress Management in Law Enforcement: Where Do We Go From Here?

James D. Sewell
Katherine W. Ellison
Joseph J. Hurrell, Jr.

It has been nearly 15 years since a series of articles appeared which led the way to the major interdisciplinary symposium on law enforcement stress held in May 1974.[1] Since then, there has been a veritable flood of publications on police stress, written by researchers and academics, police managers and police officers, and psychologists and counselors. We estimate that there are now well over 200 publications in this area. Throughout the country, numerous seminars on this critical topic have been held. Countless training courses, both specialized and as part of basic recruit curricula, have been conducted. It is an easy assumption that the awareness about the stress of law enforcement officers has increased significantly over the last 15 years.

A variety of component areas have been considered in addressing the scope of the problem, including stress on law enforcement officers in general, stress on particular segments of the law enforcement population, police "burnout," stress in the police family and traumatic incident stress. They have also dealt with stress management techniques, including the role of physical fitness and diet and nutrition, counseling and psychological services, and training.[2]

Yet there is little information about the impact of this explosion of interest and data on police managers and management techniques. With 15

---

1. Kroes, W.H., and Hurrell, J.J. (eds.) (1975). *Job stress and the police officer. Identifying stress reduction techniques*. Washington: U.S. Government Printing Office.

2. For bibliographies of this literature, see Terry, W.C. (1981). Police stress: The empirical evidence. *Journal of Police Science and Administration*, 9 (1), 61–75; Ellison, K.W. and Genz, J.L. (1983). *Stress and the police officer*. Springfield: Thomas; or Malloy, T.E., and Mays, L.G. (1984). The police stress hypothesis. *Criminal Justice and Behavior*, 11 (2), 197–224.

years of stress research behind us, law enforcement chiefs and managers must today confront two major areas of concern:

1. What do we know about the impact of stress in policing?
2. What practical use can we make of the research data?

What Should We Be Asking?

The first question in this area should be: how many agencies have implemented stress management programs and to what extent? In 1984 it was estimated that, in spite of the concern over police stress, "only 20 percent of all law enforcement agencies have any comprehensive program of stress management."[3] Such estimates, however, are not based on population surveys.

To assess accurately the impact of stress concerns on the administration of law enforcement agencies, the following questions must be asked:

1. What is the best method to define and measure individual and collective stress within a police organization?[4]
2. How many agencies have implemented stress management programs?
3. What type and size of agency is most likely to implement stress management programs?
4. What have existing stress management programs encompassed?
    a. How many consist only of training?
    b. How many involve psychological counseling?
        (1) What is the nature of such counseling? For example, does it concentrate primarily on substance abuse?
        (2) What is the relationship of the service providers to the agency? Are they also responsible for fitness-for-duty evaluations?[5]
    c. How many have involved changes in management style?
    d. How long has each program been in effect?
    e. What are the average costs per officer for each program?
    f. How have programs been evaluated? That is, what do we know about the effects of these programs, both on the organization and on its individual officers?

---

3. Sewell, J.D. (1984). Stress in university law enforcement. *Journal of Higher Education, 55* (4), 510.

4. For a discussion of some of the problems in defining the concept of stress, see Ellison & Genz (1983), *op. cit.*

5. The practical and ethical problems of this arrangement have been discussed widely elsewhere.

The Training Issue

Many additional issues arise from the question about evaluation of the effects of training programs. Most tend to center around the specific approach offered as preventives for stress-related disorders. We especially need to know *what changes in lifestyles among police officers have occurred as a result of stress management training?* As one of the authors of this article has already observed.

> ...as our knowledge of police stress has increased, many researchers and law enforcement professionals have offered a variety of mechanisms that can be used to control or reduce law enforcement stress. Increased stress management training, professional counseling for officers and their families, peer advisement, and required fitness standards and programs have been identified as important measures that should be developed and implemented at the department level. The use of relaxation responses and neutralization techniques, proper nutrition and diet, and regular exercise, particularly aerobic exercise, have been offered as remedies for the individual officer.[6]

Evaluating Components

The issue, then, is whether training aimed at the individual has led to behavioral changes, and, more important, whether behavioral change has led to a reduction in those physical and psychological problems believed to be stress-related. We need to know if the various components of stress management training programs have had the impact they have claimed. We must evaluate specific components of training, including those aimed at improving nutrition, general physical and, particularly, cardiovascular fitness and emotional well-being. The latter would involve an assessment of programs designed to teach techniques, such as biofeedback, self-hypnosis and relaxation techniques. The various techniques for cognitive behavior changes, such as those aimed at managing anger and irrational thought patterns, also must be examined.

Post-Traumatic Stress

One very specific problem has merited much special consideration in the literature on stress in law enforcement: "post-traumatic stress." It has encompassed reactions to shootings and handling very difficult cases, such

---

6. Sewell, J.D. (1986). Stress management for the police manager. *The Florida Police Chief*, 12(3), 56–65.

as the violent death of a child or severe child abuse. In our research, we need to direct questions toward *the impact of special programs aimed at post-traumatic stress disorder on the short-term stability, long-term mental health and attrition/retention rates of police officers.*

It has been noted that "every officer involved in a traumatic incident does not experience problems. *Although not a scientific study,*[7] approximately one-third have minimal, if any, problems; one-third have moderate problems; and another one-third have severe difficulty affecting the officer, his family, and often ending in divorce, combined with leaving the department because of disability or desire."[8] Yet, when it comes to shooting situations, other research indicates that "70 percent of officers involved in a killing leave the force within seven years of the incident."[9]

Regardless of the exact number of officers affected, it is generally believed that trauma experienced on the job can severely damage an officer's psychological and physical well-being. Yet there is little specific evidence about the extent and nature of this effect. Future research needs to explore the type, intensity and frequency of incidents likely to be associated with negative reactions; the responses of agencies to potentially traumatic incidents affecting their officers; and the results of these responses on the emotions and behaviors of officers.

One commonly used measure of stressfulness on the job, and particularly on specific incidents, has been attrition. To accurately study variables such as post-traumatic stress, we will need a much more careful comparison of attrition rates of officers experiencing specific incidents. To evaluate fully the effects of intervention programs, we need to compare agencies with and without post-traumatic stress management programs.

Marital Conflict

In addition to specific traumatic events, the daily hassles and pressures on the job[10] are believed to accumulate, leading to a number of chronic problems. An event that is mentioned frequently in the catalog of stress-related problems is marital conflict. One researcher noted,

---

7. The emphasis is ours. This quote is a good example of the anecdotal nature of much of the evidence from which we must wok.

8. Stratton, J.D. (1983). Traumatic incidents and the police. *Police Stress,* 6 (1), 4.

9. American Society of Public Administration (1983). Killing in the line of duty: Study examines effects. *PA Times,* 6 (5), 14.

10. These have been catalogued in many publications, including Stratton, J.G. (1978). Police Stress, Part 1: An overview. *Police Chief,* 45 (4), 58–62.

...police departments researching marriage failures among their officers find widely varying results...the Seattle, Wash. Police Department discovered 60 percent of its officers were divorced during the first 3 years on the force... the Tacoma, Wash., Police Department has been reported as having 82 percent of its force divorced, and the San Jose, Calif., Police Department estimated its divorce rate to be between 50 and 70 percent...Another survey reported divorce rates in police departments in Baltimore, Md., as 17 percent; in Santa Ana, Calif., as 27 percent; and in Chicago, Ill., as 33.3 percent.[11]

In contrast, other researchers have declared, "we know of no evidence to support the popular notion that the divorce rate on police marriages is higher than other occupations...statements or reports claiming higher divorce rates for law enforcement are based on supposition rather than fact."[12] Again, the dissonance between evidence and supposition suggests further questions. We need more precise statistics on divorce rates. Given the generation of these data, we can then ask if the divorce rate for law enforcement personnel differs significantly from other supposedly "high stress" occupational groups, or indeed, from that of the general population. Finally, we need to know whether stress management programs have an impact on the divorce rate in a given police agency. Perhaps even more specifically, we should ask if the nature of the program makes a difference.

Premature Death

Premature death has been used as yet another indicator of occupational stress. Studies have commonly focused on two very different causes: cardiovascular disease and suicide. In an early article, Richard and Fell concluded that police "have significantly higher rates of premature death and rank third among occupations in death rates. Police also are admitted to general hospitals at significantly higher rates."[13] Although these statistics, with their contention of difference, have been contested,[14] officers do suffer from these problems, and programs have been designed for their amelioration.

---

11. Depue, R.L. (1979). Turning inward: The police officer counselor. *FBI Law Enforcement Bulletin*, 48 (2), 8–12.

12. Stratton, J.G., and Stratton, B.T. (1982). Law enforcement marital relationships: A positive approach. *FBI Law Enforcement Bulletin*, 51 (5), 6.

13. Richard, W.C., and Fell, R.W. (1975). Health factors in police job stress. In W.H. Kroes & J.J. Hurrell (eds.) *Job stress and the police officer*. Washington: U.S. Government Printing Office, 78.

14. See Ellison and Genz (1983), *op. cit.* for a discussion of the methodological problems of many of the studies of police stress.

It is, therefore, appropriate to study the impact of stress management programs in these areas. Again, research should be directed to the question of the success of stress management and stress inoculation programs in reducing these problems. On the most simple level, we need to know if counseling in diet and nutrition, aimed at reducing cardiovascular problems, has led to changes in eating habits and, subsequently, to improved physical health. On a more global level, is there any relationship between training and/or counseling programs and rates of premature death, whether from cardiovascular disease or suicide?

Organizational Stress

Many articles and much published research have pinpointed organizational change as a major element of successful stress management in a law enforcement agency. It has been commonly held that effective stress management requires enlightened management practices; employee involvement in organizational direction and control; increased and observable management sensitivity about employee needs; mitigation of the paramilitary nature of the law enforcement organization; and a softening of the police character depicted as "badge-heavy" and "macho."

Under this rubric, we need to ask several questions. Can the police character's macho traits be softened without a reduction in the control qualities necessary for effective law enforcement and peace-keeping activities? Has there been any change in the attitudes and behaviors of police managers toward their employees and, more particularly, toward the stress-related problems of these employees? What is the nature of documentation for this change? How many agencies have instituted a different organizational, nonparamilitary structure and what has been the effect on employee stress reactions? Has there been an increase in employee involvement in organizational control, and what impact has this had on stress reaction, both at the individual and organizational level?

Disability Claims

A major concern for police managers has been the possibility of increases in disability pension claims and early retirements in which organizational stress is claimed to have been a factor. If there is a close relationship between the job and its stress, then it would seem to follow that heart attacks, ulcers, cardiovascular disease and similar illnesses held to be stress-related must be also job-related.

According to a study by the National Council on Compensation Insurance, claims for gradual mental stress alone now account for about 11 percent of all occupational disease claims. The study also showed that worker compensation costs for gradual mental stress reached and then surpassed average costs for other occupational disease claims in the period 1981–1982.[15] The precise level of these claims for police is unknown, but the media has indicated that, in some larger cities, there has been an increase in disability and early retirement claims related to stress.[16]

Especially for managers of police agencies facing a fiscal crisis, it is important to identify the dimensions of these claims, to find ways to minimize them, and to recognize and discourage false claims, while still responding to the legitimate need of employees.

Practical Applications

The large number of research questions that remain unanswered would suggest that the study of stressors in police work and their effects on law enforcement personnel and operations remains incomplete. Yet, if we assume that further research can bring some closure to the issues raised here, an even more critical question must be confronted: How can police organizations use the results of continued stress research?

For the law enforcement administrator, stress research would appear to have several practical implications. First, the issue of "stress," with or without empirical support, has had an important place in law enforcement thought and literature for a number of years. If research confirms that stress is a problem for the morale and productivity of police officers, then administrators would do well to undertake an aggressive program of stress management. If, however, the stress on officers is not as significant as some literature has led us to believe, perhaps it should receive less management attention. In particular, we need to avoid the development of a self-fulfilling prophecy: officers believe the job is stressful and either talk themselves into stress-related problems[17] or use vaguely defined stress "disorders" to malinger and/or inappropriately increase the size of their pensions.

15. National Council on Compensation Insurance (1985). Emotional stress in the work place: New legal rights in the '80s. New York.

16. Spiegal, C., and Welkos, R. (1985). Malingerers—Dark side of the force. *Los Angeles Times*. Special reprint of February 3–6 series, 21–6.

17. Many of the articles on this topic published by psychologists emphasize the *cognitive* aspects of stress reduction programs. The popular cliche exemplifying this view is, "Stress management is 'mind over matter: if you don't *mind*, it doesn't *matter*.'"

Second, research's finding a relation between stress management programs and organizational effectiveness would support the continued and even expanded allocation of resources to such programs. On the other hand, little to no correlation between agency productivity and a formal program of stress management might properly suggest a reallocation of existing resources and administrative priorities.

Third, improved research should allow us to identify those practices which work—or those which did not—to lessen the incidence and prevalence of stress-related disorders. Again, such knowledge is important in allocating agency resources and in determining the direction and substance of agency training efforts.

Finally, attrition rates that may be attributed to a variety of pressures are, of course, a major concern for any administrator. With a greater understanding of the problem, managers can design programs and modify organizational structure and efforts to increase retention of employees and to control the cost of officer disability claims.

In summary, despite many years of interest and a wealth of publications on the subject of police stress, our knowledge about the problem remains sketchy at best. Consequently, police agencies may be pouring their limited resources into stress management programs that may not work, and police chiefs and other law enforcement executives may be focusing their energies in the wrong direction. The need for well-controlled, comprehensive *research* on police stress is greater than ever. Once we have knowledge about *what* works, it will be up to police administrators to decide *how*—or whether—to implement programs from the information gained.

Part Three

Police Suicide

As the authors in Part One and Two have indicated, stress can severely impact individuals, especially in certain stress prone professions. We can identify a number of physical or physiological, psychological or emotional, or sociocultural manifestations of stress, which can affect an individual in a negative manner.

Suicide is, of course, the most negative, inward-directed result of stress. According to classic stress lore, with some empirical support, the most suicide-prone professionals are psychologists, dentists, and law enforcement officers.

The concern about officer suicide is not new, and administrators and academicians alike have recognized the problem for decades. Between 1934 and 1940, for instance, 93 New York City Police Officers killed themselves, and that agency's suicide rate from 1950 to 1967 exceeded the suicide rate for all males in the United States during that time period.

The critical questions in any discussion of police suicide are two-fold: Is police suicide statistically a major or unique problem in American policing? If so, how can it be prevented? The authors in Part Three, then, will focus on these concerns.

As we examine this issue, we all must acknowledge that suicide has a devastating effect on both an officer's family and the police department. Violanti examines the factors that lead officers to take their own lives and the role police departments can play in preventing such action. His recommendations center on training officers to better cope with professional and personal problems.

Examining the experience of one agency in police suicide, Josephson and Reiser reports an increase in the incidence of suicide in LAPD between 1976 and 1982. They suggest that principal among the factors for this increase are marital discord and alcohol abuse. Yet, in spite of these increases, the suicide rate of officers at the LAPD continues to remain lower than the rates for other adults in the state and nation.

Unlike others which deal with the subject of police suicide, Baker and Baker do not dwell on the rates and means of suicide but rather the kinds of support systems that can be developed by police departments to intervene *before* an officer decides to take his/her life. The article discusses the obstacles to intervention most commonly encountered (i.e.., denying a problem exists; fear of losing one's job or being demoted; and fear of having personal problems exposed for public ridicule). The authors suggest that, in order to eliminate such obstacles, police administrators and supervisors must play a non-punitive role and conclude the article with a series of suggestions on how a successful intervention strategy can be accomplished.

References

Green, James J. (1995). "Officer Needs Assistance: Suicide in the New York City Police Department." *CJ Update*, 23(2), 2.

9

The Mystery Within: Understanding Police Suicide

John M. Violanti

Although considerable obstacles hinder the study of police suicide, mounting evidence suggests that self-inflicted deaths within the law enforcement profession are continuing a dramatic upward trend that began in the 1980s. According to one study, in the years 1950 to 1979, a sample of 2,662 officers averaged one suicide every 2.5 years. From 1980 to 1990, the rate increased to one suicide every 1.25 years. These sobering findings indicate that police suicides now may be occurring at twice the rate they did in the past.[1]

Such statistics make it increasingly important for law enforcement agencies to deal with a problem that refuses to disappear, no matter how successfully it is ignored. Only by gaining a better understanding of the factors that lead to police suicide can administrators develop an effective response to this tragic cause of death among law enforcement officers. Resolving the underlying problems that hinder the research of police suicide may be the first step to gaining a better understanding of it.

Problems of Research

Considerable difficulty exists in studying police suicide. Researchers often find that information on officer suicide either is not collected or departments are reluctant to allow access to such data.[2]

In addition, police suicides may be misclassified routinely as either accidents or undetermined deaths. Because police officers traditionally subscribe to a myth of indestructibility, they view suicide as particularly disgraceful to the victim officer and to the profession.[3]

---

1. J.M. Violanti and J.E. Vena, "Epidemiology of Police Suicide" (research in progress, NIMH Grant MH 47091-02).

2. J.H. Burge. "Suicide and Occupation: A Review," *Journal of Vocational Behavior,* 21, 206–222, 1982.

3. J. Skolnick, *Police in America* (Boston: Educational Associates, 1975), 21.

The police represent a highly cohesive subculture whose members tend to "take care of their own."[4] The desire to shield victim officers, their families, and their departments from the stigma of suicide may lead investigators to overlook certain evidence intentionally during the classification process. One study of the Chicago Police Department estimated that as many as 67 percent of police suicides in that city had been misclassified as accidental or natural deaths.[5]

Failure to correct for such biases could lead to false conclusions regarding the causes and frequency of police suicides. Therefore, accurate research must go beyond official rates; the preliminary results of an ongoing study of police suicides over a 40-year period indicate that nearly 30 percent of police suicides may have been misclassified.[6]

Other problems exist in the study of police suicide. Because most research focuses on large cities, very little is known about suicides in small or rural departments. Therefore, while epidemiological data reliably indicate that police officers are at a higher risk for suicide than the general population, such results may not be generalized appropriately to the entire country. However, the research that has been conducted produced various explanations as to why police officers take their own lives.

Why Officers Commit Suicide

Studies have revealed several factors related to police suicide. Suicides have been found to be more common among older officers and are related to alcoholism, physical illness, or impending retirement.[7] Other clues have been cited to help explain the high rate of self-inflicted death among police officers: The regular availability of firearms; continuous duty exposure to death and injury; social strain resulting from shift work; inconsistencies within the criminal justice system; and the perception among police officers that they labor under a negative public image. In addition,

---

4. J.M. Violanti, "Police Suicide on the Rise," *New York Trooper*, January 1984, 18–19.

5. M. Wagner and R. Brzeczek, "Alcohol and Suicide: A Fatal Connection," *FBI Law Enforcement Bulletin*, March 1983. 7–15.

6. Supra note 1.

7. J. Schwartz and C. Schwartz, "The Personal Problems of the Police Officer: A Plea for Action," in *Job Stress and the Police Officer*, W. Kroes and J. Hurrell eds. (Washington, DC: U.S. Government Printing Office. 1976), 130–141.

research confirms a higher propensity for suicide among males, who dominate the police profession.[8]

A study of the Detroit Police Department found that the vast majority of Detroit police officers who took their lives were white young men, high school educated, and married. Alcohol abuse was fairly common among the sample (42 percent), as was a formal diagnosis of psychosis (33 percent). However, marital difficulties appeared to be the most prevalent problem among the Detroit sample.[9]

Examination of 27 cases of police suicide in Quebec found that one-half of the officers had a history of psychiatric and/or medical problems, and many had severe alcohol problems. Most officers in the sample experienced difficulties at work, and in *every case*, a notable drop in work performance had been observed in the 6 months prior to the suicide.[10]

Stress

The high stress of police work generally is cited as a primary contributing factor. The constant barrage of stressors inherent with danger, and for police managers, the pressure of administration, can overwhelm even the strongest person. When officers lose the ability to cope in normal ways, they may turn to an ultimate solution to relieve the pressures of stress.[11]

Frustration and Helplessness

Among the occupational factors surrounding police suicide, frustration often is cited as particularly important. Almost unfailingly, officers enter policing with high ideals and a noble desire to help others. Over time, this sense of idealism may transform into hardcore cynicism.

The roots of frustration emanate from the central irony of American policing: Society charges police officers with the task of regulating a public that does not want to be regulated. For individual officers, the result-

8. S. Labovitz and R. Hagehorn, "An Analysis of Suicide Rates Among Occupational Categories," *Sociological Inquiry*, 41, 1971, 67–72; also Z. Nelson and W. E. Smith, "The Law Enforcement Profession: An Incidence of High Suicide," *Omega*, 1, 1970, 293–299.

9. B.I. Danto, "Police Suicide," *Police Stress*, 1, 1978, 32–35.

10. G. Aussant, "Police Suicide," *Royal Canadian Mounted Police Gazette*, 46, 1984, 14–21.

11. F.L. McCafferty, E. McCafferty, and M.A. McCafferty, "Stress and Suicide in Police Officers: A Paradigm of Occupational Stress," *Southern Medical Journal*, 85, 1992, 233–243.

ing frustration is exacerbated by a largely unsympathetic press, a lack of community support, and a criminal justice system that values equity over expediency. A sense of societal isolation often ensues, compelling officers to group together in a defensive stance. When an officer feels that the frustration no longer is tolerable or that no coping alternative is available, suicide may become an attractive option.[12]

It also is possible that feelings of helplessness are brought about by the nature of the job.[13] A sense of helplessness is a disturbing realization for anyone, but especially for police officers who are conditioned to view themselves as superheroes capable of anything. Suicide is one way of dealing with helplessness and emotional pain. The finality of the ultimate solution may be an attempt to restore feelings of strength, courage, and mastery over the environment.[14]

Access to Firearms

Another factor that distinguishes police officers from the general population also has been implicated in the high number of police suicides. That is, most law enforcement officers carry or have access to firearms. An ongoing study of police suicides in the United States reveals that 95 percent involved the use of the officer's service weapon.[15]

Another study compared suicides in New York City and London. While the police suicide rate in New York City was twice that of the general population, the police suicide rate in London, where officers do not carry firearms, was similar to that of the city's civilian population.[16]

The police firearm holds special significance for officers. It is a very potent symbol of the power of life and death. Society entrusts law enforcement officers with the authority to use their weapons to take the life of another person in certain situations. In police suicides, officers, in effect, are claiming the right to take their own lives. After all, the weapon has

---

12. Supra note 1.

13. M. Heiman, "Suicide Among Police," *American Journal of Psychiatry*, 134, 1977, 1286–1290.

14. P. Bonafacio, *The Psychological Effects of Police Work* (New York: Plenum Press, 1991); also S. Allen, "Suicide and Indirect Self-Destructive Behavior Among Police," in *Psychological Services for Law Enforcement*. J. Reese and H. Goldstein eds. (Washington, DC: U.S. Government Printing Office, 1986).

15. Supra note 1.

16. P. Friedman, "Suicide Among Police: A Study of 93 Suicides Among New York City Policemen 1934–40." in *Essays in Self-Destruction*. E.S. Shneidman, ed. (New York: Science House, 1968)

been issued as a means to stop misery and to protect others from harm. Despondent officers may view suicide in such a way.

Alcohol Abuse

Alcohol abuse also has been implicated as a significant contributing factor in police suicides. One study documented alcohol abuse in 60 percent of the suicides in the Chicago Police Department.[17] Administrators should be aware that alcoholism may lead to other work problems, such as high absenteeism, traffic accidents, or intoxication on duty. Given the established correlation between alcoholism and suicide, these symptoms should not be ignored. They should be considered indications of a larger problem.

Fear of Separation from the Police Subculture

As officers near the end of their law enforcement careers, another potential threat appears—separation. To individual officers, retirement may mean separation from the camaraderie and protection of police peers. During their years of service, officers may have clustered with other officers due to a general isolation from society and its prejudices toward the police. Upon retirement, these officers must enter the very society that they perceive as alien and hostile.

While the benefits of retirement may be viewed positively by the majority of officers, separation from the police subculture can be a frightful and devastating prospect for others. Fear, coupled with increasing age (a definite suicide risk factor), loss of friends, loss of status as a police officer, and a loss of self-definition, leaves some retiring officers vulnerable to suicide. A recent study found a 10-fold risk of suicide among police retirees.[18]

Other Factors

Other factors have been suggested in an attempt to explain why officers take their own lives. One theory holds that officers commit suicide because of their continuous exposure to human misery and their constant

17. Supra note 5.

18. C.W. Gaska, "The Rate of Suicide, Potential for Suicide, and Recommendations for Prevention Among Retired Police Officers" (Doctoral Dissertation: Wayne State University, 1980).

giving of themselves.[19] Another study cites police bureaucracy, with its paramilitary structure, overbearing regulations, and negativism, as a primary catalyst in police suicides.[20]

It also has been suggested that "loner" officers who feel isolated from and uninvolved with the police subculture are more likely to commit suicide.[21] Another theory views police suicides as a response to confusing messages from society: Police are given great discretionary powers, but that power is routinely truncated by the courts, the press, and from time to time, administrators. Under these conditions, many officers experience a significant sense of conflict and confusion.[22]

Policing involves a continual barrage of boredom interspersed with acts of violence, deceit, and human misery. Many officers are exposed to a subculture of violence in which they encounter death almost daily. The average citizen generally does not witness in a lifetime the amount of death and violence a police officer experiences in one month. As a result of this exposure, Post Traumatic Stress Syndrome may lead to a breakdown of normal coping processes. Because the effects of stress are believed to be cumulative, officers exposed to many stressors may reach a breaking point leading to suicide. A study of the Royal Canadian Mounted Police found that 15 percent of the Mounties who committed suicide recently had been exposed to a traumatic work incident.[23]

Current research does not explain definitively what effects such exposure has on the psyche of police officers. It is possible that exposure to death and human suffering produces a numbing effect; that is, death becomes easier to accept as a possible solution to seemingly impossible problems.

Psychological trauma is associated closely with this exposure to death and violence. Many officers involved in police shootings suffer serious aftereffects as a result of these critical incidents. Similar to veterans of war, officers involved in such incidents experience posttraumatic symptoms, such as nightmares, flashbacks, and a fear of returning to duty. Suicide can be the ultimate response to this sometimes unendurable pain.

---

19. M. Heiman, "The Police Suicide," *Journal of Police Science and Administration*, 3, 1975, 267–285.

20. C. Nix, "Police Suicide: Answers Are Sought," *The New York Times*, September 15, 1986, B2–4.

21. J. Slater and R. Depue, "The Contribution of Environmental and Social Support to Serious Suicide Attempts in Primary Depressive Order," *Journal of Abnormal Psychology*, 90, 1981, 275–285.

22. Supra note 4.

23. R. Loo, "Suicide Among Police in a Federal Force," *Suicide and Life-Threatening Behavior*, 16, 1986, 379–388.

Asking for Help

Traditionally, no matter what their problems, police officers refrain from asking for help. There are various reasons for this reluctance. Officers do not wish to appear weak or vulnerable in front of their peers. Individuals who perceive themselves as problem solvers often have great difficultly admitting that they have a problem of their own. As a result, some officers who feel that they can no longer tolerate psychological pain choose to solve the problem themselves through suicide rather than by asking others for help.

Fortunately, officers' reluctance to seek out help is being abated by successful counseling programs established in many departments. For individual officers, these programs have helped remove the stigma of admitting that they have problems. Currently the domain of large and progressive departments, intervention programs should be implemented in every U.S. law enforcement agency. Because all police officers face similar challenges and pressures—regardless of the size of the agency in which they serve—every officer should have access to comparable counseling resources.

Effects on Survivors

As is true with any suicide, it is the survivors who must cope with the aftermath of a police suicide. In addition to the emotional anguish and feelings of guilt that generally haunt family members following a suicide, other difficulties often face police suicide survivors. Because suicide is perceived as "dishonorable," families may not be afforded the full honors of a police military-style funeral. To make matters worse, police departments often abandon surviving family members after 1 or 2 weeks of condolences.

Law enforcement agencies must go beyond departmental boundaries to assist the families of *all* deceased officers, including those who take their own lives. By simply maintaining contact and offering assistance with practical matters, such as finances and pension rights, agencies can help family members move through the grieving process.

Departments

In addition to the immediate family, another group experiences the wrath of suicide: Police peers. A grief wave often strikes departments after an officer commits suicide. In some cases, supervisors note a lasting negative effect on the morale and work quality of surviving officers. For this reason, agencies should arrange for psychological debriefings after the self-inflicted death of any officer.

Preventing Police Suicide

The destructive effects on survivors underscore the need to prevent suicide among police personnel. Not only can an effective intervention effort save officers' lives, but it also can safeguard agencies from the devastating effects of suicide.

Agencies must move beyond the morbidity of the subject to develop effective suicide countermeasures. Perhaps the best way to prevent police suicide is to train officers to cope better with professional and personal problems. This provides them with the means to recognize and avoid the psychological and behavioral wrong turns that eventually can lead to suicide. In addition, training supervisors to recognize the warning signs of suicide can afford agencies an opportunity to intervene before it is too late.

Conclusion

Suicide leaves survivors shaken and in search of answers that may never be found. Police suicide can devastate the morale of entire agencies and leave individual officers with intense feelings of guilt, remorse, and disillusionment.

By its very nature, suicide is an act of desperation, carried out when less drastic avenues of relief seem unavailable or inadequate. Police agencies should ensure that these other avenues are available.

Because most studies suggests that law enforcement officers are at a heightened risk for taking their own lives, police agencies also should be at the forefront of developing and implementing suicide intervention programs. As is true with addressing any problem, the first and most important step is to recognize that the problem exists. With regard to police suicide, this fact can no longer be ignored.

10

Officer Suicide in the Los Angeles Police Department: A Twelve-Year Follow-up

Rose Lee Josephson
Martin Reiser

Relatively few studies have been conducted to determine the rates or causes of suicide among police officers. Most police departments do not publish any suicide statistics. Despite the lack of credible data there has been a widespread presumption of high suicide rates among police officers by the media and in some literature on police stress (Burge 1984). One reviewer noted, "An informal consensus appears to have arisen to the effect that the suicide rate among police is appreciably greater than for other occupational groups" (Bedeian 1982). However, research done at the Los Angeles Police Department (LAPD) and the data available in the literature fail to provide support for the belief of an inordinately high suicide rate among police in general (Dash and Reiser 1978).

Background

In an earlier LAPD study, Dash and Reiser examined officer suicide from 1970 through 1976 and found an average rate of 8.1 per 100,000 for the seven-year period (1978). This rate was considerably lower than the county, state, and national suicide rates for adults.

Several factors believed to mitigate the incidence of suicide among LAPD officers were identified: (1) the use of rigorous physical and psychological screening; (2) the utilization of relevant police training programs; and (3) the availability of professional mental health services within the department.

Only one recent study could be found providing statistics on police suicide. Wagner and Brzeczek examined the records of Chicago Police Department members who died from 1977 through 1979 and found twenty officer suicides during that period, including three retirees. The au-

Table 1
Suicide Experienced at the LAPD 1977–1988

Year	Number of Suicides	Number of Sworn Personnel	Mean Ratio Per 100,000
1977	1	7,290	13.7
1978	1	6,980	14.3
1979	1	6,733	14.9
1980	0	6,670	0.0
1981	1	6,885	14.5
1982	0	6,844	0.0
1983	2 (1 female-Hispanic)	6,879	29.1
1984	1 (female-Black)	6,970	14.3
1985	1	7,025	14.2
1986	1	6,966	14.4
1987	1 (female-Hispanic)	7,039	14.2
1988	0	7,387	0.0

12-year average suicide rate = 12.0 per 100,000.

thors stated, "If one looks only at the numbers, a Chicago police officer was five times as likely during this period to take his life as a citizen of the city, based on a department strength of 13,000 and general city population of 3 million" (Wagner and Brzeczek 1983, p. 10).

Using these numbers, the three-year average suicide rate of active Chicago police officers from 1977 through 1979 would be 43.8 per 100,000. This contrasts markedly with the seven-year average rate of 8.1 per 100,000 found for Los Angeles police officers from 1970 through 1976.

Heiman recognized the existence of geographic variations in suicide rates and concluded that the east and west coasts had more suicides than the midwest and south (1977). However, the high suicide rate reported for Chicago police as compared to Los Angeles police calls this generalization into question.

Results

The present study examined officer suicide experienced in the Los Angeles Police Department from 1977 through 1988 and found an average rate of 12.0 per 100,000 (see table 1). This compares with the average rate of 8.1 found in the earlier LAPD study from 1970 through 1976 (see table 2).

In order to examine suicide trends over time, the twelve-year span of this study was divided into two time periods. The first period of seven

Table 2
LAPD Suicides 1970–1976

Year	Number of Suicides	Number of Sworn Personnel	Mean Ratio Per 100,000
1970	2	6,306	29.4
1971	0	6,994	0.0
1972	1	7,145	14.0
1973	0	7,237	0.0
1974	0	7,407	0.0
1975	1	7,506	13.3
1976	0	7,359	0.0

7-year average suicide rate = 8.1 per 100,000.

years, 1977 though 1983, yields an average suicide rate of 12.4 per 100,000. The second time period of five years, 1984 through1988, shows an average suicide rate of 11.4 per 100,000. These rates are not significantly different, suggesting that the overall rate of 12.0 for the total period examined, 1977–1988, fairly represents the current suicide experience at LAPD (see table 3).

Demographic data of LAPD officer suicides suggest that the average profiles for males would reveal a Caucasian, age 35, working patrol, abusing alcohol, separated or seeking divorce, and experiencing a significant loss (see table 4).

During the most recent five-year period studied, for the first time, there were three minority female officer suicides among the total sample.

Discussion

In order to put the results of this study into context, it seems useful to make comparisons with county, state, and national suicide rates for all adults.

Los Angeles County suicide rates for adults, age 20 to 69, were 21.3 per 100,000 in 1970; 18.2 in 1975; 14.3 in 1980; and 13.4 per 100,000 in 1987 (Department of Chief Medical Examiner-Coroner). This decreasing rate of suicide in the county also contributed significantly to the state figures.

The suicide rate in the state of California has been decreasing since the early 1970s. The California suicide rate for adults in 1970 was 18.8 per 100,000 population; 18.0 in 1975; 15.2 in 1982; and 14.8 per 100,000 in 1986 (Vital Statistics of California).

Table 3
LAPD Suicides 1977–1988

(First seven years)

Year	Number of Suicides	Number of Sworn Personnel	Mean Ratio Per 100,000
1977	1	7,290	13.7
1978	1	6,980	14.3
1979	1	6,733	14.9
1980	0	6,670	0.0
1981	1	6,885	14.5
1982	0	6,844	0.0
1983	2 (1 female-Hispanic)	6,879	29.1

7-year average suicide rate = 124 per 100,000.

(Second five years)

1984	1 (female-Black)	6,970	14.3
1985	1	7,025	14.2
1986	1	6,966	14.4
1987	1 (female-Hispanic)	7,039	14.2
1988	0	7,387	0.0

5-year average suicide rate = 11.4 per 100,000.

Nationally, the suicide rate rose over a period of two decades from an average of 9.0 per 100,000 in 1956 to 13.3 in 1977. However, since

Table 4
Demographic Data

Year of Suicide	Age	Gender	Race	Marital Status	Rank	Assignment
1977*	32	male	Caucasian	married	PII	Patrol
1978*	35	male	Caucasian	married	PIII	Investigation
1979*	34	male	Caucasian	divorced	PIII	Patrol
1981*	40	male	Caucasian	separated	Lt.	Patrol
1983*	20	female	Hispanic	separated	PII	Patrol
1984	32	female	Black	single	PI	Patrol
1985*	53	male	Caucasian	married	Det II	Investigation
1986	28	male	Black	separated	PII	Patrol
1987	26	female	Hispanic	single	PII	Patrol

* alchohol involvement

1977, the national suicide rate has remained between 12.0 and 12.7 per 100,000 population (National Center for Health Statistics).

Overall, these comparative data reveal that the average suicide rate for officers in the Los Angeles Police Department remains lower than the average rates for adults at county, state, and national levels.

Because the suicide rates for the Los Angeles Police Department are based on only fourteen cases between 1970 and 1988, caution is advised in interpreting the data.

A review of the trend at LAPD for the total nineteen-year period covered in both studies shows an increase in the incidence of suicide from 8.1 in the 1976 study to 12.0 in the 1988 study. This suggests that stressors may have increased as is reflected in the area of marital discord and alcohol abuse. The high evidence of alcohol and marital problems among police services has been discussed elsewhere (Lester 1978; Stratton 1984).

Because of the small number of female suicides, it isn't possible to infer too much at this time. The growing number of females coming into field police work would suggest a larger representation in the suicide numbers on a probability basis. In addition it is likely that the particular problems encountered by female officers would significantly impact stress levels (Greene 1985). Donovan and Howard (1979) maintain that the stress on female and minority officers is usually more severe than on nonminority male officers.

Conclusion

The suicide rate of officers at the Los Angeles Police Department continues to remain lower than the rates for other adults in the county, state, and nation. This contrasts sharply with the numbers reported for the Chicago Police Department.

The trends toward an increasing officer suicide rate in the LAPD and the representation of minority female officer suicides in recent years suggest an increase in stressors and problems unique to the groups affected. This is worthy of further study.

Research on police suicide continues to remain sparse. Until more comprehensive research is done across geographical and department-size parameters, it isn't possible to speak in broad generalities about police suicides.

References

Bedian, A.G. 1982. Suicide and occupation: A review. *J. Voc. Behavior,* 21:206–222.

Burge, J.H. 1984. *Occupational stress in policing*. La Canada, CA: American Educators Publishing.

Dash, J., and Reiser, M. 1978. Suicide among police in urban law enforcement agencies. *J. Pol. Sci. & Adm.* 6 (1): 18–21.

Donovan, E., and Howard, G. 1979. Interview with Edward Donovan on stress. Audio cassette. Hagerstown, MD: Harper and Row.

Greene, R. 1985. *Psychological well-being, physcial health and coping responses in a police population*. Los Angeles: University of California.

Heiman, M.F. 1977. Suicide among police. *Am. J. Psychiatry* 134: 1286–1290.

Lester, D. 1978. Suicide in police officers. *Police Chief* (April): 17.

National Center for Health Statistics. Hagerstown, MD: Public Health Service, United States Department of Health and Human Services.

Stratton, J.G. 1984. *Police passages*. Manhattan Beach, CA: Glennon Publishing Co.

Suicide totals, 1970, 1980, 1985, 1986, 1987. Los Angeles: Department of Chief Medical Examiner-Coroner.

Vital Statistics of California, 1970, 1975, 1982, 1986. Sacramento: State of California.

Wagner, M., and Brzeczek, R.J. 1983. Alcoholism and suicide: A fatal connection. *FBI Law Enforcement Bulletin* (August): 8-15.

11

Preventing Police Suicide

Thomas E. Baker
Jane P. Baker

Does being a police officer increase the risk of suicide? During 1994, a record 11 New York City police officers committed suicide; only two officers were killed by criminals that year. Two homicides and 11 suicides — at that rate, police officers are killing themselves faster than they are being killed by criminals.[1]

The research on police suicide is limited. Most of the studies on police deaths have addressed police killings and assaults committed by criminals. The available studies on police suicide generally focus on the number of suicides, the methods employed, the impact of having service weapons readily available, and the occupational factors that seem to contribute to the high suicide rate among officers.[2]

One research study found that the suicide rate among police officers was three times higher than that of the general population.[3] In addition, an unpublished research report recently found that the police suicide rate now has doubled.[4]

Overcoming Obstacles to Intervention

Typically, when police officers experience serious, long-term emotional problems that can lead to suicide, two reactions occur that hinder the helping process. First, everyone — from the affected officers to friends and

---

1. W. Bratton, "We Don't Want to Lose You," *Spring 3100* 57 (1994), 12–13.

2. *See, for example*, J.M. Violanti, J.E. Vena, and J.R. Marshall, "Disease Risk and Mortality Among Police Officers: New Evidence and Contributing Factors," *Journal of Police Science and Administration*, 14 (1986), 17–23; and K.O. Hill and M. Clawson, "The Health Hazards of Street Level Bureaucracy: Mortality Among the Police," *Journal of Police Science and Administration* 16 (1988), 243–248.

3. Ibid., Hill and Clawson.

4. J.M. Violanti, "The Mystery Within: Understanding Police Suicide," *FBI Law Enforcement Bulletin* 2 (1995), 19–23.

co-workers to the department's hierarchy—initially denies that a problem exists. Second, even when a problem eventually is acknowledged, the affected officers often resist seeking help for fear of losing their jobs, being demoted, or having their personal problems exposed for public ridicule. These common systemic reactions must be overcome before any successful intervention can take place.

Many officers feel that referral to a mental health professional would mean the loss of their jobs. Police supervisors have a similar value system and, because of this belief, they often fail to take the appropriate action. As a group, police officers and supervisors often have protected those officers experiencing depression and denied the existence of any problems. However, such an obvious cover-up does a disservice to affected officers by denying them the help they need.

As noted, troubled officers usually resist seeking help. Officers fear that if help is sought, employment and economic security will be threatened. This myth can be dispelled through departmental policy and the approach supervisors use when dealing with potential suicides.

Education on depression and suicide should be implemented for all personnel. Officers who receive assistance might even develop into better officers. They should be informed that seeking help does not mean the end of a career, but the start of improving a new career. Asking for help signals strength, not weakness, and that must form the foundation of any prevention program.

A suicide prevention program can work only if members of the department feel free to take advantage of it. Police administrators and supervisors must play a nonpunitive role. They must communicate to officers four clear messages: 1) Seeking help will not result in job termination or punitive action; 2) all information will be respected and kept confidential; 3) other ways exist for dealing with a situation, no matter how hopeless it seems at the time; and 4) someone is available to help them deal with their problems. Police training and departmental policy, as well as the everyday examples set by police leaders, must communicate these four messages consistently.

Recognizing the Warning Signs

Identifying at-risk officers is the first step toward helping them. Is there any common pattern to be found in police suicidal behavior? In truth, any member of the department could become depressed and commit suicide under certain circumstances. However, a long trail of evidence typically leads to the final act. Many suicidal people have mixed feelings about dying and actually hope to be rescued. About 75 percent give some kind of notice of their intentions.[5] If recognized and taken seriously, these early warning signs make prevention and intervention possible.

Typically, multiple problems plague suicidal police officer, so supervisors should look for a cluster of warning signs. These might include a recent loss, sadness, frustration, disappointment, grief, alienation, depression, loneliness, physical pain, mental anguish, and mental illness.

The strongest behavioral warning is a suicide attempt. Generally, the more recent the attempt, the higher the risk factor for the officer. Police training officers need to incorporate education about suicide warning signs as a regular part of the department's mental health program.

When officers fail to perform at the optimal level for an extended period of time, the problem could be related to a major depressive episode. Clinicians agree that depression often plays a major role in suicide.[6] While anyone can have an occasional gloomy day, people dealing with depression suffer from a deeper, long-term malaise.

Depression is a mood disorder that can be characterized as a person's overall "climate" rather than a temporary "weather condition." Significant depressive episodes last for at least two weeks. During this time, a person might experience changes in appetite or weight; altered sleep patterns and reduced psychomotor activity; reduced energy levels; feelings of worthlessness or guilt; difficulty thinking, concentrating, and making decisions; and recurrent thoughts of death or suicide. Finally, this person might plan or attempt to commit suicide.[7] Behaviors such as exhibiting persistent anger, responding to events with angry outbursts, or blaming others over minor events should be considered indicators of possible distress.

Assessing the Problem

Supervisors or managers should schedule interviews with officers who appear depressed, sad, hopeless, discouraged or "down in the dumps." During this interview, the supervisor should check the officer's body language, look for sad facial expressions, and be alert to a flat mood. The officer might complain of feeling down, not having any feelings at all, or being anxious. Complaints about bodily aches and pains might be reported to cover the officer's true feelings.

---

5. E.A. Grollman, *Suicide: Prevention, Intervention, Post Intervention* (Boston: Beacon Press, 1988).

6. American Psychiatric Association, *DSM IV Diagnostic and Statistical Manual on Mental Disorders* 4th ed. (Washington, DC: Government Printing Office, 1994).

7. Ibid.

The twin feelings of hopelessness and helplessness indicate a high risk of suicide. Officers who think and speak in these terms feel that their lives are devoid of hope, or they see themselves as unable to meaningfully alter their situations. When they reach this point, they often take action. The finality of suicide might be seen as a technique to restore feelings of former strength, courage, and mastery over the environment.[8] Supervisors should listen carefully for expressions of these feelings.

Suicidal officers might have negative influences in their personal lives as well. Supervisors should look for histories that might include suicidal behavior, mental illness, chronic depression, multiple divorces, and alcoholism. Losses in an officer's life, drug abuse patterns, and stress overload also contribute to the problem. Older officers might experience physical problems or face impending retirement and feel that they will become socially isolated.[9] Such physical and social losses can generate the destructive feelings of hopelessness and helplessness.

Taking Action

Most people have mixed emotions about committing suicide, and suicidal feelings tend to be episodic, often coming and going in cycles. Troubled officers want to be rescued, but do not want to ask for assistance or know what specific help to request. This state of confusion actually works to a supervisor's advantage because suicidal officers want a strong authority figure to direct their emotional traffic and make sense of the confusion. Therefore, supervisors should quickly assure suicidal officers that support and assistance is available.

The situational leadership style that applies here is one of directing and telling. Officers in a suicidal state of mind are open to suggestion and are likely to respond to directions. Supervisors must use their positions of authority to tell officers what action they expect. Further, supervisors should demand that officers respond to their directions.

It is important for supervisors to ask specifically whether officers are having thoughts of hurting themselves. Many find it difficult to ask such a basic question, but it must be done. Officers who indicate that they are having suicidal thoughts must not be left alone. All threats must be taken seriously. Other people might not have heard their pleas for help.

---

8. P. Bonafacio, *The Psychological Effects of Police Work* (New York: Plenum Press, 1991).

9. J. Schwartz and C. Schwartz, *The Personal Problems of the Police Officer: A Plea for Action.* (Washington, DC: Government Printing Office, 1991), 130–141.

Supervisors should plan their intervention so that it leads to a professional referral. The specific methods of intervention must be thought out as carefully as possible in order to avoid violence directed inward or outward at other employees. Without careful planning, officers confronted by supervisors could react unpredictably. Because their thought processes are garbled, they could strike out at co-workers, supervisors, or family members, resulting in a homicide followed by suicide. Even if that does not occur, a real danger of suicide exists at the point of intervention.

Supervisors should refer officers to a certified mental health professional, even setting appointments and making arrangements for the officers to be there. The department's responsibility does not end there, however. Supervisors should monitor the situation to ensure that officers are evaluated and receive continued support and counseling.

Conclusion

The research clearly indicates that being a police officer increases the risk of suicide. Appropriate intervention can occur during a specific time frame, but within the police culture, denial often delays assistance.

Police officers throughout the ranks must stop pretending that the problem of police suicide does not exist or that it will go away. Someone must break the silence of denial and take action. With further research, innovative prevention programs, and proactive training, officers' lives can be saved.

Part Four

Stress and the Police Family

The negative effects of stress discussed in Parts Two and Three cannot focus solely on the individual officer and his or her life at work. Most officers are part of a family—with spouses, children, and parents—who experience the impact of police stress on the *personal* life of that officer and on their own lives. As one NYPD officer explained his reaction under stress:

> You change when you become a cop—you become tough and cynical. You have to condition yourself to be that way in order to survive this job. And sometimes without realizing it, you act that way all the time, even with your wife and kids. But it's something you have to do because if you start getting emotionally involved with what happens at work, you'll wind up in Bellevue [psychiatric hospital] (Maslach and Jackson, 59).

A recognition of vicarious victimization is critical to our understanding of the complexity and comprehensiveness of the issue of police stress. It is toward this understanding that the authors in Part Four turn their attention.

It is generally accepted that problems can result when law enforcement officers, who are taught to behave in certain controlling and authoritarian ways on the job, continue to interact with their families in the same manner when at home. Southworth holds that transferring professional dispositions to personal situations can and often does cause conflict, fear and resentment with an officer's spouse and children. His focus is on those certain specific behaviors—professionalism, detachment, and suspicion – which when, even unintentionally, exhibited at home by police officers cause significant interpersonal problems.

It is an unfortunate fact that, in some cases, law enforcement seems to have institutionalized marital and family turmoil into the profession. The worst manifestation of such turmoil is domestic violence. In his article, Lott outlines some of the early warning signs of the potential for domestic abuse by police officers, discusses how this behavior can be detected and controlled and calls for a change in the police culture to most effectively prevent violence in police families.

Historically, police families must manage many difficult stresses and are left to their own devices to provide the necessary resources to meet these stresses. Consequently, many police marriages end in failure. In dealing with stress in non-police families, McCubbin and Figley proposed the ABCX Model as a framework to explain how stress is produced and handled within a family system. Kannady applies this model to the police family, concluding that it is possible to develop stress resistant families that not only successfully adapt to the rigors of the police career but actually grow and thrive.

In an article prepared for the first national symposium on police psychological services, Means holds that the police family is not really different than that of a civilian family. Time pressures, finances, and relationships, regardless of the occupation, are always fraught with difficulty. Yet, the highly structured atmosphere "at the station" seems to suppress the need to deal with one's feelings and, unfortunately, it is difficult for an officer to readjust this attitude upon entering his/her home. He suggests that, for the therapist, strategic therapy has been a very useful way of developing long term changes in family behavior.

Borum and Philpot acknowledge that a great deal of attention has been given to the impact of stress on law enforcement and its individual officers. However, the literature has not equally addressed the effects of police work on an officer's interpersonal relationships. According to these authors, police work can impact an officer and his/her relationships through three sets of influences: those of the organization, those of peers and the socialization process, and the police role itself. They identify some common difficulties encountered by police couples and provide basic goals and strategies for addressing these issues in couples therapy.

References

Maslach, C., and Jackson, S.E. (1979). "Burned-out Cops and Their Families." *Psychology Today*, 12(12), 58-62.

12

Taking the Job Home

Richard N. Southworth

One day, while riding in the car, my 16-year-old daughter and I began to talk seriously about our relationship. I told Michelle that at times, it appeared as though she was angry with me and that nothing seemed to ease this rage. Almost instantly she responded with tremendous force, "I am! When I needed you, you weren't there for me. When I wanted to cuddle up on your lap and talk, you were unapproachable. Now you want to be part of my life, and I resent the hell out of it. You're damn right I'm angry!"

I spent 16 years with the Virginia State Police before leaving to pursue other interests. But I also left because I was burnt out. Something was very wrong in my life, and I knew it was somehow related to being a police officer.

No one can deny being a police officer is tough. There is tremendous stress associated with the profession. Most of us have experienced it, or at least have seen it in fellow officers. We know the strain it places on marriages and families, the divorces and family break- ups it causes. We also are intuitively aware that much of this discord is a result of a family member being a police officer.

My daughter also is clearly aware of the connection. During our conversation, she admitted that she knew when to keep her distance when I first came home from work, and how she could tell when I responded to a bad automobile wreck or had been involved in a high-speed chase. Recently, when I considered returning to law enforcement, she emphatically stated to a friend, "No, I don't want my daddy doing that again!"

When looking for causes of family turmoil, we often focus on the negative aspects of the job—the shift work, being on call, the constant exposure to pain and suffering. Compounding the situation are the frustrations caused by the court system or the department's administration that seems to offer rigid discipline and little support. All have negative effects on personal relationships.

The negative aspects, however, are only part of the problem. The positive aspects, when taken home, are just as destructive. The traits and dispositions that make exceptional police officers unfortunately can also make very poor spouses, parents, and friends. To the extent that these traits and dispositions are developed and supported through police training programs and peer support systems, we seem to have institutionalized marital and family turmoil in our profession.

Dispositions

To understand what I mean, it is first necessary to understand the patterned responses police officers develop to help themselves function in similar situations. These patterned responses are called "dispositions,"[1] which help us to respond quickly and without conscious thinking to similar events. Without dispositions, we would have to evaluate every event, decide on the best course of action, or think about how to perform each action.

But, dispositions are more than habits; they include thoughts, emotions, and actions. For example, as a trooper, when I observed a vehicle being operated in a reckless manner, I would think, "That guy's dangerous. He needs a ticket!" I might feel keyed up and even somewhat apprehensive and aggressive as I prepared to stop the vehicle. Then, I would check the traffic, place my vehicle in the proper position, and stop the suspect.

These thoughts, emotions, and actions make up a disposition—a patterned response to a repeated event. Training, peer modeling, and repeated similar experiences developed my disposition to traffic violators.

Disposition Transference

Occasionally, dispositions developed for a professional life transfer to personal situations in such a way that they are destructive. Quite simply, it happens when an officer "takes the job home."

When my daughter, who is learning to drive, makes a reckless maneuver, I think, "That's dangerous, she has to be corrected!" Feeling keyed up, apprehensive, and aggressive, I respond, "If you do that again, you won't drive for a month!" It is the same response I made to a traffic violator years ago as a trooper. The disposition is still active. It may have been appropriate as a trooper on patrol, but with my daughter, it is inappropriate and destructive to our relationship. Besides, such a response does not help her to learn how to drive.

Transferring professional dispositions is a serious problem for police officers, especially since most officers are unaware that it occurs. To make

---

1. Adrian Van Kaam, *Formative Spirituality—Human Formation*, vol. 2 (New York: Crossroad Publishing, 1985), chap. 1.

matters worse, police officers usually assume these dispositions are appropriate. We cannot understand why the rest of the world does not think, feel, and act in the same manner. When my wife tells me that I am being too hard on my daughter, I respond bluntly, "She's got to learn to drive right!" Then, we are likely to argue about the appropriate way to discipline children. Not teach, mind you, but discipline. And so, the cycle goes on.

Law Enforcement Dispositions

To Be Professional

In recent years, talk has centered on the professional police officer, one who is well-trained, well-equipped, and well-paid. But, how does professionalism translate into a disposition?

As a trooper, I dressed neatly, spoke politely, and carried out my duties with authority. This seemed to capture the professional image. My professional disposition kept me alive in many situations, and there is no doubt that my professional image helped to build the public's respect and cooperation. Besides, it makes us feel good about ourselves.

Yet, this same disposition can have a destructive effect on family relationships. For example, when I came home after being on patrol for 8 hours, I walked into the house still carrying myself erect with the hat pulled down over my eyes. My kids would run up to greet me, but would stop short of jumping into my arms. In fact, they kept their distance. This professional image is at least part of what my daughter referred to as "unapproachable." The professional dispositions, which worked in a law enforcement context, were inappropriate at home. I should not have been looking for the same type of respect in my family relationships that I sought in my job.

Another detrimental effect of this disposition is that my family knows the image is a facade. At home, I dress like a slob, am known to slump on the couch watching some dumb TV program, and can be heard cursing about some chore I do not want to do. In short, they have seen me when I was anything but professional. When I act out my professional image at home, they either respond to me as being pompous or refuse to take me seriously.

All of this sets into motion a destructive spiral. As my family pulls away, I accuse them of not caring. When I perceive that they do not respect me, I fight for that respect in other destructive ways, pulling myself away even farther from my family.

As a trooper, the professional disposition built respect and self-confidence. Occasionally, it even helped to keep me alive. However, in my relationship with my family, it built a wall between us, and at times, left me feeling alienated and alone.

To Take Control

A police officer is expected to be in control, no matter what situation. We act out this disposition—taking control—every time we respond to a radio call or observe a violation. Once we decide on a course of action, there is the badge, gun, and backup to enforce it. And, although our actions may be questioned later, in the heat of the moment we are in control. Taking control is at the heart of what it means to be a police officer.

But, what happens when we take this disposition home? In varying degrees, we become dominating spouses and authoritarian parents. Take, for example, the day my wife was trying to get our son to wash the dishes. They were locked in a battle of wills. After I walked into the kitchen, I evaluated the situation and immediately took control, I admonished my wife for being bossy, talked to my son about responsibility, and told everyone else to leave the room so that the job could get done.

In less than 5 minutes, I issued a warning, dispersed the participants in the dispute, and got the job done. I acted like a good trooper. The problem was that I still had to live with these people. I could not get into my patrol car and drive away. Predictably, my wife and I argued, my daughter defended her mother, my son sulked, and I justified my actions like a good trooper. Everyone was upset, all because I took control.

My actions were totally inappropriate in the context of the family relationship. I embarrassed my wife in front of the family and undermined her authority. In the end, I alienated myself from everyone. This was not a situation that called for me to take control. Probably, it did not require any response from me at all. If it called for a response, it should have been a supportive, caring response, not an authoritative one. The disposition to take charge was destructive when acted out in my family relationships.

To Remain Detached

Police officers encounter a substantial amount of pain and suffering, and each time, we must deal with it regardless of the situation. The training to handle whatever comes our way starts early. From the first day at the academy, we are told repeatedly never to become emotionally involved. This desensitization keeps us from being devastated by the human tragedy we encounter daily. Emotional uninvolvement is part of the job.

One day, while riding with another police officer as part of a training program, we responded to a suicide. We found two old women sobbing uncontrollably, while a young man screamed and beat the wall with his fists. His brother had hung himself in the next room. The officer's only response to all of this was to threaten to arrest the women and the brother if they did not kept quiet.

The training was clear. The only way to deal with this type of situation was to remain detached, and he expected the victim's relatives to respond in the same detached way.

It's not hard to see what happens when we take this disposition to remain detached home with us. When my wife's mother died, I wanted very much to comfort her, but all I felt was impatience with the whole matter. As hard as I tried, I could not empathize with her pain, and I knew she could feel my impatience and detachment.

To remain detached in emotionally charged situations serves us as police officers in emergencies. Without it we probably could not function. But when we take this disposition home, it is destructive. For me it was a major component of what Michelle was talking about when she told me that I was not there for her when she needed me as a child.

To Question Everything

Police officers are trained specifically to be suspicious of everything. In the legitimate interest of safety, we approach every vehicle and every person as a potential threat. We frequently sit with our backs to restaurant walls and often follow regulation by carrying a weapon everywhere we go.

An investigator questions the truthfulness of every statement made by criminals, witnesses, and victims. Even when preliminary information contains no indication of deception, investigators with well-developed investigative dispositions keep asking themselves what they missed. Even as I write this article, I recognize that I am predisposed to ferret out the negative aspects of my police experience rather than the positive ones that were obviously present.

There are good and valid reasons for questioning everything. Quite honestly, it keeps police officers alive and solves cases.

Questioning everything permeates police training. Once I helped to teach a class on vehicle stops. For several days, we put the group through every conceivable situation in which they could get hurt or deceived. During the simulations, the trainees were lied to, argued with, threatened, and shot. Not one situation involved an honest person who engendered trust. Indeed, such focus on the risks involved in routine traffic stops serves to keep officers alive.

However, when applied to family situations, questioning everything quite simply makes spouses and children suspects in every family encounter. When I discovered that my hairbrush was not on the dresser where I always keep it, I caught myself going from family member to family member, basically conducting a criminal investigation. I questioned each person critically, and when no one confessed, I went back and questioned them again. The second time around the questions were even more pointed. They sounded frightfully like interrogations, complete with accusation and trick questions designed to trip them up. When my daughter got angry, ran up the stairs, and slammed her door, I simply responded, "I was just trying to find my damn brush!"

It was not wrong to ask family members what happened to my brush. The problem was in the approach and the underlying attitude of distrust. When they denied knowing where the brush was, I did not believe them. I accused them of lying to me. I responded like a trooper, not like a husband and father.

The important point to be made here is that this was not a thought-out response. I did not want to act this way. It was a patterned response that was triggered by the situation. Given the same type of situation at work, the response would have been appropriate. With my family, it served to create conflict and distance between us.

This disposition has been the most destructive in the way I handle situations involving my teenage daughters. Like most parents, one of my greatest fears is that my kids will become involved with drugs. But, there are good reasons why I trust my kids when it comes to drugs. Yet, let one of them come home late, looking even a little tired, and the disposition to question is triggered. Recently, when Michelle came home really tired and stressed out, I knew there were good reasons for her appearance. But, I immediately started looking into her eyes and asking questions that could only indicate that I thought she might have been using drugs. I really didn't think so, but I still asked the questions.

Michelle's usual response to such questioning is accompanied by anger. This time it was different. She simply looked at me and said, "You really believe I've been using drugs, don't you." The pain in her eyes overshadowed the tiredness. Of course, I denied it and tried to explain. But, the damage was done. After discussing the matter, I think she understood. But, the subconscious effects of that encounter on our relationship, and others like it, will never be fully known to either of us.

Conclusion

Transferring professional dispositions to one's personal life can have a destructive effect. With a little reflection, every law enforcement officer can find instances of this occurring either in family relationships or in other personal situations.

This transference also poses a very serious problem, one that is not recognized or dealt with in police training programs. In fact, it is often denied outright, while we argue that the rest of the world is out of step. However, professional dispositions cut at the heart of what it means to be distinctively human.

The facade of professionalism keeps family numbers and friends at a distance. Recognizing this, where do we go from here? While talking to a friend, I stated candidly, "Maybe what makes a good police officer doesn't make a good human being!" I hope this is not true, and I sincerely do not believe that it is. But, some aspects of the profession change us and cause us serious problems for the rest of our lives. If we as police officers are to live full and rewarding lives, and especially if we are to maintain meaningful relationships with our spouses, families, and friends, we must face these and other problems of our profession.

We need to work hard to deactivate those destructive dispositions when we leave the job. We must allow ourselves to become vulnerable, to show respect and concern. Most importantly, we have to find a way to trust our loved ones.

The problem is not inherent in the profession; it is not caused totally by society or the system. Yet, neither the profession nor society will find the solution apart from us. In the end, we are the only ones with the necessary motivation or insight to find a better way.

13

Deadly Secrets: Violence in the Police Family

Lonald D. Lott

Early morning telephone calls rarely signal good news: this one was no exception. A fellow officer reluctantly disclosed that one of our officers had beaten his girlfriend badly the previous night. Although I sensed the hesitation in his voice as he briefed me on the incident, we both knew we could no longer avoid the inevitable: We would have to arrest the officer.

Arresting one of your own officers is a difficult task, especially when that officer is a friend. And, although I was saddened by the news, I was not surprised. After all, most everyone in the department knew the officer was having domestic problems. But as I discovered a few days later, the officer's friends also knew that his domestic disputes had turned violent.

The Family Enigma

Through 20 years of police work, three separate law enforcement agencies, and my own failed marriage, I have come to know intimately the innumerable family problems police officers experience. In many ways, police families resemble other families. However, in addition to dealing with the same daily frustrations that confront all families, they must cope with all of the exceptional pressures that accompany police work. This extraordinary stress makes police officers more prone than average citizens to alcoholism, domestic violence, divorce, and suicide.[1]

Clashing Traits

The very nature of police work teaches officers to control their emotions. They discipline their minds to remain focused in dynamic situa-

---

1. D. Jackson, "Police Brutality Often Begins at Home," *Chicago Tribune.* March 29, 1991.

tions, no matter how bizarre or terrifying. Above all, they must prevail in the face of adversity.

Officers learn to interrogate when suspicious, to intimidate or match aggression when challenged, and to dominate when threatened. Granted, these actions are necessary for survival and control. However, when combined with the unfavorable conditions of police work—undesirable shifts, rotating work schedules, days off spent in court, exposure to pain and suffering and violent confrontations—even exceptional police officers can become very poor spouses, parents, and friends.[2]

Law Enforcement's Response

Sadly, though numerous case studies document the susceptibility of police families to domestic problems, police officers rarely receive advice on avoiding such pitfalls. For the most part, senior officers only admonish rookies to "leave the job at work."

If art intimates life, then the media's portrayal of many police officers as grumpy, quarrelsome, divorced alcoholics is right on target. Indeed, law enforcement seems to have institutionalized marital and family turmoil into the profession.[3]

Do Unto Others

Traditionally, the police have chosen not to get involved in domestic disturbances in the general population. Unless a family fight turned violent and resulted in severe injuries, the police viewed it as a civil problem inappropriate for police attention. Often, the reluctance of law enforcement to get involved led to temporary, nonlegal remedies, designed to ease the tension between the victim and the abuser.

Responding officers might make one party leave the house for a cool-down period. Or, they might convince one partner to apologize and promise not to repeat the behavior. As a general rule, though, officers did not take anyone into custody.

Gradually, however, lawsuits and political activism brought about a change in law enforcement's attitude toward domestic violence. Research indicated that arresting batterers reduced the likelihood of repeat violence, compared with police mediation or similar counseling-oriented in-

2. R.N. Southworth. "Taking the Job Home." *FBI Law Enforcement Bulletin*, November 1990. 20.

3. Ibid.

tervention techniques.[4] In the face of this emerging empirical evidence, laws dealing with family violence took an extreme turnabout.[5]

Most States enacted legislation mandating police action in cases of suspected family violence. Unfortunately, although officers increasingly become involved in private citizens' family disturbances, they were less diligent in policing their own.

Need for Specific Policy

While most law enforcement administrators claim to comply with domestic violence statutes when dealing with their own officers, they also admit to slippage.[6] Many agencies have no specific policy concerning the issue.

The absence of clear policy does not mean that police managers ignore domestic violence involving their officers. In fact, most agencies conduct both criminal and internal affairs investigations. To reduce possible allegations of a coverup, some agencies request outside assistance for such investigations. Still others require direct supervisory attention any time a law enforcement officer is implicated in a family disturbance.

The problem, then, is one of timing. Police departments properly handle domestic disputes when they become aware of them. Oftentimes, however, cases remain unreported, even though other officers may have direct knowledge of the incidents. Clearly, police administrators should focus on these cases, from both the standpoint of the officer committing the violence and those officers who know the facts but choose to remain silent.

Keeping It a Secret

A unique culture exists in law enforcement. The dangerous nature of the job, combined with the authority to use force, creates close bonds among officers.[7] They depend on one another for safety and support. As a result, they develop a code of silence that excludes outsiders. Unfortunately, hon-

---

4. J.L. Edelson, "Interventions with Men Who Batter." *Family Violence: Research and Public Policy Issues*, ed. D.J. Besharov (Washington, DC: The AEI Press, 1990), 137.

5. Ibid., *See also* J. Fagan, "Criminal Justice Policy on Wife Assault," *Family Violence: Research and Public Policy Issues*, ed. D.J. Besharov (Washington, DC: AEI Press, 1990), 54.

6. Informal survey conducted by the author at the FBI National Academy, Quantico, Virginia, April–June 1994.

7. J. Skolnick and J. Fyfe, *Above the Law* (New York: Free Press, 1993), 92.

oring the code or choosing to mediate their peers' crises themselves only exacerbates the problem.

Further, little research exists in the area of police family violence, even though information does exist on police officers and alcohol abuse, divorce, and suicide. Certainly, all of these indicate serious domestic problems.

The lack of pertinent information on violence in police families merely illustrates officers' reluctance to speak up when confronted with a peer's personal problems. As do members of most groups, law enforcement officers understand that they take a risk when they report another officer's misconduct. Short of actually killing someone, officers may exercise one of three options in enforcing the code: Shunning violators, revealing their inadequacies, or withholding assistance in emergencies. Often, however, whistleblowers' *fear* of reprisal serves as sufficient punishment. Overall, the evidence does not support most officers' feeling that they literally risk their lives when they turn in their peers.[8]

Breaking the Code

In a recent study, law enforcement officers attending a training and law enforcement inservice reported the prevalence of violence in their marital relationships. Approximately 40 percent of the officers surveyed reported at least one episode of physical aggression during a conflict with their spouse or companion in the previous year.[9] These results even may be conservative, given the tendency for individuals to underreport incidents considered socially undesirable.

Although patrol officers reported somewhat higher rates of aggression, the effects of rank were statistically insignificant. In short, police officers of all ranks may be susceptible to the risk of marital violence. Furthermore, officers who reported working excessively long hours and

---

8. Ibid. 110–112.

9. P. Neidig, H. Russell, and A. Seng, "Interspousal Aggression in Law Enforcement Families: A Preliminary Investigation," *Police Studies*, spring 1992, 30–38. In this study, volunteers completed a survey at an inservice training and law enforcement conference in a southwestern State. Respondents included 385 male officers, 40 female officers, and 115 female spouses. The researchers defined a violent episodes as "minor" incidents, such as pushing or slapping the spouse or throwing objects, and "severe" violence, such as choking or beating the spouse or brandishing or using a weapon. Respondents reported the frequency of each incident on a scale that ranged from "never" to "more than 20 times a year."

failing to take leave had higher rates of marital aggression, suggesting that increased job dedication may result in increased marital violence.[10]

Previous attempts by police to mediate family violence or to practice crisis intervention in their own families have proven unsuccessful. This means that police officers can no longer remain silent when they believe one of their own is in trouble; they must turn to others for help.

The Administrator's Role

In the case of the officer in my own department who had beaten his girlfriend, I questioned whether we, as an organization, had faltered in assisting the officer. Several resources were available for him: A chaplain, a police psychologist, an employee assistance program, and a peer counseling program. Still, early intervention did not occur. The officer's supervisor had spoken to him and directed him to seek professional counseling, but not until he nearly had reached his breaking point.

Yet, even when police supervisors suspect officers of abuse and intervene, officers often minimize the extent of their problem and resist recommendations for treatment. Indeed, voluntary treatment programs in anger control, stress management, or conflict containment techniques usually have poor attendance records. However, because the violence tends to repeat and escalate in severity over time in a substantial number of domestic abuse cases, managers should initiate mandatory treatment programs as soon as possible after they become aware of an episode of physical aggression, even if that occurs after the officer commits a criminal act.[11]

Early Detection

Early detection can prevent aggressive behavior in police families from escalating to criminal acts. Batterers can and do exhibit warning signs that may spill over into the workplace. Some symptoms of potential abuse include:

- Jealousy
- Controlling behavior

---

10. Ibid.

11. P. Neidig, H. Russell, and A. Seng, "Observations and Recommendations Concerning the Prevention and Treatment of Interspousal Aggression in Law Enforcement Families." unpublished paper. June 1994.

- Quick, romantic involvement
- Unrealistic expectations
- Isolation
- Blaming others for their feelings and/or problems
- Hypersensitivity
- Cruelty to animals or children
- Jekyll and Hyde personality
- History of battering
- Threats of violence
- Breaking or striking objects
- Use of force during an argument.[12]

Individuals who physically or emotionally abuse their domestic partners may exhibit some of these behaviors. Three or more indicate a strong potential for physical violence. The last four behaviors almost always are seen only in batterers.

Police managers, supervisors, and coworkers should watch and listen for these indicators. Although they might not be readily observable at work, a spouse, a friend, or a neighbor may have seen or heard inappropriate behavior.

A Change in Culture

Even if managers initiate prevention and treatment programs, they may remain ineffectual if not supported by the general law enforcement populace. Peer pressure often compels group members to follow standards of conduct, especially in law enforcement.[13] Accordingly, before any meaningful intervention program can curb violence in police families, members of the law enforcement profession first must acknowledge the existence of the problem. Then, they must work together to assist coworkers through intervention. In short, they must not keep it a secret.

Police managers must establish, maintain, and enforce policies that define acceptable employee conduct and performance. Further, they must educate all employees about the nature of police violence, emphasizing detection and encouraging intervention. Finally, through their words and actions, law enforcement leaders must set an example for their employees to follow.

First-line supervisors represent just that—the first line of defense against an escalation of violence in the police family. Beyond coworkers,

---

12. Adapted from the Project for Victims of Family Violence, Inc. Fayetteville, Arkansas, by the Haven Women's Center of Stanislaus County, California.

13. Supra note 7, 110.

first-line supervisors have the most direct contact with employees and are responsible for monitoring their work performance and adherence to policy and procedure. Therefore, law enforcement supervisors must look for indicators of employee domestic violence and be prepared to guide employees toward an appropriate intervention program.

Violence in police families affects all ranks of law enforcement, both directly and indirectly. Thus, all members of an organization, not just administrators and supervisors, must pay close attention to the signs of domestic problems in all of their coworkers—in recruits, experienced officers, patrol officers, and chiefs alike. Furthermore, all members of the force should take appropriate action at the first indication of improper domestic behavior.

Conclusion

When law enforcement employees become involved in domestic violence, their agencies suffer the consequences, including decreased morale, inefficiency, and poor judgement among its personnel. Further, due to a perceived lack of credibility or their own biases, officers may suffer from diminished capacity to enforce domestic violence statutes in the community. Finally, agencies face increased risk of adverse publicity.[14]

The cost of failing to intervene in police family violence situations goes far beyond monetary losses. What is the value of a career or a family or the damage of emotional scars left by unchecked family violence?

The costs are too great to allow the enigma of violence in police families to continue. Administrators must create and maintain an organizational climate that supports and assists affected employees. Finally, all employees must recognize the seriousness of the problem. It cannot be kept secret any longer.

---

14. Supra note 9, 37.

14

Developing Stress-Resistant Police Families

Grace Kannady

John and Lisa have been married two years and John has been a police officer for the past six months. Lisa has found that the daily routine the family had established has been replaced with disorder because of shift hours, over-time and on-call status. Further, she has been forced into the role of primary parent for their nine-month-old daughter. John is experiencing a great deal of pressure at work completing his rookie year and meeting the expectations of his peers and supervisors. He feels out of step with the daily rhythms of family life and emotionally isolated due to the intensity and negativity of his work environment. John and Lisa have begun to feel some strains in their marriage and a lessening of the intimacy they enjoyed a year ago. A number of events have occurred in a short period of time and they are beginning to experience some negative feelings within their marriage that were not there before.

Both John and Lisa are struggling with stress—a common situation among police families. How they cope with the stress, however, will determine the quality of their marriage and perhaps even whether or not the marriage will survive. If they use effective coping strategies, they may not only meet their stressors successfully but strengthen their marriage, as well; if not, the stressors may escalate to a point at which a marital crisis will erupt. In other words, John and Lisa's response depends on how stress-resistant their marriage is as they face their current situation. The purpose of this article is twofold: to present a model that supports the idea of a stress-resistant police family and to suggest ways to create such families.

ABCX Model

A framework that helps explain how stress is produced and handled within a family system is the ABCX model proposed by McCubbin and Figley.[1] Stress is commonly defined as a mismatch between perceived envi-

---

1. H.I. McCubbin and C.R. Figley, eds. , *Stress and the Family, Volume 1: Coping with*

ronmental demands and the resources perceived to be available to meet these demands. Using this definition, McCubbin and Figley describe three components that work together to produce the possibility of a crisis within a family. Their model is as follows:

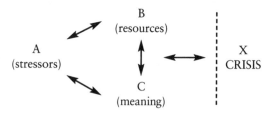

In this diagram, factor A refers to the stressor itself—the life event that creates the strain within the family unit. These events may be normative (expected changes within the family, such as the birth of a child) or non-normative (outside influences, such as the impact of a career on the family unit). Factor B refers to the resources the family can use to meet the stressors. Factor C refers to the definition or meaning the family gives to the seriousness of the stressor. If the family is able to consider the stress as a challenge rather than a threat and has adequate resources with which to meet it, the stress is met and reduced. However, if stressors occur, are defined negatively and reacted to with inadequate resources, then factor X—a crisis—is likely to occur.

The healthy family system, then, operates to keep stress within the ABC interrelationship and keep stressors from building up to a crisis point.

Stressors

The first component of this model, factor A, consists of the stressors and hardships affecting the family unit because of the choice of a police career by one or both of the spouses. There are five major ways in which the structure and organization of work can affect family life: absorption, time, rewards, world views, and emotional climate.[2] A highly absorptive occupation—such as policing—encourages close identification of an employee with his occupation, demands participation from the employee's family members and structures expectations for the behavior of both the employee and his family.

This intrusion and domination of the police role in family life can be seen in many different ways, including long hours on the job, preoccupa-

Normative Transistions (New York: Brunner/Mazel, Inc., 1983).

2. R.M. Kantor, *Work and Family in the United States: A Critical Review and Agenda for Research and Policy* (New York: Russell Sage Foundation, 1977).

tion with job-related matters even when off duty and disruption of family plans in the face of departmental demands.

Police officers tend to limit socialization to other police personnel so family socialization patterns may become narrowed. Spouses may have to make many adjustments or sacrifices in their own employment or daily activities to accommodate the needs of the police officer. Lastly, police families may indirectly be influenced to sustain a particular image within the community. For example, teenage children of police officers may feel restraints on their behavior that their peers may not feel. Thus police departments can be said to be "greedy" toward the police officer's work participation and commitment and this takes its toll on family life.

Occupational requirements in terms of time are also a critical factor in the organization of family life. Time together becomes a scarce commodity in police families because of the sheer number of hours the officer spends on the job. Also at issue are both the amount of time available for family life and the timing of daily events within the family schedule. Police families are usually "out of sync" in that daily schedules of eating, sleeping, and leisure activities among its members do not occur at the same time. Afternoon shift work generally disrupts the time police officers and their school-aged children could spend together, and night shift work generally disrupts husband-and-wife relationships.

Occupations traditionally provide money and prestige as the primary rewards of work. Unfortunately, police work falls short in both of these areas. Maynard and Maynard report:

> In many other high-demand occupations, such as law and medicine, the
> financial security and status often allow the wives to overcome many of
> their objections to the long hours and the child care with little assistance.
> Yet in this (police) occupation, there is no such support.[3]

Thus, many officers may invest in a second job, which increases income but further decreases time at home. Often, spouses do not have the option of choosing to work but must work to contribute to the family's financial resources. Promotions can be a source of reward and status to both the officer and his family. However, in the hierarchical organizational structure of most police departments, promotions are scarce and the process highly competitive. In addition, the hazardous nature of police work detracts from its appeal to the family. Worry over possible injury in accidents, bad weather, pursuits and encounters with violent individuals may contribute to family anxiety. The police career, then, does not offer many of the traditional rewards that might be found in other occupations.

---

3. P.E. Maynard and N.E. Maynard, "Stress in Police Families: Some Policy Implications," *Journal of Police Science and Administration*, 1982, 10 (3): 310.

Any occupation will sponsor not only a particular culture but also a particular outlook on the world. This "world view" not only develops within the employee but is also brought home, where it influences the family's perception of reality. The illusion of absolute safety is quickly abandoned in police families as officers bring their stories of unpredictable tragedies home every day. Further, the perceptions of the world as threatening and people as untrustworthy quickly penetrate the world view of the police officer and are assimilated within the world views of his family members. The officer and his spouse may react to the perceptions of the world as a dangerous place by becoming overprotective of each other and their children.

The view of the criminal justice system as unfair and impotent is another perception that is created as police officers are confronted with the outcomes of their cases and bring their frustrations and anger home. Because of the unique duties and demands placed on police officers, a world view is created that is different from an "average" community member's world view, thus creating a dichotomy between police officers and citizens. Families also come to share in this dichotomized world view of "them" and "us." This perception may lead to a sense of isolation within a hostile world.

An employee's work within an organization includes not only task assignments but also an emotional climate that may affect his personality and attitudes and, in turn, his family life. Kantor notes, "It is not uncommon for people in high interaction occupations to develop 'interaction fatigue' and withdraw from contact at home."[4] Thus police officers may appear distant and uncommunicative with their spouses and children. They may desire their homes to be havens of order and restfulness following the chaos of work; however, the needs and demands of family members may frustrate such unrealistic expectations.

Another personality characteristic found among many police officers is "emotional hardening" — a protective maneuver that may be successful at work but disastrous in terms of maintaining the intimacy necessary within a family system. Police also develop work and organizational cynicism and this may generalize into other settings and relationships. These personality and attitudinal changes may be positive for the role of police officer but negative for the role of parent and spouse.

In summary, the high absorption of police work, the demands on personal time and the hardship associated with the timing of family activities, the scarce rewards, the negative world view and the personality and attitudinal changes undergone by the police officer all interact to produce a great deal of stress upon the family.

---

4. Kantor, p. 50.

Resources

The next factor in the ABCX model is B—the family's resources for meeting the demands of the stressors. These include the developmental stages of marriage and career, the use of suitable coping strategies and the availability of individual family member assets. The family, of course, is not static but evolves through different transitions, crisis points and stable periods. Careers also display such evolution. Frequently, stress in a family is escalated because of the simultaneous timing of transitions in the family and career.

For example, many police families begin a police career and start a family within the same time frame. Violanti, describing the first five years of the police stress as the "alarm stage," reports that stress is high at this time as reality shock is encountered and officers struggle inwardly with the question of whether they can handle the difficult requirements of police work.[5] At the same time, the marital relationship is experiencing a drop in its quality due to the demands of giving birth and raising small children.

This clashing of developmental cycles between work and home can easily deplete family resources. Police couples need to be aware of these conflicting pressures and the strain they put on existing resources when a family and a career are begun at the same time.

The coping strategies chosen for use in meeting the stressors of a police family can either increase or reduce the strain on the family. Unhealthy strategies include such traditional reactions as avoidance, denial, blame, withholding, threat of leaving and depression. Healthy strategies include negotiation with a problem-solving orientation, handling conflict at the issue level and appropriate self-disclosure of one's views and feelings.

Personal assets available for coping with stress include financial resources (e.g., the individual's economic well-being), educational resources (such as cognitive ability and problem-solving skills), health resources (the individual's physical well-being) and psychological resources (the individual's sense of self-esteem).[6]

Thus, these three sets of variables—the family's developmental status, its repertoire of healthy coping strategies and the availability of individual

---

5. J. Violanti, "Stress Pattens in Police Work: Longitudinal Study," *Jouranl of Police Science and Administration*, 1983, 11(2): 211–216.

6. H. McCubbin, C. Joy, A.E. Cauble, J. Comeau, J. Patterson and R. Needle, "Family Stress and Coping: A Decade Review," in F.M. Berardo, ed., "Decade Review: Family Research in 1970–1979," *Journal of Marriage and the Family*, 1980, 42(4).

resources—all combine to produce a force field against incoming stressors.

Meaning

The C factor refers to the subjective definition the family gives to the stressful events. The underlying belief is that the event itself does not necessarily cause the stress so much as the interpretation given to the event. Although it is commonly believed that stress is directly transferred from the event into a stressful emotional reaction, this direct causation theory is now being challenged and replaced with the concept that the intervening internal process of evaluation actually determines the emotional reaction.

This internal evaluation process can be reality-centered or composed of irrational beliefs that distort reality. Thus, the subjective interpretation of events can lead to either a clear perception of reality and appropriate emotional reactions or a distorted view of reality and inappropriate emotional reactions. In a police marriage, such irrational ideas as "romantic love lasts throughout a marriage," "spouses should do everything together" and "marriage is a 50-50 partnership" contribute to unnecessary emotional conflict.[7] A shift from blaming the event itself for feelings of stress to examining personal interpretations of the event leads to a more controlled reaction to situations.

Health psychology has now captured these ideas and termed this process "psychological hardiness." Psychological hardiness has the following six components: the appraisal of potential stressors in such a way that they are not labeled as threatening and little autonomic nervous system reaction occurs; the presence of found meaning in one's life; the sense of commitment to work, family, and self; the belief in the individual's ability to influence and control some aspects of life; the acceptance of change as normal and positive; and the ability to perceive of day-to-day living as fitting into a larger pattern of life.[8] Psychological hardiness implies, more than anything else, a fundamental attitude change, in which the subjective meaning of an event is more important than the event itself.

The idea of individual psychological hardiness is also being translated into the concept of "family hardiness," under which the family can redefine the stressors so that issues are clarified, problem solving can occur and emotional reactions are diminished. Generally, if the family can perceive the imbalance between resources and demands as a opportunity for

7. A.A. Lazarus, *Marital Myths* (California: Impact Publishers, 1985).

8. J. Borysenko, *Minding the Body, Mending the Mind* (New York: Bantam Books, 1987).

growth for the family system instead of an immediate and fearful threat, adaptation to stress is facilitated.

In the ABCX model, if the family has sufficient resources and interprets the stressors positively, the stressors will be met in a growth-producing manner. On the other hand, if the family's resources are running low and negative appraisal occurs, the stressors will accumulate and produce a crisis. To prevent such a crisis, families need to know and understand the variety and intensity of stressors affecting the family system, build appropriate and effective coping strategies and resources and define reality without distortions and unrealistic expectations. A stress-resistant police family can avoid crisis by confronting incoming stressors with a well-fortified reserve of resources and realism.

Implications

According to the ABCX model, police families must manage many difficult stressors with their accompanying hardships. At the present time, most police families are left to their own devices to provide the necessary resources and appraisals to meet these stressors. As stressors build up, resources become scarcer, appraisal more negative and crisis more likely. The high level of divorce among police officers and the high level of dissatisfaction felt within police marriages suggest that many families are unable to adapt to the excessive demands of the police career.

Several police departments have actively addressed this issue, designing and implementing training in this area. Some departments have conducted spousal training concurrent with police recruit training.[9] Other departments have conducted marriage seminars and workshops that validate the impact of the police career on the family and offer resources for continued support. These types of interventions are even more effective if they present training to the police couple, rather than just the police spouse, and if they include skill building in the areas of coping strategies.

Policymakers within the police department need to acknowledge that the police career is a family change agent. Such acknowledgement, along with a provision for training in resource building and positive appraisal, is a firm step toward aligning the family *with* the police department instead of against it.

---

9. J.G. Stratton, B. Tracy-Stratton and G. Alldredge, "The Effects of a Spouses' Training Program: A Longitudinal Study," *Journal of Police Science and Administration*, 1982, 10(3): 297–301; and P.C. Ricks and J.D. Munger, "The Forgotten Recruit: Training the Police Spouse," *Police Chief*, November 1988, pp. 20–22.

Conclusion

Police officers do not exits in a vacuum. What occurs at work spills over at home and what occurs at home is likely to affect performance on the job. With the high absorption of the police occupation and the many demands placed on the police family, police departments, their officers and spouses must address more attention toward the health of the police family. According to the ABCX model, it is possible to develop stress-resistant families that not only successfully adapt to the rigors of the police career but actually grow and thrive.

John and Lisa's marriage is at a crossroads. Stress is affecting their family system not only as a result of the stressors inherent in the demands of police work but also because of the normative changes within their own marriage. How they will meet these stressors will depend a great deal on how they interpret their situation and what individual resources they can muster and utilize. Hopefully, they will be able to find the support and knowledge they need to preserve their marriage. A happy marriage and a good family life are the essential contrasts that provided balance to a police officer's life.

15

Family Therapy Issues in Law Enforcement Families

Mark S. Means

What I am about to present to you may seem negative, but believe me, that is not my intent. I just want to share some observations I have made in my practice as a marriage and family therapist that might have some meaning to you.

In Alabama last year there were over 35,000 divorces. 35,000! When you consider that every marriage tends to have at least two people involved, that means there are 70,000 people involved in the divorce court each and every year in Alabama. But let's go on, there are at least two children per marriage which means a total of 140,000 people directly involved in broken homes, not to mention the countless grieving grandparents and other relatives lying alongside the road of "broken relationships." Unfortunately, many of these families come from the local police force.

These are alarming facts to the marriage and family therapist, but the most frightening issue is the inability of the local police force to recognize some very important and basic facts about the police family.

I'm sure at this point I may seem negative, but families are being chewed up and spat out by a society that says, "actualize self, do your own thing, look out for number one," when this therapist feels that they really are wanting something that will help them make some sense out of a "no-sense" world.

As I see it there are five basic reasons (although there are many more) that families are suffering the deathblows of, if not a broken home, at least a chaotic one. For each authentic need I describe there is also a counterfeit that has been produced by our society...look, if you would, at some issues that this writer has observed in practice.

Authentic	Counterfeit
Sharing/Listening	Talking/Hearing
Quality/Quantity Time	Quality Time
Unconditional Love	Conditional Love
Self-Esteem	Self-Actualization
Servanthood	Self-Centeredness

1. At surface level when we think of communication, we think of someone talking in an audible fashion and someone to hear those sounds. True communications come from sharing something that you think has value to someone who not only hears your audible sounds, but interprets the meaning of them. They even help you say what it is you are trying to communicate. It has been discovered that only 10% of communication is done through verbal communication. Imagine!

That means there are about 90% more effective and maybe unconscious ways we communicate, such as body language, the tone, voice inflexions, facial expressions and attitude. I have observed through testing police officers with the MCMI (Millon Clinical Multiaxial Inventory) that come to me for marriage and family therapy that they have high scores in Compulsiveness, Narcissism and Avoidance scales. One thing we do know in family therapy: that the perfectionistic, workaholic, obsessive-compulsive individual often becomes that way in an attempt to hide or avoid dealing with inner feelings. As long as "I am busy and doing something out there, I don't have to deal with the emotional struggles that go on in and around me." The workaholic often says I stay at work and get lost there because to come home and deal with family issues and my mate's need for intimacy is very difficult," it becomes an anesthetizing affect. Many "police kids" often say, "Dad never listens, he only hears what he wants to hear." So then, listening is an active time-consuming event, rather than a passive, unconnected method of communicating. Many of the officers I have seen tell me of a father that didn't really "listen to me," a father that was afraid to hook-up to those inner feelings "I might have had." Dr. Lloyd Ogilvie states, "All of us want someone to know us, really knows and not go away." Dr. E. Stanley Jones tells us that "humans have a great need to conceal, but an even greater need to reveal." It seems we all really need someone to listen to us and know who we are inside. For the therapist, it is immensely important job to help the family provide a "safe" place where a risk can be taken for you to know me.

2. In Birmingham, therapists often meet together to discuss cases, and as we shared one day, we began to notice a basic pattern about time spent together in police families. There seemed to a justification of how time was spent with the family. Comments like, "I know I can't spend quantity time with Johnny, but I give him quality time! While I understand that there are unbelievable financial and time pressures on the police officer, and that their work schedule is demanding at times, there is still a price to pay for this concept, maybe too high a price. James Dobson in his book, "Preparing for Adolescence" gives an illustration of a man going to the finest steak-house in the city and ordering the most succulent, juicy, grain-fed, medium-rare steak in the house. After waiting 30 minutes the waitress finally brings the dinner. As the diner lifts up the cover to his entré, to his surprise he finds a one-inch square of meat. A point to be made is that

while quality is very important, so also is quantity. For an inter-personal relationship to be healthy and family dynamics to be open and nurturing, there must be quantity and quality time spent with each member. How many times do we hear kids in our office tell of how their parents have tried to compensate by giving their children things, money and permissiveness hoping to compensate for not being able to have the time to be "with" them.

3. How many of us have felt loved only if we did things a certain way? If we were thinner–heavier, taller–shorter, more hair–less hair, bigger breasts–smaller breasts, give good sex–less sex, good grades–bad grades, made lots of money-made less money, then we could be loved. If we could only change and meet the condition that others put on us we could finally be truly loved. Of course, this is called "conditional love." "Conditional love" says, "I'll love you if…when…because," and just maybe then you'll have my love. How tragic! "Unconditional love" says "I love you, period." "You don't have to be anything or do something or look a certain way." It seems to me that as families come to me, especially police families, there is an unconscious value that when you meet certain standards "you can be accepted by me, because I have had to meet those standards in the force and it's good enough for you." It seems that this quality of love is definitely taught inter-generationally. It was modeled by their parents and their parents parents; and so a dysfunctional attitude becomes pervasive not out of malice or unloving attitudes, but because no one ever taught them how to love that way.

For the therapist there is a task of "teaching the family how to love the person "unconditionally." By teaching the family that while loving people is unconditional, acceptance of behavior is conditional. Often "the baby gets thrown out with the bath water." Showing by modeling for the family how to not destroy the person while not accepting a behavior that is unacceptable. Dr. William Glasser states that "while neurologists may not find it, the desire for unconditional love is built into the nervous system."

4. We have been socialized to believe that if "I have something, if I wear Jordache Jeans, if I drive a Porsche, if I own a place in Florida, if I make so much money, if I have jewelry, somehow that will make me worth more to people. In some way that makes me of more value to others. That it will give me self-esteem — self-value — self-worth.

Again the socialization process has hurt families in that it tells them if you actualize yourself you will in some way discover who you are. You will be accepted because you have this success. But in fact, it seems to this therapist that the converse is true.

Self-esteem comes not from what you can get, but from what you can give. It comes from saying "Do I have value to someone," "Am I needed in this family or support system?" When the answer is yes, it seems that the individual finds a sense of identity of being needed, that his or her efforts have something to do with the whole.

In counseling session after counseling session we often hear, "He didn't do it right, so I did it myself." This attitude teaches a debilitating feeling of being incompetent when repeated over a lifetime. In family therapy we even see the person as an adult marrying the mate who continues the pattern and it becomes pervasive through a lifetime. Again the therapist can help the family by directing it to deal with some feelings of we "really do need each other." Of course if it is pathological, intense therapy should be applied to help the feelings rise to a conscious level of awareness.

5. This will be probably the most controversial issue discussed. We live in a society that wants to bow to no one or take time out to see from the other point of view. We have been conditioned to think highly of the young medical student who spends years and sacrifices pleasure time for the purpose of medicine; or the law student who spends hour upon hour studying legal documents to pass his bar exam; or the Olympian who for years of not socializing with friends, beating his feet to the ground to the point of bleeding day after day after day after day, and indeed these are committed, dedicated and fantastic people. But, it has become more at the attention of others that it is vitally important for a family to have a sense of "other"ness. Healthy families have a sense of knowing that they are in an economy of humanity and have a sense of destiny to the world outside them. Caring for others in the family unit, caring for friends, the older, the younger gives a sense of propriety that brings about order. If you will, a sense of "servant-hood," not slavery, but a knowing that you and your needs are important, too, teaches a lesson in responsibility that no text-book can teach.

The police family is not really different than that of the civilian family. Time pressures, finances, and relationships are difficult, but the highly structured atmosphere at the "station" does seem to suppress dealing with feelings and unfortunately it is difficult to cut off feelings that we have at work the minute we enter the home. It is difficult to leave the feelings of animosity toward the bureaucracy and not take them out on the kids. That's why we as therapists can help these folks bring to a conscious level the need to sensitize ourselves to more appropriate ways of dealing with feelings.

For this therapist, strategic therapy has been a very useful way of developing long-term changes in the family behavior. Assessing the family's agenda and what they feel their capabilities and goals are will help give way to appropriate change. Continuing education within the force is a ABSOLUTE must! Ongoing training by therapists and the helping professions would keep in the forefront the human motivation that "relationships are precious, and for life."

16

Therapy with Law Enforcement Couples: Clinical Management of the "High-Risk Lifestyle"

Randy Borum
Carol Philpot

The law enforcement profession brings tremendous pressures to bear on the family relationships of those involved in this line of work. Wide-spread recognition of this has led to a popular notion that divorce rates for police officers are considerably higher than the national average. While the empirical evidence does not support this particular idea, the variety of potential problems for these families is quite evident (Terry, 1981). Shift work, unpredictability, and physical danger are just a few of the elements that create a "high-risk lifestyle" (Depue, 1981). This chapter will provide an overview of the influences of police work, and some specific problems that may be seen when these couples seek treatment. Suggested techniques for engaging these couples in therapy and for promoting change will also be considered.

The Police Profession — The Larger System

The impact of police work on the officer can be divided into three major areas: (1) organizational influences — the demands of the departmental system and working conditions (work hours, on-call time, etc.); (2) peer socialization influences — the ideas, attitudes, and values that develop as the officer acculturates to the police subculture; and (3) police role influences — the influence of the various roles the job requires (enforcer, protector, mediator, etc.)

Organizational Influences

The organization (law enforcement agency) competes with the marriage for time and commitment. A police officer rarely works a nine-to-five, 40-hour week. Arrests made late in the shift, special details, and calls that require extensive paperwork commonly require the officer to put in sizable amounts of overtime. Specialty team assignments and supervisory positions often require 24-hour on-call status. It is expected that the officer is willing to put in the extra hours and make the job a priority. To some extent, these demands are unavoidable. In the middle of a violent domestic dispute, an officer cannot leave just because the shift is almost over. However, in addition to time demands from emergency situations, there are "requests" by supervisors for officers to extend their shift or take on additional duties. The officer's response reflects upon the perception of his/her commitment to law enforcement and the department. It is frequently the intensity of time devoted to the job that creates the image of a highly motivated and committed police officer. This image is subsequently reinforced by the organization through immediate appreciation and long-term reward.

The long-term benefits come when candidates are selected for promotion. Those who have worked hard and "gone the extra mile" for the agency are likely to receive more favorable ratings, and are therefore more likely to be promoted. When these individuals are promoted, the pattern becomes self-reinforcing. The extra time required by the job detracts from potential time the couple can spend together and may even interfere with plans the couple has previously made, creating resentment by the spouse toward the department. An additional conflict is created for the officer who wants to advance and be successful in order to provide well for the family and make them proud. However, acquiring the reputation of success frequently requires giving the job priority in a destructive competition for time and commitment. Conflicts of priority are seen in all types of industry; however, when combined with the following influences, the effects are even more powerful.

Peer/Socialization Influences

Here, the competition with the family is seen primarily in the development of attitudes and values. One spouse of a police officer gave the following account of her feelings about the changes in her husband following his entry into law enforcement: "His outlook on things has changed, his views, his opinions, his personality. He's changed, and we're not changing together. And that frightens me a lot." The impact of these influences should not be underestimated. There is a strong solidarity among police officers. This occurs not only because they are forced to rely on one another for safety (back-up), but also because there is a perceived adversarial relationship between the police and the public. Most citizen contact is made with individuals who are complaining and/or violating the law. This typical "in group-out group" conflict increases cohesiveness, and an "us and them" mentality develops which promotes trust only among members of the profession. Often this trust is even limited to members of one's own department. The result is that police officers tend to associate, on or off duty, only with other police officers. Thus, the solidarity creates an isolation which magnifies the power of the peer influence.

Typically, stereotypic masculine values and attitudes pervade the law enforcement community. This occurs in part because the profession is predominantly male, but also because the valence of the job pulls for such characteristics as control, dominance, and authority. Frequently, these are seen in the extreme. It is immediately apparent that these are in direct conflict with values that tend to be seen as more "relationship oriented." Values of power, control, competition, dominance, rigidity, rationality, independence, and transcendence are characteristic of the police population. These are accepted as the norm and are subsequently reinforced, overtly and covertly, within the officer's circle of acquaintances and colleagues. So much time is spent trying to emulate this stereotypic ideal that these values solidify in the officer's mind. It then becomes very difficult when the officer is forced to negotiate a conflict within an intimate relationship where a different mindset and alternative skills are necessary.

The officer may become increasingly uncomfortable in expressing emotion or affection or in adopting an attitude of cooperation or accommodation to resolve a conflict. These abilities are necessary to maintain a successful relationship; however, they are in direct opposition to the norms of the system with which the officer has worked so hard to identify.

Police Role Influences

The third area of impact is that of police role influences; in other words, the way that job activities and the requirements of the role of law enforcement agent influence the officer's personality. These compete with the marriage primarily in the areas of interpersonal perception and relations. The officer's role is quite complex. It requires sensitivity in dealing with lost children, calmness and assertiveness in directing emergency situations, as well as the ability to carry out the most severe law enforcement function — the use of deadly force. However, certain behaviors are so intense or so consistently required that their influence on the officer is compelling. Three primary areas where the role influences may be seen are: hypervigilance/suspiciousness, authoritativeness, and emotional control.

While on patrol, the officer must maintain a keen sense of alertness, which is characterized by a state of mental, emotional, and physical preparedness. This function is essential for officer survival and readiness to respond. It is also true that most of the people with whom an officer comes in contact during the discharge of duties are offenders of various types and view the officer very negatively during the interaction. Some of these people do, in fact, pose a real threat to the safety of the officer. Often it is difficult to make the distinction. The result is that the officer acquires a perceptual hypervigilance, and tends to view all others with some suspiciousness, possibly even evaluating them for potential threat.

This learning is quite powerful, and actually involves biological changes in the brain, as the reticular activating system is retrained to combat stimulus habituation and respond in this state of constant alertness (Gilmartin, 1986). Therefore, the effects last beyond the time spent on duty, eliciting the popular image of the cop who always sits with his back to the wall in the corner of a restaurant. This can annoy or frighten the spouse, who then perceives the officer as "paranoid." It may also interfere with the officer's perceptions of the spouse's friends or even of the spouse. Jealousy is commonly seen as a problem in law enforcement couples.

The two other police role influences result from the use of authority and emotional control. The police officer's position is clearly one of authority. Directives given and enforcement actions taken are delivered from a base of real authority which has been given to the officer by the state. Compliance is expected. If resistance is encountered, a level of force may be applied, which ranges from verbal warning to physical or even deadly force. However, when the officer arrives home, it is often difficult to make a rapid shift from authority to partnership and equality, and power struggles or conflict may ensue.

In addition to the use of authority, the officer must maintain close control of his/her emotions at all times while on duty. Considering the amount of stress and emotion generated in some police encounters, this is an ominous task. However, failure to do so could result in complaints, excessive force, injury to a citizen or to the officer. Again, this creates problems for the transition to the home situation. Complaints are frequently heard from spouses that officers are unable to emotionally connect with their partner. The officer is instructed in, and continually reinforced for, emotional control so that when he or she arrives home and emotional expression or vulnerability is required, there is not only an inability to readily identify and appropriately express emotion, but also a fear of doing so.

Common Problem Areas

The range of problems that can occur in law enforcement couples could occur for any type of couple; however, some areas emerge with consistency (Maynard & Maynard, 1982; Stenmark, et. al., 1982). Many of these are directly related to the influences of the police system that were previously discussed. The clinician should be aware of these to be certain that they are investigated; however, they should not limit the scope of therapeutic inquiry.

Structural Problems

As was previously noted, the police system facilitates solidarity and isolation. The result is that the system of the police department is characterized by an extremely rigid external boundary, which is sometimes stronger than the boundary around the couple. This may limit the spouse's sense of connection or accessibility to the officer. It may, in fact, overshadow the boundary of the couple and become a primary factor in the couple's own definition of their relationship. This is especially true where a moderate-to-high level of conflict exists within the relationship. This sets the stage for triangulation.

A triangle develops when a third party is used to stabilize the relationship between the spouses. Triangles serve to protect the individuals in the couple from having to be vulnerable and deal with one another directly about problems in the relationship or within themselves, such as strong dependency needs or overwhelming insecurity. Triangles also develop as a dysfunctional mechanism for the regulation of intimacy. One common triangle in law enforcement couples is with the job or department. Because the boundary around the officer and the department is so much stronger than the one around the officer and the spouse, the officer tends to become overinvolved with the department (and other officers) and underinvolved with the spouse. The spouse becomes jealous of the energy and commitment the officer puts into the job, and may displace resentment from the officer onto the department. However, this serves to further polarize the couple because the officer sees the spouse's resentment as a threat to his/her career and support. This triggers the officer's feelings of loyalty to the solidarity and to the department, and promotes a defensive response. So, rather than separating from the department, the officer is actually drawn closer to it as a result of triangulation, and is further distanced from the spouse because the conflict between them remains unresolved. With more severe dysfunction, triangles may also be seen with extramarital affairs and/or alcohol.

Police Attitudes

Authoritative or insensitive demands are sometimes placed upon members of the family, especially the spouse. This is a carryover from the authoritative presence the officer maintains on the street.

Cynicism is another problematic attitude which may develop over time. It becomes highly irritating to the spouse. It also reinforces the perception of emotional inaccessibility and calls attention to the negative influences of the profession. This, more than any other attitude, is a complaint of spouses who claim that their officer/spouses have changed as a result of police work.

Overprotectiveness and jealousy are two other problems which are separate, but functionally related. These stem from the officer's role of protection and need to control, in combination with a perception that the spouse is not emotionally satisfied within the relationship. Jealousy may emerge from the officer's projection of his/her own dissatisfaction with the relationship and feelings of attraction to others.

Job-Related Problems

A common concern expressed by the spouse is fear and anxiety about the safety of the officer. Very few law enforcement couples have directly negotiated this very difficult area. The attitude of most officers is: "It's just part of the job." Their own fears prevent them from comfortably confronting the topic, which leaves the spouse feeling isolated to deal with the problem on his/her own. The officer consoles him/herself by saying that the spouse will "get used to it."

Police work is also known for irregular schedules. Such schedules can be very difficult for the couple to adjust to, especially if both spouses are working. They may hardly see one another for weeks at a time. Loneliness and worry may also increase for the spouse while the officer is on a midnight shift.

Rotating schedules, overtime, and the demands of the job also produce a problem that is very common for law enforcement couples: limited time together. The officer may try to justify to him/herself that they spend "quality time" with the spouse, but developing intimacy also requires sufficient quantity of time. A related problem is that the long hours of intense stressful work produce physical exhaustion, which then detracts from the quality of time that the couple does spend together.

One specific job-related problem that may create conflict is the dilemma of weapons in the home. The spouse may feel uncomfortable having loaded guns in the house, especially if children are present. In addition the weapons tend to symbolize the aggression and danger that exist for the officer. Thus, this issue may serve as an indirect expression of the spouse's disapproval or concern about the officer's profession. Clinicians should be alert to this possibility.

Social-Interpersonal Problems

The solidarity previously noted implies that officers will be overinvolved with co-workers. Therefore, the spouse may be jealous of time spent with them and the emotional closeness the officer seems to share with them. The spouse may, in fact, feel sided against in a battle of loyalty.

Another problem that may result is isolation from the rest of the community. The overinvolvement, in combination with the "us and them" mentality, precludes the development of a strong or broad-based social network. The officer's jealousy and overprotectiveness may, directly or indirectly, limit the spouse's attempts to break the isolation and develop a personal support system.

Problematic Behaviors

The intense emtotional control required on the job may produce a store of anger and aggression. Some law enforcement couples have faced the problem of displacement of this aggression at home. This may result in an angry verbal outburst or, in more extreme cases, may erupt into physical violence. If such domestic violence does occur, the spouse may be especially ambivalent about reporting it, since the officer's colleagues may respond to the call, and such an incident is likely to result in termination.

The incidence of alcohol abuse in police officers also appears to be somewhat higher than that found in the general population (Pendergrass & Ostrove, 1986). This may be due, in part, to social norms, which frequently promote the use of alcohol as a stress reduction technique and as an integral part of social interaction. Sometimes excessive drinking is encouraged under the guise of a necessity to "unwind" after a hard shift or a stressful incident

Another behavior reported as a common concern in law enforcement couples is marital infidelity. This is related to several previously mentioned problems, such as regulation of intimacy, insecurity, fear of vulnerability, and emotional inaccessibility. Concerns in this area are reported by both officers and spouses.

Both Partners in Law Enforcement

Most of the problems and influences mentioned above also apply when both partners are involved in law enforcement. However, a number of variables may influence the intensity of the impact, including whether the officers work for the same department or work the same shift, or the nature of their current assignment (i.e., patrol, vice, narcotics, administrative, etc.). These couples do report some advantages, however. In the "us and them" mentality, both partners are on the same side. There are far fewer conflicts about the exclusivity of social contacts from within the department. They also have the unique opportunity of being able to truly understand the problems, pressures, and perspective of the partner. In addition, these couples actually have more power to combat the police role influences at home, since they both share this influence and can easily make it overt.

Clearly, the closer the working relationship, the more there is a potential for problems. Primary among them is the blurring of personal and professional roles. One example of this may be seen when the spouse's role as "protector" interferes with his/her objectivity in perceiving the partner as a police officer in an emergency situation. Another common problem is the tendency of co-workers to meddle in the couple's relationship by starting and escalating rumors or providing unsolicited advice. In other words, the relationship becomes open material for officer gossip.

Shift work creates another problem. If they work the same shift, they are more subject to the aforementioned problems. However, if they are not on the same shift, their available time together is severely limited because there are 16 to 20 working hours per day when they cannot be together. Coordination of time off can also create difficulty.

Treatment Recommendations

Thus far, we have reviewed the nature of the police role and its impact on a marital relationship. This is necessary, because it is this phenomenology that most clearly delineates this population. Without it, the effectiveness of any treatment may be reduced. But with this knowledge, many techniques may be utilized to address the problems that emerge in the relationships of law enforcement couples. Conjoint therapy would be the treatment modality of choice. However, very little has been written about this very important area (Reese, 1982). The following section will briefly introduce some suggestions for engaging these couples in therapy and also for enhancing motivation and change.

The Joining Stage

Understanding the dynamics and acquiring an "insider's view" of the police profession are among the therapist's most powerful tools for engaging these couple in therapy. If a clinician expects to do any extensive work with this population, it may be helpful to arrange for participation in a "ride along" program with a local police department. This is the only way to get a firsthand look at the true nature of police work, the officers, and the working environment. This also demonstrates an interest in the profession and in knowing what the officers really do on patrol. It may serve as a starting point in a conversation with a reluctant officer, affording the therapist a unique opportunity to meet the officer on a common ground that is not as threatening. This may facilitate the first of two primary tasks in therapy with law enforcement couples, namely, "hooking" the officer into treatment. The second and concurrent goal is to empower the spouse and instill hope, so that the relationship between therapist and officer is not seen as yet another alliance from which the spouse is excluded. An additional suggestion is to attempt to locate a police spouse support group and request permission to attend some of the meetings. This may help to sensitize the therapist to the spouse's phenomenology as well.

Being able to speak the language of police work will also increase therapeutic power. Some phrases or expressions may be picked up during ride-along sessions, others may be acquired from the officer during the course of therapy. For example, the therapist may ask to "investigate" a problem further, or refer to specific skills as a set of "policies and procedures" for handling conflict.

The emphasis here is on learning to communicate with the officers on their terms. This is important because of the uniqueness of that subculture and because the officer is typically the more difficult party with whom to connect. Part of the process of therapy is going to be showing the couple how to speak a common language, so it is beneficial for the therapist to know the language of each of the individuals in order to facilitate the initial phase of translation. Other strategies to use during the joining stage are: emphasizing confidentiality, maximizing motivation, and providing hope for a positive resolution.

Intervention

Enhancement of motivation is a useful technique for the joining phase. By the time a law enforcement couple presents for therapy, they have probably tried every common sense solution available. However, it is likely that their "solutions" have only perpetuated, and in many instances compounded, their initial problem. They are typically in true crisis as a couple. The therapist should allow the couple to relate their desperate attempts to solve their difficulties, and have them describe their present situation as intolerable. This heightens motivation and decreases the probability of premature termination. The task of the therapist is not to alleviate their sense of urgency, but to counteract their demoralization, and give them a sense that theirs is a problem that can be successfully resolved (Rabkin, 1983). One tactic might be to tell the couple that their specific difficulties are frequently encountered by police couples and that the therapist has seen many other couples work them out successfully. This serves the added function of normalizing the problem, which is a very influential reframe for these couples.

Goals and Strategies of Treatment

Although there is natural overlap between them, common goals in treatment of law enforcement couples can be organized into specific problem areas. Many strategies will address more than one goal at a time.

Structural Goals

Goal: Strengthen the boundary around the couple, relative to the departmental boundary.

Strategies

1) Use the us/them mentality as a metaphor for the police officer to begin to understand the need to create an us/them atmosphere for the marital dyad. The couple can make a list of all the stresses operating to drive them apart. This can be framed as an enemy against which they can unite.

2) Create more time together for the couple. Urge them to go out on weekly dates alone and take frequent weekend trips away from children. Have them negotiate an amount of time that is mutually agreeable, and then schedule that as time allotted specifically for that purpose. Designate a communication or decision hour once or twice a week, during which they will put aside all distractions and communicate about important issues. Certain times should be set aside when neither party is permitted to talk about the job. This may be very uncomfortable at first, especially for the officer; however, building this tolerance will strengthen the couple's relationship.

3) A "secret vacation" may be devised where the couple plans a weekend getaway that only they are to know about. Friends, family, and colleagues are not to be told anything about the adventure either before or after the fact.

Goal: Reduce triangulation

Strategies:

1) Teach the couple to deal directly and effectively with one another. This facilitates the process of detriangulation. This process can begin in session when the therapist refuses to take the role of judge and jury, instead encouraging the couple to speak with one another directly during the session. This allows the therapist to see their interaction first hand, providing a systemic understanding of the couple and preventing triangulation into the couple system. In addition, this

protects the therapist from answering questions or evaluating material that actually belongs to the couple. As the couple learns more effective communication skills (see below), they should be asked to cease sharing intimate details of the relationship with fellow workers, friends, extended family, and so on.

2) Help the couple gain insight into the use of triangulation of job, friends, family, even lovers, to gain distance and avoid intimacy. Help them find more effective ways to maintain autonomy within an intimate relationship (i.e., separate hobbies, activities, etc.). Normalize the need for both autonomy and intimacy and the need to find a balance.

Attitudinal/Affective/Cognitive Goals

Goal: Increase intimacy and bonding between the couple.

Strategies:

1) Have them describe their early dating days—what attracted them to one another, what their love was all about. Bring in old love letters and photographs. The therapist may elicit some useful information (and positive feelings) by asking each partner to recall what it was that initially attracted them to one another. Frequently the same characteristics that originally attracted them to one another have now become polarized and are presently the source of conflict. This situation can be normalized and reframed so that the couple learns to focus once again on the positive side, on what they have to each one another in a complementary fashion. For example, the very logical, emotionally stilted police officer may have originally been attracted to his wife because of her open affection and warmth, which made it easier for him to get in touch with his own emotions. Now, as she begins to show more intense emotion, which frightens him, he becomes a calm "computer" to balance her. Unfortunately, this only infuriates her, because it frustrates her need for connection and validation, so she becomes more intense. He now calls her hysterical, and she calls him unfeeling. This "schismogenesis" can be reversed if both recall their original admiration for the characteristics of the other that they need to develop within themselves.

2) Teach them how to identify and appropriately express emotion to one another. During the sessions, as the couple deal with one another directly about areas of conflict, many emotions, including anger, are likely to emerge. The therapist should help them to recognize that anger covers feelings of frustration, anxiety, and hurt. Then,

the couple can learn to get in touch with these more vulnerable feelings and to intensify them beyond their usual threshold in a safe environment. The therapist can reinforce this tolerance and process the responses of the spouse. It may also be helpful to teach them to "compartmentalize," so that they can turn on their feeling channel at home and turn it off at work.

Goal: Increase the positive feelings in the marriage, and build a sense of "connectedness" that is satisfying to both partners.

Strategies:

1) Identify, emphasize, and mobilize strengths that have thus far kept the marriage together. An obvious strength that should be reinforced is the couple's courage in seeking help.
2) Assign "caring days" homework (Stuart, 1980). Have the couple generate a list of nice things they can do for one another on a daily basis and commit to doing several each day.
3) Use reframes to place the behavior of both spouses in the most positive light. For example, a spouse's over-protectiveness can be reframed as love and concern; the officer's overwork may be framed as an attempt to provide adequately for the family.

Goal: Help the couple gain insight into larger systemic influences in their relationship.

Strategies:

1) Have the couple construct a genogram. Identify intergenerational patterns, family myths, and expectations. Teach them to break dysfunctional patterns and preserve functional ones.
2) Teach the couple about gender differences. A gender-sensitive approach to treatment can provide an understanding of basic gender differences, so that frustrations in this area may be depersonalized. It is also desirable to teach each partner how they can make this new understanding work for each in relating effectively to the partner (Philpot, 1991).
3) A spin-off from the gender differences discussion can lead to providing the couple with an understanding of how the very skills required at work are detrimental to the relationship (i.e., control, dominance, aggression, power, etc.). The couple can be encouraged to set aside a decompression period after work, during which the spouse learns to change channels and bring to the surface a different set of skills, more appropriate to intimate relationships. In other

words, the officer's tendency to compartmentalize into good and bad can be used to teach him or her to compartmentalize between home skills and work skills.

Goal: Motivate the couple for change
Strategies:

1) The strategy of "restraining" the couple is likely to be quite effective here. In this intervention, the couple is told not to change too quickly because they may not be able to tolerate the consequences of progress. Law enforcement couples are likely to rise to this challenge (Fisch, et. al., 1982).

Social-Interpersonal Goals

Goal: Teach the couple basic communication skills.
Strategies:

1) Communication training with an emphasis on active listening skills and taking responsibility for one's own emotions and actions is useful. This may be initially facilitated by a simple exchange of: "I feel _____ when you do _____ and I would prefer that you do ___," followed by the partner's reflection of what message he/she has heard. Police officers are particularly vulnerable to the stereotypically "male" characteristic of attempting to produce immediate solutions to problems rather than giving the spouse an opportunity to find his/her own solutions. Learning to listen non-defensively without interruption and with a goal of empathy for the other can be very helpful. One very effective exercise, which may be useful in teaching this skill, is that suggested by Stuart Johnson (in Scarf, 1987), in which each partner has one half hour of uninterrupted time to talk about him/herself, *not* about the relationship or the other spouse, followed by the other partner's turn to do the same. Neither partner is allowed to respond to the other, just listen.
2) Teach problem-solving/negotiation skills. Due to the atmosphere of their job, law enforcement officers are inclined to look at issues through an "either/or, right/wrong" lens, which is ineffective in a marital relationship. Problem-solving training will give the couple practice in negotiating a two-winner approach, in which the relationship is enhanced, and the typical "either/or stance" is transformed into "both/and" philosophy.

3) Teach conflict-containment skills. Here the therapist can build on the training the officer has already received regarding diffusion of conflict. Have the couple apply the same techniques to themselves, including time-out, cognitive restructuring during the cooling down phase, changing locations, identifying and avoiding hot buttons, developing cues to indicate when it is time to readdress issues, and so on.

4) Expand the couple's sphere of social influence beyond the department and their own families-of-origin. This will have the effect of loosening the departmental bond as well as expanding the officer's friendships to include people whose value systems are more worthy of trust than that of the criminal population. This may help to counteract his/her cynicism.

Job-Related Goals

Goal: Make more time for the couple.

Strategies:

1) Use communication skills and problem- solving skills (see above) to negotiate time for the couple relationship.

2) Use exercises designed to motivate the couple to focus more energy on their relationship as opposed to work and problems. These may include the Time Pie (what is most important to me vs. where I spend most of my time) or the Time Line (when will I get around to doing that which means most to me).

Goal: Openly discuss stresses on each of the spouses and on the relationship due to the job.

Strategy:

1) As the couple learns communication skills (particularly active listening and empathic skills) and the officer learns to identify and feel safe expressing emotions with the spouse, he/she can openly discuss fears, doubts, and frustrations in a supportive, bonding fashion, which will strengthen the relationship and energize rather than isolate the officer.

These techniques are offered only as a supplement to the basic clinical skills and strategies of the practicing couples/family therapist. One primary consideration, however, regardless of theoretical orientation, is to remain flexible, otherwise the patterns of therapy merely emulate the couple's own dysfunctional sets.

Conclusion

Couples therapy with law enforcement couples may be highly challenging and complex. There are myriad influences that create stress for the individuals and actually work in opposition to the goals of building an intimate relationship. The goal of the therapist is to connect with both partners in different ways without alienating either one. She/he must then guide the couple through the gauntlet of a larger, more rigid system, and have them emerge as a connected, well-functioning unit. The task is difficult for all parties involved, but the conjoint approach is the most effective mechanism for stabilizing and humanizing this high-risk lifestyle.

References

Depue, R. L. (1981). High risk lifestyle: The police family. *FBI Law Enforcement Bulletin*, 50(8), 7–13.

Fisch, R., Weakland, J., & Segal, L. (1982). *Tactics of change*. San Francisco: Jossey-Bass.

Gilmartin, K.M. (1986). Hypervigilance: A learned perceptual set and its consequences on police stress. In J. Reese & H. Goldstein (Eds.), *Psychological services for law enforcement*. Washington: US Government Printing Office.

Maynard, P.E., & Maynard, M.E. (1982). Stress in police families: Some policy implications. *Journal of Police Science and Administration*, 10(3), 302–314.

Pendergrass, V.E. & Ostrove, N.M. (1986). Correlates of alcohol use by police personnel. In J. Reese & H. Goldstein (Eds.), *Psychological services for law enforcement*. Washington: US Government Printing Office.

Philpot, C.G. (1991). Gender sensitive couples therapy: A systemic definition. *Journal of Family Psychotherapy*, 2(3), 19–40.

Rabkin, R. (1983). *Strategic psychotherapy: Brief and symptomatic treatment*. New York: New American Library.

Reese, J.T. (1982). Family therapy in law enforcement: A new approach to an old problem. *FBI Law Enforcement Bulletin*, 51(9), 7–11.

Scarf, M. (1987). *Intimate partners*. New York: Random House.

Stenmark, D.E., Depiano, L.C., Wackwutz, J.C., Cannon, C.D., & Walfish, S. (1982). Wives of police officers: Issues related to family and job satisfaction and job longevity. *Journal of Police Science and Administration*, 10(2), 229–234.

Stuart, R. (1980). *Helping couples change*. New York: Guilford Press.

Terry, W.C. (1981). Police stress: The empirical evidence. *Journal of Police Science and Administration*, 9(10), 61–75.

Part Five

The Trauma of
Law Enforcement

No discussion of police stress can occur without a full acknowledgement that the stress of law enforcement significantly differs from the stress of other occupations. While the magnitude and manifestations may parallel those of occupations, the source of the stress sets law enforcement apart. Unlike all but other crisis professions, e.g. fire and emergency medicine, only law enforcement deals on a daily basis with stress that results from the violent act of one person toward another. Only law enforcement must deal directly with the sights, sounds, smells and emotions associated with violence, whether caused by a human being or "Mother Nature." Only law enforcement must handle the impact caused by "people pain," the vicarious stress one feels because another is going through trauma.

Maslach recognized that one response of emergency workers who are required to give "too much, too often, to other people in need" was *burnout*. As she observed:

> Hour after hour, day after day, health and social service professionals are intimately involved with troubled human beings. What happens to people who work intensely with others, learning about their psychological social or physical problems? Ideally, the helpers retain objectivity...without losing their concern for the person they are working with. Instead, our research indicates, they are often unable to cope with this continual emotional stress and burnout occurs. They lose all concern, all emotional feeling for the person they work with and come to treat them in a detached or even dehumanized ways (Maslach, 16).

So what exactly is this trauma related stress? In what kind of circumstances is it likely to occur? How can we begin to mitigate it? Here in Part Five, our authors will address these questions. Within the context of their own therapeutic point of view, McCann and Pearlman discuss the therapist's reaction to a client's traumatic material. They relate the phenomenon termed *"vicarious traumatization"* both to the graphic and painful material trauma clients often present and to a therapist's own reaction to such trauma. The article suggests ways the therapist can transform and integrate the client's traumatic experience in a manner that will provide the best services to clients and minimize the impact on the therapist.

By its nature, police work often involves highly complex skills, considerable emotional strain and little recognition. Human suffering and death are often an intrinsic part of the work, and the often traumatic nature of police work has been found to render the police officer vulnerable to those more severe stress reactions characteristic of Post Traumatic Stress Disorder (PTSD). Hetherington describes a study of 306 British road traffic officers, averaging seven years experience on the force. Her findings support the need for an organizational approach to those officers vulnerable to unexpected stress reactions and to improve the ability of all personnel to handle traumatic situations.

As a result of their routine contact with death and violence, homicide investigators are subjected to sources of stress unique among law enforcement officers. Sewell focuses specifically on the stressors experienced by those officers who regularly deal with victims of violent deaths. Such stressors include the burden and constant pressure of their responsibilities, the need to deal with the significant others of the victims, difficulties with the judicial and human service systems, frustration, anger and fatigue. The successful management of such stress requires short-term responses to deal with immediate stressors, as well as long-term strategies that involve the police organization and the individual investigator.

References

Maslach, C. (1976). "Burned-out" *Human Behavior, 5*(9), 16-22.

17

Vicarious Traumatization: A Framework for Understanding the Psychological Effects of Working with Victims

I. Lisa McCann
Laurie Anne Pearlman

Introduction

Tom, a married man in his late 20s and father of two young children, was frequently disturbed by intrusive images involving danger befalling his loved ones. He became obsessed with safety precautions and was hypervigilant about strange noises in his house. As a result, he often woke up suddenly in the middle of the night, fearing that a prowler was in the house. Despite the absence of evidence of immediate danger, he would lie vigilant in his bed for several hours before finally dropping off to sleep. These recurrent feelings of impending danger disrupted his sleep pattern and left him with a pervasive sense of anxiety and vulnerability.

Joan, a single parent and mother of two school-aged daughters, often attended school functions with other parents in the community. During one event, she observed a father stroking the hair of his young daughter, an exceptionally beautiful little girl. Suddenly, she experienced a vivid image of the father forcibly sodomizing the child, an image associated with feelings of disgust and anxiety. She quickly found a friend to talk to and consciously pushed the ugly image out of her mind. She reflected later that she often found herself distrustful of other people's motives, particularly where the potential abuse of children was involved.

Ann, a single woman in her 30s, would awaken in a cold sweat after experiencing a vivid, recurrent nightmare of being raped brutally at knife point. She would turn on all the lights and lie awake until the dawn broke. After these nightmares, she reported feeling vulnerable and exposed. Over the subsequent weeks she experienced intrusive thoughts about knives and became fearful of being around knives.

What do these three people have in common? Are they experiencing the psychological aftereffects of incest, rape, or some other traumatic violation? Indeed, these people are evidencing some of the cardinal signs and symptoms of the aftermath of a serious victimization. The nightmares, fearful thoughts, intrusive images, and suspicion of other people's motives are common among persons who have been victimized. However, neither Tom, Joan, nor Ann has directly experienced a victimization or catastrophe. What they do have in common is that they are all mental health professionals who spend a significant proportion of their professional time doing therapy with or studying persons who have been victimized. Although all of them have advanced degrees and training, including supervision in the treatment of victims, they are not immune to the painful images, thoughts, and feelings associated with exposure to their clients' traumatic memories. These reactions can occur as a short-term reaction to working with particular clients, as described in the literature on countertransference in work with victims (e.g., Blank, 1987; Danieli, 1981; Lindy, 1988) or as a long-term alteration in the therapist's own cognitive schemas, or beliefs, expectations, and assumptions about self and others.

Therapists who work with victims may find their cognitive schemas and imagery system of memory (Paivio, 1986) altered or disrupted by long-term exposure to the traumatic experiences of their victim clients. In this paper, we describe this transformation and provide a new theoretical context for understanding this complex phenomenon. Through the explication of the trauma-related alterations in the therapist's cognitive schemas, we build upon the existing literature to provide a systematic basis for assessing and understanding therapists' unique responses to clients' traumatic material. Our work at the Traumatic Stress Institute, a private mental health organization devoted to the treatment of trauma survivors, has shaped our thinking about this issue as well as providing the case material presented in this paper.

In the past two decades, mental health professionals have shown an unprecedented interest in the psychological aftermath of victimization (e.g., Figley, 1985, 1988; Horowitz, 1976; Lifton, 1973; van der Kolk, 1987). This interest has extended to a wide variety of victimizing events. While an extensive knowledge base exists on the psychological consequences of traumatic experiences for victims, less attention has focused on the enduring psychological consequences for therapists of exposure to the traumatic experiences of victim clients. Persons who work with victims may experience profound psychological effects, effects that can be disruptive and painful for the helper and can persist for months or years after work with traumatized persons. We term this process "vicarious traumatization."

First, we review previous conceptualizations of the client's impact on the psychotherapist and the psychotherapeutic process. Next, we apply our constructivist, self-development theory to understanding the psychological impact of working with victims. Finally, we discuss the implications of this theory for clinicians who work with trauma victims.

Previous Conceptualizations

Burnout

Working with victims clearly has much in common with working with any difficult population, such as seriously ill persons, victims of poverty, or persons with very severe psychiatric or social problems. Burnout refers to the psychological strain of working with difficult populations. From a social learning theory (Rotter, 1954) point of view, burnout might be conceptualized as the state in which one's minimal goals are too high and are not changed in response to feedback.

The symptoms of burnout have been described as depression, cynicism, boredom, loss of compassion, and discouragement (Freudenberger and Robbins, 1979). The research on burnout among therapists suggests the following as contributing factors: professional isolation, the emotional drain of always being empathetic, ambiguous success (Bermak, 1977); lack of therapeutic success, non-reciprocated giving and attentiveness (Farber and Heifetz, 1982); and failure to live up to one's own (perhaps unrealistic) expectations, leading to feelings of inadequacy or incompetence (Deutsch, 1984). Although the burnout literature has not specifically addressed the effects of working with victims, these concepts are clearly relevant.

Working with victims may produce symptoms of burnout in mental health professionals for a number of reasons. Victims of undisclosed traumas may present chronic, entrenched symptoms that are difficult to treat and require long-term therapy. Furthermore, trauma victims may be reluctant to focus on traumatic memories, a source of potential frustration for the therapist. Finally, helpers who understand victimization as a reflection of social and political problems may feel hopeless about the potential impact of individual psychotherapy upon the root causes of crime and violence.

We believe that burnout among therapists who work with victims has special meanings. That is, symptoms of burnout may be the final common pathway of continual exposure to traumatic material that cannot be assimilated or worked through. The symptoms of burnout may be analogous to the trauma survivor's numbing and avoidance patterns in that each reflects an inability to process the traumatic material.

Although the burnout literature is relevant to working with trauma victims, we concur with others (e.g., Danieli, 1981; Haley, 1974) that the potential effects of working with other difficult populations because the therapist is exposed to the emotionally shocking images of horror and suffering that are characteristic of serious traumas.

Contertransference

The countertransference literature provides additional useful background for understanding this complex phenomenon. Countertransference traditionally has referred to the activation of the therapist's unresolved or unconscious conflicts or concerns. Freudenberger and Robbins (1979) write: "(in therapy), the therapist's old scars and injuries are constantly rubbed anew" (p. 287). Similarly, Farber (1985) suggests that the work of psychotherapy may reactivate therapists' early experiences and memories.

Within the victimization literature, countertransference has more broadly incorporated the painful feelings, images, and thoughts that can accompany work with trauma survivors. Haley (1974) originally described the intense and sometimes overwhelming emotions that can be evoked by exposure to images of atrocities or abusive violence reported by Vietnam veterans. In reporting her own reactions to hearing about atrocities experienced by her clients, Haley describes feelings "numbed and frightened" and cautions therapists to confront their own sadistic and retaliatory wishes. Blank (1984) states that persons who work with Vietnam veterans must face the darkest side of humanity and forever be transformed by it. Scurfield (1985) suggest that work with these clients may stir up ambivalent, negative, or moral/judgemetnal feelings in the therapist and suggests the importance of confronting one's own feelings of aggression, rage, grief, horror, loss of control, and vulnerability. Margolin (1984) describes therapists' reactions to Vietnam veterans as centering around existential anxiety about death and non-being. Furthermore, Blank (1987) describes cases in which therapists experience an intrusion of their own unresolved traumatic experiences, including unresolved Vietnam experiences. With regard to work with incest survivors, Herman (1981) suggests the danger for female therapists of over-identification with the victim and rage at the perpetrator. In contrast, male therapists may experience over-identification with the aggressor.

The most comprehensive models of countertransference reactions among therapists who work with victims cite the following issues and themes. In her work with therapists who work with Holocaust survivors, Danieli (1981) found empirical validation for some of the following themes; guilt, rage, dread and horror, grief and mourning, shame, inability to contain intense emotions, and utilization of defenses such as numbing, denial, or avoidance. In a similar model, Lindy (1988) identified a number of symptom patterns that emerged in therapists in their work with Vietnam veterans. These included nightmares, intrusive images, reenactments, amnesia, estrangement, alienation, irritability, psychophysiologic reactions, and survivor guilt.

Finally, within the area of victimization, there is evidence that persons close to the victim, such as family members, may suffer signs and symptoms of traumatization similar to those of the victim. This concept has been described by Figley (1983) as secondary victimization. For example, there is evidence that children of Nazi concentration camp survivors (Danieli, 1985; Freyberg, 1980) and Vietnam combat veterans (Kehle and Parsons, 1988) may experience social and psychological difficulties. Critical incident stress, an acute type of post-traumatic stress disorder (PTSD), has also been observed in emergency workers who are at the scene of environmental disasters or accidents involving loss of life (Mitchell, 1985).

Overall, the above writings suggest that exposure to the traumatic experiences of victims may be hazardous to the mental health of people close to the victim, including therapists involved in the victim's healing process. These different literatures parallel the two lines of thinking in the field of traumatic stress which place different emphases on whether characteristics of the stressor or individuals' personal characteristics determine their responses to trauma. That is, the literature on burnout parallels the focus on characteristics of the stressor in that it suggests that the therapist is distressed because of the nature of the external event (isolation, difficult client population, and so forth). On the other hand, the countertransference literature parallels the focus on preexisting personal characteristics to the extent that it attempts to explain the individual's responses as a function of his or her previous unresolved psychological conflicts. Constructivist self-development theory is interactive in that it views the therapist's unique responses to client material as shaped by both characteristics of the situation and the therapist's unique psychological needs and cognitive schemas.

In addition, we understand the effects on therapists as pervasive, that is, potentially affecting all realms of the therapist's life; commutative, in that each client's story can reinforce the therapist's gradually changing schemas; and likely permanent, even if worked through completely. This notion has been written about somewhat more broadly in the past. Jung (1966) originally conceived that an "unconscious infection" may result from working with the mentally ill. English (1976) describes this process as follows: "As the emotional needs and distresses of people in difficulty were presented to me, I not only felt them through a process of empathy, but I also found I tended to absorb them within myself as well" (p. 193).

Chessick (1978) also hypothesizes that conditions of depression and despair in one's clients (which he calls "soul sadness") can be contagious. Farber (1985) cites evidence that the client can transfer his or her pathology to the therapist. Finally, in a recent book on the personal impact of doing psychotherapy, Guy (1987) cites research which supports the notion that doing psychotherapy can be dangerous to the psyche of the therapist.

Within the area of victimization, others (Blank, 1987; Danieli, 1981; Lindy, 1988) have described a similar phenomenon, generally using the rubric of countertransference, while also raising questions about the adequacy of that construct to explain the phenomenon. Our notion of vicarious traumatization is somewhat broader than countertransference, as it implies that much of the therapist's cognitive world will be altered by hearing traumatic client material. It is our belief that all therapists working with trauma survivors will experience lasting alterations in their cognitive schemas, having a significant impact on the therapist's feelings, relationships, and life. Whether these changes are ultimately destructive to the helper and to the therapeutic process depends, in large part, on the extent to which the therapist is able to engage in a parallel process to that of the victim client, the process of integrating and transforming these experiences of horror or violation.

Constructivist Self-Development Theory

The material we present here expands upon our previous work and provides a new theoretical perspectives for understanding and working with therapists' reactions. In previous papers (McCann et. al., 1988a, b), we described a new theoretical model for understanding psychological responses to victimization. That work focused on the complex relation among traumatic life events, cognitive schemas about self and world, and psychological adaptation. We have elaborated that model into a theory of personality we call constructivist self-development theory, described more fully elsewhere (McCann and Pearlman, 1990b). In this chapter, we focus primarily on the portion of the theory that describes psychological needs and cognitive schemas.

The cognitive portion of the theory is built upon a constructivist foundation. The underlying premise is that human beings construct their own personal realities through the development of complex cognitive structures which are used to interpret events (e.g., Epstein, 1989; Mahoney, 1981; Mahoney and Lyddon, 1988). These cognitive structures evolve and become increasingly complex over the life span as individuals interact with their meaningful environment. Piaget (1971) described these cognitive structures as schemas. These schemas or mental frameworks include beliefs, assumptions, and expectations about self and world that enable individuals to make sense of their experience. Some of these basic schemas for experience involve beliefs, and assumptions about causality, the trustworthiness of sense data, identity, and self-world relations (Mahoney, 1981).

An extensive review of the literature on adaption to trauma (McCann *et al.*, 1988b) revealed five fundamental psychological needs: safety, dependency/trust, power, esteem, and intimacy. In later elaboration of our work (McCann and Pearlman, 1990b), we have expanded the needs of interest to include independence and frame of reference.

The cognitive manifestations of psychological needs are schemas. Our major hypothesis is that trauma can disrupt these schemas and that the unique way that trauma is experienced depends in part upon which schemas are central or salient for the individual. In this chapter, we assert that working with trauma survivors can also disrupt the therapist's schemas in these areas. The therapist's unique reactions will be determined by the centrality or salience of these schemas to himself or herself. In addition to the focus on schemas, our current work (McCann and Pearlman, 1990a, b) includes more emphasis on the imagery system of memory, as well as ego resources and self-capacities. In this chapter, we will focus primarily on changes in cognitive schemas and in the imagery system, both areas particularly relevant to understanding vicarious traumatization.

Cognitive Schemas

Beliefs, expectations, and assumptions about the world are central to many current notions about the effects of victimization. Janoff-Bulman (1985) asserts that victimizing life events challenge three basic assumption or beliefs about the self and the world: the belief in personal invulnerability; the view of oneself in a positive light; and the belief in a meaningful, orderly world. Similarly, Taylor and Brown (1988) have reviewed the evidence that illusions about self and world are adaptive and enhance self-esteem and mental health. Epstein (1989) presents four basic assumptions which he asserts are disrupted by trauma. These include the beliefs that the world is benign, the world is meaningful, the self is worthy, and people are trustworthy. The work of Roth and her colleagues (Roth, 1989) draws upon and provides empirical support for Epstein's conceptualization. Our work is consistent with this thinking.

Therapists may experience disruptions in their schemas about self and world when they work with trauma victims. These changes may be subtle or shocking, depending upon the degree of discrepancy between the client's traumatic memories and the therapist's existing schemas. We will now describe how disruptions in these schemas may be associated with certain emotions or thoughts in the helper.

Dependency/Trust

Through their clients, therapists who work with victims are exposed to the many cruel ways that people deceive, betray, or violate the trust of other human beings, as well as the ways people can undermine those who depend upon them, as is often the case with child victims. This may well disrupt the therapist's schemas about trust. As a result, therapists may become suspicious of other people's motives, more cynical, or distrustful. In the case example of Joan, previously discussed, we find a helper who works with many incest survivors questioning the motives of parents at her child's school function. In our case conferences about victims, we sometimes observe ourselves expecting the worst from people in our clients' interpersonal worlds. For example, a therapist reporting on a new intake said, "I bet I know how this case is going to come out. The father is probably molesting the daughter, the mother has abandoned her emotionally, and everyone else is looking the other way." Startled by what she had just said, this therapist reflected, "I can't believe I'm saying this. I used to believe that most people are trustworthy and that some people are not. Now I believe just the oppposite."

Safety

Images involving a loss of safety, including threats or harm to innocent people, may challenge the therapist's schemas within the area of safety. This will be particularly disruptive if the helper has strong needs for security. The case example of Tom, the therapist who awoke one night with fearful images of being violated by a prowler, involves a therapist who works with many victims of acute traumas, such as crime or rape. In this instance, the therapist strongly identified with his middle class suburban clients who were victims of a burglary. His own fearful images closely corresponded to the images they reported in therapy. In other instances, the connection between the client's images and the therapist's response is not as readily apparent. For example, the helper might experience increased thoughts and images associated with personal vulnerability, such as loved ones being killed in a car accident. Therapists who work with victims of rape or other crime may experience a greater need to take precautions against such a violation. Overall, clinicians who work with victims of random violence or accidents may experience a heightened sense of vulnerability and an enhanced awareness of the fragility of life.

Power

Persons who have been victimized often find themselves in situations of extreme helplessness, vulnerability, or even paralysis. Exposure to these traumatic situations through the client's memories may evoke concerns about the therapist's own sense of power or efficacy in the world. In our experience, helpers with high needs for power are likely to be greatly impacted by the powerlessness reported by their clients. This can at times lead therapists to urge clients inappropriately to take action rather than to help clients understand the meanings of their responses. It is not uncommon to hear rape counselors report that they are taking self-defense classes, no doubt to increase their own sense of power as well as safety. In addition, therapists whose power needs are threatened may find themselves becoming more dominant in social or work situations. One therapist who works with crime victims states that he often fantasizes about how he would protect his family in the event of a criminal victimization. Sometimes these fantasies are brutal or retaliatory, expressing his need to reaffirm his beliefs in his own personal power. Another therapist spoke of wondering how she would respond if she were raped. Sometimes these thoughts became obsessional, as she would replay various rape scenarios over and over in her mind. To the extent that this leads to constructive self-protective action, whether by client or therapist, it is positive. Yet it can become dysfunctional if it leads to inappropriate attempts to control others or anger about one's inability to do so.

Alternatively, a therapist may express a heightened awareness of the illusory nature of control over capricious or unexpected life events. One therapist expressed this by stating, "I realize now how little control I really have over life or death. All that I have worked for can be destroyed in an instant and nothing I do now can prevent that from happening." In extreme cases, a therapist may find himself or herself experiencing feelings of helplessness, depression, or despair about the uncontrollable forces of nature or human violence.

Independence

Trauma survivors, such as victims of rape or other crime, often experience a disruption in their need for independence, such as restriction in their freedom of movement and a diminishment in personal autonomy. One of the therapists in our setting works with many rape and other crime victims. Several of her clients are women with high needs for independence who have experienced a profound diminishment in personal freedom since the victimization. One survivor continues to be terrorized by her assailant, resulting in her decision to move back into her family's home, an event that profoundly disrupted her independence. Her therapist found herself identifying with her client's loss of independence and described experiencing dreams in which she was similarly trapped and confined. While discussing these clients in a case conference, she reflected on how painful it would be "to lose my sense of personal control and freedom in my life" while another therapist, for whom safety was a more salient issue, focused on the sense of personal vulnerability this case elicited in her. For the therapist with strong needs for independence, the identification with clients who have lost a sense of personal control and freedom can be especially painful.

Esteem

We use esteem to refer to the need to perceive others as benevolent and worthy of respect. Persons who are violated or harmed through the uncaring, cruel, or malicious intentions and acts of other human beings may experience diminished esteem for other people or the human race in general.

The helper may also find his or her own view of human nature becoming more cynical or pessimistic. A therapist who had previously held an idealistic view of human nature, reflecting her training in humanistic psychology, experienced a painful shattering of her belief systems after working at the Institute for a year. In case conferences, she would often comment "I can't believe that people treat each other like this" and describe how distressing it was to encounter so much human cruelty. The discrepancy between her own positive schemas about human beings and the reality of the terrible abuses people perpetrate made this a particularly salient and painful issue for her. This diminished view of humanity may be associated with feelings of bitterness, cynicism, or pessimism. Therapists may experience a sense of anger at other people and the world in general as they reflect on the potential malevolence of others. This is a very painful experience as it involves a loss of youthful idealism. On an existential level, therapists may find themselves reflecting on the problem of human perversity and pondering the fate of the human race.

Intimacy

Trauma victims often experience a profound sense of alienation from other people and from the world in general. This experience is most often described in Vietnam veterans who found themselves at odds with a world to which they no longer feel connected (Lifton, 1973). Therapists who work with victims may experience a sense of alienation that results from exposure to horrific imagery and cruel realities. This alienation may be reinforced by other professionals who view the work they are doing with disdain or repulsion. Too often, therapists are asked "How can you listen to such terrible things day after day?" We met a rape crises counselor at a professional meeting; when asked what kind of work she did, she paused briefly, told us, then pulled in her breath and pulled back slightly, as if waiting for a shocked response. Indeed, she eventually explained with some relief, that was the type of response she ordinarily received. Just as the victim often feels stigmatized (Bard and Sangrey, 1985), so too may the therapist exposed to these horrors experience an uncomfortable sense of separateness from family, friends, or co-workers. This sense of separateness is compounded by the requirements for confidentiality in psychotherapy, which precludes one's ability to reveal the disturbing traumatic material. This, of course, stands in the way of a sense of connection with others, and, unchecked, may grow into a deep sense of alienation. Finally, other professionals may assume that the therapist chose this particular field of study because of his or her own unresolved conflicts. This too can contribute to a sense that one is stigmatized because of one's association with the field of traumatic stress.

Frame of Reference

The need to develop a meaningful frame of reference for experience is a fundamental human need (Epstein, 1989; Fromm, 1955; Lecky, 1945; Rogers, 1951; Snygg and Combs, 1949). This need is represented cognitively in part in schemas related to causality, or individuals' attribution about why events occur. Traumatized individuals often reflect repeatedly upon the question, "Why did this happen to me?" Similarly, therapists may try to understand why an individual experienced a traumatic event. This can become destructive if it takes the form of victim-blaming. For example, a client reported that her previous therapist of several years minimized the importance of her incest experience, focusing instead on why she had allowed the incest to continue into young adulthood. Therapists can commit another serious therapeutic error by focusing on the possible motives of the assailant or perpetrator. A woman whose former boyfriend tried to murder her reported that her therapist asked her many more questions about the boyfriend, his family, and his history, than about herself. This seems to reflect the therapist's rather than the client's need to assign causality. The client interpreted the therapist's behavior as the latter's unwillingness to hear her pain, and terminated therapy prematurely.

Another, perhaps more subtle, alteration in frame of reference schemas can also be quite distressing. If therapists' schemas are continuously challenged by clients' reports of traumatic experiences, they can experience an overall sense of disorientation. Without the opportunity to process their experiences, therapists, like clients, can respond to this with a pervasive and unsettling sense of uneasiness.

The Memory System

Therapists who listen to accounts of victimization may internalize the memories of their clients and may have their own memory systems altered temporarily or permanently. The following sections describe how the therapist's memory system may be affected by exposure to the traumatic memories of the clients. These alterations in memory may become intrusive or disruptive to the helper's psychological and interpersonal functioning.

Disruptions in Imagery

The imagery system of memory (Paivio, 1986) is most likely to be altered in vicarious traumatization. Like the trauma victim, therapists may experience their clients' traumatic imagery returning as fragments, without context or meaning. These fragments may take the form of flashbacks, dreams, or intrusive thoughts (Horowitz, 1976) and constitute what some believe to be the hallmark of PTSD (Brett and Ostroff, 1985). These images may be triggered by previously neutral stimuli that have become associated with the clients' traumatic memories. In the case of Ann, presented earlier, the therapist experienced a nightmare that replicated the rape of one of her clients. Another clinician reported the uncanny experience of having a "flashback" that replicated that of one of her clients. This therapist, who works with many Vietnam veterans, found herself staring at a young Vietnamese waitress while ordering food in a restaurant. She described the following experience: "I found myself experiencing a vivid image of hiding in a rice paddy, watching for the enemy. Suddenly, a young Vietnamese girl spotted me and I knew, with horror, that I would have to kill her." The therapist recalls experiencing this as her own memory because the image was so vivid and powerful. These examples suggest that the client's memories may become incorporated into the memory system of the therapist. The images can then be triggered by what previously was a neutral stimulus.

We also believe that the imagery that is most painful to therapists often centers around the schemas related to the therapist's salient need areas. That is, a therapist for whom safety is salient will likely recall those images that are associated with threat and personal vulnerability, while another, for whom esteem is more central, may focus in on images involving extreme degradation or cruelty at the hands of others. Likewise, the imagery that is recollected can produce a temporary state of disequilibrium as the schemas accommodate or change. Thus, what is recollected in the imagery systems of memory is colored by schemas, which are encoded in the verbal representation system of memory (Paivio, 1986). Likewise, the memories (both imagery and verbal components) produce changes in the schemas as the latter accommodate to new realities.

Disruption in the imagery system of memory is often associated with powerful affective states (Bower, 1981; Paivio, 1986). Therapists may report a variety of uncomfortable emotions resulting from their work with victims, including sadness, anxiety, or anger. These feeling states may be activated and within conscious awareness or they may be repressed and out of conscious awareness. Some therapists, particularly those who are unable to process their emotional reactions, may experience denial or emotional numbing. These latter reactions may occur when therapists are exposed to traumatic imagery that is too overwhelming, emotionally or cognitively, to integrate. These feelings may be too overwhelming because the therapist's own capacities for affect regulation or self-soothing are overtaxed or because the traumatic experiences are too discrepant with the therapist's own meaning systems or schemas.

In brief, therapists may experience alterations in their own imagery system of memory through their work with traumatized clients in which they re-experience or avoid various components of their client's traumatic memories. For the most part, alterations in one's memory system are probably transient in nature. However, we believe that these traumatic memories can become permanently incorporated into the therapist's memory system. This is likely to occur when the material is particularly salient to the therapist, relating closely to his or her psychological needs and life experience, and when the therapist does not have the opportunity to talk about his or her experiences of the traumatic material.

Summary

In the previous sections, we provided a theoretical conceptualization of the profound psychological impact of working with trauma victims, which we refer to as vicarious traumatization. Elsewhere we apply constructivist self-development theory to the conceptualization of unique human beings who experience trauma (McCann and Pearlman, 199b). Just as trauma alters its victims, therapists who work with victims may find themselves permanently altered by the experience. The unique effects on therapists can be more fully understood within this theoretical framework.

The Transformation of Vicarious Traumatization

In *Civilization and Its Discontents*, Freud (1961) expresses a dim view of human nature that reflects the painful awareness of the cruelty of the world and human beings:

> ...(people) are not gentle creatures who want to be loved, and who at most can defend themselves if they are attacked; they are, on the contrary,

creatures among whose instinctual endowments is to be reckoned a powerful share of aggressiveness. As a result, their neighbor is for them not only a potential helper or sexual object, but also someone who tempts them to satisfy their aggressiveness on him, to exploit his capacity to work without compensation, to use him sexually without his consent, to seize his possessions, to humiliate him, to cause him pain, to torture and to kill him. *Homo homini lupus* (Man is a wolf to man) (p. 58).

Is it inevitable that helpers who work with victims adopt this grim view of Freud's—a view that is both realistic and despairing? Is it possible to have a more optimistic view of humanity than Freud, without denying the harsh reality of violence and aggression? How can the helper be aware of and ameliorate these potential harmful effects, transforming images of horror and violence through his or her own healing process?

Therapists may experience painful images and emotions associated with their clients' traumatic memories and may, over time, incorporate these memories into their own memory system. As a result, therapists may find themselves experiencing PTSD symptoms, including intrusive thoughts or images and painful emotional reactions. The helper must be able to acknowledge, express, and work through these painful experiences in a supportive environment. This process is essential if therapists are to prevent or ameliorate some of the potentially damaging effects of their work. If these feelings are not openly acknowledged and resolved, there is the risk that the helper may begin to feel numb or emotionally distant, thus unable to maintain a warm, empathetic, and responsive stance with clients.

Helpers must understand how their own schemas are disrupted or altered through the course of this work and also shape the way they respond to clients. Our theory can be helpful in identifying the areas within the therapist where disturbances might exist. For example, therapists for whom safety schemas are salient or disturbed may find it very anxiety-provoking to work with crime, rape, or accident victims. This work can challenge their own beliefs in personal safety, resulting in a tuning out or avoidance of the client's memories. It is thus important for the helper to assess which of the seven need areas are particularly salient for him or her. This is important because the therapist's reactions to trauma survivors will be shaped by his or her own schemas.

It is important to tap into potential sources of support in one's professional network. The helper should first avoid professional isolation by having contact with other professionals who work with victims. These contacts can provide opportunities for emotional support for one's work in addition to the professional and intellectual support they offer. Professionals within a geographical area might organize support groups for helpers who work with victims. These support groups can be facilitated by experienced professionals who are sensitive to the personal effects of working with victims. Such groups can be focused around three major issues: normalizing the reactions helpers experience in the course of this work; applying constructivist self-development theory to understanding one's specific reactions; and providing a safe environment where helpers feel free to share and work through reactions that are painful or disruptive.

In our two-hour weekly case conference, we spend the first hours discussing and conceptualizing difficult victim cases (with client consent). In the second hour, we move into more personal discussions about what this means to us and how each of us respond to the painful experiences of victims. We refer to this as "feeling" time. As we have grown to trust each other and to allow ourselves to be vulnerable with one another, we have found this time together powerful and meaningful. At times, we have had to process not only our own individual reactions, but also the way in which particularly traumatic cases can affect the entire organization. At times, we struggle with two competing needs: the need to verbalize the traumatic imagery we are attempting to work through and the need to protect our colleagues from the stress of assimilating new traumatic material. The way we have attempted to resolve this is to talk openly about this dilemma and attempt to find a balance between the two needs. At times, we have had to tell each other that we cannot handle hearing details of a particular case because our own personal resources are at a low ebb or because we have particular difficulty assimilating certain types of traumatic material, such as serious violence against children. Fortunately, because the group is large enough, there is usually at least one other clinician who can listen and talk about any particular case. Providing a safe, supportive context for processing these issues is clearly essential to making this format positive and productive.

To this end, it is important that the group members avoid pathologizing the response of helpers. Just as PTSD is viewed as a normal reaction to an abnormal event, we view vicarious traumatization as a normal reaction to the stressful and sometimes traumatizing work with victims.

While there is no doubt that countertransference reactions that arise from the therapist's own psychic conflicts are also important, we do not presume that the therapist's own unresolved issues always underlie these reactions. On the other hand, therapists' own unresolved victimizations of early childhood experiences can contribute to the process of vicarious traumatization. These reactions should not be viewed necessarily as a sign of psychopathology, but rather as an area of potential growth for the helper. Over the course of this personal exploration, the helper may conclude that he or she needs to work through these more personal issues in his or her own therapy.

Finally, the theory states that individuals will experience and construe events according to their own needs and schemas. As therapists learn more about their own psychological needs, they will be able to process traumatic material more effectively and limit its impact upon their schemas.

In essence, the process of working through vicarious traumatization is parallel to the therapeutic process with victims. We do not offer a quick fix approach to psychological issues that will require continual awareness, monitoring, and processing for those who work with many victims. As the authors were finishing the final touches on this manuscript in an office at home, workers were in the house installing a burglar alarm system. We reflected on the irony of writing an article on this topic while this was happening, as the need for the alarm system was a direct result of disruptions in safety schemas in our work with many crime victims. That our lives have changed in permanent ways must be acknowledged, along with the inherent losses and pain associated with this process.

We have found it useful to share with each other coping strategies that help us ameliorate some of the potential hazards of this work. The coping strategies that have emerged from our weekly discussions include: striving for balance between our personal and professional lives; balancing a clinical caseload with other professional involvements such as research and teaching that can replenish us; balancing victim with nonvictim cases; being aware of and respecting our own personal boundaries, such as limiting evening or weekend work; developing realistic expecations of ourselves in doing this type of work; giving ourselves permission to experience fully any emotional reactions of which we are aware; finding ways to nurture and support ourselves; engaging in political work for social change; and seeking out nonvictim-related activities that provide hope and optimism. Furthermore, it has been important for us to be aware of our conflict areas or unresolved traumas that are reactivated by the therapeutic process.

In a recent article on how mental health professionals cope with working with difficult cases, Medeiros and Prochaska (1988) found evidence that the coping strategy "optimistic perseverance" is adaptive. We concur that maintaining optimism and hopefulness in the face of tragedy is an essential component to making our work with victims possible. To this end, we also try to acknowledge and confirm the many positive experiences in our work as well as the positive impacts this has had on ourselves and our lives. It is important to remind ourselves and others that this work has enriched our lives in countless ways. In our case conferences, we also share the many personal rewards that are inherent in this work. There is a tremendous sense of personal meaning that evolves from knowing that we are involved in an important social problem by making a contribution toward ameliorating some of the destructive impact of violence on human lives. For some of us, an outcome of our enhanced awareness of social and political conditions that lead to violence has been greater social activism. Other positive effects include a heightened sensitivity and enhanced empathy for the suffering of victims, resulting in a deeper sense of connection with others; increased feelings of self-esteem from helping trauma victims regain a sense of wholeness and meaning in their lives; a deep sense of hopefulness about the capacity of human beings to endure, overcome, and even transform their traumatic experiences; and a more realistic view of the world, through the integration of the dark sides of humanity with healing images. Although we may be sadder but wiser, it is important to acknowledge the many ways this important work has enriched our own lives as well as countless others.

References

Bard, M., and Sangrey, D. (1985). *The Crime Victim's Book* (second edition), Basic Books, New York.

Bermak, G.E. (1977). Do psychiatrists have special emotional problem? *Am. J. Psychoanal.* 37: 141–146.

Blank, A.S. (1984). *Psychological Treatment of War Veterans: A Challenge for Mental Health Professionals*, Paper presented at the ninety-second annual convention of the American Psychological Association, Toronto, August, 1984.

Blank, A.S. (1987). Irrational reactions to post-traumatic stress disorder and Vietnam veterans. In Sonnenberg, S.M. (ed.), *The Trauma of War: Stress and Recovery in Vietnam Veterans*, American Psychiatric Association Press, Washington, D.C.

Bower, G. (1981). Mood and memory. *Am. Psychologist* 36: 129–148.

Brett, E.A., and Ostroff, R. (1985). Imagery and post-traumatic stress disorder: An overview. *Am J. Psychiatry* 142: 417–424.

Chessick, R.D. (1978). The sad soul of the psychiatrist. *Bull. Menn. Clin.* 42: 1–9.

Danieli, Y. (1981). Therapists' difficulties in treating survivors of the Nazi Holocaust and their children. *Diss. Abstr. Int.* 42: 4947–B.

Danieli, Y. (1985). The treatment and prevention of long-term effects and intergenerational transmission of victimization: A lesson for Holocaust survivors and their families. In Figley, C.R. (ed.), *Trauma and Its Wake: The Study and Treatment of Post-Traumatic Stress Disorder*, New York, Brunner/Mazel, pp. 295–313.

Deutsch, C.J. (1984). Self-reported sources of stress among psychotherapists. *Prof. Psychol. Res. Pract.* 15: 833–845.

English, O.S. (1976). The emotional stress of psychotherapeutic practice. *J. Acad. Psychoanl.* 42(2): 191–201.

Epstein, S. (1989). The self-concept, the traumatic neurosis, and the structure of personality. In Ozer, D., Healy, J.M., Jr., and Stewart, A.J. (eds.), *Perspectives on Personality (Vol. 3)*, JAI Press, Greenwich, Conn.

Farber, B.A. (1985). The genesis, development, and implications of psychological-mindedness among psychotherapists. *Psychotherapy* 22: 170–177.

Farber, B.A., and Heifetz, L.J. (1982). The process and dimensions of burnout in psychotherapists. *Profess. Psychol.* 13: 293–301.

Figley, C.R. (1983). Catastrophes: An Overview of family reaction. In Figley, C.R., and McCubbin, H.I. (eds.), *Stress and Family: Coping with Catastrophe (Vol. 2)*, Brunner/Mazel, New York, pp. 3–20.

Figley, C.R. (ed). (1985). *Trauma and Its Wake: The Study and Treatment of Post Traumatic Stress Disorder*, Brunner/Mazel, New York.

Figley, C.R. (1988). Toward a field of traumatic stress. *J. Traum. Stress* 1: 3-16.

Freud, S. (1930/1961). In Strachey, J. (ed.), *Civilization and Its Discontents*, Norton, New York.

Ferudenberger, H., and Robbins, A. (1979). The hazards of being a psychoanalyst. *Psychoanal. Rev.* 66(2): 275–296.

Freyberg, J.T. (1980). Difficulties in separation-individuation as experienced by offspring of Nazi Holocaust survivors. *Am. J. Orthopsychiatry* 50: 87–95.

Fromm, E. (1955). *The Sane Society*, Rinehart, New York.

Guy, J.D. (1987). *The Personal Life of the Psychotherapist*, Wiley, New York.

Haley, S.A. (1974). When the patient reports atrocities: Specific treatment considerations in the Vietnam veteran. *Arch. Gen. Psychiat.*, 30: 191–196.

Herman, J.L. (1981). *Father-Daughter Incest*, Harvard University Press, Cambridge, Mass.

Horowitz, M.J. (1976) *Stress-Response Syndromes*, Jason Aronson, New York.

Janoff-Bulman, R. (1985). The aftermath of victimization: Rebuilding shattered assumptions. In Figley, C.R. (ed.), *Trauma and Its Wake: The Study and Treatment of Post-Traumatic Stress Disorder*, Brunner/Mazel, New York, pp. 15–35.

Jung, C.J. (1966). Psychology of the transference. *The Practice of Psychotherapy* (Vol. 16, Bollingen Series), Princeton University Press, Princeton, NJ.

Kehle, T.J., and Parsons, J.P. (1988). *Psychological and Social Characteristics of Children of Vietnam Combat Veterans*, Paper presented at the Annual Meeting of the National Association of School Psychologists, Chicago, April, 1988.

Lecky, P. (1945). *Self-Consistency, A Theory of Personality,* Island Press, New York.

Lifton, R.J. (1973). *Home from The War,* Simon and Schuster, New York.

Lindy, J.D. (1988). *Vietnam: A Casebook,* Brunner/Mazel, New York.

Mahoney, M.J. (1981). Psychotherapy and human change process. In Harvey, J. H., and Parks, M. M. (eds.), *Psychotherapy Research and Behavior Change,* Master lecture series, American Psychological Association, Washington, D.C., pp. 73–122.

Mahoney, M.J., and Lyddon, W.J. (1988). Recent developments in cognitive approaches to counseling and psychotherapy. *Counsel. Psychologist* 16(2): 190–234.

Margolin, Y. (1984). *What I Don't Know Can't Hurt Me: Therapist Reactions to Vietnam Veterans,* Paper presented at the ninety-second annual convention of the American Psychological Association, Toronto, August, 1984.

McCann, L., and Pearlman, L.A. (1990a). Constructivist self-development theory as a framework for assessing and treating victims of family violence. In Stith, S., Williams, M.B., and Rosen, K. (eds.), *Violence Hits Home,* Springer, New York, In press.

McCann, L., and Pearlman L.A. (1990b). *Through a Glass darkly: Understanding and Treating the Adult Trauma Survivor through Constructivist Self-Development Theory,* Brunner/Mazel, New York, In press.

McCann, L., Pearlman, L.A., Sakheim, D.K., and Abrahamson, D.J. (1988a). Assessment and treatment of the adult survivor of childhood sexual abuse within a schema framework. In Sgroi, S.M. (ed.), *Vulnerable Populations: Evaluation and Treatment of Sexually Abused Children and Adult Survivors, Vol. 1,* Lexington Books, Lexington, Mass., pp. 77–101.

McCann, L., Sakheim, D.K., and Abrahamson, D.J. (1988b). Trauma and victimization: A model of psychological adaptation. *Counsel. Psychologist* 16: 531–594.

Medeiros, M.E., and Prochaska, J.O. (1988). Coping strategies that psychotherapists use in working with stressful clients. *Prof. Psychol. Res. Pract.* 1: 112–114.

Mitchell, J.T. (1985). Healing the helper. In National Institute of Mental Health (ed.). *Role Stressors and Supports for Emergency Workers,* NIMH, Washington, D.C., pp. 105–118.

Paivio, A. (1986). *Mental Representations: A Dual Coding Approach,* Oxford University Press, New York.

Piaget, J. (1971). *Psychology and Epistemology: Toward a Theory of Knowledge*, Viking, New York.

Rogers, C.R. (1951). *Client-Centered Therapy*, Houghton Mifflin Co., New York.

Roth, S. (1989). *Coping with sexual trauma*, Manuscript submitted for publication.

Rotter, J.B. (1954). *Social Learning and Clinical Psychology*, Prentice-Hall, Englewood Cliffs, N.J.

Scurfield, R.M. (1985). Post-trauma stress assessment and treatment: Overview and formulations. In Figley, C.R. (ed.), *Trauma and Its Wake: The Study and Treatment of Post-Traumatic Stress Disorder*, Brunner/Mazel, New York, pp. 219–256.

Snygg, D., and Combs, A.W., (1949). *Individual Behavior*, Harper and Row, New York.

Taylor, S., and Brown, J.D. (1988). Illusions and well-being: A social-psychological perspective on mental health. *Psychological Bull.* 103: 193–210.

van der Kolk, B.A. (1987). *Psychological Trauma*, American Psychiatric Press, Inc., Washington, D.C.

18

Traumatic Stress on the Roads

Angela Hetherington

Post Traumatic Stress Disorder (PTSD) is potentially stimulated by any experience that exposes the individual's vulnerability and disturbs his or her confidence in the continuity of life. The current diagnostic criteria for PTSD are shown in Table 1 (American Psychiatric Association [APA], 1987).

The predominant features of PTSD are recurrent, vivid intrusive thoughts and images of the event, numbed feelings, increased arousal, and avoidance behavior that serves to prevent the recollection of the incident. For an individual to be diagnosed as suffering from PTSD, he must fulfill all five categories of the criteria as listed in Table 1 on the following page.

PTSD may result from prolonged exposure to small scale traumatic situations. This is commonplace in a police officer's work (Kroes, 1974; Singleton, 1977). Stratton (1983) identifies four distinct types of experiences known to initiate PTSD in a police officer; threat of death to self or close colleague; shooting incident; child murder or abuse; and visually aversive scene (traffic accident, air disaster or aftermath of mutilation).

For a police officer, the most stressful critical life event to be dealt with, is reported to be the death of a child (Sewell, 1981). The sight of a child crushed by a truck tire is inevitably deeply disturbing and is often faced repeatedly by a road traffic patrol officer. The experience of reporting an accident victim's death to their family and dealing with bereavement are also considered to be one of the more stressful aspects of police work (Perrier & Toner, 1986).

There has been little systematic research into severe stress reactions in police officer within the United Kingdom. The traumatic effects on police officers of constant exposure to 'small scale' trauma was first recognized in the Police Mobile Reserve Unit, who respond to emergency calls. The officers experienced 'unexpected reactions' in response to one, or an accumulation of traumatic situations (Smith, 1983). Current research into the everyday trauma of police work is largely exploratory in nature, documenting subjective reports (Newton, 1989). The current study seeks to establish, by the use of survey data, the incidence of traumatic stress in the every day work of road traffic patrol officers.

Table 1
Criteria for Post-Traumatic Stress Disorder

A. The individual has experienced an event that is outside the range of usual human experience and that world be markedly distressing to almost anyone.

B. The distressing event is persistently re- experienced in the form of intrusive, disturbing thoughts, images or dreams of the event. The individual may experience intense psychological distress on exposure to events symbolic of the traumatic experience/s. He/she may also experience sensations of the event recurring (flashbacks) and/or feelings of guilt associated with behavior at the time of the event.

C. Persistent avoidance of thoughts, feelings, activities or situations reminiscent of the event or numbing of responsiveness to others, and to activities. The individual may also experience an inability to feel warmth toward others, an inability to recall aspects of the event, and a sense of foreshortened future.

D. Persistent symptoms of increased arousal. This may take the form of physiologic reactivity at exposure to events that are reminiscent of an aspect of the event, difficulty concentrating or sleeping, irritability, hypervigilance or increased startle response.

E. Duration of the disturbance of at least one month. Symptoms may not be immediately evident but may be exhibited some time after the event. In this instance they would be classified as delayed.

Method

Subjects

Three hundred and six road traffic patrol officers from six police districts in the United Kingdom participated in the study. The officers had an average of seven years experience in road traffic patrol. No further demographic information was asked of the officer in order to assure anonymity.

Procedure

The study was of a survey nature, with self-completion questionnaires being distributed to six road traffic patrol units comprised of 612 officers.

Each questionnaire was accompanied by a cover letter and a freepost envelope addressed directly to the researcher to ensure confidentiality of response.

Instruments

The questionnaire was composed of the GHQ-12, a hardiness scale and a modified version of the Impact of Event Scale. This chapter discusses the results of the Impact of Event Scale which is a 15-item questionnaire designed to assess current subjective stress related to traumatic events (Horowitz, 1976). It is considered to be a reliable measure of post traumatic stress (McFarlane, 1989).

The scale is designed to be anchored to any particular life event and to tap the two most commonly reported specific categories of reactions to traumatic incidents: intrusion and avoidance. Intrusion and avoidance are the central defining characteristics of PTSD (APA, 1987) and remain at the core of research into traumatic stress (Zilberg, Weiss, & Horowitz, 1982).

The Impact of Event Scale used for this study was of an abbreviated form, omitting two questions (one from each subscale) which referred to only one event. This allowed for the assessment of cumulative stress. For this reason, the scores on this scale are not entirely comparable to that used in other studies (although the scores have been computed to accommodate for the missing items from each subscale). The questionnaire also invited officers to relate individual experiences of incidents which they had at the time, or afterwards, found to be traumatic.

Results

This report refers to three hundred and six officers in the British Police Force and as such the results cannot be considered to be necessarily representative of the entire workforce. Although a response rate of 50% compares favorably with other studies of this nature (Mitchell, 1990), it is possible that there might be a response bias inherent in the data collected. The study serves to illustrate the distressing nature of road traffic patrol work and the impact of traumatic incidents upon the road traffic patrol officer.

The mean score on the modified version of the Impact of Event Scale was 19.3 (SD 15.3, Cronbach's alpha .87), with a mean of 10.1 on the intrusion subscale (SD 6.9, Cronbach's alpha .71).

The recomputed scores on the impact of event (allowing for the missing questions) were 22.8 (SD 14.4) for total impact of event, 11.8 for intrusion (SD 8.2), and 11.1 for avoidance (SD 7.9). These scores are more directly comparable with those of other studies.

Comparison with other studies must be undertaken with caution given the difference in the nature of the trauma, the samples and the timing of data collection.

Table 2
Scores for Victims and Helpers in Traumatic Incidents

	Intrusion		Avoidance		Total	
	x	sd	x	sd	x	sd
Davidson & Baum (1986)						
Three Mile Island	10.4	9.2	8.5	8.7	18.9	17.0
McFarlane (1988)						
Ash Wednesday Bushfire	19.2	9.3	12.6	8.0	32.7	14.3
Creamer et al. (1989)	9.0	7.8	9.8	9.1	18.8	5.6
Queen St. Shootings	(1.5)*	(2.9)	(2.0)	(4.0)	(3.4)	(6.5)
Duckworth (1990)	23.47	17.45	40.9			
Hillsborough	(4.8)*	(4.4)	(9.2)			
Hetherington (1992)						
Occupational trauma	11.8	8.2	11.1	7.9	22.8	14.4

* Denotes contrast group of non-trauma victims selected in each case from the same population.

Studies using the IES are currently confined to disasters. For the purpose of comparison, Table 2 shows IES scores for victims of such trauma. Davidson and Baum (1986) report scores for residents experiencing the Three Mile Island Disaster, 5 years post-trauma. McFarlane (1988) assessed 45 firefighters involved in the Ash Wednesday bushfires, 8 months post-trauma. Creamer, Burgess, Buckingham, and Pattison (1989) used the IES with survivors of the Queen St. shootings, and also with a contrast group of subjects in a similar office block who had not been involved in the shootings. Duckworth (1990) gives scores for those police officers who sought counseling following the Hillsborough football stadium disaster.

Forty percent of officers related an event in their careers which they had found to have a disturbing effect upon them. These subjective accounts supported the quantitative data in their description of avoidance behavior and intrusive imagery. A typical sample of qualitative data follows, to illustrate the subjective nature of the impact of event.

The reality of the traumatic experiences is vividly described by a number of officers.

> ...air crash...four young children died. I didn't sleep for 3 days and was treated by a doctor with Valium for 2 weeks. Very distressed by needless loss of four such young lives.

> Attended an RTA (road traffic accident) where a six year old girl had been knocked over and split her head open and I had to hold her head together for some 15 minutes prior to the ambulance attending. It took me some 2 months to completely get over the incident.

The experiences the officers relate serve to illustrate the symptoms of avoidance and intrusion, characteristic of PTSD.

> Attended a fatal road traffic accident where a driver had lost control of his car whilst speeding and ran down a 15-year-old youth. The youth, when struck, hit his head face down on a 6" square, wooden post demolishing half his face. I dealt with the accident in a correct manner but the remainder of the week was quite harrowing. I had recurring nightmares for a week, constantly seeing the youth's face eventually waking up in a sweat. I avoided using that section of road for some time, finding an alternative route.

> I dealt with an accident involving a motor-cyclist about three years ago. There was a leg severed at the knee lying in the road. The body was some 100 yards away with the skull smashed. By the leg was a tiny piece of skin on the road surface. It had goose bumps and the hairs were raised. It reminded me of chicken skin and put me off that meat for some time. Pictures of the leg and skin flashed into my mind quite often.

Incidents involving a sense of helplessness often add to the impact of the event, particularly where children are involved. One officer describes such a scene:

> Two cars collided head-on. Two families each alive and conscious, but both were trapped in their cars. We couldn't get them out. The cars set alight and we watched the two families burn alive. You don't get over something like that.

Identification with the victim or family can also increase the officer's susceptibility to the impact of the event (Raphael, 1986). This reactions is also found in Accident and Emergency staff when similarities appear between the victim and the helper's own personal experience which make it more difficult for the individual to dissociate from the incident (Hetherington & Guppy, 1991). One officer describes such an experience:

> An eleven year old male pedal cyclist was run over and completely crushed, mutilated and killed by a large truck at a roundabout. The boy's mother arrived at the scene by chance, minutes afterwards, just as I arrived, and collapsed and became hysterical... I dealt with the accidents and on arriving home late (due to the accident), I burst out crying on seeing my own son and couldn't sleep that night. Every time I pass the scene I think about the accident, although I am no longer upset by it, as I was at the time, and had been for some weeks afterwards.

The natural consequence of such feelings is mostly accepted by officers, many of whom describe similar incidents, largely involving children, which have drawn them to tears. Accidents to children, universally render humor an ineffective means of reframing the distress. At such times, officers derive considerable support from family.

Table 3
Mean Scores of Air Crash Survivors on IES over 12 Months

Time in months scale	Initial	2	5	10	12
IES	30.3	14.3	11.6	13.6	13.7
Intrusion	16.0	9.1	6.6	6.1	7.5
Avoidance	14.0	4.3	4.8	7.2	4.7

...I later went home and burst into tears talking to my wife about it. My wife is my main release from stress in these situations. Once I have related the event to her, whatever it might be, I can then forget it.

Discussion

The mean scores for this group on the Impact of Event Scale (IES) seem relatively but not extremely high. Nevertheless, for a non-clinical population, there would seem to be a high incidence of avoidance behavior and intrusive thoughts pertaining to work-related events. This cannot be taken to be conclusive evidence of post traumatic stress disorder but reflects the potential psychological sequalae of handling traumatic incidents and the vulnerability of this occupational group to PTSD.

Horowitz's (1976) theory predicts that the alternating symptoms of intrusion and avoidance will diminish in magnitude over time in the normal stress response. If, however, the process is blocked, then the individual is vulnerable to post traumatic stress disorder.

The rapid and gradual decrease of scores on the IES over the first eight weeks following the traumatic experience is illustrated in a study of plane crash survivors (Sloane, 198). Table 3 shows the immediate high scores on intrusion and avoidance, and their subsequent decline.

This pattern of recovery has implications for the police, who may repeatedly experience traumatic incidents without always receiving adequate psychological support. The relatively high IES scores of the police officers may reflect their not having been able to completely process and recover from the traumatic events they encounter. If they have not fully recovered from the impact of a traumatic incident their vulnerability to subsequent trauma is increased (Dunning, 1990; Gersons, 1990).

In a similar vein, Kolb (1989) found that a re-arousal of symptoms could occur in those having experienced traumatic stress, as the result of further emotionally disturbing events such as a bereavement or threat of violence. He reports police officers and emergency service workers as being more likely to fall into this category. In the course of their work they will encounter emotionally disturbing events on a more frequent basis.

The organizational culture often encourages denial of the psychological impact of traumatic incidents, promoting the "John Wayne" stereotype (Reese & Goldstein, 1990; Silva, 1990). This organizational attitude to distress is changing. The increasing employment of debriefings and peer counseling strategies in police forces helps to legitimize stress, rendering it more readily acknowledgeable (Kristofferson, 1990; Mitchell & Bray, 1990).

Conclusions

The road traffic patrol officers of this sample relate occasions on which they have experienced severe traumatic stress reactions as a result of one particular incident, or an accumulation of incidents. The impact of these events is demonstrated by the officers' reports of intrusive thoughts and dreams relating to particular accidents, and the occasions on which they have employed avoidance behavior in an attempt to dispel the disturbing experience/s from memory.

Although many officers contend with trauma and tragedy and suffer no adverse effect, this should not detract from the need for an organizational response towards those who, for a combination of factors, find themselves vulnerable to 'unexpected reactions' (Hetherington, 1992). Providing automatic help and support for police officers in the event of an 'unexpected reaction' or 'critical incident' has proved of considerable value (Reese & Goldstein, 1986; Silva, 1990). This support may take the form of:

1. psychological debriefing. This is often the most effective means of mobilizing support between the group and providing psychological support (Hetherington, 1992; Kristofferson, 1990).
2. increasing the awareness of officers to the possible emotional reactions to attending serious accidents; times at which they might find themselves more vulnerable to such reactions; and effective means of coping (Dunning, 1990; Gersons, 1990).
3. training selected staff members (with appropriate aptitudes) in counseling skills, and formalizing peer support systems. This will also help to influence attitudes and norms within the force (Mitchell & Bray, 1990).
4. increasing responsibility and competency of supervisors for the emotional welfare of their staff, by providing training in the identification and management of traumatic reactions (Googins & Kurtz, 1981; Peters-Bean, 1990).

Such strategies, undertaken by the employing organization, might serve to reduce the unnecessary strain and anguish of those officers who, together with the stresses of their own life events, also contend with the horrors and tragedies of our own.

References

American Psychiatric Association. (1987). *Diagnostic and statistical manual of mental disorders.* (3rd. ed., Rev.), Washington, DC: Author.

Creamer, M., Burgess, P., Buckingham, W., & Pattison, P. (1989). *The psychological aftermath of the Queen Street shootings.* Parkville, Victoria, Australia: University of Melbourne.

Davidson, L.M., & Baum, A. (1986). Chronic stress & post-traumatic stress disorders. *Journal of Clinical & Consulting Psychology.* 54(3), 303–308.

Duckworth, D.H. (1990). *The nature and effects of incidents which induce trauma in police officers.* Publication of the Research and Scientific Unit, The Home Office, London, UK.

Dunning, C. (1990). Mitigating the impact of work trauma: Administrative issues concerning intervention. In J.T. Reese, J.M. Horn, & C. Dunning (Eds.), *Critical incidents in policing.* Washington, DC: Federal Bureau of Investigation.

Dyregrov, A. (1989). Caring for helpers in disaster situations: Psychological debriefing. *Disaster Management, 2,* 25–30.

Gersons, B.P.R. (1190). *PTSD & the police scope of the issue.* Paper presented at the Second European Conference on Traumatic Stress, Utrecht, Netherlands.

Googins, B., & Kurtz, N.R. (1981). Discriminating participating and non-participating supervisors in occupational alcoholism programmes. *Journal of Drug Issues, 11,* 29–38.

Hetherington, A. (1192). *Human resource management in times of stress.* Publication of the Research & Scientific Unit, The Home Office, London, UK.

Hetherington, A., & Guppy, A. (1991). *Traumatic stress in accident and emergency personnel.* Paper presented at the Fifth European Congress of the Psychology of Work and Organization, Rouen, France.

Horowitz, M.J. (1976). *Stress response syndromes.* New York, NY: Jason Aronson.

Kristofferson, J.I. (1990) *Psychological debriefing with police officers.* Paper presented at the Second European Conference on Traumatic Stress, Utrecht, Netherlands.

Kolb, L.C. (1989). Chronic post-traumatic stress disorder. *Psychological Medicine, 19,* 821–824.

Kroes, W.H. (1976) *An analysis of job stress in society's victim — The policeman.* Springfield: Charles Thomas.

McFarlane, A.C. (1989). The treatment of post-traumatic stress disorder. *British Journal of Medial Psychology,* 62, 81–90.

Mitchell, J.T., & Bray, G.P. (1990). *Emergency service stress.* Englewood Cliffs, NJ: Prentice-Hall.

Mitchell, M. (1990). *Symptoms experienced by police officers after body handling at the site of the Lockerbie air disaster.* Paper presented at the British Psychological Conference, London, UK,

Newton, R. (1989). *The incidents of stress reactions in individual operational police officers to line of duty crisis.* Home Office report, Scientific Research and Development Branch, The Home Office, London, UK.

Perrier, D., & Toner, R. (1984). Police stress: the hidden foe. *Canadian Police College Journal,* 8(1), 17–24.

Peters-Bean, K. (1990). *Recent developments in occupation health and welfare.* Paper presented at the Second European Congress on Traumatic Stress, Utrecht, Netherlands.

Raphael, B. (1986). *When disaster strikes.* London: Hutchinson.

Reese, J.T. & Goldstein, H.A. (1986). *Psychological services for law enforcement.* Washington, DC: U.S. Government Printing Office.

Sewell, J.D. (1981, September). Police stress. *FBI law enforcement bulletin,* Washington, DC.

Silva, M.N. (1990). Delivery of mental health services to law enforcement officers. In J.T. Reese, J.M. Horn, & C. Dunning (Eds.). *Critical incidents in policing.* Washington, DC: Federal Bureau of Investigation.

Singleton, G.W. (1977). *Effects of job related stress on the physical and psychological adjustment of police officers.* Doctoral dissertation, Wayne State University, Detroit, MI.

Sloane, P. (1988). Post-traumatic stress in survivors of an airplane cash-landing: A clinical and exploratory research intervention. Journal of Traumatic Stress, 1(2), 211–229.

Smith, B.M. (1983). *The effects of stress on police employees.* Unpublished report, Leicestershire constabulary, UK.

Stratton, J.G. (1983). Traumatic incidents and the police. *Police Stress,* 6, 12–18.

Zilberg, N.J., Weiss, D.S., & Horowitz, M.J. (1982). Impact of event scale: A cross validation study and some empirical evidence supporting a conceptual model of stress response syndromes. Journal of Consulting and Clinical Psychology, *50(3), 407–414.*

19

The Stress of Homicide Investigations

James D. Sewell

Over the last several years, law enforcement administrators and academicians have shown a major interest in the phenomenon known as police stress. It is now apparent that the manifestations and effects of police stress can be dangerous to individual law enforcement officers, their families, their departments, and the communities they serve. As part of the effort to combat this critical problem, a number of researchers, including Kroes, Margolis, and Hurrell (1974) and Sewell (1983), have identified sources of stress within the field of law enforcement. On the basis of such general studies, Sandy and Devine (1978), Scott (1979), and Sewell (1984) have focused on those problems experienced within unique or specialized police roles.

The latter inquiries offer a beginning point for discussing the stress that affects investigative personnel and, in particular, specific types of investigators whose unique stressors vary with the scope, intensity, and type of their assignment. From such analysis and understanding can come more effective programs of training and stress management tailored to the needs of specific segments of the law enforcement workforce.

Stress and the Homicide Investigator

Although homicide investigators experience many of the stressors already described in the literature on law enforcement and investigator stress, there are several stressors unique to their specific job responsibilities. However, current research in this area is limited (Sewell, Ellison & Hurrell, 1988). Consequently, descriptive analyses drawn from the working world of police officers can offer a point of departure for further quantitative research and, ultimately, effective stress management and mitigation. The particular stressors described in this section were identified in discussions with seasoned investigators at training sessions and professional conferences or are taken from the author's experiences as an investigator and administrator.

Responsibility of the Job: The "Awesome Burden"

Citizens and detectives alike have ranked murder as the most important crime (Rossi, Waite, Bose, & Berk, 1974; Sanders, 1977). In line with such findings, a seasoned homicide investigator once remarked, "You can't restore life, but you can right the wrong. It is an awesome burden... life is the most precious right given by God." The public's acknowledgment of the seriousness of murder reinforces the importance of the investigator's role and the need to bring a case to a successful conclusion. Many detectives feel a personal commitment to solve such cases; to not disappoint the victim's family; and, ultimately, to protect society. After a year of observation with a homicide unit, Simon (1991) spoke for these investigators:

> In a police department of about three thousand sworn souls, you are one of thirty-six investigators entrusted with the pursuit of that most extraordinary of crimes: the theft of a human life. You speak for the dead. You avenge those lost to the world. Your paycheck may come from fiscal services but, goddammit, after six beers you can pretty much convince yourself that you work for the Lord himself. If you are not as good as you should be, you'll be gone within a year or two, transferred to fugitive, or auto theft or check and fraud at the other end of the hall. If you are good enough, you will never do anything else as a cop that matters this much. Homicide is the major leagues, the center ring, the show. It always has been. When Cain threw a cap into Abel, you don't think the Big Guy told a couple of fresh uniforms to go down and work up the prosecution report. Hell no, he sent for a fucking detective. And it will always be that way, because the homicide unit of any urban police force has for generations been the natural habitat of that rarefied species, the thinking cop. (p. 17)

Reality of Violent Death

Dealing with violent death becomes a way of life for homicide investigators. These detectives regularly experience the violence and inhumanity perpetrated by one individual against another. For many persons, violent crime is news or entertainment; for the homicide investigator, it is reality, with the incumbent sights, sounds, smells, and survivors. This constant exposure to death and reflection on the tenuousness of life increase the "normal" stress associated with the law enforcement profession. Stroud (1987) has identified some of these feelings:

> It's an oddity of life that most people who fantasize about working on a big-city homicide squad, or who pretend to do it for CBS or NBC, don't seem to realize that at the heart of every homicide investigation is a dead body, and the essence of the job is to be able to confront that body in all

its grim carnality, its stolid and perfect distance, and its sensory intimacy. You walk up to the thing and you step in its blood and juices, you smell it and you feel it, and your job is to get down onto the ground with it and slip underneath the skin and inhabit the skull and make its last seconds live and live again. Every cop maintains that detachment is the key, but the truth is that he gives up a section of his soul to every corpse and he dies a little death at the beginning of every case. If he were truly detached he could never see what has to be seen. The key to the thing is intimacy without emotion. Even the ones who have that quality never keep it for long. A few years on the job, and you're either out of homicide or well into the process of freezing solid forever. For cops, homicide work is the top of the ladder. You become a boss and drive a desk, you go to the FBI or Drug Enforcement or the Department of Investigation. Now and then you kill a glass of Johnnie Walker Black with a .357 chaser and your widow has to call in a workman to get your brains off the wood paneling. (p. 20)

Constant Pressure

With the investigation of a violent death comes a pressure to provide for its speedy solution. Such pressure is twofold. First, especially in high-profile cases, the departmental administration, citizenry, and media all call for a quick resolution of the case. Second, from an internal perspective, the investigator is interested in solving the case to resolve this affront; protect the community; and, to a lesser degree, eliminate a case from the open files.

This pressure for solution is accompanied by the additional pressure to be continually available to respond. Homicide detectives live, as do many other specialists, with constant communications access by their department—via pager, telephone, radio, and, increasingly, mobile telephone. The beeper one is wearing serves as a reminder for the investigator and his or her family that it is difficult to escape the inevitable call to duty, that the department has higher priority than one's personal life. Consequently, there is little or no down time for the investigator to cope effectively with stress.

Impact of Time

Law enforcement training has always suggested that the first 48 hours are the most critical to the successful conclusion of a homicide investigation. The attempt to pursue as many leads as possible within this time period places significant pressure on the officer. Such time constraints demand that the lead detective coordinate multiple investigative and forensic activities, maintain complete communication between all involved police personnel, ensure that adequate reports are written, and communicate with both the media and the victim's family.

From a different perspective, the lengthy nature of many homicide investigations generates another type of stressor. Patrol officers often race from call to call, gaining immediate gratification from incidents handled successfully. For the homicide investigator, gratification is slow in coming; many cases are not quickly resolved, and court proceedings, especially if appeals are involved, can add years to the investigation of a case, which, although it deals with death, often feels as if it has a life of its own.

Dealing with Significant Others

It is often difficult to deal with the survivors of a homicide victim. Especially when the crime is stranger-on-stranger with no logical motive, the next of kin is often distraught, angry, and frustrated and lacks understanding of the crime and the criminal justice process. Despite having little training in death notification and the impact of the grief process, the detective must face the stress of dealing with the emotional elements of the situation. Concurrently, there is often a role conflict between the need for sensitivity in dealing with the victim's significant others and the emotional hardening required for the investigator's own mental self-preservation. This relationship becomes even more complicated when, as frequently occurs, a significant other is the identified offender or primary suspect in the homicide. Especially when evidence against such a person is limited or inconclusive, the investigator must balance what is known with what is felt and continue to maintain an appropriate and professional, albeit strained and strange, relationship with this individual.

Interagency Rivalry

Interagency rivalries may surface during an investigation, particularly when several jurisdictions share the site of a murder. These may arise from long-term political issues; from one agency's sense that it more professional or better respected than another; from a snobbery fostered by differences in experience, education, or training; or from the desire not to share the "glory" of a major homicide investigation.

Regardless of the motivation, the impact of interagency rivalry is virtually always negative. As classically illustrated in the Manson murders (Bugliosi & Gentry, 1974), such rivalry may effectively eliminate communication between agencies, engender harmful feelings and jealousy, and reduce the cooperation and communication necessary to solve cases expeditiously. It is a sad commentary that, although the investigative staffs of agencies may work well together, it is often at the administrative and managerial levels that such disputes and conflicts are fostered.

Judicial System Support

Becasue of continued prosecutorial caseload, overburdened court dockets, and the time necessary to prepare and present adequate homicide cases, prosecutors may, in the perception of a detective, appear reluctant to file information unless evidence beyond probable cause exists. The investigator may feel that the proof the prosecutor requires even to file an indictment is to the exclusion of not every reasonable doubt, but *any possible* doubt.

In addition, the judicial system encourages plea bargaining as a means to expedite the legal process, which often serves to frustrate the investigator. Too often, it appears that the victim is forgotten and the ultimate goal of justice is sacrificed to ensure system efficiency and judicial/political expediency.

The length of time required to ensure justice can also be a stressor. Although corrections theory may assume that, to be effective, punishment must be swift, sure, and certain, the trial stage actually may be delayed for months, and the appellate process can add years to the process. An example from the author's own experience is a multiple murderer who was arrested within 6 weeks of his crime. His criminal trial did not occur until nearly 18 months after his indictment, and the appellate process, including multiple hearings through the system to the U.S. Supreme Court, took 9 years before he was finally executed for his crimes. For the homicide investigator, delay in the application of his or her concept of justice perpetuates further frustration with the judicial system and fosters the perception that the judicial system fails to support its primary mission.

Human Service System Support

The failure of social support services, such as juvenile, probation, and mental health agencies, is a common source of stress for law enforcement officers. For homicide investigators, this is particularly true when they perceive that the law enforcement response was adequate and appropriate and support systems were inadequate, unresponsive, or unavailable. As an example from the author's experience, a 21-year-old man was taken into custody under Florida's mental health act, but he was released by a psychiatrist after less than 12 hours. Two days later, he killed and burned his grandmother. When dealing with the stress of such investigations, it is difficult for the homicide investigator not to blame the other components of social services.

Frustration and Anger

Problems also arise in communities where there is a high or increasing number of homicides. Although a detective may still feel a personal commitment to solve a case, the sheer number of cases in an investigator's caseload may limit the scope and length of an investigation and preclude the time necessary for sustained follow-through, particularly in whodunits. This frustration increases in situations in which the investigator knows who committed the crime but lacks sufficient proof, time, or resources to bring charges or, more particularly, to sustain a conviction.

The constant exposure to violence frequently reinforces the frustration an investigator feels that stems from deeply held feelings that society is lawless beyond control, communities are too insensitive to sights of violence, and little effective rehabilitation or punishment exists. With the reported increases in violent juvenile behavior and with their awareness of children as victims and offenders, many investigators may perceive little hope in the juvenile justice system and view too many children as lacking a conscience.

The very emotion resulting from stress can simmer and cause further stress. Frustration, especially that resulting from failures in other parts of the system or a belief that non-drug-related homicide investigation is underfunded and undersupported, often materializes in anger and hostility directed against superiors, suspect, the system, and even the uninvolved, such as an investigator's spouse, significant other, or family. Simon (1991) observed a gripe session held by a group of seasoned homicide detectives:

> Suddenly no one in the room was typing or collating anymore as voices competed with one another in a recitation of long-standing grievances. They complained about the equipment, about cars without radios and about a major urban department that still doesn't provide a polygraph examiner suitable for criminal investigations, requiring detectives to use the state police facilities. They complained about the cutbacks in overtime, about the department's reluctance to pay for pretrial preparation so that good cases wouldn't come unglued in the months between arrest and trial. They complained about the lack of money to pay informants. They complained about the inability of the trace and ballistics labs to keep up with the violence, about how the state attorney's office no longer charged anyone with perjury when they lied to a grand jury, about how too many prosecutors allowed witnesses to back up on their grand jury testimony. They complained about the growing number of drug-related murders, about how the days of the domestic dunker and 90-plus clearance rates were long gone. They complained that the phone didn't ring the way it used to after a murder, that fewer people were willing to drop a dime and risk becoming a witness to an act of violence. (pp. 191-192)

Fatigue

The reality of homicide investigation is that it is tiring. The physical and mental demands placed on homicide investigators, closely tied to time demands and the overall pressure to solve such cases, can cause serious fatigue in assigned personnel. Such fatigue often manifests itself in case errors, shortcuts, difficulty in working relationships, and severe domestic problems.

In *Balefire*, the fictionalized account of a terrorist multiple murderer, Goddard (1983), a forensic scientist in real life, captures the sense of such fatigue in his protagonist's perceptions of his officers:

> After working on the investigation without rest for slightly more than twenty hours—which included a grueling nine-hour autopsy session—the detectives and lab team were out on their feet. They weren't stumbling or dozing or exhibiting any of the other external body signals most often associated with fatigue. Those symptoms wouldn't begin to show up among the investigators for another four to six hours. Andersen had simply realized his detectives were no longer alert to the subtle but critical bits of investigative information being continuously gathered for evaluation.
>
> The deterioration was mental rather than physical, and the warning signals were not all that apparent. One of the first involved a seemingly casual response made by a witness, which Andersen discovered when he made a routine playback of an interrogation tape. The comment wasn't significant by itself, but the detective asking the questions should have followed up immediately with a couple of sweep questions to see if there was anything else in the background worth discussing. He hadn't, so Andersen sent him back into the field to recontact the witness in the faint hope that the individual would still be cooperative. He wasn't.
>
> There were other similar incidents, each by itself was relatively insignificant, but they formed a growing pattern of sloppiness that would eventually result in the loss of significant information. The unspoken worry on Andersen's part was that the diminished awareness of his investigators would result in another officer's death if they ran across another suspect involved in the shooting. (pp. 88-89).

Traumatic Stress of Multiple Murder Investigations

For homicide investigators, as well as other police officers, America's growing violence has brought additional stress. As the phenomenon of serial, spree, and mass murders has been increasingly publicized in the United States in the last few decades, the investigation of such crimes has been accompanied by significant stress on responding law enforcement personnel. The violence and dehumanization associated with these crimes often exceed the preparation given the typical responding law enforcement officer or even that of a well-prepared and experienced homicide investigator. Such visual and emotional stress is magnified by what can be divided into organizational and event stressors (Sewell, 1993). Organizational stressors include administrative pressure to solve the crime and yet to carry on with business as usual, the work environment of such crimes, and conflicts within an officer's role and responsibility. Event stressors include the traumatic stimuli of the incident itself; personal loss or injury; the impact of mission failure, including an inability to bring closure to the crime; and human error.

Dealing with the Stress of Homicide Investigations

Short-Term Responses

Once the sources of stress have been established, two key questions remain: How are homicide investigators currently handling stress? How can we improve their ability to manage the stress of each particular law enforcement assignment?

As a framework for understanding investigators' short-term responses to stress, it is appropriate to review the work of researchers who have identified the strategies used by other crisis workers to cope successfully with both day-to-day stress and death and dying. Taylor (1989), for instance, has documented some general community and individual responses that allow for successful recovery after disaster. Palmer (1983) has reviewed the strategies commonly used by paramedics in coping with death. These include desensitization processes that are a part of paramedic training, the use of humor and dark comedy as an escape valve, reliance on technical jargon and a special working language as a coping mechanism, the ability to fragment scientifically and escape into paramedical work, and rationalization of the importance of both the emergency medical function and the condition of the patient (i.e., the fact that the patient could not have been saved regardless of their efforts) at the time of response (Palmer, 1983).

Police officers, particularly homicide investigators, classically adopt similar methods of coping with stress. Beginning with the initial training at the academy, the profession emphasizes the need to distance oneself from an emotional response. Graphic slides, videotapes, and war stories are used to desensitize the novice, to force him or her to acquire the beginning of a protective shell. These underpinnings are reinforced by the treatment of new officers at their first violent scenes, in which seasoned personnel verbally reward the less emotional and punish those who display a less than professional demeanor. As one rookie detective discovered,

> The male detectives were not very sympathetic to the rookie's plight. After joining the squad, Carolann had to pay a second visit to the morgue with

one of her colleagues. The male detective could not resist a bit of ghoul-ish hazing. Slipping his hand into a rubber glove, he peeled back the sheet from a murder victim who had been shot so many times that he looked like Swiss cheese. "Hmmmmm," said the detective, gingerly poking his fingers into each of the bullet holes, "guess the shots came from this angle."...Carolann headed straight for the door: (Hirschfield, 1982, p. 33)

Detectives add a particular dimension to the techniques used by their medical colleagues: image. The aura of the homicide detective conveys a message of professionalism, competence, and self-control. Again, Hirschfield (1982) has captured the mixed feelings underlying this out-ward composure:

> Detectives usually don't wear their emotions on their sleeves. Baring one's innermost feelings while on the job is considered unprofessional conduct, a sign of weakness in the eyes of one's peers, and most detectives have mastered the art of maintaining that no-nonsense, thick skinned veneer. But sometimes it's really no more than an act. For deep inside, under those tough exteriors, there are some things—the murder of a child, the rape of a young girl, the beating of an elderly widow—that do get to them. Touch them. Leave them feeling whipped...There are even a few things that make them want to cry. (p. 49)

During homicide investigations, dark comedy further allows an officer to develop distance from his or her emotions. As a former police reporter explained through a character in a fictionalized account of law enforce-ment.

> That's why the uniforms...make bad jokes. You have to when things like this become such a damn routine in your life. I mean, if you start thinking about the lives of all these lonely people here in New York— like if you start trying to figure out each time exactly what crazy thing it was that drove them into a closet, for God's sake—then you're going to go nuts yourself pretty quick.
>
> Those guys back there are waiting for the morgue unit now and they're probably making more jokes. Let me tell you, it's scary thing walking into some place where you know you're there to look for the dead body. So can you blame those guys? You have to whistle in a graveyard, you know? (Adcock, 1984, p. 121)

The uniqueness of the police vocabulary and its use as a method of communication and shorthand within the law enforcement culture are well documented.[1] Such vocabulary is also used by investigators dealing

---

1. Manning (1977, 1980, 1992), Martin (1973), Van Maanen (1978), and Lombardi (1991) provide extensive discussion of the unique vocabulary of law enforcement and the critical role interpersonal communication plays in the police organizational environment.

with murder. Bodies are depersonalized as "stiffs," "signal 5's," and "DBs." Individuals are not necessarily killed; they are "wasted," "capped," "smoked," "done," or "blown away." These alternative terms allow a controlled verbal and mental response to the reality of death and violence.

As previously indicated, homicide investigators believe in the importance of their mission within the scope of the criminal justice system, a trait they share with paramedics. This belief in their role is a critical factor in allowing individual investigators to assert their professionalism and maintain an emotional distance between victims and themselves. However, although the "intimacy without emotion" (Stroud, 1987) necessitated by their unique function may produce a short-tem ability to manage cases, it may result in a long-term difficulty in managing life. Other strategies, then, must be included in a comprehensive stress management approach.

Long-Term Strategies

Any effective long-term strategy of stress management begins with the administrators' recognition that they have the responsibility to care for the mental and physical well-being of their officers.[2] With this recognition comes a willingness to accept responsibility and make a commitment to deal actively with the issue of police stress by structure and budget. Such a commitment is manifested in the maintenance of an appropriate organizational climate, development and implementation of support programs, and training.

Organizational climate. Organizational climate rests on institutional practices that encourage communication, recognize individual as well as organizational needs, and emphasize individual stress management. Such organizational practices include (a) effective supervision; (b) fair, consistent, and enlightened personnel practices; (c) provision of appropriate equipment and investigative resources; and (d) a supportive organizational environment.

Support programs. Organizational support can take many forms. First, the use of critical-incident stress debriefing is an appropriate intervention strategy to deal effectively with the trauma many scenes may produce.[3] Although it must be recognized that violence and traumatic crime scenes are simply part of a homicide investigator's job, it also must be acknowl-

---

2. Both Sewell (1986) and Ayres (1990) have discussed organizational practices that support the proper management of law enforcement stress. Other institutional programs have been detailed by Reese and Goldstein (1986) and Walima and Kirschman (1988).

3. Explanations of the debriefing process have been provided by Mitchell (1985); Walker (1990); Kirshcman (1992); and Reese, Horn, and Dunning (1990).

edged that there are effective ways to deal with the emotions caused by these scenes and to prevent the development of a permanent, impenetrable shell. The institutionalization of a mandatory debriefing program eliminates any stigma associated with the need for assistance, while assuring a regular, formalized process of emotional ventilation and group support. Debriefings can also be expanded to include investigators, responding uniformed personnel, supervisory personnel, medical examiners, crime scene technicians, and prosecutors, allowing for not only successful stress management, but also nonjudgmental analysis and critique of the handling of the case and elimination of some of the issues causing interagency rivalry and breakdowns in communication.

As effective as critical-incident stress debriefings may be, their use after each homicide or violent crime scene is both impractical and potentially disruptive to the mission of an agency. Periodically scheduled debriefing sessions, however, may allow an agency to deal more effectively with the compilation of routine stressful incidents that cause long-term emotional and physical damage. Furthermore, these sessions allow for a structured outlet that can reduce the build-up of frustration, anger, and the sense of impotence that can accompany law enforcement and investigative efforts. The feedback from such sessions may be used to correct some of the human support and judicial system support problems perceived by investigators.

Other support resources, including psychologist and grief counselors, are appropriate for investigative personnel and their families. To be most successful, mental health professionals must understand the work of homicide investigators, be familiar enough with the department to not be considered outsiders, and be effective in trauma debriefing.

As in other organizations, administrators in law enforcement agencies tend to find the proper job fit for an employee, and, absent promotion, requested transfer, or disciplinary problems, allow that person to remain in that position for as long as possible. Such a practice allows an agency to maximize the use of the skills an employee acquires on the job and to continually benefit from the application of job experience, and it provides the employee with job security. However, there can be detriments to the individual. Without proper stress management practices, the accumulation of stressors associated with long-term exposure to violence and death can exacerbate the emotional and physiological damages normally associated with police stress.

One solution to this type of job burnout is regular job rotation. Upon establishment of an average maximum desired stay in "homicide," investigators could be routinely rotated to other less stressful assignments; investigators who are exhibiting negative manifestations of stress would be moved more quickly. Such rotation would not only minimize the negative effects of overexposure to death/violence investigations, but also expand the departmentwide expertise available for the investigation of such crimes.

Another rotational alternative in larger departments would be to move homicide investigators from the active-duty roster, with its constant call demands, to a cold-case squad working on whodunits. From there, they could rotate to administrative duties or specialized task forces before returning to the active-duty roster. Such a practice would allow highly trained investigators to continue to use their skills with less danger of burnout.

Training. One of the most critical elements in a long-term strategy is effective, ongoing training. This training must focus on the investigators, allowing them to understand, before the fact, the assault that violent crime scenes make on their senses; on the normalcy of feeling emotional reactions to scenes; and on specific techniques that reduce, mitigate, or control the stress associated with homicide investigation. In addition, training can help the investigator to handle the grief experienced by victims' families more effectively.

Such training should emphasize the individual investigator's responsibility for his or her own stress management. In addition to the standard discussions about diet, nutrition, and physical fitness, attention should be devoted to the need to keep a balance in one's life; to understand one's physical, mental, and emotional limits; and to use emotional outlets outside of the profession. It should be pointed out that many officers, including homicide investigators, are now taking great pride in maintaining their health and physical well-being through diet, exercise, and changes in life-style. For many law enforcement professionals, it is no longer glamorous to smoke incessantly, drink excessively, and fail to exercise.

Parallel training for the significant others of homicide investigators is equally critical. Too often, agencies fail to recognize the impact of professional stress on an officer's personal life, and stress on the job is magnified by problems that an investigator is dealing with in his or her home, family, and social life.

At the same time, the training of other managers and supervisors cannot be overlooked. Such administrative personnel must understand not only their role in mitigating stress, but also their practices that often cause it. It is important that they learn to recognize symptoms and develop methods to assist their personnel in coping with the stress brought on by this highly necessary, but potentially emotionally damaging, job.

Research Implications

The need for further research on stress in the law enforcement field has been documented by Terry (1981), Dantzer (1987), and Sewell et al. (1988). As these researchers have emphasized, anecdotal and qualitative analyses of sources and symptoms of stress need to be verified; the impact of suggested stress management practices need to be assessed; and the relationships among institutional, organizational, and individual stress and effective law enforcement activities need to be determined.

Such research should also be conducted for subgroups, including homicide investigators, in the law enforcement field. This article has identified both sources of and potential solutions for the stress experienced by police officers who investigate violent death. The first item in a research agenda would be to assess quantitatively the impact of stress-causing and stress-reducing practices on position incumbents.

At the same time, officers charged with the investigation of a variety of crimes share many stressors, especially those whose work continually exposes them to the violence one person can commit against another. Future analysis may identify the similarities and differences in the occupational stress experienced by child abuse, rape, and robbery detectives, as well as the crime scene personnel who support them.

A second issue goes beyond specific practices to the nature of the police role. In a society characterized by violence and a structured system of criminal justice, specific individuals will always be required to deal with violence and its aftermath. The job of homicide investigator carries with inherent stress and significant emotional and physical demands, few of which can be effectively and permanently eliminated. The research issue, then, is the identification of the most effective methods to support those individuals who face major ongoing stress and, ultimately, the translation of such research into effective agency policy.

References

Adcock, T.L. (1984). *Precinct 19*. Garden City, New York: Doubleday.

Ayres, R.M. (1990). *Preventing law enforcement stress: The organization's role*. Alexandria, VA: National Sheriff's Association.

Bugliosi, V., & Gentry, C. (1974). *Helter skelter*. New York: Bantam Books.

Center for Mental Health Studies of Emergencies. (1985). *Role stressors and supports for emergency workers*. Rockville, MD: National Institute of Mental Health.

Dantzer, M.L. (1987). Police-related stress: A critique for future research. *Journal of Police and Criminal Psychology, 3*(3), 43-48.

Geberth, V.J. (1992). Secondary victims of homicide. *Law and Order, 40*(9), 91-96.

Goddard, K. (1983). *Balefire*. New York: Bantam Books.

Hartsough, D.M., & Myers, D.G. (1985). *Disaster work and mental health: Prevention and control of stress among workers*. Rockville, MD: National Institute of Mental Health.

Hirschfield, N. (1982). *Homicide cop: The true story of Carolann Natale*. New York: Berkley Books.

Kirschman, E.F. (1992). Critical incident stress. *Law Enforcement Technology, 19*(3), 22-27.

Kroes, W.H., Margolis, B.L., & Hurrell, J.J. (1974). Job stress in policemen. *Journal of Police Science and Administration, 2,* 145-155.

Lawson, B.Z. (1987). Work-related post-traumatic stress reactions: The hidden dimensions. *Health and Social Work, 12,* 250-258.

Lombardi, J.H. (1991). Street language. *Minnesota Police Chief, 11*(2), 47-51.

Malloy, T.E., & Mays, L.G. (1984). The police stress hypothesis. *Criminal Justice and Behavior, 11,* 197-224.

Manning, P.K. (1977). *Police work: The social organization of policing.* Cambridge, MA: MIT Press.

Manning, P.K. (1992). *The narcs' game.* Cambridge, MA: MIT Press.

Manning, P.K., & Van Maanen, J. (Eds.). (1978). *Policing: A View from the Street.* Santa Monica, CA: Goodyear.

Martin, J.A. (1973). *Law enforcement vocabulary.* Springfield, IL: Charles G. Thomas

Mitchell, J.T. (1985). Healing the helpers. In Center for Mental Health Studies of Emergencies (Eds.), *Role stressors and supports for emergency workers* (pp. 105-118). Rockville, MD: National Institute of Mental Health.

Palmer, C.E. (1983). A note about paramedics' strategies for dealing with death and dying. *Journal of Occupational Psychology, 56,* 83-86.

Reese, J.T., & Goldstein, H.A. (Eds.). (1986). *Psychological services for law enforcement.* Washington, DC: U.S. Government Printing Office.

Reese, J.T., Horn, J.F., & Dunning, C. (1990). *Critical incidents in policing.* Washington, DC: U.S. Department of Justice.

Rossi, P.H., Waite, E., Bose, C., & Berk, R. (1974). The seriousness of crimes: Normative structure and individual differences. *American Sociological Review, 39,* 224-237.

Sanders, W.B. (1977). *Detective work.* New York: Free Press.

Sanders, W.B., & Daudistel, H.C. (1976). Detective work: Patterns of criminal investigation. In W.B. Sanders (Eds.), *The sociologist as detective* (pp. 186-203). New York: Praeger.

Sandy, J.P., & Devine, D.A. (1978). Four stress factors unique to rural patrol. *Police Chief, 45*(9), 42-44.

Scott, S. (1979). Stress and the female cop. *Police Stress, 1*(3), 31-34.

Sewell, J.D. (1983). The development of a critical life events scale for law enforcement. *Journal of Police Science and Administration, 11,* 109-116.

Sewell, J.D. (1984). Stress in university law enforcement. *Journal of Higher Education, 55,* 515-523.

Sewell, J.D. (1986). Administrative concerns in law enforcement stress management. *Police Studies, 9*, 153-159.

Sewell, J.D. (1993). Traumatic stress of multiple murder investigations. *Journal of Traumatic Stress, 6*, 103-118.

Sewell, J.D., & Crew, L. (1984). The forgotten victim: Stress and the police dispatcher. *FBI Law Enforcement Bulletin, 53*(3), 7-11.

Sewell, J.D., Ellison, K.W., & Hurrell, J.J. (1988). Stress management in law enforcement: Where do we go from here? *Police Chief, 55*(10), 94-98.

Simon, D. (1991). *Homicide: A year on the killing streets*. Boston: Houghton Mifflin.

Stratton, J.G. (1979). Police stress and the criminal investigator. *Police Chief, 46*(2), 22-26.

Stroud, C. (1987). *Close pursuit*. New York: Bantam Books.

Taylor, A.J.W. (1989). *Disaster and Disaster Stress*. New York: AMS Press.

Terry, W.C. (1981). Police stress: The empirical evidence. *Journal of Police Science and Administration, 9*, 61-73.

Terry, W.C., & Luckenbill, D. (1976). Investigating criminal homicides: Police work in reporting and solving murders. In W.B. Sanders & H.C. Daudistel (Eds.). *The criminal justice process: A reader* (pp. 79-95). New York: Praeger.

Van Maanen, J. (1978). The asshole. In P.K. Manning & J. Van Maanen (Eds.), *Policing: A view from the street*. Santa Monica, CA: Goodyear.

Wagner, M. (1986). Trauma debriefing in the Chicago Police Department. In J.T. Reese & H.A. Goldstein (Eds.), *Psychological services for law enforcement* (pp. 399-403).

Walima, S.E., & Kirschman, E.F. (1988). Human resource coordinators: Organizational consultation services. *Police Chief,55*(10), 78-81.

Walker, G. (1990). Crisis-care in critical incident debriefing. *Death Studies, 14*, 121-133.

Part Six

Coping with Stress

By now, the reader should have developed an understanding of the nature, severity and complexity of police stress. The solutions to this complicated problem, especially assuring that the individual officer learns and utilizes successful coping strategies, are equally complex.

Many researchers and practitioners have identified a variety of mechanisms that can be used to control or reduce law enforcement stress. Increased stress management training, professional counseling for officers and their families, peer advisement, and required fitness standards and programs have been identified as important measures at the department level. The use of relaxation responses and neutralization techniques, proper nutrition and diet, and regular exercise, particularly of an aerobic nature, have been offered as remedies for the individual officer.

So what works? How can police officers effectively cope with the effects of stress? Our authors in Part Six offer some suggestions.

Defining critical incidents as *"sudden, powerful events that fall outside the range of ordinary human experiences,"* Kureczka examines those common physical, emotional, and cognitive reactions to critical incident stress. His particular emphasis is on the role administrators, peers and mental health professionals can play in helping officers deal with the traumatization involved in responding to critical incidents and in recognizing the vicarious effect of such stress on police families.

In her discussion of critical incidents, Walker includes recognized disasters, natural acts, or other significant events involving death or serious injury and necessitating rescue or emergency care; or other crisis situations that energize unusually strong emotions. Participants in such incidents respond with predictable systematic stress reactions involving normal and pathological grief patterns and may develop post-traumatic stress disorder. As she explains, effective mental health services include pre-incident preparedness, early intervention with psychological first-aid, and post-disaster treatment using critical incident stress debriefing, grief counseling, brief multi-modal therapy, referral to traditional therapy or counseling if necessary, and regular follow-up.

In one large police department, a 1983 survey of officer reactions to post-shooting trauma led to the establishment of a Critical Incident Response Team and specific training for police officers. Ten years later, Gentz again surveyed the members of that department. His article discusses the results of those two studies. His analysis reflects that most of the common reactions documented in the earlier study were also reported in the later survey and, significantly, in roughly the same frequency. It thus appears that the reactions to a critical incident are fairly predictable between individuals, an important recognition for both training and treatment.

Janik discusses the concept of peer support and the advantages for public safety personnel and their families to confidentially discuss personal and/or professional problems with one of their own. The researcher concludes that the non-professional peer supporter not only cares a great deal about the well being of fellow officers but also has a first-hand understanding of the situations they experience. He discusses the philosophy underlying a peer support program, as well as the methods employed in the selection and training of individuals who will provide such services. The reader will find the guidelines developed by IACP's Psychological Services Section to be of particular use.

Holding that peer supporters have three major responsibilities—"listening, assessing, and referring"—Finn and Tomz offer an extensive analysis of the use of peer support mechanisms to handle specific types of law enforcement stress. Their article provides a detailed discussion of recruiting, screening and training peer supporters and identifies the strengths and weaknesses of such an approach. They conclude that, while professional psychological services will always be necessary in handling police stress, peer support systems can complement and enhance such systems, especially with certain officers and in specific stressful incidents.

Each year, nearly 150 law enforcement officers die in the line of duty. Drawing from his personal experiences as a police executive, Haddix examines how, on a daily basis, law enforcement officers must cope with an inordinate amount of stress brought on by the constant conflicts with violators, complaints, irate citizens, and demanding supervisors. Recognizing that death could be just the next call away, all law enforcement officers must deal with this burden every working day. Haddix recommends that each department develop a comprehensive response strategy to help relieve officers of the burdens associated with line of duty deaths and to allow the agency to more effectively handle the death of one of its own.

Drawing from their experiences as sworn officers and from their involvement in stress management for other law enforcement personnel, Vasquez and Band examine the survival behavior and traits that will most likely result in a police officer surviving in combat. Using a survey of the 207 federal, state, and local law enforcement officers, these researchers identified 33 specific survival behaviors and traits directly related to survivability. They perceive five as most critical: self-confidence in performance; training; effectiveness in combat; decisiveness; and perseverance under stress.

20

Critical Incident Stress in Law Enforcement

Arthur W. Kureczka

A patrol officer observes a car with three teenagers speed through a rural intersection. The officer pulls out in an attempt to stop the vehicle, knowing that at its current speed, the car cannot navigate the series of sharp turns coming up in a few short miles.

The driver accelerates out of the officer's range of sight. The officer slows to round the first curve and hears screeching brakes, followed by a sickening thud and the crunch of crumpling metal. As the wreck comes into view, what the officer sees confirms what the sounds reported: The driver lost control of the vehicle and careened off the road. The car smashed into a tree before coming to rest on its side several yards down the embankment.

The officer immediately calls for assistance, parks the cruiser, and runs toward the car. Two of the occupants were thrown from the vehicle when it flipped over. The veteran officer momentarily freezes in horror as he recognizes them—his daughter's high school classmates. He feels sick seeing their broken, bloody bodies lying lifeless in the muddy weeds. Fearing the worst, the officer rushes to check the victim trapped inside the crumpled wreck. His brief sigh of relief that his own daughter was not in the car quickly vanishes as he sees her best friend, crushed in the wreckage. No one survived, "If only I could have stopped them," he thinks, shaken, while he waits for the ambulance to arrive.

The officer suffers no physical injury as a result of the incident, but the emotional trauma can be just as painful, if not more so. The actions taken by the department in the ensuing weeks and months will determine in large part whether he copes effectively with the stress induced by this critical incident or whether its effects become debilitating.

Every year, hundreds of officers experience intense, traumatic events that can have serious long-term consequences for them, their families, and their departments. It is incumbent upon police administrators to ensure that their officers and their departments have the tools at hand to cope with such critical incidents.

Critical Incidents

In the past, most studies of stress in law enforcement focused exclusively on post-shooting trauma. Recently, however, the research has expanded to encompass stress induced by other traumatic events, collectively known as critical incidents. A critical incident is any event that has a stressful impact sufficient to overwhelm the usually effective coping skills of an individual.

Critical incidents typically are sudden, powerful events that fall outside the range of ordinary human experiences. Because they happen so abruptly, they can have a strong emotional impact, even on an experienced, well-trained officer.

In law enforcement, any situation in which an officer's expectations of personal infallibility suddenly become tempered by imperfection and crude reality can be a critical incident.[1] Such events include a line-of-duty death or serious injury of a coworker, a police suicide, an officer-involved shooting in a combat situation, a life-threatening assault on an officer, a death or serious injury caused by an officer, an incident involving multiple deaths, a traumatic death of a child, a barricaded suspect/hostage situation, a highly profiled media event (often in connection with another critical incident), or any other incident that appears critical or questionable.

The definition of a critical incident must remain fluid because what affects one officer might not affect another. An officer who has children, for example, might be affected by responding to the death of a child more than an officer who has no children. In addition, the circumstances of an event, the personality of the officer, and the way the event is handled by the department, the media, and the officer's family all affect the officer's reactions to an incident.

Critical Incident Stress

Many U.S. soldiers returned from war "shell-shocked" and suffering from the effects of critical incident stress, often referred to as "battle fatigue." In 1980, the American Psychiatric Association formally recognized the civilian version of battle fatigue, which became known as post-traumatic stress disorder (PTSD).

Post-traumatic stress is defined as "...the development of characteristic symptoms following a psychologically distressing event that is outside the

---

1. W. Fowler, "Post Critical Incident Counseling: An Example of Emotional First-aid in a Police Crisis," in *Psychological Services for Law Enforcement*, eds., J. Reese and H. Goldstein (Washington, DC: U.S. Government Printing Office, 1986).

range of human experience."[2] Symptoms are characterized by intrusive recollections, excessive stress arousal, withdrawal, numbing, and depression. The signs and symptoms must last more than 20 days for an individual to be diagnosed with PTSD. An estimated 4 to 10 percent of individuals who experience a critical incident will develop a full-fledged post-traumatic stress disorder.[3]

Research also has shown that critical incident stress affects up to 87 percent of all emergency service workers at least once in their careers.[4] In many cases, the stress from one incident can be compounded by two or more factors. For example, an officer involved in an armed confrontation exchanges gunfire with a suspect. The officer is wounded, the suspect dies, and the incident becomes a media event. The injury to the officer, the use of deadly force, and the media scrutiny—conceivably three separate critical incidents – multiply the stressors on the officer.

Critical incident stress manifests itself physically, cognitively, and emotionally. The officer might experience some or all of these reactions immediately, or perhaps not until after a delay. While in most instances the symptoms will subside in a matter of weeks, a few of those affected by such stress will suffer permanent emotional trauma that will adversely affect their continued value to the department and cause acute serious problems in their personal lives.

Administrative Support

Clearly, administrators can no longer afford to ignore the issue of traumatic stress caused by involvement in a critical incident. Such stress impairs officers' ability to perform their duties and impacts on the operation of the department.

Police agencies can be held liable in court for ignoring lingering stress-related problems or for disciplining workers who exhibit the behavioral effects of trauma from a job-related critical incident. Courts have made significant cash awards to officers whose departments did not provide them with professional assistance. Thus, it is in the best interests of police administrators to identify stressful situations and address effects early.

2. *Diagnostic and Statistical Manual of Mental Disorders*, 4th ed., rev. (Washington, DC: American Psychiatric Association, 1994).

3. R. Blak, "Critical Incident Debriefing for Law Enforcement Personnel: A Model," in *Critical Incidents in Policing*, eds., J. Reese, J. Horn, and C. Dunning. rev. ed. (Washington, DC: US Government Printing Office, 1991). 23–30.

4. T. Pierson, "Critical Incident Stress: A Serious Law Enforcement Problem," *The Police Chief*, February, 1989, 32–33.

Failure to do so could prove detrimental to the department, not only operationally but also financially.

The most important aspect of managing critical incident recovery is for the administration to understand that police duties can result in psychological injury. Departments should be proactive and develop a critical incident response that addresses the likelihood of psychological injury with the same attention and concern as the likelihood of physical injury. Critical incidents can inflict mental harm just as they inflict physical wounds.

Administrators should design policies and standard operating procedures for officers involved in critical incidents. Well-planned intervention programs can prevent bad relations between the department and affected employees, reduce compensation costs from potentially divisive litigation and, in turn, build morale and make employees feel valued by the department.

Unfortunately, police officers typically resist seeking available assistance because they do not want to be stigmatized as weak or crazy. By mandating a visit to a mental health professional, administrators provide officers the opportunity to express themselves and ask questions without appearing to seek help. Still, officers have the option of remaining silent while the mental health professional provides information about critical incident stress.

Budgetary Impact

One law enforcement expert stated that 70 percent of the police officers who use deadly force leave law enforcement within 5 years.[5] The impact, therefore, of an overstressed officer can be far reaching. Stress affects the officer, other employees, the department, the public, and the officer's family. It can lead to faulty decisionmaking, disciplinary problems, excessive use of sick leave, tardiness, on-the-job accidents, complaints from citizens, and high officer turnover. All of these cost the department time and money.

It costs a department approximately $100,000 to replace a 5-year veteran. This figure includes the expense of retraining, overtime, benefits, testing for replacements, and knowledge that is lost when an officer leaves the department.[6]

---

5. Jerry Vaughn, former director of the International Association of Chiefs of Police. quoted in J. Horn, "Critical Incidents for Law Enforcement Officers." in *Critical Incidents in Policing*, eds., J. Reese, J. Horn, and C. Dunning, rev. ed. (Washington, DC: U.S. Government Printing Office, 1991). 143–148.

6. R. Fuller, "An Overview of the Process of Peer Support Team Development," in *Critical Incidents in Policings*, ed. (Washington, DC: US Government Printing Office, 1991), 99–106.

In contrast, one study showed that the average cost of intervention when PTSD was detected soon after the event totaled $8,300 per victim. When detection and treatment were delayed, the average cost rose to nearly $46,000. Even though that is almost six times more than the cost of early treatment, it still is less than half the cost of replacing an officer.

As a group, employees who received prompt treatment averaged 12 weeks of recovery before returning to work and had a low incidence of permanent disability. In comparison, the delayed treatment groups required an average of 46 weeks of recovery and displayed significant long-term effects.[7]

These figures represent costs incurred when employees actually developed PTSD subsequent to traumatic work event and do not include the money spent in cases where less serious secondary trauma occurred. In addition, the computed cost of an intervention program also should take into account the number of victim-survivor employees who did not develop PTSD as a result of the treatment approach.

Clearly, the expense of a few sessions for everyone involved in an incident, especially if conducted as a group, would be significantly less than long-term treatment and/or disability leave for those significantly involved few. Preventive intervention, then, appears to be less expensive than waiting until psychological injuries deteriorate to the point where personal and occupational life suffers.

In some larger cities, full-time psychological services units or police psychologists might already be in place. For those departments that do not employ a full-time mental health professional (i.e., counselor, psychotherapist, psychologist, or psychiatrist), such services can be contracted or retained on a per-hour or per-incident basis. It is a minimal expense and a wise investment for administrators to secure the services of a mental health professional and train peer support officers.

Pre-Incident Stress Education

Perhaps the most important element of combating critical incident stress is pre-incident stress education. Providing education before a crisis strikes helps to reduce the impact of traumatic events. Educated officers who later became involved in critical incidents generally are better able to avoid or at least control stress reactions. Pre-incident stress education

---

7. R. Freidman, M. Framer, and D. Shearer, "Early Response to Post Trauma Stress," *EAP Digest*, February 1988, 45–49.

helps officers recover from acute stress reactions better because they recognize the symptoms early and seek assistance more quickly.[8]

Stress management training should begin with new recruits, who generally accept the message that they are vulnerable and need to take precautions to control stress. In addition, all police officers should receive stress management training as part of inservice or recertification programs. Command personnel should learn how to recognize officers exhibiting symptoms of stress so that intervention can take place early.

Pre-incident stress education should be provided by the people with whom an officer will be dealing in the event of a critical incident—the department's peer support officer and the mental health professional employed by the department. This essential introduction provides the foundation for building the trust and rapport that will come into play later between an affected officer and the assistance providers.

Peer Support

Generally speaking, law enforcement officers have been slow to recognized the positive contribution that can be made by mental health professionals. Police officers often have difficulty trusting and confiding in someone outside the close circle of sworn personnel. They also fear that seeking professional help in dealing with a traumatic event will mark them among their co-workers as incapable in some way. To counter such resistance, while still getting help for officers who need it, many police departments have established peer support programs.

Peer support officers are trained to recognize problems and make the appropriate referrals. Peers learn basic counseling skills. They use a client-centered approach that builds a climate of trust through empathy, genuine concern, and an unconditional positive regard for the employees seeking help.

Often, the most important function of a peer support officer is simply to act as a sounding board for troubled officers. Peers provide a safe place for troubled officers to ventilate and to begin to understand and articulate their feelings in a confidential, nonjudgmental environment. In a few minor instances, no other assistance is needed. With critical incidents, however, officers have problems beyond the abilities of the peer, who refers them to the appropriate mental health professional.

Peer support officers do not conduct any clinical therapy; only trained and certified professionals who are insured against malpractice can pro-

---

8. S. Miller and A. Birnbaum, "Putting the Life Back Into 'Life Events': Toward a Cognitive Social Learning Analysis of the Coping Process," in *Handbook of Life Stress, Cognition and Health*, eds., S. Fisher and J. Reasons (New York: John Wiley and Sons, 1988).

vide therapy and determine the proper course of treatment for an affected officer. Peer support officers work under the supervision of a mental health professional to ensure that officers who need help get it.

Police administrators should take several factors into account when choosing peer support officers. Selected individuals should exhibit a genuine willingness to help their coworkers. They must be trusted and respected within the ranks. Racial diversity, gender, and multicultural issues within the department also should be considered. The size of the department would determine how many peers to train.

Officers who personally have been involved in a critical incident and have successfully resolved their problems provide an excellent pool of candidates for the peer support team. Not only can they empathize but they also can relate to a troubled officer.

Support officers, however, must be strongly cautioned on the issue of counter-transference. This develops when peers begin to over-identify on both a personal and professional basis with the officers being helped.

Peers must be prepared to navigate the difficult course of showing sufficient caring, understanding, and empathy without becoming overwhelmed by the familiarity of any given critical incident. Peer support officers need to remember the basic techniques of listening in order to be effective helpers and to let the officers involved in critical incidents express their own emotions.

Mental Health Professionals

Delivering mental health care to members of the law enforcement community is difficult. Police officers often resist counseling for several reasons. Frequently, they have a strong sense of self-sufficiency and insist that they can solve their own problems. Officers generally possess great skepticism of outsiders and have difficulty trusting counselors. At the same time, counselors sometimes do not understand police work, nor can they easily grasp the daily stresses faced by officers. For these reasons, law enforcement administrators must choose mental health professionals carefully and work to ensure that they provide the best service for the department's employees.

Counselors must have a thorough understanding of policing, as well as comprehensive knowledge of the police force and its demographics. They must be familiar with the organization of the police department and its power structure so they can understand the work environment of affected officers.

Because of their background and experience, some mental health professionals find it hard to understand who the law enforcement officer is and what the occupation entails. For example, police officers often are seen as having a warped sense of humor, sometimes referred to as "gallows humor."[9] The condition results from the many negative aspects of human nature that confront officers on a regular basis.

Officers use humor to vent anger and frustration. Those outside of law enforcement might see it as sarcastic, callous, and insensitive. They may even have problems empathizing with those in public safety. Sensing this, the police officer in turn might refuse to trust or confide in the counselor, thus defeating any chance for effective therapy to occur.

When mental health professionals start to work with law enforcement officers, they soon discover that the officers evaluate them as much as they evaluate the officers. Often, the officer-patients might want to know about the counselors' familiarity with policing, their opinions of police officers, and their previous work with police personnel. Counselors must be cautioned not to display anger or annoyance at the officers' apparent lack of trust. Instead, they should work to establish a relationship based on mutual respect.

An important dynamic in the relationship between officers and mental health professionals is that officers often fear being betrayed. Self-disclosure frequently intimidates them because of what it might reveal about themselves. More intimidating is the fear that counselors will divulge what the officer shares with them.

Building rapport and assuring officers of the confidentiality of the information revealed take time and diligent effort on the part of the mental health professionals. Only by taking this time will the therapeutic effects of counseling be realized.

Family Reactions and Support

Some incidents in the careers of police officers leave a profound effect not only on the involved officers but also on their family members. Side effects of traumatic events might surface at home in the form of anger, depression, frustration, grief, insecurity, confusion, and disillusionment. Family members frequently become the convenient targets of officers' misplaced emotions.

In addition, the families of officers involved in critical incidents might show similar signs of stress. Spouses might adopt the roles of either supporter or victim. Frequently, they find themselves alternating between those roles, at times being able to support and nurture the officer, while at

---

9. M. Silva, "The Delivery of Mental Health Services to Law Enforcement Officers," in *Critical Incidents in Policing*, eds., J. Reese, J. Horn, and C. Dunning, rev. ed. (Washington, DC: US Government Printing Office, 1991), 335–342.

Common Reactions to Critical Incident Stress

Physical Reactions	Emotional Reactions	Cognitive Reactions
• Headaches	• Anxiety	• Debilitating flashbacks
• Muscle aches	• Fear	• Repeated visions of
• Sleep disturbances	• Guilt	the incident
• Changed appetite	• Sadness	• Nightmares
• Decreased interest in	• Anger	• Slowed thinking
sexual activity	• Irritability	• Difficulty making decisions
• Impotence	• Feeling lost and	and solving problems
	unappreciated	• Disorientation
	• Withdrawal	• Lack of concentration
		• Memory lapses

other moments feeling terribly vulnerable, alone, and in need of support themselves. As the children of officers who suffer from post-traumatic stress disorder mature, they also might exhibit the same fears, emotions, and cynical attitudes as their affected parent.

To help officers and their families prepare for the stress of a critical incident, a "significant other" stress course can help. Conducted when officers first enter the department and again periodically during the course of their careers, such a course can allow spouses to feel less excluded and to gain valuable insights into the behaviors and reactions of their loved ones.

Families need support and intervention, and they must not be forgotten. While conceivably few municipal authorities would endorse police departments providing counseling for family members, police administrators might consider referring families to mental health professionals familiar with police-related issues.

Conclusion

No one can predict how powerful an incident will be or what effects it will have on them. It is incumbent upon police administrators to prepare their employees for such incidents by teaching them the signs and symptoms of critical incident stress and establishing policies that enable them to get help when they need it.

The officer who responded to the terrible accident described earlier need not succumb to the debilitating effects of critical incident stress. With the proper support from his department and counseling from a certified professional, he and his family will learn to deal with the trauma, and the department likely will keep a valued employee.

21

Crisis-Care in
Critical Incident Debriefing

Gail Walker

A critical incident can be a recognized disaster, such as an airplane crash or a hotel fire; an act of nature, such as an earthquake or tornado; or any event involving death, injury, destruction, and disruption. In December 1988 above Lockerbie, Scotland, Pan Am Flight 103 exploded at 31,000 feet, crashed into a row of tenement houses, dug a flaming tunnel for several thousand feet, and landed in pieces in a pasture. All 258 passengers and crew members were dead; some bodies were dismembered, many cremated in the fireball; several townspeople were dead, more were critically injured. The global community was stunned. Sympathy and support poured out for the victims—living and dead. Critical incidents can be less dramatic, but still individually significant events. Such cases may involve death or injury of an emergency responder team member or an innocent bystander; or call for prolonged rescue or crisis care; or elicit extensive media exposure. They always energize unusually strong emotion. A critical incident is any crisis situation that causes emergency personnel, family members, or bystanders to respond with immediate or delayed stress-altered physical, mental, emotional, psychological, or social coping mechanisms.

The people who generally provide emergency care are emergency medical technicians and paramedics, firefighters, and police officers. They often incorporate the paradoxical personality traits of resilient survivors. These traits include commitment to important values, a sense of personal control, capability and understanding personal limitation, perception of crisis as challenge, and courage and caution. First responders may be trained or untrained bystanders who try to the best of their ability to help at the scene.

The conditions are, by definition, difficult in a critical incident. The hardships include external factors such as locale, weather, time of day or night, ease of scene access, and proximity to emergency service necessities. The human factors include variables such as extent and severity of injuries and deaths; number of people involved, demographic characteristics of the affected people, responder crew characteristics, and the cumulative effect of the number and kind of noncritical and critical incidents in the past years of service for individuals on the response teams. In one instance, two college students were involved in a drinking and driving accident. The young man had not been wearing a seatbelt, and had been impaled on the broken steering column. He was porpoising on the ground, covered in blood. His girlfriend was trapped in the car, her face shattered by the windshield. Finally, the young man was past screaming and could only look into the eyes of the crew member holding his head. He said, "Help me," and then he died. That crew member has since been unable to deal with any event that involved blood. In time, and with care, his crew hopes he will once again be effective with trauma patients.

People involved in a critical incident—some catastrophe resulting in human suffering beyond the normal range—may be at risk to develop posttraumatic stress disorders and pathological grief reactions. The reactions to critical incidents involve the general system stress response with predictable symptomatology and more individualistic response patterns. According to Selye (1), the alarm reaction to a situation of high emotional stress invokes mobilization of the body's resources to cope with the agent of stress. If adaptation or effective resistance is not possible, the unresolved distress reaction may manifest itself physically and psychologically. Some physical reactions include gastrointestinal, respiratory, or cardiovascular distress, or chronic fatigue. Some psychological reactions include anxiety, irritability, depression and moodiness, numbing of affect, involuntary flashbacks, and recurrent dreams. As described by Lilfeld (2), the predominant styles of response to perceived stress are direct action, rationalization with stressor avoidance, and passive acceptance. People who prefer direct coping act to alter the sources of stress; they provide emergency interventions as appropriate for their skills, participate in disaster debriefing or seek psychological counseling, and actively reconstruct their personal, family, and social lives. People who use indirect coping may try to alter the perceived significance of the stressor event.

Some dysfunctional strategies that reduce short-term severity contribute to the intensity of long-term crisis reactions. These include chemical coping, markedly increased environmental and interpersonal vigilance, a flight into activity, increased personal cynicism or interpersonal hostility, and sexual hyperactivity or incapacity. A variety of traditional psychological defense mechanisms such as denial, regression, reaction-formation, intellectualization, and rationalization may be used. Personality factors that may make an individual more susceptible to post-traumatic stress disorder symptomatology include higher levels of anxiety, chronic or reactive apathy or depression, overt interpersonal hostility or repressed anger, and an experiential history of learned helplessness. A higher level of anxiety may occur as a reaction to trauma events perceived as central stressors, events that embody the of loss of self-esteem, symbolically suggest loss of a significant other, or have components that make horror personal.

Intervening Variables

Intervening factors can moderate the degree of stress vulnerability. Green, Lindy, and Grace (3) describe the severity of the catastrophe as one variable in the formation of posttraumatic stress disorder. Walker and Maiden (4) include psychological profile and experiential history as factors impacting life span attitudes toward death. The lack of predictability in some specific emergency situations and across situations may compound helper distress. Advance practice sessions can prepare team members for predictable events, but no amount of training can insulate people from the smell of human flesh burning, or the sight of dismemberment, or from carnage and other tragic consequence. The more central and significant an experience or relationship, the more intense will be the reactions.

Other intervening variables that influence patterns of stress vulnerability are the presence or absence of social support networks, availability of peer counseling and critical incident stress debriefing, and the quality of posttrauma environments. For example, in one incident a farmer left the combine idling and hopped across the guard plate on his way to the house for a second cup of coffee. His cuff snagged and the blades pulled him in, amputating both feet and one hand. His screams brought his wife and children, as the combine processed him into the second level where the machinery pinned him and stalled. Rescue workers opened a space large enough for the smallest woman emergency medical technician (EMT) to enter, provide oxygen, apply pressure dressings, and talk to him. For six hours they worked to free him. When they managed to release the breaker bar, blood geysered from his stumps and he died. Body reclamation took another hour. One crew member walked the EMT to the house and held her in the shower until the water no longer ran pink and her shuddering sobbing quieted. That night, the team members and their families visited the bereaved, expressed their condolences, assisted in the chores and practical arrangements, and offered continuing contact. During debriefing, the crew expressed feelings of sadness and regrets about the untimely death of their neighbor and the effects it would have on his family. Team members knew they had done everything possible. The incident was objectively and subjectively severe, yet the effects were mitigated by efficient medical and psychological interventions, peer interdependence and debriefing, and continuing social support.

Social factors can moderate the amount of stress experienced by team members. Factors that reduce frustration include efficient coordination of the delivery of emergency services by fire, police, and ambulance crews. The impact of the 1964 Alaskan earthquake was detailed by Anderson (5), who noted that postdisaster relief was complicated not only by stressor patterns originating in civilian response to the disaster, but also by the conflict between relief agencies in protocols of proper emergency procedures, authority disputes, and interagency competition. Also useful are available representatives from utility and power companies to provide control of hazards at the scene, access to backup relief crews, and standby specialized tools and equipment. Medical and psychological crisis-care and follow-up are necessary. Frederick (6) suggested that survivors will need psychological first aid in response to the initial emergency and long-term interventions as individuals seek to integrate the crisis into their emotional or mental equilibrium.

Emotional Response to Critical Incidents

Critical incident participants respond with predictable, systematic stress reactions during each phase of the event. Although wide individual variation in behavior may occur in a critical incident, victims often respond during the initial impact phase with disorientation, shock, confusion, apathy, and emotional lability. Emergency responders attempt to assess the scene and the extent of the disaster, prepare and deliver search and rescue operations, provide needed intervention, and prevent escalation in physical and human terms. In the recoil phase, victims attempt to cooperate with emergency personnel. Hargreaves (7) warns they may express altruism and gratitude to the extent of minimizing their own injuries. Survivors may harbor feelings of resentment toward those spared serious loss or toward care givers. Many will suffer feelings of self-blame with accompanying depression. They may transfer feelings of anger, originating from the emergency situation, into hostility toward significant others. For some individuals these feelings will be expressed as suicidal or homicidal attempts.

In the postdisaster phase civilian and emergency responders may manifest survivor euphoria and survivor guilt. They may deal with the crisis by participation in physical and psychological reconstruction efforts, or may show posttraumatic stress disorder symptomatology. Commonly observed postdisaster stress disorder syndrome includes recurrent thoughts, dreams, or classically conditioned emotional trauma responses. Participants may manifest emotional numbness or marked agitation, initial apathy, depression with accompanying sadness, negative cognitions, learned helplessness responses, and low self-esteem. The survivor may show hypervigilance, feelings of imminent danger, and conscious or unconscious reenactment behaviors. A variety of other symptoms may be present, depending on the individual's characteristic coping style.

Interventions for Emergency Responders

The Emergency Services Branch of the National Institute of Mental Health (8) has devised effective interventions for emergency responder personnel that take place prior to, during, or after the actual disaster. Predisaster interventions include the development of liaison teams comprised of emergency services personnel, mental health professional, disaster planning, and cooperative drills. This allows professionals and volunteers to become familiar with one another, promotes awareness of potential stressors in relation to specific events, and provides the opportunity for informal debriefing and counseling.

During the disaster, crew members are encouraged to share factual information, which allows psychological preparedness. Team managers should rotate workers from high stress assignments such as triage or morgue duty, or physically dangerous rescue operations, to moderate stress assignments that allow for physical and psychological decompression, to low stress assignments with coworker debriefing and support. Mental health workers must be prepared to use psychological triage and attend to acute mental health needs. Initial crisis care will necessarily be limited to specific needs of the survivors, including emotional ventilation and practical assistance, crisis counseling and reorientation, and resource referrals. Tuckman (9) asserts that active intervention during a disaster or emergency may prevent the formation of posttraumatic stress disorder.

In providing psychological first aid to victims and emergency responders, the crisis worker should remain calm, providing information and honest reassurance. However, emergency care providers must be sure to inform involved people within customary limits of tolerance, to tell them the truth tempered with compassion, and to give appropriate counseling, reassurance, advice, and guidance. Emergency workers should tell family members nothing that might promote psychopathology; for example, the detail of dismemberment, decay, or other forms of extreme trauma are often omitted in the interest of mental health. Crisis workers should not expect to take the pain away completely; there is no magical amnesia. Emergency workers should expect to encounter volatile emotional reactions, such as intense burst of ventilated grief, expressed feelings of helplessness, and possible hostility. They should accept the situation, tolerate the ventilation, and encourage physical and verbal support for those particularly affected. Crisis workers providing psychological first aid should try to legitimize and normalize the experience, the participants' reactions, and coping strategies that promote resolution. Simultaneously, crisis workers should avoid endorsing destructive or dysfunctional strategies, such as emotional repression, chemical coping, or denial of secondary losses. These secondary losses may include loss of an element of self-concept, loss of the illusion of invulnerability for oneself or significant others, or loss of faith in a "just world," where only good things happen to good people.

Conversation with certain types of victims can be problematic. For instance, some emergency workers prefer not to work with incoherent alcohol and/or drug abuse victims or perpetrators of violent or criminal acts. Effective communication and intervention is more difficult with mentally ill people, such as hysterically expressive or catatonically withdrawn victims, or people whose lifestyle or language is markedly different from the caregiver's own. Crisis workers should operate on a buddy system and rotate care of difficult victims, while also monitoring one another for signs of fatigue, stress symptoms, or inappropriate conduct. They should not allow negative emotional responses to compromise personal integrity, professional ethics, or humane delivery of psychological services.

The majority of participants in a critical incident want to talk about the event and their part in it. Given the opportunity, they talk about the stressors present in the situation, the disturbing sights and smells and sensations and thoughts they experienced, and their emotional and behavioral reactions. Some describe techniques they use at the scene to maintain an emotional distance from gruesome events, such as imagining the dead as animals or impersonal cargo. Some participants use depersonalization strategies to convince themselves that these events are not real, that this is only a dream or a movie, and life will be different when they wake up. If mental health specialists are part of the disaster relief team, they can directly observe participants manifesting stress reactions and initiate practical and psychological first aid measures.

Practical first aid includes providing needed medical care, answering questions, locating significant others, and making an initial triage decision about the necessity of continuing care. Both victims and crisis workers may need bathroom facilities, food and water, shelter from the elements, a place to rest that is physically removed from the scene, and an opportunity to talk about their feelings with coworkers or mental health specialists. Crisis workers can defuse some stress reactions through use of the following techniques of psychological first aid:

- Gather information about the event and significant stressors.
- Assess the participant's stress response pattern.
- Provide information about the cognitive, emotional, and interpersonal aspects of normal grief reactions.
- Describe realistic processes for grief reactions.
- Devise an action plan that mobilizes the individual's resources.
- Encourage physical activity and good health practices of adequate nutrition and rest.

- Attempt to ascertain the predominate sources of social support available to the victim, and encourage contact with those individuals.
- Make appropriate referrals.
- Provide follow-up.

Critical Incident Debriefing

If necessary, after the disaster a formal debriefing for involved emergency personnel should be arranged within 24 to 48 hours. Debriefings may be restricted to emergency personnel, but currently can also include people such as bystanders, family, and classmates of victims, coworkers and supervisory personnel, or those directly involved in or affected by the incident. Some differences in procedures and concerns will be mandated by the constituency and the specific nature of the event. Separate debriefings are advisable for identifiably coherent groups, such as care providers or the families of deceased victims.

The appropriate use of critical incident stress debriefing procedures, crisis intervention techniques, and brief therapy coupled with referral to traditional therapies when necessary can aid in resolving issues related to critical incident crisis-care. The psychological interventions and ethical considerations most appropriate for each situation vary. The therapeutic procedures used in a specific critical incident debriefing generally reflect the practitioner's theoretical framework, areas and levels of competence, and familiarity with the special demands of emergency crisis intervention.

The process of critical incident stress debriefing described by Mitchell (10) includes the elements of factual description of the event, emotional ventilation, and identification of stress response symptoms. Stress education is provided that emphasizes the normalcy of stress response syndromes. Plans of action are devised, and referrals are made if necessary. The physical and psychological environment must be conducive to intensive therapy. Representatives from the media are excluded unless they are present only as participants in the incident. No written notes, tape recordings, or video documentation should be allowed, thus protecting the group's right to confidentiality and privacy. The facilitator should anticipate predictable response patterns and provide tissues.

Procedurally, an efficient approach is to seat the members of each of the emergency response teams together, with all involved parties arranged in a large circle. This arrangement allows team members to gain mutual support, to experience familiar interdependence, and to reinforce feelings of self-worth. They can exchange physcial gestures of comfort, and the more quiet or restrained members can express themselves in the relative safety of their team. The facilitator encourages the chronological description of the event, from first dispatch through all procedural steps of all involved teams. The events should be told in the present tense, as though they were happening in the moment, to reenergize feelings that people may be defending themselves against with denials, avoidance, and intellectualization. The facilitator may use newspaper photographs of the incident, if available, to function as linking objects. If there were multiple victims or accelerating levels of horror, the facilitator may deal with each one separately or continue the chronological unfolding. Emphasis is maintained on factual descriptions, stressor sources, and emotional ventilation aspects. This is not a competitive comparison between teams or areas of expertise, nor an incident critique. The *empty chair* technique can be used to provide a format for emergency responders to deal with the "I should have...," "I shouldn't have...," "I wish...," and "I regret..." feelings. The facilitator places an empty chair in the center of the circle and encourages participants to share those feelings as though the involved persons could hear the dialogue. The facilitator may include dream material and/or spontaneous drawings of participants, depending on the theoretical orientation and areas of expertise of the facillitor and the characteristics of the working group.

The facilitator should assess the nature and extent of critical incident stress responses in the areas of somatic disturbances, affective and cognitive distress patterns, changes in personal and interpersonal behavior, or other reported areas of complaint. The techniques of psychological first aid described for disaster defusing are also effective in critical incident stress debriefings. Although originally developed for grief counseling of the bereaved, with adaptation and synthesis for techniques of guided imagery described by Melges and DeMaso (11), regrief therapy as developed by Volkan (12), behavioral therapy as discussed by Ramsey (13), and existential psychotherapy as practiced by May and Yalom (14) are also useful. Although any of these formats can be effective, the multimodel therapy approach developed by Lazarus (15) allows the design of specific treatment programs to alleviate disturbances in behavior, affect, sensation, imagery, cognition, interpersonal relationships, and disordered biochemistry. The facilitator should encourage the participants to devise action plans that include constructive coping strategies, and to develop decompression routines incorporating physical activity, health maintenance, emotional defusing, physical and mental relaxation techniques, and reestablishment of normal routines.

Ethical concerns that may be discussed during crisis-care commonly include issues of personal response to tragedy, acts of commission or omission, issues of responsibility or confidentiality or integrity, and larger questions concerning the consequences of life and death decisions. For example, as a father stood beside his children waiting for a school bus on a frosty morning the week before Christmas, a car skidded out of control on the ice and sustained a head-on collision. In the back seat of the nearer car he found a young woman slumped with her head at an odd angle,. He reached in and took her by the chin, and said, "Are you all right? Are you okay?" and turned her head so she could look at him. She focused on his face, her eyes dilated, and she died. In the debriefing, the father asked if he had killed the young woman when he turned her head. The facilitator replied that although she was critically injured, the immediate cause of death was the broken neck vertebra which sliced through her spinal cord in a spiral fashion. He asked for referral to discuss "how these hands which helped my children into life could have helped someone else's child into death."

The facilitator should establish some means of monitoring the effectiveness of debriefing in promoting recovery from critical incidents. People with special issues, unshared trauma, or unresolved grief will often stay after the debriefing to explorer these issues, either voluntarily or by request. They may be candidates for referral. A follow-up meeting with involved individuals, or with the group, can be scheduled at the conclusion of the initial debriefing session. A routine follow-up session approximately 4 to 6 weeks after the incident will identify team members who are continuing to experience stress symptoms. These people should be referred to mental health professionals who understand the special issues of emergency service personnel. The facilitator also has the option of scheduling a session on the anniversary of the incident or shortly thereafter, to reassess intervention outcomes and to deal with any long-term effects.

Individuals who request referral to either traditional or specialized therapy often manifest difficulty with either prolonged or chronic grief, or experience distress because of the form of grief expression, or have not been able to resolve the traumatic aspects of the death or the associative complex of related issues. The facilitator must use clinical judgement in deciding who among these individuals would benefit more from action plans for stress management, who needs various types of counseling and therapy, and who requires referral to pastoral counseling to explore issue of a spiritual or ethical nature, such as forgiveness for irreversible acts, or adjustment in their ideas of the nature and essence of God.

The procedure for brief therapy with critical incident survivors is similar to traditional counseling approaches in process, although the content issues may be outside usual areas of crisis intervention. Some emergency personnel or incident victims will already be in a counseling relationship; they will generally explore crisis reactions within the context of this existing therapeutic alliance. Some will accept referral to therapists whose practice is specific to one of the many psychotherapeutic modalities. The unit of treatment will generally be the distressed individual, with intermittent counseling of the couple, family, or the emergency response team.

Although anyone can be affected by a critical incident and need psychological care, emergency responders and crisis care workers intervene in situations of high stress to mitigate the suffering of others. In the process, they assume the risk of immediate or delayed difficulties with their life-support patterns of body maintenance, psychological and emotional stability, occupational well-being, family and social relationships, and spiritual equanimity. Effective provision of mental health services to critical incident survivors must include predisaster preparedness, early intervention using psychological first aid, and postdisaster treatment using critical incident stress debriefing grief counseling, brief multimodal therapy, referral to traditional therapies, and follow-up. Appropriate critical incident crisis-care can provide needed emergency mental health services, prevent the formation of some postdisaster stress disorders, and therapeutically modulate the long-term effects of calamity for victims and emergency care providers.

References

1. Selye, H. (1976). *The stress of life*. New York: McGraw Hill.
2. Lilfeld, S.W., Jr. (1980, June). Coping styles. *Journal of Human Stress, 6*, 2–10.
3. Green, B.L., Lindy, J.M., & Grace, M.C. (1985). Post-traumatic stress disorder: Toward DSM-IV. *Journal of Nervous and Mental Disease, 173*, 406–411.
4. Walker, G., & Maiden, R. (1988). *Lifespan attitudes toward death*. Arlington, VA: Eastern Psychological Association. (ERIC Document Reproduction Service No. ED 289 086).
5. Anderson, W.A. (1969). *Disaster and organizational change: A study of long-term consequences of the 1964 Alaska earthquake* (Monograph Series No. 6). Columbus: Ohio State University Disaster Research Center.
6. Frederick, C.J. (1977). Crisis intervention and emergency mental health. In W.R. Johnson (Ed.), *Health in action* (pp. 376–411). New York: Holt, Rinehart, and Winston.
7. Hargreaves, A.C. (1980). Coping with disaster. *American Journal of Nursing, 80*(4), 683.
8. National Institute of Mental Health (1988). *Human problems in major disasters: A training curriculum for emergency medical personnel*. Rockville, MD: U.S. Department of Health and Human Services.

9. Tuckman, A. (1973). Disaster and mental health intervention. *Community Mental Health Journal, 9*(2), 51–57.
10. Mitchell, J.T. (1983, January). When disaster strikes...The critical incident stress debriefing process. *Journal of Emergency Medical Services, 8,* 36–39.
11. Melges, F.T., & DeMaso, D.R. (1980). Grief resolution therapy: Reliving, revising, and revisiting. *American Journal of Psychotherapy, 34,* 51–61.
12. Volkan, V. (1975). Re-grief therapy. In B. Schoenberg, I. Gerber, A. Wiener, A.H. Kutscher, D. Peretz, & A.C. Carr (Eds.), *Bereavement: Its psychosocial aspects.* New York: Columbia University Press.
13. Ramsey, R.W. (1977). Behavioral approaches to bereavement. *Behavioral Research and Therapy, 15,* 131–135.
14. May, R. & Yalom, I. (1984). Existential psychotherapy. In R.J. Corsini (Ed.), *Current psychotherapies* (3rd ed.). Itasca, IL: F.E. Peacock Publishers.
15. Lazarus, A.A. (1976). *Multimodal behavior therapy.* New York: Springer.

22

Critical Incident Reactions: A Comparison of Two Studies Ten Years Apart in the Same Police Department

Douglas Gentz

In April 1983 a group of police officers and the police department's psychologist began work on designing a survey to collect information about officer's reactions to what was then called "post shooting trauma." The survey was distributed to officers of the police department in May, 1983. Of the 730 surveys distributed, 164 were returned (22%).

The questions on the 1983 survey asked officers to describe their involvement (if any) in shooting situations, their reactions during and immediately after the shooting situation over the next four to six hours, and their long-term reactions to the situation. The survey also investigated a number of other questions regarding such topics as how many times officers told their story to investigators, how they would like their family to be notified, who they wanted to talk to about the situation, and how they assessed their chances of being involved in a similar incident in the future.

As a result of the findings of that survey, as well as other factors, the department authorized the formation of a Critical Incident Response Team. This group of officers has the responsibility of responding to officers when appropriate and also has the responsibility of providing In-Service Training to other officers. As the years passed after the 1983 survey it became clear that shooting situations account for only a portion of those situations that can be referred to as "critical incidents."

In an effort to update knowledge regarding police officers' responses and reactions to critical incidents, the Critical Incident Response Team began planning in the spring of 1993 to repeat the survey. The Team members worked together to revise the original survey to expand the definition of a critical incident to include more than just shooting situations. The revised survey had three basic purposes:

1. To insure that the Team's knowledge regarding officers' responses to critical incidents was current and accurate.
2. To ascertain the perceptions and attitudes of officers toward the Critical Incident Response Team.
3. To acquire information to disseminate to police officers as a part of In-Service Training.

In mid-September, 1993, 720 surveys were distributed to all officers of the department. Of those 720 surveys, 356 were returned and tabulated. This represented a 49% return rate which is more than two times greater than the 22% return rate in the 1983 survey. This increase in the response rate suggested to the Team that there was a greater awareness as well as an increased acceptance of the phenomenon of critical incidents by the officers. Another obvious factor leading to a greater response rate was the change from asking about post shooting trauma to asking about involvement in a critical incident. The 1993 survey defined a critical incident as: "An incident with the capacity to generate profound emotion and/or distress." In order to further clarify this definition the following additional description was provided on the first page of the survey.

Characteristics of a Critical Incident:

A sudden and unexpected event, not a normal, frequent event. Evokes feelings not normally a part of everyday life experiences. Can generate distress in a normal, healthy person. Involves some lingering aftereffects which may be physical, emotional or psychological.

Critical incidents are not limited to officers involved shooting or fatality accidents. They may include investigations of SIDS deaths or gruesome crime/accident scenes, and confrontations where the officer perceives himself or herself to be in great danger - whether or not injury occurs. What becomes a critical incident to one officer may not be a critical incident to another officer.

The 1993 survey asked respondents to list the number of years they had worked for the department. Years of service ranged from less than one year to 30 years. The 1993 survey also asked officers if they felt they had experienced at least one critical incident as defined above at some time during their career. Fifty-nine percent (211) responded that they had experienced a critical incident.

A subsequent question on the 1993 survey asked officers to give a brief description of their most significant critical incident and time on the department when the incident occurred. The clear majority (57%) reported that their most significant critical incident occurred sometime during their first five years on the department. The following table shows a breakdown of years officers had been on the department when the most significant critical incident occurred:

0 to 5 years	85	57%
6 to 10 years	34	23%
11 to 15 years	17	11%
16 to 20 years	10	7%
21 to 24 years	2	.01%

Note. Not all officers who described a critical incident provided the number of years they had been on the department when the incident occurred.

The most frequently reported kind of critical incident was "Death or serious injury of a fellow officer." It should be noted that approximately five months prior to the time that the survey was distributed, an officer was shot and killed during a routine traffic stop. This was the first violent death in the line of duty on this police department in over 10 years.

The descriptions of the kinds of critical incidents fell into seven categories as follows:

1. Death or Serious injury of an officer   57 cases
2. Gruesome scene   45 cases
3. Officer shooting a suspect   39 cases
4. Shot at by suspect OR shot at suspect,
   but no one was injured   38 cases
5. Deadly force justified but not used   27 cases
6. Near death incident not involving a
   shooting   18 cases
7. Miscellaneous   11 cases

The 1993 survey asked officers to endorse items on a list of possible reactions which occurred during or immediately after the critical incident. A sense of slow motion was the most frequently reported, followed by a sense of detachment, followed by tunnel vision as the third most frequent reaction reported.

A similar question in the 1983 survey yielded very similar results—slow motion, sense of detachment, and tunnel vision were also reported in that order as the most frequently occurring reactions. Other experiences reported in the 1983 study included a sense of disorientation, apathy, hearing deficiency, profuse sweating, increased auditory sensitivity, and a sense of serenity and/or calmness.

Officers were asked in the 1993 survey to endorse items from a list of possible physical and emotional reactions experienced beginning with the incident until approximately four to six hours afterwards.

The most frequently reported physical reaction by officers was an adrenaline surge (57%), followed by crying (18%), and tremors (15%). Other reactions included profuse perspiration, dizziness, involuntary laughter, vomiting, affected vision, involuntary urination, extreme fatigue, headache, and "cotton mouth."

A similar question in the 1983 study yielded similar results—the most frequently reported reaction was an adrenaline surge and the second most frequently reported reaction was tremors.

The most frequently reported emotional reaction by officers in the 1993 study was disbelief (44%), the second was anger (28%) and the third was fear (24%). Others included guilt, elation, shame about any physical reactions, loss of patience, preoccupation with the event, and sadness and/or depression.

Results from the 1983 survey showed the same top three reactions but in reverse order. In the earlier study the most frequently reported reaction was fear, followed by anger, followed by disbelief.

An item on the 1993 survey asked officers to respond by identifying, from a provided list of delayed reactions, those which they had experienced, or were still experiencing. Among the responses to this question, the most commonly reported delayed reactions were flashbacks (voluntary or involuntary) reported by 92 (44%) of the officers who had experienced a critical incident. The other most frequently reported reactions included insomnia, feelings of depression/sadness, feelings of anxiety, and fear of a similar incident. A partial list of less frequently reported delayed reactions included social withdrawal, fatigue or lethargy, denial (stating "it doesn't bother me at all" even though it really does), impaired concentration, family withdrawal, increased tendency to criticize self, and avoidance of the scene of the incident.

The 1983 study found that flashbacks were also the most commonly reported delayed reaction, followed by fear of a similar situation, denial of an existing concern, social withdrawal, fear of "freezing up" in a similar situation, a family withdrawal, feelings of anxiety, increase in insomnia, alcohol consumption. and fear of overreaction.

The 1993 study asked officers to describe how they dealt with the aftereffects of their critical incidents. These descriptions seemed to fit into seven general categories. The most frequently reported way of dealing with the aftereffects was talking with fellow officers, followed by acceptance. Other responses (in descending order of frequency) were engaging in denial: "no effects to deal with"; talking with family, friends, clergy; negative responses (alcohol, sleeping pills, fatalistic attitude, etc.); and professional counseling.

The 1983 study asked officers if they felt a need to speak personally about a shooting incident with another officer. A majority of officers at that time reported having had that desire.

The 1993 study did ask officers to list with whom they discussed their reactions, if with anyone at all. Most officers (135 of 211) spoke with a fellow officer, followed closely by those who spoke with a family member/spouse (120 of 211). Other responses included speaking with a civilian friend (40), "no one" (36), CIRT Team member (23), psychologist or psychiatrist (19), and clergy (18).

Officers were asked in the 1993 study if they were involved in future critical incidents would they prefer to remain at the scene or leave the scene as soon as possible. Of the officers who responded to this question, 59% (161 officers) reported a preference for leaving the scene as soon as possible, while 41% (110) said they would prefer to remain at the scene longer. In the 1983 study 57% wanted to leave the scene as soon as possible and 43 % wanted to stay longer.

An item on the 1993 survey asked officers their preference about having a CIRT member available after a critical incident. Of those that responded to this item 252 (78%) expressed a preference to have CIRT support as soon as possible. Sixty-three (19%) of those that responded to this item did not want a CIRT response, while 10 officers (3%) were undecided. This question was not asked on the 1983 survey because there was no Critical Incident Response Team in existence at the time.

Conclusions

The results of the 1993 survey can be interpreted as a validation of the findings of the 1983 study. Most of the common reactions to critical incidents that were documented in the earlier study were also reported in the later survey. It is certainly of interest to note that not only were most of the same reactions reported 10 years later, they were also reported in roughly the same frequency. This supports the idea that although what constitutes a critical incident varies from person to person, the reactions to critical incidents are fairly predictable.

The number of surveys completed and returned in this study was over twice as great as the number returned in the 1983 study (a 49% return rate as compared to a 22% return rate in 1983). This significant increase in the number of surveys returned suggests a greater awareness by officers regarding critical incidents. It may also suggest an increased willingness on the part of the officers to identify reactions to critical incidents as predictable and "normal." This shift in perception compared to perceptions in 1983 may be a result of the educational efforts of the Critical Incident Response Team members in Apprentice Police Officer Training, In-Service Training, and other informal training over the last 10 years. The core of that training has been to communicate the concept that reactions to critical incidents are normal, temporary, and treatable. It is hoped that training can continue to provide this "inoculation effect" which seems to reduce the possible negative, long-term impact of critical incidents on police officers who have been exposed to such situations.

23

Who Needs Peer Support?

James Janik

Virtually everyone has experienced a significant and stressful situation in their lifetime. Traditionally, it was family and friends who provided support, reassurance and the resources necessary to get through the crisis. However, the resources of families have been strained by divorce, and work and friendships have been isolated by occupational mobility. At the same time, the problems of daily life have become more common, more complicated and more often exacerbated by social and environmental pressures.

Peer support provides an opportunity for public safety personnel and their families to confidentially discuss personal and/or professional problems with one of their own. This non-professional peer supporter not only cares a great deal about their well-being, but also has a first-hand understanding of their situation.

Dr. Nels Clyver of the Los Angeles, California, Police Department and Dr. Robin Kline of the Long Beach, California, Police Department are two police psychologists who recognized early the advantages of using immediately accessible and resourceful support officers when troubled peers might be reluctant to discuss their situation with outsiders. Law enforcement officers have reported avoiding contacting professional counselors because of the potential impact upon employment or promotion, the desire to avoid reliving the stressful experiences they have "forced" out of their minds, the feeling that asking for help is an admission of weakness and a lack of confidence in employee assistance programs (EAPs) and mental health professionals who neither understand nor appreciate the context in which police decision are made.

Similarly, in an attempt to protect their families from the ugliness of the street, police officers are sometimes reluctant to be candid with them, which creates significant barriers to open, trusting and sharing partnerships. Thus, officers may unwittingly become tough and aggressive when dealing with their families—growing less involved emotionally and more suspicious, distrustful, rigid, cynical and opinionated.

Officers' spouses often comment on the unwritten law that fellow police officers rarely intervene in each other's domestic disturbances. Similarly, officers may be reluctant to report a coworker's brutality to a senior officer, especially if that person is someone who acts as back-up at the officer's potentially dangerous calls.

Family relationships tend to suffer as officers gravitate towards spending more time with fellow officers who do not criticize them; often this time is spent drinking together. Hurrell and Kroes estimate that 25% of all police personnel are dependent to some degree on alcohol as a stress reliever.[1] Wolford reports that in a 1990 survey of police officers by the National Institute of Occupational Safety, 37% reported severe marital problems.[2] My own research has found that officers who are referred for fitness-for-duty evaluations are 4.8 times more likely to attempt suicide if they complain of marital problems and 6.7 times more likely if they had been suspended for abusing citizens; they were 37 times more likely to make a suicide attempt if both conditions were present.[3] Perhaps not surprisingly, McCafferty, et al., reported that a dissolution of marriage through divorce/angry separation is the most common event preceding suicide in an alcoholic.[4] Specifically, Danto found that marital problems may be a concomitant—if not precipitating—factor in police officer suicides.[5] Given the degree of legal precision required in officers' work, the unsettling circumstances they are called to and the erosion of family supports that can occur, there can be no question that there is a need for peer support among police officers.

Ideally, peer support begins when an officer initiates a contact with an identified peer supporter. At other times, peer supporters may reach out individually or educationally in roll-call meetings to discuss common problems and solutions to situations facing police officers. For example, peer supporters often get involved following family tragedies, shootings, mass disasters, severe injury to a child, or the injury or death of another officer.

Officers also find peers helpful in discussing communication difficulties with their supervisors and low job satisfaction, as possibly reflected in

1. J. Hurrell, and W. Kroes, "Stress Awareness," in W.H. Kroes and J.J. Hurrell, (eds.), *Job Stress and the Police Officer: Identifying Stress Reduction Techniques*, HEW Publication (NIOSH) No. 76–187 (Washington, DC: U.S. Department of Health, Education and Welfare, 1975), pp. 234–246.

2. R. Wolford, *The Relationship Among Police Stressors, Coping Strategies, Alcohol Expectancy and Drinking Patterns for Law Enforcement Officers*, unpublished doctoral thesis, Northern Illinois University, DeKalb, Illinois, 1993.

3. James Janik, "Police Suicides: The Trouble Starts at Home," in J. Reese and E. Scrivner (eds.), *Law Enforcement Families: Issues and Answers* (Washington, DC: S. Department of Justice Publication, 1994).

4. F. McCafferty, C. McCafferty, and M. McCafferty, "Stress and Suicide in Police Officers: A Paradigm of Occupational Stress," *Southern Medical Journal*, 1992, (85): 233–243.

5. B. Danto, "Police Suicide," *Police Stress*, 1970, pp. 1, 32–36, 38, 40.

performance evaluations, use of sick leave, tardy problems, disciplines or transfers. Officers may doubt their own effectiveness when they receive citizens' complaints and simply not understand how to effectively manage citizens' behavior. They may become fearful of changes in society around them or worried about changes in themselves or their coworkers. Young officers may simply have questions about how to be happier in their jobs, while older officers may be experiencing more profound existential dilemmas about the meaning of their lives.

At times, officers can self-refer with problems that later involve experiences of psychopathology (which must be referred to a mental health professional); at others, the referral may not even directly involve them. For example, Maslach and Jackson reported that the spouses of police officers who score high on their burnout scale were very likely to report using alcohol as a device to cope with their stress.[6]

Peer support is a very effective tool to foster problem solving. However, using departmental personnel as peer supporters can raise many significant ethical, legal and confidentiality questions. For example, how should peer supporters be selected? Should unions or management run the program? How far can confidentially be extended? What of dual relationships—e.g., being both a confidant told of illegal behavior and a sworn officer of the court who is loyal to departmental and ethical standards? Where, how, when and to whom should referrals be made? How are peer supporters supervised?

These and other concerns have occupied the Psychological Services Section of the IACP for the past three years. Dialogue with representatives from police departments across the country, including the various perspectives of officers, therapists and spouses, has enabled the section to offer the association the enclosed guidelines for peer support programs.

The section endorses the use of peer support programs in all law enforcement departments. Peer support may be used to assist with such relatively small problems as finding babysitters for officers on rotating shifts, balancing checkbooks and getting along with neighbors, as well as larger problems that may compromise an officer's effectiveness, possibly producing agitation, anxiety, depression and panic. The section especially advocates its use for seemingly insurmountable multiple problems that can be prioritized and addressed with the assistance of a helping friend.

The object of peer support is to make small interventions, before crises develop. Peer support is best at stimulating personal and social resources that may have temporarily broken down. Peer support is not psychotherapy, of course, and peer supporters are officers first and last.

---

6. C. Maslach and D. Jackson, "The Measurement of Experienced Burnout," *Journal of Occupational Behavior*, 1981, 2: 99–112.

But they can provide important help and support when the usual problem-solving devices are not working. A peer supporter might intervene in self-defeating behaviors, clarify perceptions of a problem, bolster self-esteem, help modify behavior, develop new skills and find alternatives. The problem is always jointly explored, within a supportive relationship built on mutual trust, truth and commitment. With peer support, there is potential for significant self-growth, and concrete stress reduction is an achievable reality.

Peer support can complement services already provided within and outside your agency. Peer supporters work with EAPs, chaplains and mental health professionals, expanding available agency resources by providing greater choices and immediate and informal access to help. A form of emotional first aid, peer support helps individuals help themselves.

Many police departments across the country have found distinct advantages in establishing peer support programs. A number of federal law enforcement agencies, as well as private organizations, are embarking on this process in an attempt both to improve the relationship between management and employees, and to improve efficiency, product quality and worker satisfaction. There are anecdotal reports that peer support also reduces the utilization of health benefits since problems are addressed and resolved before they reach the crisis stage.

Departments that wish to establish peer support programs and have questions that may not be addressed in the following guidelines may contact the author or any member of the IACP Psychological Services Section. Some departments, such as the Illinois State Police, have modified the initial LAPD model for their local needs; other models are applicable when there is great geographical distances between officers. Interested readers are referred to Trooper Kim Castro of the Illinois State Police in Springfield, Illinois; Dr. Steve Curran of Greenside Psychological Associates in Cockeysville, Maryland; Lieutenant Al Brenner, Ph.D., of the San Francisco, California, Police Department; Dr. James Shaw of the Thurston County, Washington, Sheriff's Department; and Dr. Nancy Bohl of The Counseling Team of San Bernardino, California, all of whom have been very involved in the establishment of peer support programs.

Peer Support Guidelines

1. The goal of peer support is to provide all public safety employees within an agency the opportunity to receive emotional and tangible peer support though times of personal or professional crises and to help anticipate and address potential difficulties. A peer support program must have a procedure for mental health consultation and training. A peer support

program is developed and implemented under the organizational structure of the parent agency.

2. To ensure maximum utilization of the program and to support assurances of confidentiality, there should be participation on the Steering Committee of relevant employee organizations, mental health professionals and police administrators during planning and subsequent stages. Membership on the Steering Committees should have a wide representation of involved sworn and non-sworn parties.

3. Sworn peer support officers are officers first and peer supporters second. Any conflicts of roles should be resolved in that context.

4. A Peer Support Person (PSP), sworn or non-sworn, is a specifically trained colleague, not a counselor or therapist. A peer support program can augment outreach programs—e.g., employee assistance programs and in-house treatment programs—but not replace them. PSPs should refer cases that require professional intervention to a mental health professional. A procedure should be in place for mental health consultations and training.

Selection

1. PSPs should be chosen from volunteers who are currently in good standing with their department and who have receive recommendations from their superiors and/or peers.

2. Considerations for selection of PSP candidates include but are not limited to previous education and training, resolved traumatic experiences and desirable interpersonal qualities, such as maturity, judgement, and personal and professional credibility.

Training

1. Relevant introductory and continuing training for a PSP could include:
   a. Confidentiality issues
   b. Communication facilitation and listening skills
   c. Ethical issues
   d. Problem assessment
   e. Problem-solving skills
   f. Alcohol and substance abuse
   g. Cross-cultural issues
   h. Medical conditions often confused with psychiatric disorders
   i. Stress management
   j. AIDS information
   k. Suicide assessment

l. Depression and burnout

m. Grief management

n. Domestic violence

o. Crisis management

p. Nonverbal communication

q. When to seek mental health consultation and referral information

r. Traumatic intervention

s. Limits and liability

Administration

1. A formal policy statement should be included in the departmental policy manual that gives written assurances that within limits of confidentiality PSPs will not be asked to give information about members they support. The only information that management may require about peer support cases is anonymous statistical information regarding the utilization of a PSP.

2. A peer support program shall be governed by a written procedures manual that is available to all personnel.

3. Individuals receiving peer support may voluntarily choose ro reject a PSP by any criteria they believe are important.

4. Management could provide non-compensatory support for the PSP program.

5. Departments are encouraged to train as many employees as possible in peer support skills.

6. A peer support program coordinator should be identified who has a block of time devoted to program logistics and development. This individual would coordinate referrals to mental health professionals, collect utilization data and coordinate training and meetings.

7. The peer support program is not an alternative to discipline. A PSP does not intervene in the disciplinary process, even at a member's request.

8. The steering committee shall identify appropriate ongoing training for PSPs.

Consultation Services from Mental Health Professionals

1. PSPs must have a mental health professional to consult.

2. PSPs should be aware of their personal limitations and should seek consultation when determining when to disqualify themselves from working with individuals who have problems for which they have not been trained or about which they may have strong personal beliefs.

3. PSP should be required to advance their skills through continuing training, as scheduled by the program coordinator.

Confidentiality

1. PSPs must inform department members of the limits of their confidentiality and consider potential role conflicts (e.g., supervisor providing peer support). These should be consistent with law and departmental policy and may include:
   a. threats to self
   b. threats to specific people
   c. felonies as specified by the department
   d. serious misdemeanors as specified by the department
   e. child, spouse and elder abuse

2. PSPs should be trained to be sensitive to role conflicts that could affect future decisions and recommendations on assignments, e.g., to investigations, transfers and promotions. PSPs cannot abdicate their job responsibility as officers by participating in the program.

3. PSPs do not volunteer information to supervisors; they advise supervisors of the confidentiality guidelines established by the department.

4. PSPs must advise members that information told to them is not protected by legal privilege and that confidentiality is administratively provided and may not be recognized in court proceedings.

5. PSPs should avoid conflicting peer support relationships. For example, PSPs should not develop peer support relationships with supervisors, subordinates or relatives. PSPs should avoid religious, sexual or financial entanglements with receivers of peer support and avoid espousing particular values, moral standards and philosophies.

6. PSPs must not keep written formal or private records of supportive contacts.

24

Using Peer Supporters to Help Address Law Enforcement Stress

Peter Finn
Julie Esselman Tomz

Police officers in crisis often seek help from their peers, and in every department, a few individuals who prove adept at helping others are turned to repeatedly. Law enforcement agencies attempt to capitalize on this natural phenomenon by establishing peer support programs. In doing so, they provide training to increase the effectiveness of these natural peer helpers while marketing their services so that as many individuals as possible become aware of the peer supporters' availability. Organized peer support programs also help agencies choose just the right individuals to meet the needs of employees in trouble.

A number of law enforcement agencies currently use peer supporters to help employees prevent and deal with stress.[1] Their experiences can help other agencies implement their own peer support programs.

---

1. The information in this article is based on a literature review on law enforcement stress and stress programs, as well as in-person and telephone interviews with program directors, mental health providers, law enforcement administrators, union and association officials, officers, family members, and civilians associated with law enforcement stress programs at a number of agencies. The programs researched for this article were selected based on the suggestions of an advisory board consisting of police psychologists and practitioners and the recommendations of law enforcement mental health professionals gathered at an FBI law enforcement symposium in Quantico, Virginia, in January 1995. This research project was supported by the U.S. Department of Justice, National Institute of Justices, Contract OJP-94-C-007. *See* Peter Finn and Julie Esselman Tomz, *Developing a Law Enforcement Stress Program for Officers and Their Families* (Washington, DC: U.S. Government Printing Office, 1997). and "Reducing Stress: An Organization-Centered Approach." *FBI Law Enforcement Bulletin,* August, 1997, 20–26.

Justifying Peer Support Programs

Peer supporters serve two major functions. First, they provide a source of help for officers who are unwilling to bring their problems to mental health professionals because they mistrust "shrinks," would feel stigmatized for not being able to handle their problems on their own, or are afraid that entering therapy might hurt their careers. While peer supporters cannot provide the level of service professionals can, they still can help considerably.[2] Furthermore, peer supporters usually are more accessible than professional counselors.

Second, peer supporters can refer receptive officers to professional counselors. Many officers are more likely to take advantage of professional counseling services when a referral comes from a trusted peer than if they have to make an appointment on their own or follow the suggestion of a family member. In this regard, peer supporters act as a bridge to professionals.

Like professional counselors who are also sworn officers, peer supporters offer instant credibility to empathize. A large cadre of trained peer supporters can match fellow officers with those who have experienced the same incident, thus heightening the empathy inherent in the peer relationship. For example, the Bureau of Alcohol, Tobacco and Firearms (BATF) operates three peer programs, each with a separate focus, linking officers with peer supporters who are critical incident survivors, victims of sexual assault, or recovering alcoholics.

In addition, because of their daily contact with fellow officers, peer supporters are in a better position to detect incipient problems before they become full blown. As a result, peer support programs are "proactive and preventative in nature."[3]

Defining Peer Supporter Responsibilities

Peer supporters have three major responsibilities: *listening, assessing,* and *referring.*[4] By *listening,* peer supporters provide an opportunity for

2. Law enforcement therapists emphasize that officers who become peer supporters are not trained to provide counseling and, to avoid misunderstanding about their role, should be called, "peer supporters," not "peer counselors."

3. M. McMains, "The Management and Treatment of Postshooting Trauma: Administration Programs," in James T. Reese, James M. Horn, and Christine Dunning, *Critical Incidents in Policing* (Washington, DC: U.S. Department of Justice, 1991), 191–196.

4. Nancy Bohl, Director, The Counseling Team, San Bernardino, California, interview with the authors, July 27, 1995.

officers under stress to express their frustrations, fears, and other emotions to another person who understands from personal experience how they are feelings and why they are upset. As one peer supporter said, "Most of the calls I get are about work-related anxiety due to department problems, not street problems. I became a sounding board, giving them an opportunity to vent."[5]

By listening, peer supporters also can assess whether the officer's problem is of a nature or severity that requires professional—and immediate—help. With proper training, peer supporters can note the signs that indicate an officer may be suicidal, homicidal, severely depressed, abusing alcohol or other drugs, or have other serious problems. If the officer has a serious problem, the peer can refer the person for professional help. Professional stress programs provide peer supporters with information about available referral resources in addition to the department's own stress services. For example, when a peer supporter in San Bernardino was asked by another officer whether he could contract AIDS after cutting himself while subduing an HIV-positive suspect, the peer arranged for an expert in HIV exposure from a local hospital to talk to the officer.

Identifying Appropriate Issues

Experts agree that peer supporters prove especially appropriate for assisting officers involved in shooting incidents and officers with drinking problems. Many peer supporters are recoving alcoholics who can link fellow officers with detoxification programs, inpatient treatment, and Alcoholics Anonymous groups. These peer supporters may also attend support group meetings with officers beginning the recovery process and, as sponsors, may follow up on their attendance and help them to avoid or deal with lapses.

Officers who have been involved in critical incidents themselves can provide effective support to fellow officers who become involved in shootings. These officers often feel that no one can understand their turmoil except another officer who has experienced a similar incident. Furthermore, after being relieved of their weapons, interrogated, and subjected to a departmental investigation and possibly a civil suit, these officers often feel equally or even more disturbed by what they perceive as their department's lack of support. Reflecting the valuable role fellow offi-

---

5. Peer supporter who requested confidentiality, interview with the authors, July 26, 1995.

cers can play, BATF mandates that all special agents in charge use the agency's peer supporters after every shooting that results in death or injury. While peer supporters should not provide counseling they can and do help other officers realize that the fear, anger, and other emotions they may experience after a critical incident are normal under the circumstances.

Peer supporters help officers and their families during times of crisis not only by spending time with them but also by performing services for them. Peer supporters in San Bernardino painted one widow's house and cut another widow's grass. When a wounded officer was hospitalized, peer supporters fed the officer's cat. Supervisors in several departments call on peer supporters to stay with the family around the clock for a week after an officer is killed.

Stress can come from a variety of situations, even those that do not result in injury or death. Illinois State Police peer supporters refer officers with money management problems to the state's credit bureau for assistance. Officers having trouble making credit card payments can work out an arrangement in which the credit cart issuer prohibits further use of the card but imposes no additional interest on the money owed until the officer can pay it back. According to a peer supporter with the Michigan State police behavioral science section, "Money problems are a sign of or a source of stress for many officers, so it's entirely appropriate for peer supporters to link them with organizations that help them manage their money."[6]

Connecting Peers

Peer support can occur in a variety of settings. Peer supporters may respond to other officers' requests to meet and talk. A peer supporter in San Bernardino may get a radio call asking, "Are you clear for an 87?" — a request to talk that does not reveal the purpose of the meeting. In the New Haven, Connecticut, Police Department, officers can page the peer supporter of their choice 24 hours a day.

Some peer supporters always wait for other officers to come to them, but many will approach a fellow officer when they observe the person having difficulty. Usually, their approach is subtle. Rather than announcing, "I'm a peer supporter, and I'm here to help you," they say something like. "It seems like you've been coming on duty late the last few days. What's up?" A great deal of peer support takes place spontaneously

---

6. Jeffrey Atkins, Michigan State Police, behavioral science section, interview with the authors, June 20, 1995.

around the water cooler, over coffee, or wherever an officer and a peer supporter happen to run into each other.

Officers who take time off to recover from a serious injury or illness often feel isolated and frightened. As a result, employees from the Palo Alto, California, Police Department receive training in workers' compensation law so they can visit at home officers who are disabled to provide support, information about their rights to workers' compensation, and assistance in navigating the complex reimbursement system. Officers involved in a shooting also can feel upset over their change of duties and the legal procedures that often follow. Peer supporters in the San Antonio Police Department prepare officers for these events, emphasizing that, while the change may last several months until a litigation has been resolved, it is only temporary.

Recruiting, Screening, and Training Peer Supporters

Recruiting and Screening

Program directors use different approaches to recruit peer supporters. Some announce the position in police department and association newsletters, departmentwide memos, at roll call, and at union or association meetings. The Erie County, New York, program received several referrals from police associations when the vice president of the Western New York Police Association, a network of law enforcement unions in the region, sent letters to its union members promoting the concept of peer support and inviting members to apply. BATF reviews its files to identify agents who have survived critical incidents. Reviews of past alcohol-related adverse actions identify possible candidates for the bureau's alcohol peer support program. Bureau staff counselors sometimes identify candidates from among their clients.

A police department in Texas combined several steps for recruiting peer supporters. First, the agency asked officers to volunteer. Then, it gave all officers in the agency a peer survey form to complete and return anonymously on which they ranked every officer in the department on a 1 to 5 scale (1 = totally unqualified) in terms of how effective each would be as a peer supporter. The form provided a short description of what peer support was and a brief overview of the activities peer supporters would conduct. Before analyzing the responses, a team of three psychologists interviewed the applicants about why they wanted to be peer supporters and what skills they could bring to their roles. The psychologist also asked a series of situational questions designed to assess the volunteers' communication and listening skills, as well as their ability to solve problems and empathize. To qualify, volunteers had to be approved by a psychologist and ranked highly by their colleagues. Interestingly, the six individuals selected by the psychologists also had the highest average ratings among their colleagues.[7] Peer supporters who have been recommended by their fellow officers are more likely to be accepted in their new roles than if sworn personnel had no say in the selection.[8] However, rejected applicants may become resentful and damage the peer support component by criticizing it in front of other officers.

An agency's command staff should approve the selections, as well. Administrators who disagree with the selections often do not encourage their use or make referrals and even may not allow peer supporters to spend on-duty time helping other officers.

Some law enforcement agencies accept applicants for peer supporter positions solely on the basis of a desire to help troubled colleagues. This is a mistake; instead, the program director needs to develop selection criteria and institute recruitment procedures to ensure than only qualified officers are chosen and accepted. An effective peer program depends on screening out inappropriate officers. Peer supporters should be selected based on some combination of the following criteria:

- A reputation as someone whom others already seek out for informal peer support and who keeps information confidential
- Quality of social skills and ability to empathize
- Previous education and training
- Several years of experience on the street
- Nomination by other officers
- Approval or recommendation from the chief or other command staff
- Previous use of the program
- Information provided in a letter of interest
- Ability to complete the training program successfully.

While some officers who have recovered successfully from critical incidents should be chosen, peer supporters should also have a variety of experiences so that it becomes possible to match peer supporters with officers under stress based on the similarity of their critical incidents. In addition to officers who have experienced shootings, officers can be se-

7. W.C. Mullins, "Peer Support Team Training and Intervention for the Police Family," in James T. Reese and Ellen Scrivner, *Law Enforcement Families: Issues and Answers* (Washington, DC: U.S. Department of Justice, 1994), 205–212.
    8. Ibid.

lected who have experienced the death of a police partner, been alcoholics, or lived through family traumas, such as the death of a child or spouse.

Because officers usually are extremely reluctant to turn to anyone of a different rank for peer support, individuals of all ranks should be encouraged to become peer supporters. The International Association of Chiefs of Police recommends that peer supporters not assist "...supervisors, subordinates, or relatives."[9] Program staff should try to train several sergeants and lieutenants as peer supporters so that senior officers have someone of their rank they can go to for assistance, as well as to increase support for the peer program among command staff. It also is important to recruit nonsworn employees and family members as peer supporters. Civilian personnel may feel uncomfortable sharing problems with officers, while family members may feel that they can receive empathetic treatment only from other family members.

In the past, some programs have required that officers have counseling certificates or degrees in order to become a peer supporters. At one time, the Dallas Police Department required that peer supporters be state-licensed counselors. The New York City Police Department required its peer supporters, most of whom worked with other officers with drinking problems, to have completed all of the requirements leading to state certification as alcoholism counselors. However, most programs do not have such stringent requirements, and such certification is not necessarily a prerequisite to becoming an effective peer supporter. Still, in many states, certification serves an advantage by making conversations between peer supporters and other officers privileged communications.

Finally, officers should volunteer to be peer supporters, and no external rewards should come with the position, such as enhanced chances for promotion. Only truly voluntary participation can ensure that the assistance peer supporters give will be perceived as genuine and, therefore, will prove beneficial.

Initial Training

Peer candidates generally receive 3 to 5 days of training. The DEA provides 64 hours of initial training, leading to certification of peer trauma team members, who then must receive 24 to 40 hours of additional training every 3 to 4 years to remain certified.

Training should focus on developing skills for active listening; recognizing and assessing officers' problems; determining the need for referral to

---

9. International Association of Chiefs of Police, Peer Support Guidelines, Alexandria, Virginia, 1993.

professionals; and selecting the proper resource to provide professional assistance. Training also may cover problem-solving techniques, dealing with death, and responding to relationship problems.

Training must emphasize the need for peer supporters to avoid providing therapy, to know their limits as to what they can offer and do, and to contact professionals freely and immediately if they have questions about how to proceed. Training also should stress the need for peer supporters to maintain strict confidentiality unless employees pose a threat to themselves or others or have committed crimes. In such cases, peer supporters must explain what information cannot remain confidential.

Training typically involves lectures, demonstrations, and role-play exercises. In some programs, staff members videotape simulated support sessions and critique the interchange. The 3-day training program provided by the Long Beach, California, Police Department is divided into three parts: explanation, demonstration, and performance. During the training, instructors present psychological principles and later demonstrate them in a simulated counseling settings. The class then breaks into small groups to practice the skills under the instructors' supervision.[10] Trainers in the Rochester, New York, Police Department assess trainee proficiency using a 5-point scale to rate the officers on such parameters as openness to learning and supervision, self-awareness, listening skills, objectivity, and the ability to maintain confidentiality. The trainees must achieve a defined level of proficiency before being allowed to work as peer supporters.[11]

The San Bernardino program invites staff members from a county employee assistance program that serves law enforcement officers to attend at least part of the training so they will not feel as though the peer supporters are competing with them for clients. Staff members from another program encourage peer supporters to meet with private practitioners to allay fears about taking away their business.[12] In fact, peer supporters will need to refer some individuals to area professionals and these professionals should attend at least some of the training so they understand the nature of the peer support program.[13]

---

10. R. Klein, "Police Peer Counseling: Officers Helping Officers," *FBI Law Enforcement Bulletin*, October 1989, 1–4.

11. G. Goolkasian, R. W. Geddes, and W. DeJong. *Coping with Police Stress* (Washington, DC: U.S. Department of Justice, 1985), 57.

12. E. Schmuckler, "Peer Support and Traumatic Incident Teams: A Statewide Multiagency Program," in James T. Reese, James M. Horn, and Christine Dunning. *Critical Incidents in Policing* (Washington, DC: U.S. Department of Justice, 1991), 318.

13. Supra note 4.

Follow-up Training and Program Monitoring

Most programs provide follow-up to the initial training to reinforce or expand the peer supporters' skills, enable them to share and learn from their experiences, and monitor their activity. The peer supporters for the Rhode Island Centurion Program meet every 2 months for 2 hours of additional training provided by clinical staff from the inpatient hospital the program uses when clients need hospitalization. The training addresses topics in which the peer supporters have expressed interest, such as confidentiality and suicide indicators. Every 3 months, the Counseling Team, a group of professional therapists in San Bernardino, California, that provides stress services to a variety of area law enforcement agencies, offers a free, 3-hour follow-up training session to all peer supporters.

Staff from the Counseling Team and some other programs require that peer supporters complete contact sheet logs.[14] The Counseling Team also asks peer supporters to complete a simple checklist for each support session. The checklist includes a case number and an indication of whether the person was sworn or nonsworn; male or female; management or nonmanagement; and on-duty or off-duty. Also included is a list of stress-related issues for which the employee received support, ranging from problems with co-workers to financial concerns to substance abuse. The forms serve as a means to determine whether any peer supporters are being overworked, not only on the basis of the numbers of hours they have been spending on support but also as a result of transfers. By using these forms, the director of the Counseling Team learned that two of three homicide detectives serving as peer supporters in one agency had been transferred, leaving the entire responsibility for peer support with one remaining detective. By asking peer supporters to record their current shift assignments, the forms can also detect if too many peer supporters are working the same shift, leaving other shifts uncovered.

Finally, the forms may point to temporary departmentwide problems that may need to be addressed. For example, in one department, three-fourths of all peer support hours were being devoted to relationship problems; within a few months, 19 officers had gotten divorced. As a result, the Counseling Team offered a seminar on marriage and family support to the peer supporters.

Stress programs must monitor burnout among peer supporters, both in terms of the ongoing, everyday support and also following particularly in-

---

14. For an example of a detailed peer log, which may ask for more information than most peers can or will provide, see Blau, *Psychological Services for Law Enforcement* (New York: John Wiley and Sons, 1994), 181.

tense incidents. If peer supporters seem overwhelmed with their care taking responsibilities, the program manager may need to get outside help. Local victim/witness assistance programs and chaplains can meet this need. To help prevent peer burnout, the DEA offers an annual workshop called "Healing the Healer" for all clinicians and peer trauma teams members who have responded to a critical incident in the previous year.

Overcoming Limitations

Several potential weaknesses of peer programs exist. First, peer supporters cannot substitute for the services of mental health professionals. Just as some officers are reluctant to seek professional help, others are unwilling to talk with peer supporters because they want to be counseled by a professional or because they fear a lack of confidentiality in talking with peer.

Indeed, confidentiality stands as perhaps the knottiest issue related to using peer supporters. Failure by peer supporters to maintain—and for management to respect—the confidentiality of what other officers say to a peer supporter can sabotage a peer supporter program. Some agencies try to ward off such threats. BATF emphasizes that peer supporters "are *mandated* to maintain total and complete confidentiality...no written reports are made or maintained." Unfortunately, the officer grapevine may spread word of an employee's troubles, inadvertently damaging a peer supporter's reputation. Georgia's peer support program may solve this dilemma. There, the Peace Officer Standards and Training Council staff set up peer support teams in each of the state's 10 emergency health regions. Members of each regions' team provide peer support to the public safety agencies within its jurisdiction, so employees need not turn to a co-worker for help.[15]

More important, however, communication between peer supporters and officers is usually not considered privileged conversation under the law, regardless of department rules, because peer supporters are not licensed mental health processionals. As a result, courts and police supervisors have the legal right to ask what was said during these interactions. This lack of confidentiality under the law can present a major barrier to peer support during critical incident debriefings.

For example, during stress debriefings after critical incidents, officers who participate in the incident sometimes make statements that could be construed as admissions of wrongdoing, including comments that begin with such phrases as "I should have..." or "If only I had..." Law en-

---

15. Supra note 12, 315–323.

The Benefits and Limitations of Peer Supporters

Benefits	Limitations
• Provide instant credibility and ability to empathize	• Cannot provide the professional care that licensed mental health practitioners can
• Assist fellow employees who are reluctant to talk with mental health professionals	• May try to offer full-scale counseling that they are not equipped to provide
• Recommend the program to other employees by attesting credibly to its confidentiality and concern	• May be rejected by employees who want to talk only with a professional counselor
• Provide immediate assistance due to accessibility	• May be avoided by employees because of the fear that problems will not be kept confidential
• Detect incipient problems because of their daily contact with co-workers	• Require time, effort, and patience to screen train, and supervise
• Less expensive than professionals	• May expose themselves and the department to legal liability.

forcement agencies cannot offer immunity from civil and criminal litigation to clinically unlicensed officers who participate in a debriefing to offer social support and are asked later to testify at departmental hearings or in civil and criminal proceedings about what they heard. As a result, program staff must warn officers who obtain counseling not to say anything incriminating during a counseling or debriefings session with other officers or when speaking privately with a peer supporter. Because peer supporters can be subpoenaed to testify during officer use-of-force trials and administrative hearings, they should not participate in group or individual debriefings following such incidents. However, licensed professional program staff who conduct debriefings and who are protected under certification law in state statute and by Rule 501 of the Federal Rules of Evidence cannot be forced to testify.

Even peer supporters who have considerable training in counseling—but still are not licensed—may not be protected by a confidentiality laws, depending on the definitions of various types of counselors in state statutes. A Massachusetts state trooper had nearly 300 hours of formal training in stress management, psychology, and related courses and several years of counseling experience both at a local chemical-dependency treatment center and his department's employee assistance unit before being assigned to the unit full time. Although he was not licensed, he considered himself a social worker. Moreover, because his department's policy deemed confidential all counseling provided through the employee assistance unit, the peer supporter told his help that their communication would be kept in confidence.

In March 1995, a woman filed assault and battery and other criminal charges against a trooper whom the peer supporter had assisted; the trooper was suspended from active duty. The peer supporter subsequently provided additional help to the trooper on several occasions the peer supporter's records were subpoenaed for the trooper's trial, but the supporter petitioned for a protective order, alleging that because he was a social worker employed by the state, his conversations with the trooper were privileged communication.

Disagreement centered on the state's definition of a social worker. The law specified that "all communications between...a social worker employed in a state, county or municipal governmental agency and a client are confidential,"[16] but the court maintained that the peer supporter was not, in fact, a social worker because he was not licensed. The Massachusetts Supreme Judicial Court later upheld the confidentiality of the trooper's conversations with the peer supporter.[17]

Finally, communication between peer supporters and other officers is never confidential if the officers being offered support appear to be a danger to themselves or to others, have engaged in child or spousal abuse, or have committed other crimes. To minimize legal complications, agencies should consult with a local attorney regarding their state laws and court rulings pertaining to confidentiality.

Confidentiality issues notwithstanding, in some situations, using officers to provide peer support to colleagues in the same agency may not prove effective. BATF officials prefer not to use peer supporters who are located in the jurisdiction of critical incidents involving large numbers of agents because the peer supporters may be too severely affected themselves by the incident to be able to help their colleagues. For example, after the bombing of the federal building in Oklahoma City in 1995, the BATF flew in eight peer supporters who contacted affected agents, their family members, and agents from other jurisdictions assigned to investigate the explosion. In the initial stage, the peer supporters allowed the visiting agents to continue their work without debriefing them but tried to remain visible, a task facilitated by the number of agents who already knew some of the peer supporters. Peer supporters also stayed with survivors and their families at hospitals and in homes.

About three-fourths of the agents' spouses attended the first voluntary meeting with the peer supporters in Oklahoma City. At this meeting, the peer supporters discussed the symptoms of stress the agents and their spouses could expect to experience. A second meeting with spouses included their children. Next, the peer supporters approached all of the BATF employees, starting with those who had been in the building at the

---

16. Ma. St. 112 Section 135A.

17. *Gilbert M. Bernard v. The Justices of the District Court of Cambridge*, 424 Mass. 32, 673 N.E. 2d 1220.

time of the explosion. Anticipating that some employees might be intimidated by mental health professionals, only peer supporters ran these initial sessions. Individual-level contact continued as the peer supporters encouraged everyone to approach them voluntarily. The employee assistance program mental health professionals were then integrated into the process.

Finally, in some jurisdictions, general issues of legal liability may make it unwise to establish a peer support program at all. For this reason, the Metro-Dade Police Department's stress program does not include a peer component, while the New York City Police Department requires that its peer supporter become certified alcoholism counselors. Agencies need to examine the issue of liability carefully to determine whether they will be immune from lawsuits if a peer supporter trained by their agency is accused of causing harm to another officer.

Conclusion

Professional stress services will remain essential for helping law enforcement officers cope with the pressure of police work. However, peer support programs can provide outlets for officers who are unwilling or not yet ready to seek professional help, make professional services acceptable to reluctant officers, and furnish assistance that only peers may have the time or understanding to provide. A number of law enforcement agencies already have demonstrated that officers will welcome—at least over time—the help peer support programs can provide. Moreover, when employees get the help they need, their agencies also benefit. Sensitively and conscientiously implemented, peer support programs can provide a significant source of assistance in every law enforcement agency.

25

Responding to Line-of-Duty Deaths

Roger C. Haddix

An average of 143 law enforcement officers are killed in the line of duty annually in the United States.[1] Whether the result of an adversarial action or an accident, the trauma caused by each death is felt by family survivors and department personnel for many months, or even years, after the event.

Still, most law enforcement agencies have not experienced a line-of-duty death. Perhaps for this reason, less than one-third of the agencies responding to a recent survey reported having any policy dealing with this sensitive issue.[2]

It is little wonder, then, that agencies dealing with a line-of-duty death for the first time often respond inadequately to the needs of survivors. This may stem from several factors, including the lack of information available regarding actions that agencies should take after the funeral. This article discusses some of the policy issues involved and recommends appropriate responses to family survivors and coworkers of officers who are killed in the line of duty.

Background

The subject of departmental response to survivors remained a largely uncharted and undocumented area until the mid-1980s. Before that time, only a few metropolitan agencies that had experienced line-of-duty deaths developed policies for such situations. This began to change on May 14, 1984, when 110 survivors formed Concerns of Police Survivors, Inc. (COPS), while attending a National Police Week seminar sponsored by

---

1. Timothy Flanigan and Kathleen Maguire, eds., *Sourcebook of Criminal Justice Standards, 1991*, U.S. Department of Justice, Bureau of Justice Statistics, U.S. Government Printing Office, Washington, DC, 1992, 413, 417.

2. Suzanne F. Sawyer, *Support Services to Surviving Families of Line-of-Duty Death*, Concerns of Police Survivors, Inc., March 1994.

the Fraternal Order of Police. This represented the first effort to form a national networking organization to aid survivors in the healing process and to provide guidance to agencies concerning line-of-duty death policies.[3]

Since that time, an increasing number of administrators have come to understand the importance of adopting line-of-duty death policies. As the threat to officers becomes more menacing and the list of police fatalities grows each year, the need for such policies becomes more apparent. The highly sensitive nature of on-duty deaths and the long-term response to survivors that agencies must provide underscores the need to formulate a policy *before* a tragedy occurs.

Preparing for Tragedy

No one wants to contemplate their own death. But, because law enforcement is a high-risk occupation and the very real possibility of death from accidents and felonious assaults exists, agencies have an obligation to their officers and officers owe it to their families to prepare for such tragedies.

Preparation should include educating offices about emergency notification of family members, funeral arrangements, survivor benefits, counseling options, and departmental support to survivors. Officers should take considerable comfort from knowing what benefits and support their families will receive in the event they are killed. Although the tragedy of losing a loved one will not be lessened, with preparation and forethought, the grieving process will not be aggravated by uncertainties and a lack of information.

Emergency Notification Forms

Agencies should use employee emergency information forms not only to obtain critical personal information from their officers but also to record officers' desires for notification of family members in the event of serious injury or death. While departments commonly notify the spouse of an officer after injury or death, they usually fail to contact the parents or grown children of an officer simply because that information is not available. In the absence of prior instructions from the officer, agencies should provide official notification to surviving parents and grown children, or make arrangements with another department if the distance prohibits notification by the officer's agency.

---

3. Ibid.

One of the procedural orders of the Charleston, South Carolina, Police Department, entitled *Handling a Law Enforcement Death or Serious Injury*, includes the "employee emergency information form," which is used to record notification information. The form also reserves space for special notification instructions and special family considerations. These forms are periodically updated and kept in the personnel section.

The National Association of Chiefs of Police publishes helpful line-of-duty death guidelines that contain a comprehensive officer questionnaire. The confidential questionnaire allows officers to record information about wills, insurance policies, funeral wishes, and the distribution of possessions. After the officer completes the questionnaire, it is sealed in an envelope to be opened only in the event to the officer's death or serious injury.[4]

Death Benefit Information

Agencies also should make sure to provide complete death benefit information to all officers so that they can prepare their families. This includes information about death benefit life insurance paid by the employing agency, survivor death benefits or annuities paid by a retirement plan, State and/or Federal death benefits, social security benefits, fraternal or labor group benefits, and financial benefits provided by civic organizations or special law enforcement support groups. Still, officers should review the benefits periodically because they may change over time.

The Mobile, Alabama, Police Department provides a comprehensive death benefits booklet for surviving family members. Officers who have this information possess an added degree of peace of mind knowing that their families will be provided for in the event of their death.

Family Support Team

Because of the complexity of issues surrounding a line-of-duty death, every agency needs to develop a family support team to provide a structured response to survivors. The Dallas, Texas, Police Department created such a team. The 10 team members handle everything from family services to ceremonial considerations.

Although few agencies require a team as large as the one in Dallas, every agency should develop a team to address five critical areas. Team members should be designated by their specific roles: Command liaison,

---

4. G.S. Arenberg, *Line-of-Duty Death of Law Enforcement Officer: Easing the Pain for the Family and Fellow Officers* (Washington, DC: National Association of Chiefs of Police, 1988).

benefits coordinator, financial coordinator, chaplain or minister, and family liaison.

Command Liaison

A senior command officer should head the family support team. This officer ensures that team members receive an appropriate level of training in their duties and supervises the team response. The command liaison officer also keeps the department head informed of problems or needs of the family.

The command liaison officer must possess ample rank and authority to implement fully the department's response to the survivors. This officer also should maintain a log of actions and prepare a calendar of significant dates that should be observed. These include the officer's birthday, spouse and children's birthdays, marriage anniversary, and graveside memorials.

Benefits Coordinator

The benefits coordinator may be a line officer, supervisor, or command officer from the administrative unit. As the title suggest, the benefits coordinator compiles all information on funeral payments and financial benefits provided to the family. This officer also explains other benefits and assistance programs that may be available. The benefits coordinator should meet with the primary survivor a day or two after the funeral.

Financial Coordinator

The financial coordinator may be an attorney or financial consultant who has been hired by the department or has volunteered to assist the officer's family. This person provides financial advice and assistance to family members so that they can make informed decisions concerning the amounts of money and benefits they will receive.

Chaplain or Minister

Chaplains or ministers provide comfort and support both to the family and to the department. Skilled in dealing with death and dying, they can offer insight and advice to survivors trying to cope with the trauma of loss. Many chaplains from larger agencies possess considerable experience with line-of-duty deaths and can provide invaluable assistance to chaplains of smaller department.

Family Liaison Officers

Family liaison officers—assigned either permanently or on a rotating basis to this duty—maintain frequent, scheduled contact with the family. They remain available on a standby basis to respond to any special request by family members.

Administrators should grant them broad latitude and flexibility in the initial months of the grieving process. However, they should keep the command liaison and/or agency head fully apprised of the emotional state of the family and inform them of any problem that they have encountered. They also should maintain a record of activities that they perform for survivors.

The Survivors

Family

In the aftermath of an officer's death, agencies often ask, "Who are the survivors?" The answer is anyone in the immediate family—spouse, children, siblings, mother, and father. Too often, agencies focus on a married officer's spouse and children and forget the parents. Because of the unexpected circumstances involved in law enforcement deaths, agencies should give special attention to notifying all immediate family members, and especially to anyone listed on the officer's emergency notification documents.

Officers may leave instructions to exclude some immediate family members from the official notification process. While this leaves the task of notification to primary survivors, an agency representative still should contact these family members later with condolences and to offer assistance. Law enforcement agencies have only one opportunity to provide a proper and caring response to family members. Departments should spare no effort in assisting them.

Fellow Officers

In the wake of an officer's death, law enforcement agencies must also respond to another group of survivors—the police family. Officers spend a great portion of their lives on the job with fellow officers and employees. This close contact results in strong bonds of friendship and camaraderie among agency personnel.

The loss of an officer in the line of duty affects every department member. Without adequate support, some may develop emotional and performance problems that adversely impact the department.

Response Issues

Support to survivors—both family and departmental—includes regular contact by members of the family support team, members of the department who knew the deceased officer, and department commanders. These contacts should be both formal and informal, planned and spontaneous.

Studies show that in the months following an officer's death, survivors frequently feel abandoned by the department that was supposed to be so close to their loved one but now seems to have forgotten the officer after death.[5] Members of the family support team and agency officials should make special efforts to call, visit, or send cards on birthdays, anniversaries, and holidays.

The agency also should give special attention to surviving children. While members in the department often make offers to get involved with the fallen officer's children, other obligations may soon take precedence. Officers must avoid making promises they cannot keep.

Counseling

In addition to a compassionate, understanding response from the department, some family and police survivors may require professional counseling. A report published by the National Institute of Justice (NIJ) states that the reactions of police survivors (i.e., spouses, parents, siblings, friends, and coworkers) may be so profound as to be diagnosed as post-traumatic stress disorder.[6] This psychological disorder is associated with traumatic events considered outside the usual range of human experience.[7]

In the past, police survivors often suffered prolonged psychological stress because they did not seek help, or agencies did not extend offers of assistance in this area. Traditionally, most law enforcement agencies have not considered the emotional and psychological needs of survivors to be a part of their responsibility. However, the NIJ report indicates that sensitivity and effective agency response procedures have a definite impact on the well-being of survivors.

---

5. Frances A. Stillman, "Line-of-Duty Deaths: Survivor and Departmental Responses," *National Institute of Justice Research in Brief*, January 1987.

6. Ibid.

7. *Diagnostic and Statistical Manual of Mental Disorders* (3rd edition) (Washington, DC: American Psychiatric Association, 1980).

Uniform Response

Reserarch into police deaths also reveals that spouses of officers killed accidentally experience the same level of stress as do spouses of homicide victims. At the same time, research indicates that parents of officers killed accidentally respond differently than do parents of those who are murdered. The latter were found to be more traumatized, hostile, and depressed.

Survivors also reported a differences in the response they received from departments. Researchers found that the survivors of homicide deaths received more preferential treatment than survivors of officers who died as a result of accidents.

Although some insensitive observers may question the heroism of an officer's accidental death, the department's response must be identical, regardless of the nature of the death. As with any memorial, it is the heroic life and the recognition of the supreme sacrifice made by the officer that is being honored, not the officer's death.

Court Proceedings

Deaths that result from adversarial actions create additional concerns, primarily relating to the attendance of family members at court proceedings. While the department should make every effort to honor the wishes of the family, agency commanders must address other considerations.

The media pose a particular concern because any appearance of family members in court will most likely be recorded in print and on film. Reporters understandably will seek interviews with survivors to capture their feelings and reactions. To deal with these possibilities the prosecutor should be consulted and should help develop a plan for family members to attend hearings and trials.

A prearranged plan is essential to satisfy the family's need for representation at court, as well as the prosecution's concern that the jury pool not be unduly influenced by the family's attendance. If family members do attend the hearings and trial, the department should offer to provide transportation and escorts.

The department and the prosecutor also must coordinate whether agency personnel should be present at hearings and the trial. Procedural rules in some States prevent involved officers from being present in the courtroom during testimony.

Whatever the case, some effort should be made to protect the officer's memory at the trial. If neither the family nor the agency represent the fallen officer, who will? Considering the support groups that exist for other types of victims, it is an unacceptable irony that police officers may be forgotten victims when suspects come to trial.

Continued Support

For the family, the months following an officer's death become particularly traumatic and stressful. As the initial shock begins to wear off, the reality of loss sets in. The department's actions during this period—what it does and does not do—will greatly impact the long-term recovery process for survivors.

No time limit exists for how long it should take a family to recover. Everyone deals with death and grieving differently. Perhaps the most important thing to remember is that the department now stands in the fallen officer's place.

Unfortunately, some agencies have done little or nothing for officer's families after the funeral. In contrast, other agencies have purchased and installed appliances, made arrangements for officers to mow the lawn, taken family members shopping, cared for children, provided transportation to and from school, or performed other simple, inexpensive, but meaningful tasks that the slain officer once did.

Of course, departments should not overwhelm survivors with attention. Nor should they devote an unreasonable amount of time and effort to providing support to survivors. No matter what a department does to assist the family and to compensate for the absence of the officer, a great feeling of loss remains inevitably.

However, departments can and should take steps to provide an ongoing response to survivors. The following time line incorporates aspects of policies and guidelines from several law enforcement agencies, as well as other sources.

First Month

For a month following the funeral, agency officials should make daily phone calls to check in with family members to see if they need anything. Family liaison officers should make regular visits; the command liaison officer, weekly visits. These visits need not be lengthy but are meant to reassure the family that they have not been forgotten.

The agency head should also place telephone calls and make personal contact with primary survivors when possible. In addition, department personnel might encourage their spouses to contact the surviving spouse or parents.

Second Through Sixth Month

The family liaison officers should continue to maintain regular contacts with the family. If the family indicates that the contacts can be reduced, the agency should honor their wishes, but the contacts should not be discontinued altogether.

Sixth Month and Beyond

Family liaison officers should continue to make calls and visits and provide any assistance necessary to family. The agency should continue to invite family members to department functions and events. Research indicates that as time goes on, survivors take great comfort simply in knowing that the department will be there if they need assistance.[8]

Memorials

When an officer dies in the line of duty, the department, fraternal and civic organizations, friends, neighbors, and concerned and caring members of the community often feel the need to create a memorial in the officer's honor. Such acts of remembrance represent a fitting and lasting tribute to officers who have fallen in the service of their communities.

Law enforcement agencies can provide several appropriate memorials to an officer's family. Departments can:

- Lobby for a special resolution from the State legislature or the city/county council.
- Arrange for special certificates from law enforcement-related organization
- Mount the officer's service weapon, handcuffs, badge, patches, and/or medals in a shadowbox for presentation to the family
- Assemble a scrapbook of photos, articles, and personal stories about the officer. Children especially value such mementos in later years.

In addition, the department and local governing body can create more public memorials, such as:

- Renaming a street, building, park, or bridge after the fallen officer
- Placing the officer's photograph in the lobby of police headquarters or another public building
- Publishing, on the anniversary of the officer's death, a story of the officer's life.

---

8. P. Radford, Concerns of Police Survivors, Inc. (COPS) National Trustee, interviewed December 5, 1994.

The community can also provide a memorial by establishing a scholarship fund for the surviving children or for students of criminal justice at a local university.

Conclusion

After the line-of-duty death of an officer, citizens often ask the chief of police if the department has gotten "back to normal." The fact is, a department that experiences the line-of-duty loss of an officer will never be the same. As long as the fallen officer's coworkers remain with the agency, the memory of the officer will be kept alive.

On a daily basis, law enforcement officers must cope with an inordinate amount of stress brought on by constant conflicts with violators, complainants, irate citizens, and demanding supervisors. Compounding this burden is the fact that death could be just the next call away. All law enforcement officers deal with this burden every working day.

Officers should not have to bear the additional worry that their department will fail to care for their family adequately if a tragedy should occur. By developing a comprehensive response strategy, agencies can relieve officers of this burden.

26

The Will to Survive*

Stephen R. Band
I. John Vasquez

Shots are fired! One subject is down, and three police officers are wounded. Another armed subject appears in the doorway, and two of the officers, stunned at the sight of their wounds, are unable to defend themselves. But, the third officer fights on, firing until the second subject is incapacitated.

This scenario could be an excerpt from a movie, but unfortunately, it is all too real. Each day, law enforcement officers across the nation face life-and-death situations. In fact, between 1979 and 1988, 841 police officers were feloniously killed in scenarios such as this.[1]

Can law enforcement officers encounter a life-threatening, violent confrontation and go home at the end of the day? Do they have the will to survive and fight on when faced with death? The answers to these questions go beyond combat tactics and accuracy with a weapon. One element is still missing: Survivability—the mental preparation and personal will to survive.

The Operations Resource and Assessment Unit (ORAU) at the FBI Academy, Quantico, Virginia, conducted a pilot study and sought expert opinions in order to identify the human attributes associated with survivability. This article will discuss the available background research and will review the FBI's findings.

Background Research

In the media, astronauts and pilots have often been referred to as having "the right stuff"—personality characteristics that would aid their survival in critical situations.[2] In fact, as part of their ongoing research, the National

---

* (Published by the Federal Bureau of Investigation, U.S. Department of Justice) Reprinted from the FBI Law Enforcement Bulletin, August, 1991.

1. *Uniform Crime Reports—Law Officers Killed and Assaulted—1988.* U.S. Department of Justice, Federal Bureau of Investigation, 1989.

2. T. Wolfe, *The Right Stuff* (New York: Bantam Books, 1983).

Aeronautics and Space Administration (NASA) and the University of Texas attempted to identify "right stuff" personality traits in pilot selection.[3] As a result, the following two prominent personality orientations were linked with successful pilot behavior under dangerous flying conditions: (1) Goal-oriented behavior, and (2) the capacity to empathize with others.

Combat psychiatry also offers insight into human performance under battle conditions.[4] Research in this area has examined the causes and prevention of combat stress reaction (CSR) in relation to surviving life-threatening circumstances. CSR, sometimes referred to as "battle fatigue," prevents soldiers from fighting and may be theoretically viewed as behavior that opposes survival.

Further research identified leadership, devotion to duty, decisiveness, and perseverance under stress as significant attributes.[5] And, in his studies into the area of survivability, S.E. Hobfol states, "…counting your losses when preserving resources is fatal…"[6] In essence, preoccupation with thoughts about loss may negatively affect one's capacity to survive a possibly lethal confrontation. Thus, merely avoiding thoughts associated with loss may enhance survivability.

This concept of preserving resources can be exemplified best through the comments of Gunnery Sergeant Carlos Hathcock, U.S. Marine Corps (Retired). Hathcock is credited with 93 confirmed kills as a sniper during two combat tours in South Vietnam.[7] A soft-spoken, unassuming man of honor, Hathcock compared his behavior just prior to and during an operation as isolating himself into an "invisible bubble." This state of mind would "block thoughts of physiological needs, home, family, etc., except the target." The amount of time in the "bubble," lasting from a few hours to several consecutive days, depended not only on the circumstances surrounding his objective but also on adjusting to conditions where a trivial mistake could cost him his life.[8] As he reflected on his distinguished military career, Hathcock also mentioned a number of other attributes he

---

3. R. L. Helmreich and J.A. Wilhelm, "Validating Personality Constructs for Pilot Selection: Status Report on the NASA/UT Project," NASA/UT Technical Memorandum 89-3, Department of Psychology, The University of Texas at Austin, 1989.

4. G. Belenky, ed., *Contemporary Studies in Combat Psychiatry* (New York: Greenwood Press, 1987).

5. R. Gal, "Courage Under Stress," in S. Breznitz, ed. *Stress in Israel* (New York: Van Nostrand Reinhold Company, 1983).

6. S.E. Hobfol, *The Ecology of Stress* (New York: Hemisphere Publishing Corporation, 1988).

7. C. Henderson, *Marine Sniper* (New York: Berkeley Books, 1986).

8. I.J. Vasquez, "An Interview with Carlos Hathcock," unpublished interview notes, Virginia Beach, Virginia, 1989.

considered necessary for survival. Among these were patience, discipline, and the ability to concentrate completely on a specific task.

Theory

Cognitive/behavioral psychological theory offers insight into the benefits of mentally rehearsing possible reactions to life-threatening situations. According to one theory, developing a plan of action could enhance one's perception of effectiveness, and therefore, affect an officer's ability to survive. In fact, as A. Bandura states:

> "People who believe they can exercise control over potential threats do not conjure up apprehensive cognitions and, therefore, are not perturbed by them...those who believe they cannot manage potential threats experience high levels of stress and anxiety arousal. They tend to dwell on their coping deficiencies and view many aspects of their environment as fraught with danger. Through some inefficacious thought they distress themselves and constrain and impair their level of functioning."[9]

A classic example of cognitive rehearsal in law enforcement is provided by C.R. Skillen.[10] According to Skillen, successful patrol officers imagine the best approach to emergencies that could occur during a tour of duty. They then decide upon the best and fastest route from one location to another, should the need arise. These officers also imagine "what if" situations and develop effective responses in case a similar confrontation occurs.

This type of cognitive rehearsal activity has proven to be effective in relieving fears and in enhancing performance in stressful encounters. However, mental preparation can work against officers who believe that if shot, they will certainly die. When reinforced by appropriate training and one's value system, these attributes and behaviors may provide a law enforcement office with the ability to survive a life-threatening situation.

FBI's Research and Preliminary Findings

Behavior identified in the background research and theoretically linked to survivability was later summarized to develop a pilot study question-

---

9. A. Bandura, "Human Agency in Social Cognitive Theory," *American Psychologist,* No. 44, 1989, pp. 1175–1184.

10. C.R. Skillen, *Combat Shotgun Training,* (Springfield, Illinois: Charles C. Thomas, 1982).

Table 1
Survival Behaviors and Traits

- Honor
- Physical fitness
- Useful training
- Emotional stability
- Aggressiveness
- Hatred for adversary
- Street Savvy
- Confidence in weapon
- Duty
- Fear of death
- Decisiveness
- Intelligence
- Patriotism
- Self-esteem
- Anger
- Religious convictions
- Personal leadership ability
- Anticipated reward or recognition
- Believing oneself effective in combat
- Loyalty (to the law enforcement agency)
- Perseverance under stress

- Having a leader/supervisor who is trusted
- Having a leader/supervisor who is a positive role model
- Having a law enforcement agency that is supportive to personnel and backs up officers' decisions made on the street
- A mutual responsibility among officers working together
- Individual morale/supportive family and/or friends at home
- Maintaining a winning attitude
- Confidence in one's ability to perform in a confrontation
- Previous combat experience
- Weather conditions
- Strong interpersonal bonds among a squad or shift that works together
- Mental rehearsal of combat action prior to action
- A belief that one's destiny is controlled by oneself and not outside forces

naire. The FBI then distributed this questionnaire in late 1989 and early 1990 to a broad group of federal, state, and local law enforcement officers attending the FBI Academy in Quantico, Virginia. The questionnaire was also administered at work or training sites in Illinois and California. In all, a total of 207 questionnaires were administered and completed.

Questionnaire

The questionnaire asked respondents to rank various behaviors and traits, developed from background research. Not all the behaviors and traits are associated with law enforcement, but every one has been linked to survival (see table 1). Ranking ranged from little or no importance to extremely important. Law enforcement officers rated each factor in terms of its overall importance for effective performance in a short-term, violent law enforcement confrontation. Effective performance was defined as a violent confrontation that requires a lawful, combative response where the officer continued to function even though the final outcome could be death for the officer or adversary.

Findings

Analyses of the pilot study data revealed the items listed below as those perceived to be most critical to officer survival. The items appear in order of importance, except for items 3 through 5, which are of equal value.

1) *Self-confidence in performance*—The officer's belief that a critical task can be performed effectively with a high probability of success.

2) *Training*—The officer's belief that prior training has been effective, and if applied, will increase the possibility of survival in deadly confrontations.

3) *Effectiveness in combat*—The officer's mental frame of reference in which the officer can visualize victory in a deadly confrontation.

4) *Decisiveness*—The officer's ability to make rapid and accurate decisions when confronted with a critical situation.

5) *Perseverance under stress*—The officer's ability to continue to perform critical tasks mentally and physically when confronted with stressful situations.

Discussion

The concept of survivability represents a dynamic set of behaviors that should be considered in relation to certain law enforcement environments. Life-threatening events associated with undercover operations, uniformed patrol, SWAT operations, and other specific hazardous law enforcement missions require personnel who can survive the virulent stressors associated with these unique operations.[11]

Self-confidence in performance, training, effectiveness in combat, decisiveness, and perseverance under stress as tantamount to law enforcement officer survival. However, these findings are preliminary and should not be considered conclusive. Further research, in the form of an enhancement/enrichment course offered to new FBI Agents in training, is planned for 1991. The data compiled during this course will then be analyzed and will, hopefully, lead to more indepth research focusing on the five behaviors mentioned previously that are most often associated with survivability. It is hoped that law enforcement officers who have been exposed to such training opportunities will increase their potential for survival in life-

---

11. S. R. Band and C.A. Manuele, "Stress and Police Officer Job Performance: An Examination of Effective Coping Behavior," *Police Studies*, No. 10, 1987, pp. 122–131.

or-death situations. Only through proper training in behaviors that ensure survival can law enforcement prepare to meet the anticipated occupational challenges of the future.

Part Seven

Psychological Services for Law Enforcement Personnel

But what if diet, exercise and talking to one's peers just don't work? What if an officer's emotional stress is so deep and his manifestations so severe that routine techniques are not successful? What comprehensive services are or should be available to assure that "good" officers remain high performers *and* their life outside of law enforcement is relatively stable?

There are, of course, professional resources available to support an agency's efforts to mitigate the stress experienced by its police personnel. Many departments have developed their own psychological services units, and others have contracted with outside providers. Increasingly, psychological services are becoming a more important and common part of the organization, with recognized success stories, accepted within the police subculture. In Part Seven, then, our authors explore the successful utilization of psychological services in policing today.

In 1979, a study on the use of psychological services by urban police agencies predicted limited current and minimal future use of such services. Ten years later, Delprino and Bahn conducted a similar national survey of 336 municipal and state police departments which was intended to identify the current use, perceived need, and anticipated future use of psychological services by police agencies. This article documents their principal finding: there has been a substantial growth in the use and range of psychological services in police departments.

American law enforcement officers appear enamored with the tough guy image of heroes like John Wayne, Humphrey Bogart, and Clint Eastwood. In his piece, Miller describes the type of stresses and problems experienced by police officers, firefighters, and paramedics. He suggests that, as a result of their self-concept and professional image, emergency personnel are often resistant to psychotherapy in its traditional forms and outlines the psychotherapeutic strategies that may prove most effective in helping the helpers.

Fischer's article is the accumulation of practices and techniques, thoughts and experiences pulled together while the author functioned as a police psychologist over a ten-year period with various departments in the Denver, Colorado metropolitan area. In this article, while acknowledging the police psychologist cannot be all things to all people, he discusses what he perceives as the value of utilizing crisis intervention techniques in police psychological services. He shares with the reader some of the adjunctive techniques and programs that are available to police psychologists in their therapeutic work with officers, spouses, and other family members.

Watson holds that the "ultimate cure for police pathological problems is not found in counseling the disturbed police officer, the answer is in preventing the disease from taking root in the police officer." To this end, his article discusses the kinds of stresses a police officer will encounter and suggests they will vary during the following six stages of his career: selection; probation; early-career; mid-career; late-career; and retirement. Each stage has certain unique features that require a department psychologist to utilize specific programs, strategies, and techniques of intervention to assure success.

Substance abuse is one of the most critical issues confronting law enforcement agencies. In his article, Gilbert describes the manner in which the social workers and substance alcohol counselors of the Chicago Police Department Professional Counseling Service combine their efforts. In each case, their therapeutic goal is for the alcoholic to achieve total abstinence from alcohol within the recovery system of Alcoholics Anonymous. Similarly the program seeks to actively involve spouses and family members in the Alanon Family Recovery Group.

27

National Survey of the Extent
and Nature of Psychological
Services in Police Departments

Robert P. Delprino
Charles Bahn

Recent legal and social developments have defined new rules for psychologists working with law enforcement agencies and have substantiated current existing roles. Police organizations must deal with the possibility of being held negligently responsible for the inappropriate actions of employees who had not been adequately trained for the job. Also, a police department may be found negligent for accepting individuals who are not psychologically fit for the position or for jeopardizing the public by retaining police officers who are not functioning adequately. Psychologists can assist by screening and testing applicants to determine their probable future success as police officers, or can apply therapeutic skills to help officers cope with the stressful nature of their job (Stratton, 1980).

To all levels of society, the police are the visible symbol of the legal system and may often be the only element of the criminal justice system with which a major segment of the population ever comes into contact. Changes in societal and organizational expectations of the police have enhanced the role of police officers as providers of social services. Heightened awareness of the potential role of social institutions in determining the general quality of life has led to recognition of the police as a major help-giving resource to the community (Mann, 1980). The majority of the modern police officer's duty time is dedicated to some type of interpersonal service or maintaining order; a small percentage of duty time involves actual law enforcement or crime investigation (Bard, 1969; Wilson, 1968). In addition to the traditional skills of police work, the officer is expected to be knowledgeable in other areas such as dealing with the mentally ill, rape victims, and family disputes and assessing suicide risk. The police officer has come to be seen as an applied primary prevention professional who requires the knowledge and skills of the behavioral sciences.

The recognition of the stressful nature of police work has also led to psychologists' involvement in police agencies. The police officer functions in a highly supervised situation in which an elaborate set of legal and organizational guidelines limit autonomy. At the same time, the officer on patrol is required to make critical decisions with little opportunity for supervision or consultation with an expert. The modern police officer functions daily as an executive in a wide variety of situations (Reiser, 1974). These situations are rarely well structured and do not neatly conform to a preconceived letter of the law. However in all circumstances, an officer is expected to take appropriate action and operate within accepted legal boundaries. Failure to do so may result in a departmental reprimand or have more serious consequences such as endangering oneself, a partner, or a member of the public. There is no room for minor mistakes.

Increased involvement of psychologists in police work is indicative of the recognition by both police administrators and psychologists of the expertise needed to deal with the many difficult issues confronting police organizations. The many potential contributions of psychologists to law enforcement have been presented by Brodsky (1972), Reiser (1972), and Loo (1986). These and other recent reports (Chandler, 1986; Fisher, 1986; Gentz, 1986; Green, 1986; Swink & Altman, 1986) provide a thorough description of the various uses of psychologists in law enforcement agencies. The majority of the reports are based on personal experience in specific police departments, or are speculations abut the potential role of psychologists in police work. They do not, however, present a representative account of psychologists' involvement in police agencies nationally.

In this study, through a national survey, we identified the current use, perceived need, and anticipated future use of psychological services by urban and state police agencies.

The only published study to date in which the researchers attempted to identify the then-current use and perceived needs for psychological services by large urban police agencies nationally was conducted in 1979 (Parisher, Rios, & Reilly, 1979). Those authors, on the basis of the survey results, predicted a minimal future use of psychological services in police departments. They reported that of the 112 departments that responded to the question concerning future use, only 18% indicated plans to enlarge or start psychological services in the next two years; 62% had no such plans; and 21% did not know.

There is a discrepancy between those findings and the general positive trend that is indicated by the literature on this topic. The literature indicates a high level of interest in the use of psychological services by police officers and agencies (Brown, Burkhart, King & Solomon, 1977; Burkhart, 1980; Somodevilla, 1978). In addition, the use of psychological services is perceived as a needed area of growth (Engle, 1974; Keller,

1978; Loo, 1986; Reiser, 1978; Wagner, 1976). There exists an obvious need for studies in which the current extent and nature of psychological services in police departments is investigated on a broad base.

Method

Subjects

The sampling frame consisted of 287 large municipal police agencies and the 49 primary state police agencies. (The state of Hawaii is unique in that it does not have a state police organization). Municipal agencies included in this study were police departments administered by a municipality that served a population of 100,000 or greater. The source used for city selection was the *Statistical Abstracts of the United States, 1984* (United States Bureau of the Census, 1983). Primary state police agencies consisted of departments that are administered by the state and have general law enforcement authority throughout the state. These agencies were titled Division of Public Safety, Highway Patrol, or State Police. Of the 336 police agencies invited to participate in the survey, 232 (69%) of the departments returned completed questionnaires. The respondents included 193 municipal police departments and 39 state police agencies.

Procedure

The questionnaire, "Psychological Services in Police Departments Questionnaire," which we developed for this study, consists of 17 items. From a review of the literature on the use of psychological services by police agencies, we compiled a list of the 25 most commonly cited services (see Table 1), and it served as the basis for four questions about the department's current use, perceived need, future use, and providers of psychological services. The remaining questions concerned the agency's plans to enlarge or implement the use of psychological services in the next 2 years, qualifications required of the providers of services, the obstacles and advantages related to the use of these services, and the job title of the individual who completed the questionnaire.

Five judges with experience in the criminal justice system, police work, or test construction were instructed to review the questionnaire for content, clarity, and ease of response. We made minor modifications that included altering item presentation so that less threatening questions, such as number of officers employed and current use of services, preceded questions dealing with future use of obstacles to the use of psychological services.

Initially, the survey instrument was sent to the chiefs of police of the 336 agencies in the sample. A second mailing was sent to nonrespondents 5 weeks after the initial mailing. In the cover letter that accompanied the questionnaire, we instructed that the survey be completed by a member of the psychological service branch of the department or other appropriate personnel. In the survey instrument we requested the job title of the person who completed the questionnaire. Of the 232 respondents to the survey, 224 identified their job titles. The job titles ranged from Sergeant (assigned to the psychological services unit) to the mayor of the city. The more frequent titles included Chief of Police, Police Legal Advisor, Psychologist, Coordinator of Psychological Services, and Personnel Director.

Telephone interviews were conducted with a selection of the municipal and state police agencies who did not respond to either of the two mailings. The purpose of the structured telephone interview was to determine whether the content of the responses of the nonrespondent group was similar in its variability to that of the respondents, or whether any consistent bias resulted from these agencies' refusal to participate in the study. The tenor of nonrespondents' experiences and attitudes of psychological services were similar to those of respondents. Agencies indicated that their inability to respond to the initial inquiry was due to changes in administration or the processing of new recruits that were occurring when the questionnaire was received.

Results

Results are reported by percentage, indicating the variability of responses to each item.

We made an initial inquiry of the specific qualifications of those who provide services in police departments; slightly more than one third (36.92%) of 214 respondents to the question did not specify qualifications of providers of psychological services. For the 135 agencies that indicated specific requirements for providers of psychological services, the preference was toward licensed psychologists with a clinical background. The most frequently cited group of providers of psychological services were consultants. Doctoral-level psychologists, the most frequently used consultants (40.60%), were also identified as the primary providers of each of the 25 psychological services presented in the questionnaire.

More than one half of the departments reported the use of psychological services for the assessment of recruits and to provide personal, family, and job-related stress counseling.

In terms of general use, the range of training functions currently provided by mental health professionals includes training in crisis interven-

Table 1
Police Agencies' Current Use, Perceived Need, and Future Use of Psychological Services

Services	Currently used %	n^a	Perceived need %	n^a	Perceived future use %	n^b
Counsel police officers for job-related stress	53.18	220	78.51	228	57.14	35
Psychological assessment of police recruits	52.29	218	90.39	229	62.50	40
Counsel police officers for personal and family problems	52.25	222	71.62	229	53.33	45
Develop curriculum for training programs	45.33	225	59.91	227	34.50	58
Counsel police officer's spouse and family members	41.70	223	63.60	228	50.00	70
Train police personnel in crisis intervention techniques	41.15	226	73.01	226	57.14	35
Special examination for suspended and problem police officers	38.91	221	67.11	225	43.39	53
Train police personnel to deal with the mentally ill	36.89	225	71.49	228	59.62	52
Assist in crisis intervention	36.77	223	46.05	228	31.51	73
Provide workshops/seminars	36.11	180	62.35	162	59.94	34
Special problems of police work	33.18	214	69.20	224	66.10	59
Alcohol abuse	25.36	209	61.99	21	57.89	57
Abnormal behavior	22.97	209	61.44	223	53.57	56
Drug abuse	22.12	208	59.09	220	60.00	60
Cultural awareness	18.96	211	54.75	221	55.71	70
Personal growth	20.67	208	60.18	221	51.90	79
Retirement from the job	9.57	209	59.15	222	55.43	92
Train police personnel to deal with hostage negotiations	35.39	226	61.23	227	51.16	43
Train police personnel in human relations techniques	35.27	224	75.98	229	46.16	31
Train police personnel to deal with suicide situations	30.40	227	66.67	228	56.63	83

a Number of responses to each item.
b Number of responses from agencies who do not currently use service or plan to expand current use of service.

tion (41.15% of 226 respondents), hostage negotiations (35.39% of 226), and handling both suicide situations (30.40% of 227) and the mentally ill (36.89% of 225). Other services used by more than a third of responding departments include special examinations for suspended and problem police officers, and curriculum development for training programs.

Table 1 (continued)

Services	Currently used %	n^a	Perceived need %	n^a	Perceived future use %	n^b
Assist in hostage negotiations	29.91	224	44.30	228	27.78	72
Assist in suicide situations	29.46	224	42.73	227	30.12	83
Act as liaison with other behavioral scientists or consultants	26.87	227	40.09	227	28.57	112
Assist in developing community relations	25.44	228	48.25	228	36.45	107
Assist in improving department command and leadership techniques	24.89	225	55.56	225	41.30	92
Psychological assessment of civilian employees of police department	22.57	226	48.24	228	42.06	126
Develop psychological profiles for crime investigations	22.32	224	37.61	226	43.21	81
Research and programs evaluations	21.49	228	42.04	226	39.09	110
Assist in management development	18.50	227	46.02	226	31.90	166
Counsel crime victims and their family members	14.60	226	50.00	226	31.29	131
Assist in investigations through hypnosis of witness or suspect	12.44	225	20.61	228	21.35	89
Evaluations of candidates for promotion	9.29	226	77.63	228	38.99	154

[a] Number of responses to each item.
[b] Number of responses from agencies who do not currently use service or plan to expand current use of service.

The only services showing low usage were some innovative areas such as hypnosis (12.44% of 225), retirement counseling (9.57% of 209), promotion evaluation (9.29% of 226), and victim counseling (14.60% of 226).

In most cases the perceived need for a particular service was almost twice as great as the percentage of the departments who indicated using that service. For some, the recognition of need far outweighed its current use; for example, in the area of victim counseling, 14.60% of departments reported current use of such counseling, whereas 50% indicated a need for this service. The most drastic contrast was in the sacrosanct area of promotion evaluation, in which 9.29% (of 226) reported using this service, but 77.63% (of 228) of respondents recognized the need for such evaluations.

Almost all respondents affirmed the need for psychological evaluation of recruits (90.39% of 229), in most cases conforming with a specific legislative requirement. The perceived need for counseling services was also quite high, particularly for job-related stress (78.51% of 228).

The statement of perceived needs represented an idealized future. The statement of current use indicated pragmatic limitations. Questions addressing the likelihood that agencies not currently using a particular service would do so in the future were also presented. To the general question concerning plans to enlarge or implement the use of psychological services in the next 2 years, 36.74% (n = 79) of 215 respondents indicated plans to do so. This is an increase over the 18% of the 112 respondents in Parisher et. al.'s (1979) study who gave this affirmative response.

When asked to indicate the level of acceptance of psychological services on a 7-point scale (1 = *highly accepted* and 7 = *not accepted*), 82.2% of 225 responses to the question indicated acceptance at 4 and above; 46.66% of respondents indicated a very high acceptance level (1 or 2). Also, more than 70% of respondents indicated that the use of psychological services could be of great help in the prevention of and dealing with problem police officers, improving the quality of police screening, and supervising police officers. Although there appears to be a high acceptance among police organizations of the use of psychological services, the moderate number of departments that indicated plans to expand or implement services may be due to a budgetary problem, which was reported by 64% (of 225) of departments as the greatest obstacle related to the use of psychological services.

Discussion

In this study we report the current state of psychologists' involvement in police agencies on a national level. The principal finding is that between 1979 and the present, there has been an enormous growth in the use of psychological services in police departments. Parisher et. al. (1979) found that only 20% of the police departments surveyed used psychological services. Our results indicate that more than half of all departments surveyed are currently using some type of psychological service.

As in the earlier study (Parisher et. al., 1979), we found that assessment of applicants is the primary service used. Parisher et. al. (1979) also reported personal counseling as a main duty of police psychologists. Our results also indicate that officer counseling is a commonly used psychological service; job-related stress counseling was reported by 53% of respondents. It is not surprising that police agencies and officers have recognized the usefulness of counseling services in preparing for and dealing with stress experienced as a result of the job, considering that over the last 15 years more than 100 articles, numerous books, and manuals that deal with the police stress problem have been published (Loo, 1986; Reiser & Klyver, 1987).

One area of counseling that seems to have been neglected is counseling for the victims of crimes. Only a small number of police departments reported the current use of this service. There appears to be very little change or prospect of change since that earlier study (Parisher et. al., 1979), in spite of the fact that Knudten and Knudten (1981) demonstrated the extent of dissatisfaction with current police dealings with crime victims and suggested possibilities for police counseling with crime victims to alleviate negative effects. In our study, 50% ($n = 226$) of respondents indicated a need for victim counseling. It appears that this service is commonly provided by voluntary organizations, support groups, and self-help programs that are not affiliated with police agencies (Walker, 1987).

One area of projected changes is in the use of psychologists for various training programs. These programs include instruction in dealing with the mentally ill, dealing with alcohol and drug abuse, and cultural awareness. Approximately 60% of those responding to each of these items indicated a need for more effective workshops and seminars in these areas and plan to introduce such services in the near future. Although the police officer has always provided a first aid role in dealing with the mentally ill, family disputes, and victims of crimes, it is only recently that the officer has come to be seen as an applied social scientist. Because an officer may potentially have a great impact of the attitudes of the community toward police, it is essential that officers develop applied behavioral skills to maximize their effectiveness. Also, the officer who acquires an understanding of interpersonal situations that may be encountered while on the job will be better prepared to handle such situations.

There appears to be a substantial growth in the use of psychological services by police agencies. Although earlier researchers speculated about the potential use of psychological services in police agencies, this study has demonstrated an increase in the range of the current uses and a high perceived need for many of the 25 specific psychological services presented in the questionnaire. Some of the psychological services presented have been used for a long enough time that their effectiveness can be measured. Evaluation studies in which researchers use outcomes such as officers' injuries, indices of police officers' mental health, and efficiency of officers' handling of specific situation are needed.

The extent and nature of psychological services in police agencies seem to be influenced by a unique mixture of political, social, technological, and economic forces. The future impact of psychologists on police officers and police organizations will be greatly determined by the goals of the organization. Innovations in policing do not necessarily lead to improvements until they are matched against specific agency objectives (Heaphy, 1978). Therefore, the successful implementation of psychological services in police departments may rest heavily on the police administration. Equally important is the ability of the provider of psychological services to work effectively in the quasi-military, bureaucratic structure of the police organization. If a service that comes from police needs is provided, it is less likely to be perceived as being imposed on the officers and the department and therefore has a greater chance of success. From the results of this study, it appears that once providers of psychological services have had the opportunity to demonstrate their value to the organization, they become an established arm of the police agency.

References

Bard, M. (1969). Family intervention as a community mental health resource. *Journal of Criminal Law, Criminology and Police Science, 60,* 247–250.

Brodsky, S. (1972). *Psychologists in the criminal justice system.* Chicago: University of Illinois Press.

Brown, S., Burkhart, B., King, G., & Solomon, R. (1977). Roles and expectations for mental health professionals in law enforcement agencies. *American Journal of Community Psychology, 5,* 209–215.

Burkhart, B. (1980). Conceptual Issues in the development of police selection procedures. *Professional Psychology, 11,* 121–129.

Chandler, J. (1986). A statewide police psychology program: Guidelines for development. In J.T. Reese & H.A. Goldstein (Eds.), *Psychological services for law enforcement: A compilation of papers submitted to the national symposium of police psychological services. FBI Academy, Quantico, Virginia* (pp. 225–230). Washington, DC: U.S. Government Printing Office.

Engle, D. (1974). Police training in non-crime related functions. *The Police Chief, 41*(6), 61–65.

Fisher, C. (1986). Some techniques and external programs useful in police psychological services. In J.T. Reese & H. A. Goldstein (Eds.), *Psychological services for law enforcement: A compilation of papers submitted to the national symposium of police psychological services. FBI Academy, Quantico, Virginia* (pp. 111–114). Washington, DC: U.S. Government Printing Office.

Gentz, D. (1986). A system for the delivery of psychological services for police personnel. In J.T. Reese & H.A. Goldstein (Eds.), *Psychological services for law enforcement: A compilation of papers submitted to the national symposium of police psychological services. FBI Academy, Quantico, Virginia* (pp. 257–258). Washington, DC: U.S. Government Printing Office.

Green, J. (1986). Genesis—Beginning of a psychological services unit. In J.T. Reese & H.A. Goldstein (Eds.), *Psychological services for law enforcement: A compilation of papers submitted to the national sympo-*

sium of police psychological services. FBI Academy, Quantico, Virginia (pp. 283–285). Washington, DC: U.S. Government Printing Office.

Heaphy, J. (1978). The future of police improvement. In A. W. Cohen (Ed.), *The future of policing* (pp. 275–295). Beverly Hills, CA: Sage.

Keller, P. (1978). A psychological view of the police officer paradox. *The Police Chief, 45*(4), 24–25.

Knudten, M., & Knudten, R. (1981). What happens to crime victims and witnesses in the justice system? In B. Galaway & J. Hudson (Eds.), *Perspectives on crime victims* (pp. 52–62). St. Louis: C. V. Mosby.

Loo, R. (1986). Police psychology: The emergence of a new field. *The Police Chief, 53*(2), 26–30.

Mann, P. (1980). Ethical issues for psychologists in police agencies In J. Monahan (Ed.), *Who is the client? The ethics of psychological intervention in the criminal justice system* (pp. 18–42). Washington, DC: American Psychological Association.

Parisher, D., Rios, B., & Reilley, R. (1979). Psychologists and psychological services in urban police departments. *Professional Psychology, 10*, 6–7.

Reiser, M. (1972). *The police department psychologist.* Springfield, IL: Charles C. Thomas.

Reiser, M. (1974). Mental health in police work and training. *The Police Chief, 41*(8), 51–52.

Reiser, M. (1978). The police department psychologist. *Police, 23*, 86–94.

Reiser, M., & Klyver, N. (1987). Consulting with police. In I.B. Weiner & A.K. Hess (Eds.). *Handbook of forensic psychology* (pp. 437–459). New York: Wiley.

Somodevilla, S.A. (1978). The psychologist's role in the police department. *The Police Chief, 45*(4), 21–23.

Stratton, J. (1980). Psychological services for the police. *Journal of Police Science and Administration, 8*(1), 31–39.

Swink, D., & Altman, K. (1986). The use of mental health professionals in the implementation of action training models. In J.T. Reese & H.A. Goldstein (Eds.), *Psychological services for law enforcement: A compilation of papers submitted to the national symposium of police psychological services. FBI Academy, Quantico, Virginia* (pp. 299–301). Washington, DC: U.S. Government Printing Office.

United States Bureau of the Census. (1983). *Statistical abstract of the United States, 1984 (104th ed.).* Washington, DC: U.S. Government Printing Office.

Wagner, M. (1976). Action and reaction: The establishment of counseling services in the Chicago police department. *The Police Chief, 43*(1), 20–23.

Walker, L. (1987). Intervention with victims/survivors. In I. B. Weiner & A.K. Hess (Eds.). *Handbook of forensic psychology* (pp. 630–649). New York: Wiley.

Wilson, J. Q. (1968). *Varieties of police behavior.* Cambridge, MA: Harvard University Press

28

Tough Guys: Psychotherapeutic Strategies with Law Enforcement and Emergency Services Personnel

Laurence Miller

Every time we dial 911, we expect that our emergency will be taken seriously and handled competently. The police will race to our burgled office, the fire-fighters will speedily douse our burning home, the ambulance crew will stabilize our injured loved one and whisk him/her to the nearest hospital. We take these expectations for granted because of the dedication of the workers who serve the needs of law enforcement, emergency services, and public safety.

These "tough guys"—the term includes both men and women—are routinely exposed to special kinds of traumatic events and daily pressures that require a certain adaptively defensive toughness of attitude, temperament, and training. Without this resolve, they couldn't do their jobs effectively. Sometimes however, the stress is just too much, and the very toughness that facilitates smooth functioning in their daily duties now becomes an impediment to these helpers seeking help for themselves.

This article describes the types of stresses and problems experienced by police officers, firefighters, and paramedics, and outlines the psychotherapeutic strategies that may prove most effective in helping these professionals. Inasmuch as an important component of any effective psychotherapy, especially for nontraditional groups, is an adequate understanding of the nature of the therapist's clinical case material (Miller, 1990, 1991, 1993a, b, c), the experiences and dynamics of this patient group will first be described.

Stress and Coping in Law Enforcement and Emergency Services

Although there is some overlap in services—for example, police sometimes have to perform emergency medical first aid, and firefighters and paramedics are often cross-trained—there are some issues that are specific to each group, and the present section will therefore consider each of these groups separately.

Police Officers

Even people who do not like cops have to admit that theirs is a difficult, dangerous, and often thankless job. Police officers regularly deal with the most violent, impulsive, and predatory members of society, put their lives on the line, and confront miseries and horrors that the rest of us view from the sanitized distance of our newspapers and TV screens. In addition to the daily grind, officers are frequently the target of criticism and complaints by citizens, the media, the judicial system, hostile attorneys, "do-gooder" clinicians and social service personnel, and their own administrators and law enforcement agencies (Blau, 1994).

Police officers generally carry out their sworn duties and responsibilities with dedication and valor, but some stresses are too much to take, and every officer has a breaking point. For some, it may come in the form of a particular traumatic experience, such as a gruesome accident or homicide, a vicious crime against a child, a close personal brush with death, the death or serious injury of a partner, a mistaken shooting of an innocent civilian, or an especially grisly or large-scale crime, leading, in some cases, to the development of a full-scale posttraumatic stress disorder (PTSD) (McCafferty, McCafferty, & McCafferty, 1992). For other officers, there may be no singular major trauma, but the mental breakdown caps the cumulative weight of a number of more moderate stresses over the course of the officer's career. Most police officers deal with both the routine and exceptional stresses by a variety of situationally adaptive coping and defense mechanisms, such as repression, displacement, isolation of feelings, humor—and generally toughing it out. Officers develop a closed society, an insular "cop culture" For many, "The Job" becomes their life, and crowds out other activities and relationships (Blau, 1994).

Apparently, police pressures and their responses to them are remarkably similar in most Western societies where these have been examined, including Australian police officers (Evans, Coman, Stanley, & Burrows, 1993) and Scottish constables (Alexander & Walker, 1994). Action-oriented coping strategies, alternating with displacement and self-blame, appear to characterize these officers' efforts to deal with job stress. In the U.S., two-thirds of officers involved in shootings suffer moderate or severe problems, and about 70 percent leave the force within seven years of the incident. Police are admitted to general hospitals at significantly higher rates, have significantly higher rates of premature death, and rank third among occupations in death rates (Sewell, Ellison, & Hurrell, 1988). Interestingly, however, despite the popular notion of rampantly disturbed police marriages, the empirical evidence does not support a higher-than-average divorce rate for police officers (Borum & Philpot, 1993).

Perhaps the most tragic form of police casualty is suicide (Hays, 1994; Seligmann, Holt, Chinni, & Roberts, 1994). Twice as many officers, about 300 annually, die by their own hand as are killed in the line of duty. In New York City, the suicide rate of police officers is more than double the rate for the population. In fact, these totals may actually be even higher, since such deaths are sometimes underreported by fellow cops to avoid stigmatizing the deceased officers and to allow the families to collect benefits. Most victims are young patrol officers with no record of misconduct, and most shoot themselves off-duty. Often problems involving alcohol or romantic problems are the catalyst, and easy access to a lethal weapon provides the ready means; indeed, physicians and pharmacists, with access to potentially deadly prescription drugs, have even higher suicide rates. Cops under stress are caught in the dilemma of risking confiscation of their guns, transfer to desk duty, or other career setbacks if they report distress or request counseling.

Aside from the daily stresses of patrol cops, special pressures are experienced by higher-ranking officers, such as homicide detectives, who are involved in the investigation of particularly brutal crimes, such as multiple murders or serial killings (Sewell, 1993). The societal protective role of the police officer becomes even more pronounced, at the same time as their responsibilities as public servants who protect the rights of individuals become compounded by the pressures to solve the crime.

Moreover, the sheer magnitude and shock effect of many mass murder scenes and the violence, mutilation, and sadistic brutality associated with many serial killings, sometimes involving children, often exceed the defense mechanisms and coping abilities of even the most seasoned officers. Revulsion may be tinged with rage, all the more so when fellow officers have been killed or injured. Finally, the cumulative effect of fatigue results in case errors, poor work quality, and deterioration of home and workplace relationships. Fatigue also wears down the officer's normal defenses, rendering him/her even more vulnerable to stress and failure.

Firefighters

Every child hears the story about brave firefighters rescuing citizens from burning buildings. For the most part, firefighters display exceptional skill and courage in the performance of their duties, but as in any role which involves dealing with life-threatening emergencies, stress can take its toll. According to the National Commission on Fire Prevention and Control, firefighting is the single most hazardous occupation in the United States. Everyday, approximately 280 firefighters are killed or injured, and each year, over 650 are forced to retire due to occupational illness, including psychological disability (Hildebrand, 1984a, b).

In addition to fires, crimes, suicides, accidents, medical emergencies, toxic waste experiences, and bombs are among the traumatic experiences that firefighters must deal with. In a study of the Toronto Fire Department (DeAngelis, 1995), fire-fighters confronted an average of 3.91 such experiences per year. In the last year of the study, these included rescuing people from an ammonia cloud, dealing with stabbings and suicides, and recovering a woman's severed head in an industrial accident. Compared to a one percent rate for the general population, the prevalence rate of diagnosable PTSD for firefighters was 16.5 percent— one percent higher than PTSD rates for Vietnam veterans. Firefighters battling a huge bushfire in Australia showed even higher rates of PTSD (McFarlane, 1988).

In some cases, firefighters, police officers, paramedics, or other rescue personnel may appear to emerge from a dangerous situation or series of emergencies emotionally unscathed, only to later break down and develop a full-blown PTSD reaction following a relatively minor incident like a traffic accident (Davis & Breslau, 1994). The fender-bender, certainly far less traumatic than the horrific scenes encountered in emergency work, seems to have symbolized vividly the personal risk, sense of human fragility, and existential uncertainty that their job-related activities entail, but that they are unable to face directly if they are to maintain their necessary defenses to get the job done. The stifled affect may then be projected onto the minor incident, which is a "safer" target to blow up at. Unfortunately, this may instigate a fear of losing control and going crazy, further propelling the vicious cycle of increased stress but greater reluctance to report it.

Paramedics

Within the medical field, the Emergency Medical Services (EMS) experience is somewhat unique (Becknell, 1995). Whereas most other branches of medicine practice in the controlled, sterile environment of the hospital, clinic, office, or even busy emergency room, paramedics find their victims in their homes, on the street, under wrecked cars, in demolished buildings. The deaths they witness are not the neat, sedated passings of the hospital bed, but are typically sudden, messy, noisy, agonized, and undignified. Although capped by many heroic and lifesaving events, for many paramedics the more common succession of tragedies and occasional stark horrors takes a grim psychological and existential toll, especially if the incident resonates with events from the worker's personal history (Becknell, 1995).

In coping with death, paramedics use a number of coping strategies reminiscent of those employed by other tough job workers (Palmer, 1983). These include desensitization processes that are an actual part of some paramedic training, the use of dark humor and crass joking, overuse of technical jargon and a special working language, the ability to cognitively fragment scientifically and escape into paramedical work, and rationalization as to both the importance of the emergency medical function and the condition of the patient, that is, that the patient would have died no matter what.

Once again, the strain sometimes becomes too much, and, like police officers and firefighters, some paramedics take their own lives, although precise suicide statistics for this population are unavailable. There are a number of reasons why paramedics commit suicide (Mitchell, 1987), including romantic troubles, major illness, death of a close family member, economic problems, job failure or failure to achieve career goals, humiliation in the presence of peers, or boring retirement after an active career. The stresses are usually multiple, diverse, and cumulative, and only rarely do job-related factors alone lead to suicide. Again, there exists the dilemma that requesting psychological help may lead to failed fitness-for-duty ratings and other stigmatizing consequences.

Dispatchers and Support Personnel

In addition to the on-line police officers, firefighters, and paramedics, a vital role in law enforcement and emergency services is played by the workers who operate "behind the scenes," namely the dispatchers, complaint clerks, clerical personnel, crime and fire scene evidence technicians, and other support personnel (Holt, 1989; Sewell & Crew, 1984). Although rarely directly exposed to actual danger or catastrophe (except where on-scene and behind-scene personnel alternate shifts), several high-stress features, characterize the job descriptions of these workers. These include: 1) dealing with multiple, often simultaneous, calls; 2) having to make time-pressured life and death decisions, often with 3) low information about, and control over, the emergency situation; 4) intense, confusing, and sometimes hostile contact with frantic and outraged citizens; and 5) exclusion from the status and camaraderie typically enjoyed by on-scene workers who "get the credit."

After particularly difficult calls, dispatchers may show many of the classic post-traumatic reactions and symptoms, including numbed responsiveness, impaired memory for the event alternating with intrusive, disturbing images of the incident, irritability, hypervigilence, sleep disturbance, and interpersonal hypersensitivity. As with other tough jobs, these individuals require proper treatment and support.

Intervention Services and Psychotherapeutic Strategies

To avoid "shrinky" connotations, mental health intervention services with tough job personnel are often conceptualized in such terms as "stress management," and "critical incident debriefing" (Belles & Norvell, 1990; Mitchell & Bray, 1990). In general, one-time, incident-specific interventions will be most appropriate for handling the effects of overwhelming trauma on otherwise normal, well-functioning personnel. Where post-traumatic sequelae persist, or where the psychological problems relate to a longer-term pattern of maladaptive functioning, more extensive individual psychotherapeutic approaches are called for. To have the greatest impact, intervention services should be part of an integrated program of services within the department and have full administrative commitment and support from commanders and the department (Blau, 1994; Sewell, 1986).

Critical Incident Stress Debriefing (CISD)

Although components of this approach comprise an important element of all therapeutic work with traumatized patients, *critical incident stress debriefing*, or CISD, has been organizationally formalized for law enforcement and emergency services by Mitchell (1983, 1988; Mitchell & Bray, 1990), and is now implemented in public safety departments throughout the United States, Britain, and other parts of the world (Dyregrov, 1989). CISD is a structured intervention designed to promote the emotional processing of traumatic events through the ventilation and normalization of reactions, as well as preparation for possible future experiences. Although initially designed for use in groups, it can also be used with individuals, couples, and families.

According to Mitchell & Bray (1990), after a critical incident, there are a number of criteria on which peer support and command staff might decide to provide a CISD to personnel after a critical incident: 1) many individuals within a group appear to be distressed after a call; 2) the signs of stress appear to be quite severe; 3) personnel demonstrate significant behavioral changes; 4) personnel make significant errors on calls occurring after the critical incident; 5) personnel request help; 6) the event is extraordinary.

The structure of a CISD debriefing usually consists of the presence of one or more mental health professionals and one or more peer debriefers, that is, fellow police officers, firefighters, or paramedics who have been trained in the CISD process and who probably have been through critical incidents and debriefings themselves. A typical debriefing takes place within 24–72 hours after the critical incident, and consists of a single group meeting that lasts approximately 2–3 hours, although shorter or longer meetings are determined by circumstances.

The CISD process consists of several phases:

Introduction: The introduction phase of a debriefing is the time in which the team leader gradually introduces the process, encourages participation by the group, and sets the ground rules by which the debriefing will operate. Generally, these involve confidentiality, attendance for the full group, nonforced participation in discussions, and the establishment of a noncritical atmosphere.

Fact phase: During this phase, the group is asked to describe briefly their job or role during the incident and, from their own perceptive, some facts regarding what happened. The basic question is: "What did you do?"

Thought phase: The CISD leader asks the group members to discuss their first thoughts during the critical incident: "What went through your mind?"

Reaction phase: This phase is designed to move the group participants from the predominantly cognitive level of intellectual processing into the emotional level of processing: "What was the worst part of the incident for you?"

Symptom phase: This begins the movement back from the predominantly emotional processing level toward the cognitive processing level. Participants are asked to describe their cognitive, physical, emotional, and behavioral signs and symptoms of distress which appeared 1) at the scene or within 24 hours of the incident, 2) a few days after the incident, and 3) are still being experienced at the time of the debriefing: "What have you been experiencing since the incident?"

Education phase: Information is exchanged about the nature of the stress response and the expected physiological and psychological reactions to critical incidents. This services to normalize the stress and coping response, and provides a basis for questions and answers.

Re-entry phase: This is a wrap-up, in which any additional questions or statements are addressed, referral for individual follow-ups are made, and general group bonding is reinforced: "What have you learned?" "How can you help one another from now on?" "Anything we left out?"

Despite the enthusiasm for this form of intervention, the CISD approach has come under criticism, especially when used indiscriminately or regarded as the only necessary and sufficient form of intervention. Bisson and Deahl (1994) have reviewed the literature suggesting some of the limitations, pitfalls, and drawbacks of the CISD approach. They note that even Mitchell (1988) acknowledges that not everyone in every critical incident situation will benefit from CISD. In some cases, more extensive, individual intervention may be called for.

Timing and clinical appropriateness are important. There is a general consensus that debriefing is most effective if carried out sooner rather than later, and clinical experience supports the holding of debriefing sessions toward the earlier end of the recommended 24–72 hour window (Bordow & Porritt, 1979; Solomon & Benbenishty, 1988). Although all involved personnel should participate in a debriefing, mandatory or enforced CISD can lead to passive participation and resentment among workers (Bisson & Deahl, 1994; Flannery, Fulton, & Tausch, 1991), and the CISD process may quickly become a boring routine if used indiscriminately after every incident, no matter how "critical," thereby diluting its effectiveness for those situations where it really could have helped.

There may also be some negative side-effects of inappropriate CISD. In the Australian bushfire study, McFarlane (1988) found that, while fire fighters who received CISD shortly after the incident were less likely to develop acute post-traumatic stress reactions than nondebriefed workers, they were more likely to develop delayed PTSD. McFarlane (1989) expressed the concern that overreliance on quick-fix, primary prevention methods may delay the diagnosis and effective treatment of those workers who suffer more serious psychological sequelae and require more extensive follow-up treatment.

As is the case for any wholesale application of a promising psychological treatment modality, further research and clinical experience typically narrow and refine the appropriate therapeutic applications, and point up certain limitations and even potentially deleterious side-effects. This has been the case, for example, with cognitive rehabilitation (Hall & Cope, 1995; Miller, 1992), relaxation training (Lazarus & Mayne, 1990), biofeedback (Silver & Blanchard, 1978), and behavioral medicine approaches (Miller, 1994a). It is therefore the responsibility of departmental administrators and the mental health clinicians who advise them to ensure that debriefing modalities are used responsibly, and that workers who require more extensive psychotherapeutic intervention will have these available.

Tough Guy Psychotherapy

Tough job personnel, cops especially, have a reputation for shunning mental health services, perceiving its practitioners as softies and bleeding hearts who help rotten criminals go free with wussy excuses or over complicated psychobabble. Other tough guys fear being "shrunk," having a notion of the psychotherapy experience as akin to brain-washing, a humiliating, infantilizing experience in which they lie on a couch and sob about their toilet training. More commonly, the idea of needing "mental help" implies weakness, cowardice, and lack of ability to do the job. In the environment of many departments, some workers realistically fear censure, stigmatization, ridicule, impaired career advancement, and alienation from coworkers if they are perceived as the type who "folds under pressure." Finally, others in the department who have something to hide may fear a colleague "spilling his guts" to the shrink and blowing the malfeasor's cover.

Administrative Issues

There is some debate about whether psychological services, especially therapy-type service, should be provided by a psychologist within the department, even a psychologist who is a sworn officer or active-duty emergency services worker, or whether such matters are best handled by outside therapists who are less answerable to departmental politics and less likely to be in the gossip loop (Blau, 1994; Silva, 1991).

On the one hand, the departmental shrink is likely to have more knowledge of and experiences with the direct pressure faced by the personnel he/she serves; this is especially true if the psychologist is also a sworn officer or active-duty worker, or has had formal training and ride-along experience. On the other hand, in addition to providing psychotherapy services, the departmental psychologist is likely to also be involved in performing work-status and fitness-for-duty evaluations, as well as the assessment or legal roles which may conflict with that of the effective therapist. An outside therapist may have less direct experience with departmental pressures, but may have more therapeutic freedom of movement.

My own experience has been that the tough job personnel who come for help—especially if they haven't been "forced" into treatment—are usually less concerned with the therapist's extensive technical knowledge of "The Job," and more interested that he/she demonstrate a basic trust and a willingness to understand the worker's situation — they'll be happy to provide the details. These workers expect us mental health professionals to give "110 percent" to the psychotherapy process, just as the workers do in their own fields, and for the most part, they do not want us to be another cop or fire-fighter, they want us to be a skilled therapist — that is why they are talking to us and not their colleagues. Many are actually glad to find a secure haven outside the fishbowl atmosphere of the department and relieved that the therapeutic sessions provide a respite from shop talk. This is especially true where the referral problem has less to do with direct job-related issues and more with outside pressures, such as family or alcohol problems, that may impinge on job performance. In any case, the therapist, the patient, and the department should be clear about issues relating to confidentiality and chain of command at the outset, and any changes in the "ground rules" should be clarified as needed.

Trust and the Therapeutic Relationship

As is obvious from the above discussion, trust is a crucial element in doing effective psychotherapy with police officers (Silva, 1991), a lesson that can be applied to clinical work with all tough job personnel. Difficulty with trust appears to be an occupational hazard for workers in public safety with a strong sense of self-sufficiency and insistence on solving their own problems, and therapists may find themselves frequently "tested," especially at the beginning of the treatment process. As the therapeutic alliance begins to solidify, the patient will begin to feel more at ease with the therapist and finds comfort and a sense of predictability from the psychotherapy session. Following Egan (1975), Silva (1991) outlines the following requirements for the establishment of therapeutic mutual trust:

Accurate empathy: The therapist conveys his/her understanding of the patient's background and experience (but beware of premature false familiarity and phony "bonding").

Genuineness: The therapist is spontaneous yet tactful, flexible yet impulsive, and tries to be as nondefensive as possible.

Availabilty: The therapist is available, within reason, whenever needed, and avoids making promises and commitments he/she cannot keep.

Respect: This is both tough-minded and gracious, and seeks to preserve the patient's sense of autonomy, control, and self-respect within the therapeutic relationship. It is manifested by the therapist's overall attitude, as well as by certain specific actions, such as indicating regard for rank or job role by initially using formal departmental forms of address, such as "officer," "detective," "lieutenant," until trust and mutual respect allow the patient to ease formality. Here it is important to avoid the dual traps of overfamiliarity, patronizing, and talking down to the worker on the one hand, and trying to "play cop" or force bogus camaraderie by assuming the role of a colleague or field commander.

Concreteness: Therapy with tough job personnel should, at least initially, be goal-oriented and have a problem-solving focus. These workers are into action, and to the extent that it is clinically realistic, the therapeutic approach should empasize active, problem-solving approaches.

Therapeutic Strategies and Techniques

Since most law enforcement and emergency services personnel come under psychotherapeutic care in the context of some form of post-traumatic stress reaction, the clinical literature reflects this emphasis (Blau, 1994; Fullerton, McCarroll, Ursano, & Wright, 1992). In general, the effectiveness of any intervention technique will be determined by the timeliness, tone, style, and intent of the intervention. Effective interventions share in common the elements of briefness, focus on specific symptomatology or conflict issues, and direct operational efforts to resolve the conflict or to reach a satisfactory conclusion.

In working with police officers, Blau (1994) recommends that the first meeting between the therapist and the officer establish a safe and comfortable working atmosphere by the therapist's articulating: 1) a positive regard for the officer's decision to seek help; 2) a clear description of the therapist's responsibilities and limitations with respect to confidentiality and privilege; and 3) an invitation to state the officer's concerns. A straightforward, goal-directed, problem-solving therapeutic intervention approach for this patient group includes the following elements: 1) creating a sanctuary; 2) focusing on critical areas of concern; 3) identifying desired outcomes; 4) reviewing assets; 5) developing a general plan; 6) identifying practical initial implementations; 7) reviewing self-efficacy; 8) setting appointments for review, reassurance, and further implementation.

Blau (1994) delineates a number of effective individual intervention techniques for police officers that can be adapted to therapeutic work with all tough job personnel. These include the following:

Attentive listening: This includes good eye contact, an occasional nod, and genuine interest without inappropriate comment or interruption.

Being there with empathy: This therapeutic attitude conveys availability, concern, and awareness of the turbulent emotions being experienced by the traumatized patient. It is also helpful to let the patient know what he/she is likely to experience in the days and weeks to follow.

Reassurance: This is valuable if it is reality-oriented, and should take the form of reassuring the patient that routine matters will be handled, premises and property will be secured, deferred responsibilities will be handled by others, and that he/she has organizational and command support.

Supportive counseling: This includes effective listening, restatement of content, clarification of feelings, and reassurance, as well as community referral and networking with liaison agencies, as necessary.

Interpretive counseling: This type of intervention should be used when the patient's emotional reaction is significantly greater than the circumstances of the critical incident seem to warrant. In appropriate cases, this therapeutic strategy can stimulate the patient to search for underlying emotional stresses that intensify a naturally stressful traumatic event. In some cases, this may lead to ongoing psychotherapy.

Not to be neglected is the use of humor. Humor has its place in many forms of psychotherapy (Fry & Salameh, 1987), but may especially be useful in working with law enforcement and emergency services personnel (Fullerton et. al., 1992; Silva, 1991). In general, if the therapist and patient can laugh together, this may lead to the sharing of more intimate feelings. Humor serves to bring a sense of balance and proportion to those circumstances in which the emotional world seems chaotic, stunted, or warped by horror. Humor, even sarcastic, callous, or crass humor — if handled appropriately and used constructively — may allow the venting of anger, frustration, and resentment and lead to productive reintegrative therapeutic work.

Departmental Support

Even in the absence of formal psychotherapeutic intervention, following a department-wide critical incident, such as the death of a worker, or a particularly stressful rescue event, the mental health professional can advise and guide law enforcement and emergency service departments in encouraging and implementing several organizational response measures, based on the available literature on individual and group coping strategies for these groups (Alexander, 1993; Alexander & Walker, 1994; Alexander & Wells, 1991; DeAngelis, 1995; Fullerton et al., 1992; Palmer, 1983). Many of these measures are applicable proactively, that is, as part of training before a disaster or critical incident occurs, as a means of preparation. Some specific measures include the following:

- Encourage mutual support among peers and supervisors. The former typically happens anyway, the latter may need some explicit reinforcement. Public safety workers often work as "partners" and find that the shared decision-making and mutual reassurance actually enhances effective job performance.
- Utilize humor as a coping mechanism to facilitate emotional insulation and group bonding. The first forestalls excessive identifica-

tion with victims, the second encourages mutual group support via a shared language. Of course, the line between adaptive crass humor and maladaptive nastiness may need to be monitored.

- Make use of appropriate rituals to give meaning and dignity to an otherwise horrific and existentially disorienting experience. This need not include only religious rites related to mourning, but such things as a military-style honor guard to attend bodies before disposition, and the formal acknowledgment of actions above and beyond the call of duty. Important here is the role of "grief leadership," that is, the supervisor's or commanding officer's demonstrating by example that it is okay to express grief and mourn the death of fallen comrades or civilians, and that the appropriate expression of one's feelings about the incident will be supported, not denigrated.

Conclusion

Psychotherapy with law enforcement and emergency personnel typically entails its share of frustration as well as satisfaction. A certain flexibility is required in adapting traditional psychotherapeutic models and techniques for use with this group, and clinical work frequently requires both firm professional grounding and seat-of-the-pants therapeutic maneuverability. Incomplete closures and partial successes are to be expected, but in a few instances, the impact of successful intervention can have profound effects on morale and job effectiveness that may be felt department-wide. In sum, working with these tough guys takes skill, dedication and sometimes a strong stomach, but for therapists who are not afraid to tough it out themselves, this can be a fascinating and rewarding aspect of clinical practice.

References

Alexander, D.A. (1993). Stress among body handlers: A long-term follow-up. *British Journal of Psychiatry*, 163, 806–808.

Alexander, D.A. & Walker, L.G. (1994). A study of methods used by Scottish police officers to cope with work-related stress. *Stress Medicine*, 10, 131–138.

Alexander, D.A. & Walker, A. (1991). Reactions of police officer to body-handling after a major disaster: A before-and-after comparison. *British Journal of Psychiatry*, 159, 547–555.

Becknell, J.M. (1995). Tough stuff: Learning to seize the opportunities. *Journal of the Emergency Medical Services,* March, pp. 52–59.

Belles, D. & Norvell, N. (1990). *Stress Management Workbook For Law Enforcement Officers.* Sarasota: Professional Resource Exchange.

Bisson, J.I. & Deahl, M.P. (1994). Psychological debriefing and prevention of post-traumatic stress: More research is needed. *British Journal of Psychiatry,* 165, 717–720.

Blau, T.H. (1994). *Psyhcological Services for Law Enforcement,* New York: John Wiley.

Bordow, S. & Porritt, D. (1979). An experimental evaluation of crisis intervention. *Psychological Bulletin,* 84, 1189–1217.

Borum, R. & Philpot, C. (1993). Therapy with law enforcement couples: Clinical management of the "high-risk lifestyle. *"American Journal of Family Therapy,* 21, 122–135.

Davis, G.C. & Breslau, N. (1994). Post-traumatic stress disorder in victims of civilians and criminal violence. *Psychiatric Clinics of North America,* 17, 289–299.

DeAngelis, T. (1995). Firefighters' PTSD at dangerous levels. *APA Monitor,* February, pp. 36–37.

Dyregrov, A. (1989). Caring for helpers in disaster situations: Psychological debriefing. *Disaster Management,* 2, 25–30.

Egan, G. (1975). *The Skilled Helper.* California: Brooks/Cole.

Evans, B.J., Coman, G.J., Stanley, R.O. & Burrows, G.D. (1993). Police officers' coping strategies: An Australian police survey. *Stress Medicine,* 9, 237–246.

Flannery, R.B., Fulton, P., & Tausch, J. (1991). A program to help staff cope with psychological sequelae of assaults by patients. *Hospital and Community Psychiatry,* 42, 935–938.

Fry, W.F. & Salameh, W.A. (Eds.). (1987). *Handbook of Humor and Psychotherapy.* Sarasota: Professional Resource Exchange.

Fullerton, C.S., McCarroll, J.E., Ursano, R.J., & Wright, K.M. (1992). Psychological responses of rescue workers: Firefighters and trauma. *American Journal of Orthopsychiatry,* 62, 371–378.

Hall, K.M. & Cope, D.N. (1995). The benefit of rehabilitation in traumatic brain injury: A literature review. *Journal of Head Trauma Rehabilitation,* 10, 1–13.

Hays, T. (1994). Daily horrors take heavy toll on New York City police officers. *The News,* September 28, pp. 2A–3A.

Hildebrand, J.F. (1984a). Stress research: A perspective of need, a study of feasibility. *Fire Command,* 51, 20–21.

Hildebrand, J.F. (1984b). Stress research (part 2). *Fire Command,* 51, 55–58.

Holt, F.X. (1989). Dispatchers' hidden critical incidents. *Fire Engineering*, November, pp. 53–55.

Lazarus, A.A. & Mayne, T.J. (1990). Relaxation: Some limitations, side effects, and proposed solutions. *Psychotherapy*, 27, 261–266.

McCafferty, R.L., McCafferty, E., & McCafferty, M.A. (1992). Stress and suicide in police officers: Paradigm of occupational stress. *Southern Medical Journal*, 85, 233.

McFarlane, A.C. (1988). The longitudinal course of post-traumatic morbidity: The range of outcomes and their predictors. *Journal of Nervous and Mental Disease*, 176, 30–39.

McFarlane, A.C. (1989). The treatment of post-traumatic stress disorder. *British Journal of Medical Pscyhology*, 62, 81–90.

Miller, L. (1990). Neurobehavioral syndromes and the private practitioner: An introduction to evaluation and treatment. *Psychotherapy in Private Practice*, 8(3), 1–12.

Miller, L. (1991). The "other" brain injuries: Psychotherapeutic issues with stroke and brain tumor patient. *Journal of Cognitive Rehabilitation*, 9(5), 10–16.

Miller, L. (1992). Cognitive rehabilitation, cognitive therapy, and cognitive style: Toward an integrative model of personality and psychotherapy. *Journal of Cognitive Rehabilitation*, 10(1), 18–29.

Miller, L. (1993*a*). Family therapy of brain injury: Syndromes, strategies, and solutions. *American Journal of Family Therapy*, 21,111–121.

Miller, L. (1993*b*). Psychotherapeutic approaches to chronic pain. *Psychotherapy*, 30, 115–124.

Miller, L. (1993*c*). *Psychotherapy of the Brain-Injured Patient: Reclaiming the Shattered Self*. New York: Norton.

Miller, L. (1994*a*). Behavioral medicine: Treating the symptom, the syndrome, or the person? *Psychotherapy*, 31, 161–169.

Miller, L. (1994*b*). Civilian post-traumatic stress disorder: Clinical syndromes and psychotherapeutic strategies. *Psychotherapy*, 31, 655–664.

Miller, L. (1994*c*). The epilepsy patient: Personality, psychodynamics, and psychotherapy. *Psychotherapy*, 31, 735–743.

Mitchell, J.T. (1983). When disaster strikes... The critical incident stress process. *Journal of the Emergency Medical Services*, 8, 36–39.

Mitchel, J.T. (1987). By their own hand. *Chief Fire Executive*, January/February, pp. 48–52, 65, 72.

Mitchell, J.T. (1988). The history, status and future of critical incident stress debriefings. *Journal of the Emergency Medical Services*, 13, 47–52.

Mitchell, J.T. & Bray, G.P. (1990). *Emergency Services Stress: Guidelines for Preserving the Health and Careers of Emergency Services Personnel*. Englewood Cliffs: Prentice-Hall.

Palmer, C.E. (1983). A note about paramedics' strategies for dealing with death and dying. *Journal of Occupational Psychology, 56,* 83–86.

Seligman, J., Holt, D., Chinni, D., & Roberts, E. (1994). Cops who kill—themselves. *Newsweek,* September 26, p. 58.

Sewell, J.D. (1986). Administrative concerns in law enforcement stress management. *Police Studies: The International Review of Police Development, 9,* 153–159.

Sewell, J.D. (1993). Traumatic stress of multiple murder investigations. *Journal of Trauamtic Stress, 6,* 103–118.

Sewell, J.D. & Crew, L. (1984). The forgotten victim: Stress and the police dispatcher. *FBI Law Enforcement Bulletin,* March, pp. 7–11.

Sewell, J.D., Ellison, K.W., & Hurrell, J. J. (1988). Stress management in law enforcement: Where do we go from here? *The Police Chief,* October, pp. 94–98.

Silva, M.N. (1991). The delivery of mental health services to law enforcement officers. *In* J.T. Reese, J.M. Horn, and C. Dunning (Eds.), *Critical Incidents in Policing* (pp. 335–341). Washington, DC: Federal Bureau of Investigation.

Silver, B.V. & Blanchard, E.B. (1978). Biofeedback and relaxation training in the treatment of psychophysiologic disorders: Or, are the machines really necessary? *Journal of Behavioral Medicine, 1,* 217–239.

Solomon, Z. & Benbenishty, R. (1988). The role of proximity, immediacy, and expectance in frontline treatment of combat stress reactions among Israelis in the Lebanon War. *American Journal of Psychiatry, 143,* 613–617.

29

Some Techniques and External Programs Useful in Police Psychological Services

Charles R. Fisher

This chapter is an accumulation of practices and techniques, thoughts and experiences, pulled together while functioning as a police psychologist over the past ten years with various departments in the Denver, Colorado Metropolitan area. For the past three years this psychologist has functioned essentially full-time as Department Psychologist for the Aurora Police Department, Aurora, Colorado.

I intend to share a brief overview concerning my particular style in working clinically with officers and then share some adjunctive programs or services available within most communities, which I feel can be of significant importance in assisting police psychologists dealing with some of the more stressful aspects of officer's lives; especially in those situations where the psychologist is working alone or may not be able to provide a service required due to time and caseload constraints.

It is not unusual for the law enforcement officer to present as a multi-problem crisis requiring adjunctive/supportive/auxiliary services that are not frequently available through traditional mental health/psychotherapeutic approaches. These problems frequently are in areas outside the realm of time, training, or expertise for many police psychologists, and too often, adequate resolution of crises cannot be fully realized without addressing the "whole problem" in all aspects.

Frequently, in my practice a crisis intervention format is required, especially if it is the male marital partner that seeks assistance for his marital/personal relationships. Traditionally, law enforcement officers strive to accept and live by the myth that they solve other people's problems and are not supposed to have any of their own, as this somehow makes them unfit to be a professional caretaker, i.e., a law enforcement officer. Partially because of this mythical attitudinal set which denies their own humanness, an officer in marital trouble waits until an eleventh hour crisis erupts before seeking professional help. He may have talked with, or complained to, peers or supervisers regarding the state of his relationship, but any suggestion that he avail himself of professional psychological services would usually be met with "I'm not crazy," thereby voicing the perpetuating myth that psychologist deal with controlling crazy people versus primarily or secondarily preventing emotionally based maladaptation.

A crisis intervention approach is also frequently appropriate in response to the level of emotional disruption experienced or demonstrated by an officer under severe stress in his marital/personal relationship. Too often, if an employee is not an emotionally aloof or non-empathic person at the start of his law enforcement career, he too often assumes those characteristics in relationships with others at some point during his career. It is not unusual for an officer to rigidly concretize the academy's teaching that he "must always remain objective in all dealings with citizens" and he misinterprets this to mean he should never feel, and, if that should ever happen, he must never let his feelings be brought to awareness and never exhibit it. "Be objective and don't let your feelings get in the way" becomes learned as "Don't feel"—setting the stage for a high probability of emotional disruption at some possible point in his future. In fairness, police academies do try to get recruits to understand the benefits derived from being able to respond to the feelings of victims and witnesses, but in the face of years of dealing with the criminal or greatly disturbed portion of society, previously empathic officers frequently develop a more aloof, unfeeling, or callous demeanor as a defensive means of preventing their reacting emotionally or, out of bitterness at constant exposure to what physical and emotional damage people can do to each other. Too often, this unfeeling attitude towards others also takes precedent with the officer's family, frequently generating difficulties through all relationships within the family structure.

My experience indicates that those officers who have adopted a non-feeling approach to their world, frequently deteriorate emotionally to a greater degree when faced with marital/personal crises such as infidelity of a spouse, extra-marital relationships, separation/divorce, severe illness, injury or death of a child, critical incident trauma, etc., etc. These officers have never introjected, or have discarded, their capacity for emotional response and thereby are not equipped with the experiential training in dealing with their emotions, to the point that they can become dysfunctional in the face of their own personal crisis. They are not familiar with their emotionality and experience the quality and intensity of their emotional response in a crisis as "going crazy" or "having a nervous breakdown." They associate a moderate level of emotional disturbance as "going crazy" as they have led a life of emotional insulation such that feelings were repressed and denied. Their language frequently betrays their uncomfortableness with feelings—they can never identify or acknowledge the feelings of anger, and similarly don't accept being depressed well. They will talk about feeling "upset" which can run the semantic gamut from being enraged, angry, frustrated, or down, sad, depressed. They will not accept anger or depression as legitimate adult feelings but tend to view their appearance as a sign of weakness or sickness.

Officers finding themselves in these personal emotional situations are frequently dysfunctional on the street, finding themselves as grossly preoccupied with their problems and feelings, sometimes to the point that they may not be aware of how they got from one point to another in their city district. Drinking may increase as an attempt at self-medication or as acting out, which exacerbates the problem. These officers are ready to work therapeutically and when they finally contact the department psychologist they are grasping at straws in desperation. Crisis intervention involving two to three appointments per week are appropriate, and the officer is usually willing to negotiate time off or temporary reassignment as indicated and appropriate, and may be willing to have the psychologist negotiate with supervisors with or for him. Consultation for psychotropic medication may be indicated as well as consultation or involvement with spouse, supervisor, or significant others, all of which the officer may be willing to accept at a time of crisis that he might have declined at other times. It is for these reasons that a department psychologist, if possible, provide crisis intervention services available to the officers on a twenty-four hour basis, given that, too often, it may literally be their request for services at the eleventh hour.

A crisis intervention format may begin with an initial meeting lasting longer than the traditional hour. It may be expedient and efficient to utilize one and one-half to two and on-half hours for the initial consultation, especially if a spouse or other significant party may be involved at the outset. This can play havoc with an appointment schedule but is appropriate and effective when expedient therapeutic gains can be realized during a crisis situation while the officer is desperate for relief and motivated to work. Two to three subsequent meetings per week may continue for two or three weeks as indicated and beneficial, incorporating conjoint or separate meetings with others as indicated and with the permission of the primary client. Monitoring of any medications utilized as well as the officer's performance on the street often requires meeting more than once a week when the primary client is in crisis but trying to maintain on the job as appropriate. The process of the crisis intervention is a directive, problem oriented focus dealing with the current problematical issues, the individuals involved, and the nature of those relationships. History is not disregarded, especially history relative to similar situation in the client's past, i.e., previous relationship problems in this or other marriages. A concise family history is taken as well as a drug/alcohol history.

It is helpful if the police psychologist can be comfortable with the unorthodox and be flexible and eclectic enough to deal with novel problems frequently encountered in providing police psychological services. But, as stated above, the police psychologist cannot possibly be all things to all people and at times a multifaceted approach to a multiproblem situation is required and adjunctive services or programs can be extremely beneficial to the therapeutic process working toward resolution and relief.

I will now deal briefly with two programs and a technique which I believe are beneficial in working with specific problematical areas frequently evidenced in working with law enforcement offices. The problem areas have to do with communication in a marital relationship, family finances and budgeting, and conflict resolution relative to custody and visitation in divorce situations. The two programs available nationwide which I will overview are Marriage Encounter and Consumer Credit Counseling Services. The conflict resolution technique is mediation intervention, techniques and skills learned from the history of management/labor relations negotiation, and conflict resolution in strike situations.

The background to Marriage Encounter is that it comes from marital communications training from a pastoral counseling viewpoint. Marriage Encounter is a non-denominational program and participants do not have to be oriented to religion as a part of their lives. The Marriage Encounter program is available within all the Protestant denominations, the Roman Catholic church, as well as within the Morman and Jewish faiths. It is non-evangelical and does not attempt to bring people into any church. It does incorporate a representative from the sponsoring church who speaks to the spiritual aspects of the topics concerning relationship being presented throughout the program. Marriage Encounter is a positively oriented program in that it does not focus on negatives or problems or problem resolution. It is not marriage counseling. The time format for a Marriage Encounter program is a weekend retreat beginning on a Friday evening and progressing through Sunday afternoon. It is an extremely structured program in that it begins in dealing with the less emotionally charged relationship issues on the Friday evening at the beginning of the weekend and graduates toward deeper more meaningful aspects of relationships toward the Sunday afternoon conclusion. It is also extremely structured in that presentations from the three training couples are from a written format and as such, does not wander loosely from topic to topic.

"Encounter" in Marriage Encounter does not signify group interaction as the weekend training is structured so that each of the couples in the entire group are repeatedly instructed that the only other person they will relate to from Friday evening to Sunday afternoon is their spouse and only their spouse. Socializing with other couples is actively discouraged and there is no expectation that any couples will interact with the three training couples or the church representative. The program teaches couples about feelings, about accepting feelings, and about talking about feelings in a constructive way that can allow for differences between individuals in a couple. The weekend teaches couples how to get in touch with their feelings relative to many different aspects of marital relationships, how to express feelings in written and verbal form, and how to constructively deal with each others feelings in a way which promotes communication and enhances relationship.

Marriage Encounter does have follow-up activities and group evening or weekend experiences which are available but not required. Marriage Encounter is a good program when one or both members of a couple are experiencing awkwardness in acknowledging feeling, expressing feelings, and allowing themselves to get emotionally close to their partner. It is a program designed for couples who have reached the "plateau" in their marital relationship such that they need to enhance their communication and interactions in new directions. Marriage Encounter can be contacted through most large congregations nationwide, and is listed under Marriage Encounter or Worldwide Marriage Encounter in the telephone book.

It has been my experience in working with law enforcement officers that a characterization that frequently fits is that they tend to be upward mobile individuals who are competitive, and who have an average to above-average difficulty in dealing with delayed gratification. They, like many of us, tend to live up to the saying that "the basic difference between men and boys is the cost of their toys," and the toys of preference among law enforcement officers are often exotic and expensive gun collections, motorcycles, the latest model car, boats, etc., etc. The often readily available extra-duty work available to police officers sometimes becomes a trap wherein they work the "extra" job for "extra" money, without staying in control of their financial life style; they frequently get into a position whereupon they must depend on extra-duty jobs and sometimes become financially overwhelmed. Needless to say, financial strain within a law enforcement family with all its other stressors adds an additional burden which can frequently be seen by the couple as insurmountable. In situations such as this, where severe financial strain is one of the symptoms of a family's dysfunction, I have found it beneficial to utilize referrals to the nationwide program called Consumer Credit Counseling Services which can be found in most major cities. This program has two levels of intervention in dealing with families with problematical financial issues. Approximately 10 to 15% of all their referrals simply need training relative to home and family budgeting which the Consumer Credit Counseling Services provides at no charge to the client. The other 85 to 90% of their clientele require the second level of intervention which essentially entails the counseling service taking over the financial dilemma of the family, contacting creditors, and arranging repayment schedules over a longer term yet insuring that creditors have their account paid. The counseling service works out a budget for the family including monthly payment to the counseling service with which to take care of the family's creditors. The bulk of the cost of the program is borne by the creditors who pay back to the counseling service 7% of their collections, an arrangement much more favorable to the creditor than going through collection agencies. The only cost to the client is $1 per month fee to maintain records and any postage necessary to mail out checks to creditors. Consumer Credit Counseling Services deals directly with the creditors securing their agreement to take part in the payment program. As long as the creditors' accounts are closed there is no damage to the credit rating for any client using their services. Creditors usually agree to the extension of the repayment time because of the involvement of Consumer Credit Counseling Services in the case. The Consumer Credit Counseling Services can be contacted in any city within the U.S. by referring to the yellow pages under Credit or Credit Counseling.

The last modality I wish to present as an adjunctive technique or service which can be of assistance to law enforcement officers and to police psychologists has to do with the technique of mediation as it applies specifically to visitation, custody, and divorce agreements. With the divorce rate within the law enforcement career what it has been, periodic stressors erupt in an officer's life dealing with a previous or pending divorce involving the highly emotional issues of custody and visitation, and sometimes dealing with modification of existing divorce agreements. Historically, people in such situations have had one recourse when they couldn't work things out themselves — their lawyers and the courts — a costly, time-consuming, adversarial system which frequently polarizes the parties to further extremes and worsens the emotional climate between them. Court involvement frequently results in a judgement that both parties feel as unfair and unjust to them; a judgement is reached but there is no resolution to the problem and in fact the problem is exacerbated.

Mediation is an alternative to the traditional legal system, its purpose being to assist people involved in disputes satisfy their needs without making enemies of opponents. Mediation advocates the amicable settlement of disputes through the intervention of a neutral third party. Mediation is more efficient in terms of cost and time than the traditional legal system and it resolves disputes privately versus in open court. Mediation is a non-adversarial process which resolves emotional conflict as well as legal issues. Mediation utilizes those techniques historically proven effective in the labor relations field and in the conflict management between management and labor in strike situations in industry. Mediation results in a written agreement that both parties in the dispute can feel comfortable with, live with, and agree to. Attorneys may be consulted prior to the signing of any mediation agreement, and mediation agreements may be legally enforceable should the need arise. Mediation research claims that if both sides of a dispute are willing to work out a resolution they have an 80% chance of succeeding. Mediation in divorce, custody, visitation agreements can frequently be better accomplished utilizing a team approach of two mediators, keeping in mind that the process of mediation is significantly different from that of marital therapy. With the coming trend of mediation being an alternative to the adversarial judicial system in divorce/custody/visitation matters, there are numerous centers for dispute resolution or centers for conflict management offering training to those in the helping professions as well as the legal professions to assist couples to work out their divisive issues in a more constructive non-adversarial process. Mediation as a service available within police psychological services has been found to be very beneficial to officers in providing them an alternative to resolve disputes with current or former spouses and does much to minimize the anxiety and anger levels frequently encountered by officers through such stressful procedures.

In summary, I have shared with you my particular value in utilizing crisis intervention techniques in police psychological services and, realizing that the department psychologist cannot be all things to all people, I have herein shared some of the adjunctive techniques and programs that are available to the department psychologist in his/her therapeutic work with officers, spouses and families.

30

Thoughts on Preventive Counseling for Police Officers

Gil Watson

In the early 1970's Dr. John Calhoun, a research psychologist, conducted an interesting experiment at the National Institute of Mental Health. Over the space of 2½ years Dr. Calhoun carefully reduced all mortality factors possible, except aging, in raising a colony of mice from a population of 8 to 2200 in a nine foot square cage. As they reached the optimum population of 2200, some unusual occurrences became evident in this "Mouse Society."

- Adult cliques of about 12 mice formed and within each group specific mice performed specific tasks.
- Usually aggressive males became passive and nonaggressive.
- The young became very passive and self indulgent only eating, sleeping, and grooming themselves.
- The "Mouse Society" gradually died off after 5 years and not one mouse survived, although there was an absence of disease and plenty of food, water, and resources.[1]

Certainly one would be treading in dangerous waters by paralleling a "Mouse Society" and a police department. Some interesting analogies can be drawn, however.

A typical police officer upon starting his/her career perceives the career as lasting at least the full twenty years needed for retirement. During that time the officer expects to progress in the paramilitary structure at least to the rank of Sergeant and hopes to attain a higher rank and expects to find good leadership, professionalism, justice, camaraderie, training, excitement, fulfillment and social acceptance. These uncontrollable stressors are well documented and now well known in the Police field through the writings and work of Reiser, Richard and Fell, Stratton and Kroes, Margolis and Hurrell.[2] As the police officer proceeds in his/her career,

---

1. Frank Sartwell, "The Small Satanic Worlds of John Calhoun" *Smithsonian Magazine*, April, 1970, p. 66.
    2. Kroes, William H., Margolis, Bruce L. Hurrell, Joseph J., "Job Stress in Policemen" *Journal of Police Science and Administration*, Vol. 2, No. 2, 1974, pp. 145–155.

he/she is incorporated into a structure that is both exciting and boring, exact and unclear, just and unjust. The officer becomes confronted with having to deal with his unrealistic expectations of job satisfaction during the first to five years on the job. It might be added that most Police Departments have an initial one year probationary period (Illinois) that allows liberal dismissal causes for the "Police Rookie" and forces the "Rookie" into an extended unrealistic honeymoon period. During these first five years the police officer begins to make choices congruent with his/her normal personality and the socialized model forced upon the officer by the law enforcement field.[3] The officer begins to face and deal with a job that has no concrete solutions in the court room, no specific "yes and no" on the street, minuscule hopes for promotion, and long boring hours of patrol. The police officer will reach a point of choice somewhere around the fifth year and will choose to accept the shortcomings of the job and its related stress factors and rechannel his/her energy in appropriate ways or will choose a defensive system that is not mentally healthy in which to deal with the reality. The police officer might indeed become a "mouse," become a clique member, lose aggressiveness, become self indulgent, and figuratively "die off" at the five year mark. Of course this comparison is full of holes and any reasonable person with "common sense" can discount this analogy as being ridiculous immediately. But the analogy does bring us to a question regarding healthy adjustment to the Police role versus abnormal adjustment to the same role.

This abnormal adjustment to the Police role and the incumbent stress is well documented in the many writings of the past decade by noted researchers, resident Police psychologists and clinicians such as; Reiser, Roberts, Stratton, Reese and Bard. Popularization of the abnormal adjustments of police officers can be found in many of Joseph Wambaugh's novels and the current Emmy award winning TV show "Hill Street Blues." Identification of the unique problems incurred by Police Officers seem to be well identified and have found acceptance among Police management circles progressively during the 70s and early 80s.

In keeping with our role as clinicians, having identified the psychopathology, we (the Police Psychology field) have made significant gains in terms of treatment during this period of time. Most of the large metropolitan police departments (Chicago, Los Angeles, San Diego, Dallas, etc.) have counseling programs available for use by their personnel. The emphasis of these programs has changed slightly over the past decade but almost categorically they deal with pathology, focusing on the presenting problems referred to the "counseling unit" such as; alcohol

---

3. Robert W. Balch, "The Police Personality: Fact or Fiction," *Journal of Criminal Law, Criminology and Police Science*, Vol. 63, No. 1, 1972, p. 106.

abuse, drug abuse, physical abuse to arrestees, severe mood swings and radical changes in performance. After entering treatment with a clinician the presenting problems are sorted out, a treatment plan is developed, and the police officer eventually returns to full duty upon successful completion of the program or fails the program and incurs other consequences. Most major metropolitan police departments have found in-house counseling programs to be effective in saving trained personnel, lost service time, disciplinary action and subsequent legal fees. This experience is quite similar to major corporations in the private sector in their development of Employee Assistance Programs (EAP's).[4] Recently major metropolitan counseling programs have become involved in the training of rookie police officers during their basic school and in the initial selection and screening process for hiring. It is obvious that the role of the counselor has expanded and is becoming an accepted part of the police management team. Full acceptance by ordinary patrol officers will take time and some changes in use by the same management team, as the patrol officers perceive the counseling unit as being a tool owned and used by management.

The experience of smaller suburban and rural police departments has been less notable and certainly harder to trace. The growing awareness of the need to provide counseling has been evident to the smaller police departments and although resources are limited, attempts have been made. Most of these departments have resorted to using private practitioners, local agencies, or consulting police psychologists/counselors. There are probably several hundred slightly different program designs used by these departments. Again, these departments deal almost entirely with pathological problems; drunk cops, abusive cops, disturbed cops, etc.

The ultimate cure for pathological problems is not found in counseling the disturbed police officer. The answer is in preventing the disease from taking root in the police officer. As a clinician working and counseling with police personnel for almost ten years, I have found that in almost every case simple changes in priorities by the officer can allow the officer to deal effectively with both the controllable and uncontrollable stressors of their jobs.

Life can be treated as a marathon race. Too often it is viewed as a 100 meter dash with all the rewards coming very quickly. Few contestants will win these kinds of races. They are won by very talented people or by those in the right place at the right time. The key to successful completion of a marathon is the prevention of breakdown during the race by preparation and training. The key to successful completion of a law enforcement

4. Lynn Lambuth, "An Employee Assistance Program that Works," *Police Chief,* January, 1984, pp. 36–38.

career is prevention of breakdown in the emotional, behavioral and physical aspects of the occupation.[5]

For any human being to successfully complete the task of life, they
must have their priorities in order. After many years of marital counseling
and clinical work with the Police Officers, it can only be concluded that
the establishing of priorities are the same for police officers as for the general public.

1. Spouse
2. Family
3. Occupation
4. Other talents and interests

In other words, the job should not be the first priority of the police officer. This common error of law enforcement management will only lead to
dysfunction with spouse and family. The subsequent collapse of the officer's support system (family) will lead to the eventual dysfunction of the
officer on the job.

> ..., in police work, the family takes second place to the job. In many cases,
> the family unit never recovers from the resulting strain.[6]

The Kroes, Margolis, and Hurrell study cited previously found 79 of
81 married officers surveyed to have strained relationships due to the occupation. Police management must acknowledge that an officer's home
life, spouse and family, have a direct reflection on the job and provide
needed relief and understanding for the officer and his/her family.
Management must address the problem of shift work, offer counseling assistance (EAP), assist with social groups of officer's spouses, and provide
periodic training for family members as well as the officers.

A full scale prevention program could begin in more police departments
with adjustments of design for the various sizes of the departments. The initially envisioned program would call for on-going counseling throughout the
career of the police officer. An employee assistance program would need to
be established with the idea that it would incorporate the following elements:

A. Treatment of identified pathology for the officer and his/her family.
B. Periodic training (quarterly) for all personnel and their families.
C. Preventive counseling on a once a month basis for all personnel, chief
executives included.

---

5. James T. Reese, "Life in the High-Speed Lane: Managing Police Burnout" *Police
Chief*, June, 1982, p. 50.

6. Hilda F. Besner and Sandra J. Robinson, "Police Wives—The Untapped Resource"
Police Chief, August 1984, p. 62.

D. Establishment of family groups and spouse groups.

The adherence to Part C would be of primary importance to the overall success of a preventive program. The issues that would need to be addressed would fall into categories or stages:

1. Selection of Police Personnel
2. Probation
3. Early Career
4. Mid Career
5. Late Career
6. Retirement

Let us take a closer look at what a counselor might be trying to deal with during these six stages.

Selection

The police counselor would start the relationship with the officer right in the beginning with the ordinary psychological testing and interviewing procedure used to screen police personnel. If this process is done by an outside agency, provisions must be made to introduce the police counselor in the process.

Probation

Most police departments have probationary time period of up to one year to evaluate new officers. The counselor must make good use of this year to establish rapport with the new officers and their families. Police management must make it clear that they will not use or involve the counselor at all in the evaluation period of probation. The counselor should focus attention with the probationary officer on these issues; adjustment to shifts, perception of the job to the reality of the job, reality of the court system, a program for stress reduction, social acceptance by other officers, and establishing the priorities of "life's marathon." The counselor needs to work with the new officer's spouse and family on the physical, emotional, psychological adjustment to having a cop in the family. The counselor must work with changes in friends and social contacts due to shift work and a career not widely accepted by the public (certainly a paradox!), developing sensitivity and establishing of a support group for the family's use.

Early Career

During the officer's early career the counselor would need to address and focus on the worth of the family system and would address with the officer the reality of advancement in the police department. The counselor and officer would set realistic goals for accomplishment. A stress management program should be begun. A physical fitness program should also be initiated with appropriate goals and request. Investigation should be started as to the officer's other talents and hobbies.

Mid-Career

At this point the officer is about ready to take their first promotional exam and is at a high point in job satisfaction if the officer has been emotionally stable. The counselor is faced at this point with re-affirming the priority of the family, stress management and physical fitness programs. The counselor must also assist the officer in readjusting career goals, because during this period of time most officers realize that they will or will not be promoted. For those with future promotions obtainable, the counselor must temper these high hopes with reality and other options. For those who will not be promoted, other realistic goals must be established. Goals that will fulfill the individual in such a way that job performance is not hindered. At this point the well adjusted officer must be presented with alternatives such as hobbies and second careers upon retirement. This is also an excellent time for additional emotional investment in family goals and outings. For the department, the counselor needs to zero in on the accomplishments the officer has made and enhance the specialties and talents he/she is good at (evidence collection, traffic enforcement, training, etc.), caution must be taken because mid-career is the beginning of the manifestations of the dysfunctional officer because of little positive guidance in a police department.

Late Career

Whereas, late career for a businessperson is the latter fifties, early sixties, for a police officer late career can be early forties. The police counselor must face preparation for retirement with the realization that true retirement may be almost twenty years away! If there has been progression through the ranks and the officer holds a command position, re-evaluation of future goals may be in order. Again, the ultimate goal of the police counselor is to affirm the role of the spouse and family as the top priority and ultimate support system for the police officer. If the officer is truly going to retire and take the "20" then hopefully adequate preparation has been made by the police counselor for a new career or other interesting alternatives for the retiree.

Retirement

This is a time for the counselor to evaluate the fruit of the program. There is little doubt of the pathological health problems of police officers, especially cardiovascular and digestive disorders, and there seems to be continued early death among retired officers, it would seem that periodic follow-up counseling would see an improvement in health and quality of life among retired officers. A retirement study would be the beginning of an answer to such a preventative program.

Conclusion

Since preventive programs in mental health continue to be placed on the back burners of the mental health system itself, there can be no illustrations that career oriented prevention counseling programs for police officers will gain widespread acceptance soon. We have long been a pathology oriented culture that has a great deal of trouble accepting that sometimes we must abstain and discipline ourselves in order to eliminate a pathology. Just look at the warnings of probable cancer given to those who smoke cigarettes and yet millions of people continue to accept this easily prevented disease.

Certainly the future holds programs incorporating preventive ideas. Already the law enforcement field has begun to embrace the counseling professions of psychiatry, psychology, and social work albeit with some fear and trepidation on the part of both professions. But the basic approach must change eventually because:

> the main tools and models for primary prevention are provided by education, social engineering, and social change. Primary prevention efforts are based on the assumption that reducing stress and giving people better resources for coping are effective ways to prevent social difficulties; so are helping them find support groups and developing good self esteem.[7]

---

7. George W. Albee, Sol Gordon, Harold Leitenber, editors, *Promoting Sexual Responsibility and Preventing Sexual Problems*, from the series "Primary Prevention of Psycho-pathology," Vol. VII, 1983, p. XVII.

31

A Coordinated Approach to Alcoholism Treatment

Rory Gilbert

The Chicago Police Department Professional Counseling Service is a free, voluntary, and confidential counseling service available to members of the Department and their families. It consists of a substance abuse counseling unit and a general individual, marital, and family counseling unit. The substance abuse unit is staffed by specially selected police officers who have received advanced training in substance abuse counseling. The individual and family therapists are clinical social workers. These two units must co-ordinate their efforts in order to provide a high quality service. Many counseling requests are made for individual adjustment or relationship problems, when, in fact, alcoholism is the primary problem. This chapter will explore several key aspects of alcoholism as it affects the police officer and the officer's family, especially as it relates to the families where the alcoholism is "hidden" behind other issues. The chapter will also describe the clinical interventions employed by the Professional Counseling Service that combine the expertise of the substance abuse counselors and social workers.

Alcoholism is a major problem for police departments across the country. No solid statistics exist but the incidence rate is high. In the general population, it is estimated that one out of every ten adults who drink are alcoholics. The percentage rate among police officers is, in all likelihood, higher because of the social milieu that supports and encourages drinking. The negative effects this has on police departments is tremendous. It can be measured in terms of absenteeism, apathy toward the job, reduction in performance levels, and liability when on-duty drinking occurs.

Alcoholism is a complex illness. It affects the whole person. This includes one's physical and emotional self. It exists when the drinking of alcohol causes problems in any major area of an individual's life such as job, family, or health. Alcoholism does not necessarily affect all these areas simultaneously or to the same degree. Many police officers, whose excessive drinking is creating severe family problems, are functioning well on the job.

The disease is considered to be a primary illness. That is, it is an entity in and of itself, and not a symptom of underlying psychological or interpersonal problems. The role that environmental factors play in the etiology of the disease varies from person to person. It is a myth that police stress causes alcoholism. The true "cause" is not entirely clear although it is apparent that physiological, psychological, and sociological factors all play a contributing role.

Alcoholism is a chronic condition. It is permanent and cannot be reversed. It can, however, be arrested. The alcoholic individual can abstain from drinking and participate in a "recovery program" that will prevent the disease from having a further adverse effect on his/her life.

The disease of alcoholism also gets progressively worse when it is untreated. The course and pace the progression takes is unique to each individual, but, if it goes unchecked, the eventual result is premature death. Alcoholism is the third leading cause of death in this country.

A major symptom of alcoholism is denial. This psychological defense mechanism blocks the unacceptable realities associated with the disease from entering the individual's awareness. This is the mechanism that permits alcoholism to progress. The denial, which can take several forms, serves as a means of protecting the disease from attempts to alter its course. Thus, it is this aspect of the disease that makes successful therapeutic intervention difficult. Furthermore, the disease is such that the alcoholic's family employs denial perhaps as intensely or even more intensely than the alcoholic.

The alcoholic's denial exists in part because of the need to protect one's self-image from his/her definition of alcoholism. The stigma and misconceptions commonly attached to this illness force the individual to go to greater lengths to avoid being labeled in this manner. Police work can also reinforce the myth that "all alcoholics are winos and/or criminals" and make the stigma that underlies the denial that much more ingrained.

Similarly, a family employs denial to avoid the shame and embarrassment of identifying one of its members as alcoholic. The connotations associated with such statements as "my husband is a drunk" or "my mother can't hold her booze" are often too painful to experience without a defense. Also, the spouse can feel personal shame and degradation for having selected and being associated with an alcoholic partner. The same can apply to parents, children, and even employers. In addition, misinformation about the causes of alcoholism place an additional burden on the family members. They have to contend with self-blame and guilt over a belief that they are responsible for their loved one's drinking.

When crises develop in these families, the magnitude of the denial is intensified. The defense needs to be stronger when problems erupt in order for the individual or family to avoid concluding that it is alcoholism that is having an adverse effect upon their lives. At these times families will frequently minimize drinking and blame other factors for the present predicament. It is common case scenario for a person with an alcoholic spouse to request counseling to resolve severe marital difficulties. The spouse may describe violent confrontations, sexual dysfunction, and other chronic interpersonal problems, but the shame associated with alcoholism prevents him/her from disclosing its presence. A case example will illustrate this:

> Ms. A. is a 35-year-old professional businessperson who has been married for five years. Her husband is a 45-year-old homicide detective who has been with the Chicago Police Department for 22 years. Ms. A. called the counseling office in tears requesting to be seen as soon as possible. She indicated that her husband had accused her of infidelity and became violent. She did not know what she should do, but was contemplating divorce. The social worker suggested she make an appointment for the two of them to be seen conjointly, but Ms. A. stated her husband refused to come. Thus, an individual appointment was made with Ms. A.
>
> During the session, Ms. A. stated that she and her husband had been having a pleasant evening following her husband's day off and then her husband's mood began to change without any apparent provocation. He became increasingly more irate and then began accusing her of sexual affairs. She stated there was no truth to his comments. Mr. A. then began pushing her around and throwing objects. She called the police for assistance and two uniformed officers were needed to subdue her husband.
>
> Ms. A. went on to explain that she very much loved her husband but feared for her safety. This social worker attempted to determine if drinking had been a factor in this incident. Ms. A. was vague and inexplicit in her response. The social worker had the impression that she was being evasive regarding the role alcohol had played. This contrasted with her previous behavior during the session. Up to this point she had been very open and expressive about a range of material of a sensitive nature. The therapist repeatedly asked her to be as explicit as possible. Eventually, statements Ms. A. made about her husband's drinking such as, "I'm not sure, but I think he had a couple of drinks," evolved into a detailed pattern. It came out that Mr. A. had completed three six-packs of beer in the afternoon and after dinner he had consumed approximately a pint of scotch.

During the initial phase of treatment it is the responsibility of the Professional Counseling Service social worker to assess the situation and determine if alcoholism is a factor in the case. The substance abuse counselor is not involved until the client is openly able to perceive that drinking is, at least partially, involved in the family problems. The social worker must be sensitive to the possibility that alcoholism exists if he/she is to make an accurate assessment. Although the need for the therapist to be sensitive to alcoholism seems obvious, it is, nevertheless, important to underscore. Alcoholism can be easily overlooked if the therapist is not actively looking for it. In the initial interview with Ms. A., for example, the therapist had to employ crisis intervention techniques, assist Ms. A. in developing a protection plan for her personal safety*, and strategize ways to involve the resistant spouse. It would have been easy for the social worker to neglect to explore for alcoholism in an assertive fashion when trying to balance so many therapeutic tasks. This is especially true when it is remembered that Ms. A. was not volunteering alcohol related information.

The therapeutic task at this early stage of treatment is to elicit from the client a factual account of the drinking that is suspected of interfering with the family's functioning. The therapist must intervene in a manner that reduces the client's denial. The therapist attempts to communicate his/her understanding that the client perceives a need to minimize the extent of the drinking and is not deliberately attempting to impede the therapist's efforts. In this way the therapist emphatically communicates respect for the client's efforts to cope with an out of control situation.

The therapist also adopts a non-judgmental attitude toward alcoholism which, in turn, helps to reduce the client's denial. The client has less of a need to protect his/her character, or in Ms. A.'s case the character of her husband, when excessive drinking and drunken behavior are approached as symptomatic of a disease. This approach reduces the stigma associated with alcoholism and debunks some of the myths. Furthermore, hope is generated in the client when alcoholism is approached as a treatable illness and not as a social taboo or psychiatric disorder.

The substance abuse counselor is brought into the treatment process when the client's resistance is lowered to the point where the individual or family is openly able to consider the possibility that alcoholism may be present. This is usually accomplished in the first session that the alcoholic family member attends if the therapist has empathically intervened in a straightforward fashion. This was the case with the A.'s:

> Mr. A. came to the next session with his wife. Initially, he was openly opposed to treatment and somewhat hostile to the social worker for "intruding" in his personal affairs. The therapist, by employing empathic and reassuring comments, was able to elicit Mr. A.'s perspective on his marital difficulties in general and the incident where the police were called in particular.
>
> Mr. A. explained that he felt his marital difficulties were the by-product of work problems. He explained that his unit had a new commander who he was having trouble getting along with. He feared being "dumped" from the detective division into patrol. Mr. A. went on to

---

* The authors are not implying that domestic violence and other problems do not exist as real problems in and of themselves in families where alcoholism is present. The interconnection between alcoholism and domestic violence is complex. Common sense dictates that both need to be addressed and monitored throughout the treatment process.

state that these work pressures cause him to be irritable at home. This situation came to a head the night he "lost his temper."

The therapist attempted to obtain a detailed account of this incident. Mr. A. did not mention drinking and, when asked if he had been drinking, he stated he had not. Ms. A. brought herself into the conversation and stated that he was lying. Mr. A. then admitted that he had "a couple of cocktails."

The therapist pointed out that since there obviously was a lack of clarity concerning the role alcohol was playing in the problem, it would be helpful to bring an alcoholism specialist into the session.

The therapist needs to make a decision concerning the timing of informing the family that he/she believes the problem is alcoholism. He/she can share this information with the family prior to the introduction of the substance abuse counselor when there is no doubt about the assessment and the family displays relatively little resistance. The substance abuse counselor has the responsibility of sharing the assessment with the family when it is not totally clear that the problem is alcoholism and the resistance is high. The therapist had no doubt that Mr. A. was, in fact alcoholic, for example, but it was felt that Mr. A. was not ready to handle this assessment in a beneficial fashion. The therapist anticipated that the substance abuse counselor could elicit a clearer pattern of alcoholism. The therapist also hoped that Mr. A. would be more receptive to the substance abuse counselor because he was a fellow police officer, than he had been to the "professional therapist." This latter point raises an interesting issue concerning the differentiation of roles of the substance abuse counselor and the social worker. Some police officers respond to the professional posture of the social worker with mistrust, but are open to the substance abuse counselor because he is a police officer. Others, on the other hand, invest the social worker with unrealistically high qualitites because of the position and discount the substance abuse counselor for not having an advanced degree. The unit attempts to be sensitive to this dynamic and use it to a therapeutic advantage.

The substance abuse counselor's initial task is to perform an evaluation for alcoholism on the family member who is suspected of having the problem. The counselor uses the evaluation to make a determination of the presence or absence of alcoholism. This clarifies any uncertainties the social worker may have or provides confirmation when the social worker believes alcoholism is present. The evaluation includes a detailed account of the individual's current drinking habits as well as the individual's drinking history. An attempt is made to obtain the most objective information possible. The substance abuse counselor utilizes the other family members to verify the facts and clarify sketchy information although an effort is made to avoid placing the family members in a situation where they feel as if they are tattling on their loved one. The following information was obtained from Mr. A.:

> Mr. A. described himself as a heavy drinker although he underscored his belief that he was not alcoholic. He stated that he enjoys drinking and the camaraderie associated with the tavern. In addition, he indicated that drinking provides him with relief from the pressures of work and home.
>
> Mr. A. was able to admit that he was a "little high" the night Ms. A. called the police. It eventually became evident that alcohol was involved in the other two incidents that Ms. A. had mentioned in her first session. Once this was established. Mr. A. stated that he had not been involved in any other alcohol related incidents in the recent past. Ms. A., however, described two weddings and a "change of watch party" this year where Mr. A. had become intoxicated to the point that he needed assistance getting home. Mr. A. defended his behavior during these incidents by stating that this was normal, common, acceptable behavior at weddings and police parties.
>
> Mr. A. then reiterated that his drinking was, in fact, not a problem.
>
> He described several times when he had "proven" this by abstaining from any alcohol consumption for two and three weeks at a time. He also stated that his drinking was generally confined to the tavern and not a problem for anyone because he usually goes home and goes to bed on the occasions that he did drink.
>
> Mr. A. indicated that there was a time in his past, prior to his relationship with Ms. A., that he had been concerned about his drinking. He felt that his entire lifestyle was getting out of control in his final years as a bachelor. He was "doing the town" and drinking to excess almost every night. He was concerned about his potential for developing an alcohol problem at that point. However, he stated that this all changed when Ms. A. came into his life. He greatly reduced the amount he drank when they became involved with each other. He was able to moderate his alcohol consumption by limiting the occasions he was drinking.

In the alcoholism evaluation an attempt is made to isolate the drinking patterns of the individual from the rest of his/her life in order to make a definitive determination of the presence of alcoholism. Alcoholism is considered to be present if it produces problems in a significant area of an individual's life. The conflicts in the A.'s marriage, for example, reach a dysfunctional level when Mr. A. is under the influence of alcohol.

The evaluation also provides information about the manner in which the individual and his family have attempted to cope with the alcoholism. This provides clues concerning the most effective ways of intervening to reach the treatment goal of recovery. Mr. A., for example, has attempted to avoid the adverse affects of the disease by placing external controls on his behavior. This is, when he exposes himself to drinking situations he cannot exercise control over his consumption and difficulties will occur that he cannot predict or regulate. He is able to reduce the problems, however, by limiting the contact he has with these situations, e.g. avoiding the tavern. This provides only modest success because without internal control the occurrence of future problems is inevitable. Furthermore, although Mr. and Ms. A.'s love for one another seems sincere, the marriage, itself, served as an external control for Mr. A.'s drinking in the way it provided a means of diminishing the out of control nature of Mr. A's life prior to the marriage.

The evaluation also provides a picture of the alcoholic individual's denial system and that of his/her family. Mr. A., for example, utilized his ability to abstain from alcohol for various periods of time as a means of providing evidence that he was not alcoholic. Abstinence is not contra-indicative of alcoholism. Alcoholics not in a recovery program who abstain from drinking for extended periods of time are considered to be actively alcoholic because their whole lives revolve around their abstinence. They lack a means of regulating their tension and anxiety without alcohol. Frequently, they attempt to reduce this excess tension by remaining active, and, in essence they attempt to "burn off" their anxiety. Thus, the surly "workaholic" who has several extra jobs is often an alcoholic not permitting himself/herself access to alcohol.

The design and implementation of a treatment plan follows the positive diagnosis of alcoholism. The ultimate goal in all cases is for the alcoholic individual to be involved in the Alcoholics Anonymous recovery program, and for the other family members to be involved in Alanon Family Recovery Group or, when appropriate, Alateen. The substance abuse counselor is primarily responsible for determining what intermediate steps are indicated to increase the likelihood that the treatment goal will be met. Hospitalization at an alcoholism rehabilitation center is frequently indicated. These settings are the most effective means available of helping people obtain sobriety because an in-patient setting is able to provide the most comprehensive educational and therapeutic milieu. Individuals who do not perceive alcoholism as the primary problem are best able to benefit from these intensive programs. Physical complications due to chronic, excessive drinking and withdrawal symptoms also require the medical supervision rehabilitation centers provide. The substance abuse counselor monitors the individual's progress when he/she is a patient in a rehabilitation center. This is done through formal employee conferences and informal conversations and visits with the patients and their counselors at the hospitals.

Occasionally, the alcoholic is directly referred to Alcoholics Anonymous and his/her loved one to Alanon. This is indicated in cases where the individual and family members are highly motivated for change and the resistance is relatively low. There are also situations where in-patient treatment is not a practical alternative. The social worker and the substance abuse counselor monitor the progress of the family and the alcoholic when they refer directly to A.A. and Alanon through additional marital sessions. This was the case with the A.'s:

> The substance abuse counselor shared his assessment with the A.'s that it did, in fact, appear that the problem was alcoholism. In-patient treatment was recommended. However, limitations in the A.'s insurance coverage ruled this out as a possibility.
>
> Mr. A., initially, wanted nothing more to do with treatment, Ms. A., however, was very open to the idea of Alanon, and in fact, seemed empowered by the process of openly discussing Mr. A.'s drinking for the first time. She made it clear to Mr. A. that she was going to follow the advice of the experts, and she was not going to allow herself to be abused any longer. Mr. A. did agree to attend an A.A. meeting with Ms. A's strong statements as impetus.
>
> The substance abuse counselor arranged for Mr. A. to go to an A.A. meeting heavily attended by police officers. He came to the next session stating that the meeting was not as bad as he had expected. He also expressed surprise that so many "stand-up" guys were involved with A.A. Ms. A. also reported having had a positive experience at Alanon. They were both praised for the work they were doing and encouraged to attend as many meetings as possible in the following week.
>
> The A.'s continued to progress at a rapid rate. They were seen for a total of five more sessions. Mr. A. became increasingly more honest regarding the manner in which alcohol had affected his life. He was able to admit that he could not control his drinking and he reported several ways has had tried to cover up this fact. Simultaneously, the assertive attitude Ms. A. had displayed when she declared that she was planning to attend Alanon became increasingly more refined. She described herself as feeling "free and unburdened" for the first time in her marriage. They both reported an increased amount of satisfaction from their relationship and more love for one another.
>
> In addition, as Mr. A. obtained sobriety, the A.'s began to address issues in their relationship they had previously avoided. Specifically, Ms. A. expressed long held resentments she had regarding Mr. A.'s family. They were able to discuss this issue and make progress toward a resolution of this problem.

There are also a significant number of clients who are not willing to enter a treatment center but who are willing to become involved in A.A. The timing with which an individual is introduced to A.A. is crucial. An alcoholic will frequently develop a negative opinion of A.A. if he/she attends meetings to placate others, e.g. spouse or therapist. The social worker and substance abuse counselor will conduct alcoholism focused marital and family sessions in this situation in an effort to reduce this resistance.

It is also fairly common for one family member, usually the non-alcoholic spouse, to be motivated for additional help while his/her partner refuses treatment. The social worker and substance abuse counselor will work with the person on an individual basis while he/she becomes involved in Alanon. It is possible in many cases for an individual to obtain relief while remaining with an actively alcoholic spouse. Often, if the non-alcoholic spouse changes, his/her partner is faced with additional pressures to alter the problematic behavior. This creates a crisis for the active alcoholic and can impel him to change.

This chapter has described the manner in which the social worker and substance alcoholism counselors of the Chicago Police Department Professional Counseling Service combine their efforts. The goal in all of these alcoholism cases is for the alcoholic to achieve total abstinence from alcohol within the recovery program of Alcoholics Anonymous. Similarly, active involvement in the Alanon Family Recovery Group is the goal for the spouses and the other family members. This goal was readily realized in the case involving the A.'s, which was discussed throughout this paper. This goal is achieved in approximately half the cases. Some measure of success can be charted in the remaining cases. This can take the form of temporary abstinence, more vigorous attempts at control, and/or active involvement in Alanon by the non-alcoholic family members. Regardless of the individual's response to treatment, the diagnosis of alcoholism has been explicitly stated. This plants a seed that is difficult to ignore. Therefore, when drinking related crises reoccur, there is an increased likelihood that the alcoholic will return to counseling with a more favorable prognosis.

References

Anonymous (1975), *Dealing With Denial—The Caring Community Series No. 6*. Center City, Minnesota: Hazeldon Foundation.

Kinney, J., and Leaton, G. (1978), *Loosening The Grip: A Handbook of Alcohol Information*. St. Louis: C.V. Mosby Company.

Milt, H. (1977), *The Revised Handbook on Alcoholism*. Maplewood, New Jersey: Scientific Aids Publications.

Vaillant, G.E. (1983), *The Natural History of Alcoholism*. Cambridge, Mass: Harvard University Press.

Part Eight

Management Issues in Dealing with Police Stress

Ayres (1990) has emphasized that the creation and maintenance of a healthy workplace is critical as an organizational goal within a law enforcement agency and serves as an effective barrier against organizational and individual stress damage. Of particular importance is a recognition by the law enforcement organization's administration that it has a responsibility for the mitigation and management of the stress of its employees.

Administrative support takes a variety of forms. An environment that encourages communication and facilitates an officer's ability to access stress management services is, perhaps, the most important. Well-defined missions and goals, clear policies and procedures, and state of the art training, equipment and management techniques are equally important. Here in Part Eight, our authors expand on the interaction between the police administration and stress management.

Over the last several years, research into law enforcement stress has dramatically underscored the problems experienced by police officers throughout this country and the significant efforts devoted to programs of stress awareness identification and management. Sewell suggests that, to have the greatest impact, the implementation of stress management efforts must be part of an integrated program of psychological services within a department. In addition to the professional considerations normally associated with such services, a number of management issues must be analyzed and successfully resolved to increase and insure program effectiveness.

Finn reflects that, in light of the often-neglected effects that organizational stress has on agencies and officers, managers should change stress-inducing policies. Citing the tendency to treat the symptoms rather than the cause, he specifies steps that several agencies have taken to effectively reduce organizational stress and thus enhance the productivity and job satisfaction of their officers.

In her NIJ-sponsored research, Scrivner surveyed police psychologists to examine the types of services they provide and how those services are used to counter police use of excessive force. These professionals were able to identify five categories of officers: those with personality disorders that place them at chronic risk; officers whose previous job related experience places them at risk; officers who have problems at early stages in their career; officers who develop inappropriate patrol styles; and officers with personal problems. These profiles suggest a number of strategies which departments can use to prevent the inappropriate or excessive exercise of force by their personnel.

Finally, in an appropriate ending as we discuss stress, we must recognize that retirement is a traumatic event confronting every veteran "baby-boomer" officer. Rhem examines a number of important retirement issues, including career challenges outside the confines of the department; the finances needed to maintain a comparable standard of living after retirement; and some of the physical and psychological manifestations of retirement. The author enumerates ways in which a police department may better help officers in preparing for retirement.

References

Ayres, R.M. (1990) *Preventing Law Enforcement Stress: The Organization's Role.* Alexandria, VA: National Sheriffs Association.

32

Administrative Concerns in Law Enforcement Stress Management

James D. Sewell

Over the last several years, law enforcement administrators and academicians have shown a major interest in the phenomenon know as "police stress." It now seems apparent that both the manifestations and effects of police stress can be dangerous to the individual officer, his family, his department, and the community at large. Within academic and professional literature, many researchers have attempted to identify and categorize sources of stress in the field of law enforcement (Eisenberg, 1975; Sandy and Devine, 1978; Ellison and Genz, 1983; Sewell, 1983). On the basis of such preliminary research into law enforcement stress, as well as efforts in other occupations, a growing body of literature now identifies and offers management techniques for the individual officer as well as the department (Teten and Minderman, 1977; Moore and Donohue, 1978; Stratton, 1978; Hageman, Kennedy, Price, 1979).

The use of psychological services to assist police agencies is, of course, expanding within the profession. An estimated 20-25% of this nation's law enforcement agencies now have stress management programs designed to better enable their officers "to protect and to serve." Yet, with the growth of police psychological services, especially stress management, there are a number of administrative concerns which should be addressed in order to assure the best services for our communities and our personnel.

Among those which law enforcement managers must recognize and resolve are:

1. The appropriate advisory role of the police psychologist
2. Administrative commitment to stress management programs
3. The moral and ethical responsibility of criminal justice managers for their personnel
4. Increased and more realistic training
5. The use of stress management programs as an "easy out" for incompetent or weak officers
6. The balancing of on-the-job demands and professional expectations with off-the-job outlets

7. The need for organizational reform
8. The education of community governing bodies and citizens about their role in the stress management of public employees
9. The identification and management of the stress of personnel beyond the line officer.

1. The Appropriate Advisory Role of the Police Psychologist

The valuable support which can be provided to law enforcement agencies by psychologists has been shown in a variety of areas, including selection, stress management, psychological profiling, job evaluation, and training. Although a number of articles have spoken to the role from the psychologist's perspective (Brodsky, 1973; Brodksy, 1974; Brodsky, 1977; Morrison, 1978; Stratton, 1980; Reiser, 1982), there are other issues for consideration by police managers. First, today's manager should recognize the value of psychological services, especially in the areas of personnel management and crime resolution. At the same time, one must acknowledge the expense of such services and their ultimate cost-effectiveness in reduced personnel turnover, disciplinary and emotional problems, and, hopefully, an improved solution rate in crimes against persons.

Second, the usefulness of police psychological services has specific limitations. Primarily, the administrator should restrict those expectations associated with psychological evaluation and with the degree of understanding of the human mind and behavior. As in the law enforcement profession and its interaction with citizens, expectation greatly exceeds reality, and predictive capabilities, especially where no past pattern of behavior exists, are more limited than many police administrators understand. Menninger's words of caution to the legal profession are equally applicable to law enforcement managers:

> ...most lawyers have no conception of the meaning or methods of psychiatric case study and diagnosis. They seem to think that psychiatrists can take a quick look at a subject...and thereupon be able to say definitely, that the awful 'it'...the loathsome affliction of insanity...is present or absent. Because we all like to please, some timid psychiatrists fall in with this fallacy of the lawyers and go through these preposterous antics (Murphy, 1973, pp. 137-38).

Third, Truman's phrase "the buck stops here" is particularly true for administrators of a police agency. The appropriate role of the police psychologist is similar to that of the departmental attorney: he or she provides guidance, counsel, advice, and predictions, all based on education, training, experience, and an understanding of research and behavior. Yet, the psychologist cannot — and should not — make final decisions for managers. Consequently, to avoid conflict and confusion, the proper role for all parties should be clearly defined, with an emphasis that administrators never abrogate their primary responsibility for the agency.

2. Administrative Commitment to Stress Management Programs

Subsequent to identifying the proper role of psychological services within a law enforcement agency, it is incumbent upon departmental managers to openly express and demonstrate their commitment to organized, departmentally-sanctioned stress management programs. Over the last several decades, many police administrators who perceive themselves as "top cops" rather than modern managers have dealt with stress through a variety of ineffective mechanisms. Many of these have resulted in ignoring the problem or in considering stressed individuals as less manly and not worthy of law enforcement positions (Stratton, 1978). Such overtly-conveyed attitudes are too frequently perceived and supported by the "super-cops" within the department who earnestly believe "if you can't stand the heat, get out of the kitchen." Although researchers and professionals in the stress management field generally assume that modern managers agree with an enlightened philosophy, the significant majority of departments still lack an organized stress management program. Consequently, the education of police administrators and supervisors to the problems and implications of police stress could allow the phenomenon to be addressed more directly and effectively, for the benefit of both the profession and the public.

3. The Moral and Ethical Responsibility of Criminal Justice Managers for their Personnel

For many years, particularly with the development of police collective bargaining and union activity, there has been a distinct line separating police managers and their personnel. Consequently, the responsibility of "bosses" for the stress management of their officers has become clouded and has centered primarily on legal and administrative issues. While the latter are critical to fostering the development of stress management programs, it is equally important that police managers recognize their moral responsibility to assure the mental health of persons under their command, that they too are police officers carrying a badge, that they too can be victims of police stress, and that they be willing to admit that the commonality of "blue corpuscles" in one's professional bloodstream requires them to be involved in the successful development of stress programs for their agency. At the same time managers are expected to demonstrate responsibility for their officers, police unions must also recognize their role and assume an active part in supporting stress management for the benefit of all officers, their communities, and their professions.

4. Increased and More Realistic Training

From an administrative point of view, the knowledge gained through on-going research should allow for the development of more comprehensive programs of stress recognition and management and will affect both police training academies and institutions of higher education. Yet, at a time when most educational training courses have emphasized theoretical frameworks or basic practical skills, the officer actually affected by occupational stress has too frequently been overlooked. In Florida, for example, out of 320 hours required as the minimum training for entry level officers, only four must be devoted to stress recognition and management. Research completed over the past several years underscores the need for increased education in stress management, interpersonal awareness, interpersonal communication, aerobic/physical fitness, and diet. Hopefully, such programs will result in more comprehensive training for officers, better control of the problem of police stress, and, ultimately, better protection and service to the citizens who employ these officers.

Additionally, this increased knowledge can serve as an educational tool for police families. Police training has too often failed to recognize the impact of stress on the officer's home, and too many agencies fail to adequately prepare the officer or the spouse for this effect. Consequently, stress on the job is magnified by problems which must be confronted in an officer's home, family, and social life (Stratton, 1975; Depue, 1981). To reduce the continuing pressures on officers on all their psychological fronts, the development of stress-awareness programs which can more directly affect the high rate of domestic problems, particularly divorce, related to this difficult job should be encouraged (Stratton, 1976; Stratton and Stratton, 1982; Reese, 1983).

In discussing training, it is appropriate to recognize that training in stress management techniques has only developed within the last decade. During that time, the efforts of many training facilities have focused on traditional methods, including human relations, diet and nutrition, and physical fitness (Burgin, 1978; Hageman, Kennedy, and Price, 1979; and

LeDoux and McCaslin, 1981). While such training underlies a successful stress management program, line officers at times see little benefit from these measures, particularly when their training is limited to only a few hours. Once initial training has provided a basis for understanding in these areas, regular in-service and specialized training can actually apply the techniques of communication, diet and nutrition, and physical fitness to the individual officer. The most effective training programs will be those which indicate specific methods of physical fitness which an officer can use to control body weight and ensure his/her own physical condition; which identify foods and even establishments, especially those available on evening and midnight shifts, which will assure the best nutrition for an officer; which provide practical ways to communicate with a spouse or other individuals: and which can be used both on and off duty to reduce stress. No longer can police training in stress management be theoretical and generalized; instead, administrators must demand programs which are specialized and applicable in the daily life of an officer.

At the same time, effective stress management training suggests on-going reinforcement; field personnel cannot afford to be exposed to this critical information only in refresher schools conducted every few years. Instead, the development and implementation of a continuous and comprehensive regimen, with a strong agency support and peer reinforcement, can produce the greatest long-term benefits.

5. The Use of Stress Management Programs as an "Easy Out" for Incompetent or Weak Officers

At the same time that administrators and law enforcement professionals recognize the need for stress management programs, perhaps there is a concurrent need for a word of caution. As it has been noted, "the state-of-the-art does not allow us to draw a fine line between the malingerer and the person who is really suffering from psychological stress" (Spiegal and Welkos, 1985, p. 23). Consequently, this new buzz word "stress" offers an easy out to excuse the conduct of unreliable, undesirable, incompetent, or poor officers, who may not belong in a law enforcement career. In many agencies, personnel who, because of their own inadequacies, are incapable of handling the "job" are shifting the blame to the pressures of the occupation. The "anguish disability" is becoming increasingly common as a method for separation from the department which assures continuing income. In a profession where the police are responsible for enforcing laws which hold persons individually accountable for their conduct, perhaps it is equally important that law enforcement personnel be held responsible for their behavior, with the recognition that the individual, not just the work, creates problems.

6. The Balancing of On-the-Job Demands and Professional Expectations with Off-the-Job Outlets

During much of the recent history of law enforcement in the United States, administrators have demanded an on-the-job commitment as well as an off-the-job devotion to the profession. In many cities, a formal policy requires officers to carry firearms at all times in their jurisdiction and to be prepared to take law enforcement action at any moment. In other jurisdictions, such edicts, while not formalized rules and regulations, are part of subcultural expectations. Regardless of the approach, when one considers these management programs which emphasize the importance of outlets outside law enforcement and the necessity of getting away from the job, managers are sending out mixed messages to their troops. Perhaps it is time to reassess the philosophy and demands placed on law enforcement personnel.

7. The Need for Organizational Reform

As a strongly traditional organization structured along paramilitary lines, law enforcement, like similar established bodies, is not always readily receptive to change. While many effective management strategies have been implemented within the private sector and some have even been applied in law enforcement, the police organization remains generally unchanged in terms of organizational alignment, responsibility, and management philosophy.

As we progress through the 1980s, it may be time to recognize the need for management philosophies more similar to progressive business and private corporations. Modern techniques, such as the Japanese style of management, suggest a way for the future which can encourage both law enforcement efficiency and effectiveness and assure successful personnel management (Carter and Gragey, 1985).

Within such approaches to management, a number of techniques may actually reduce stress. Decentralization of management authority and responsibility is, of course, a major contemporary thrust. In other current concepts, such as team policing, Management of Criminal Investigations, and Integrated Criminal Apprehension Programs, professional and productive alternatives to traditional law enforcement are emerging.

The facilitation of interpersonal communication is equally important to reduce stress experienced by law enforcement personnel. The paramilitary structure of law enforcement fosters a class system which is further complicated by unions representing distinct groups of officers, including managerial personnel. With these distinct classes, especially as a result of collective bargaining, it is critical that administrative, supervisory, patrol, and support personnel have regular exchanges which can moderate the pressures caused by interpersonal conflict. Because of the human reluctance to easily and openly communicate, administrative or structured encouragement may be necessary. It must be recognized that such efforts will initially be viewed as suspect and must be shown to be good faith, productive efforts.

Involvement in the departmental decision-making process is also necessary to reduce stress of personnel. All staff must believe they have a voice in the direction and policies of the agency. It is thus important to include all personnel as part of intra-agency task forces, policy development and quality of work-life groups, and personnel selection and benefit committees. When such approaches are implemented, however, only management can assure that all personnel understand the appropriate role of such vehicles and that false expectations are neither encouraged nor developed within nonmanagerial personnel. In attempting to manage stress caused by the organization, a department cannot afford to increase stress by policy statements or actions which result in misunderstanding, confusion, or uncertainty. In the final analysis, managers must still be managers. While the input and involvement of line personnel are necessary for an effective decision-making process, it is still the administrator who must decide and is accountable for agency actions.

A widespread perception by all personnel that promotional alternatives exist within the agency can also serve to reduce occupational stress. Step-pay plans, successful in many agencies, may be one alternative to meet the financial needs of all personnel. Professional and personal development through department-sponsored education and increased in-service training offers another valuable incentive to reduce the effects of occupational stress. In general, sworn and support staff must believe that their occupation is not strictly a dead-end street, but that there is a way to grow and develop within the job.

8. The Education of Community Governing Bodies and Citizens about Their Role in the Stress Management of Public Employees

Not long ago, at a conference on stress management attended by law enforcement officers and administrators and representatives of municipal governments, a presenter suggested the importance of physical fitness requirements and the provision of in-house physical fitness facilities to reduce the stress related to law enforcement. During the subsequent question-and-answer session, a mayor of a mid-sized south Florida city stated that she doubted the need in her community because her union had never asked for it. As a result, she was hesitant to recommend such facilities for fear of giving them an issue at the bargaining table!

The issue is whether municipal administrators outside the law enforcement agency understand the potential effects of stress on police officers. It would appear that law enforcement administrators simply have not educated their bosses to its impact on the municipal bottom line: successful stress management means fewer citizen complaints, fewer liability claims, fewer worker compensation claims, and improved productivity for and service to citizens.

In a country where the media regularly paints officers on a continuum from villain to hero to buffoon, communication of the real problem experienced by officers and the continuing stress of the job should also be effectively made to the public. An open admission of human qualities in law enforcement officers may more realistically set the level of expectation of the public, an expectation grounded in fiction and best characterized by a classic case in Tallahassee in the early 1970s. In that incident, following a particular brutal rape and assault, officers made an arrest and identified a number of pieces of forensic evidence which clearly pointed to the guilt of the suspect. The jury remained unconvinced, however. It was their considered opinion that the major item lacking was fingerprints and that "McGarrett would have found fingerprints;" consequently the suspect was found not guilty. Through an active program of community education and awareness, perhaps some of the frustration underlying stress may be significantly curtailed.

9. The Identification and Management of the Stress of Personnel beyond the Line Officer

For many years, the primary focus for efforts in stress research, identification, and management has been the line officer, with some limited effort devoted to the problems of the investigator and undercover personnel (Stratton, 1979; Yablonsky, 1979). Yet, in the law enforcement arena, there are other participants whose stress is just as real and just as deadly as the "star" who has received the spotlight. The specialty officers — whether unique because of their responsibilities or their communities — suffer from stresses different from most line officers and which must be addressed in a unique manner (Sandy and Devine, 1978; Scott, 1979; Sewell, 1984). Perhaps even more serious are the stress-related problems of the forgotten victims—dispatchers, complaint clerks, crime scene and evidence technicians, and even secretaries—who are oftentimes treated as second class citizens, yet are critical to the accomplishment of the law enforcement mission (Sewell and Crew, 1984). In an effective stress management program of the future, administrators must expect and demand a comprehensive approach to the stress of all their agency personnel.

Such a comprehensive program cannot afford to overlook a group normally neglected: the police manager. Agency administrators suffer from the same stress as executives in other occupations. Their pressure and frustration are further compounded by the stress they sustain as law enforcement bosses—a magnification of the stress experienced by line officers.

Summary

Over the last several years, research into law enforcement stress has dramatically underscored the problems experienced by police officers throughout this country, and significant effort has been devoted to programs which promote awareness, identification, and management. As has been previously noted,

> ...as our knowledge of police stress has increased, many researchers and law enforcement professionals have offered a variety of mechanisms that can be used to control or reduce law enforcement stress. Increased stress management training, professional counseling for officers and their families, peer advisement, and required fitness standards and programs have been identified as important measures that should be developed and implemented at the department level. The use of relaxation responses and neutralization techniques, proper nutrition and diet, and regular exercise, particularly aerobic exercise, have been offered as remedies for the individual officer (Sewell, 1984; 520).

At the same time, one should recognize that, for the greatest impact, the implementation of stress management efforts is part of an integrated program of psychological services within a department. In addition to the professional considerations normally associated with such services, a number of management issues require analysis and successful resolution to increase and assure program effectiveness. Law enforcement administrators should recognize and accept their critical role in maintaining the highest quality programs which officers demand and communities deserve.

References

Brodsky, Stanley C. The Ambivalent consultee: The special problems of consultation to criminal justice agencies. In Stanley C. Plog and Paul I. Ahmed (Eds.). *Principles and Techniques of Mental Health Consultation.* New York: Plenum Publishing Corporation, 1977.

————. After the courtship: Psychologists and policemen work together. Presented as part of a symposium on "The Psychologist within the Police Department" at the 82nd Annual Meeting of the American Psychological Association. New Orleans, Louisiana, September 3, 1974.

————. The unlikely partnership: Psychology and law enforcement. Presented at a Conference on Law Enforcement Management and the Behavioral Sciences, University of Alabama, April 24, 1973.

Brinegar, Jerry L. Nutritional stress in policing. *Police Chief,* 1981, 48(12), 28-29.

Burgin, A. Lad. The management of stress in policing. *Police Chief,* 1978, 45(4), 53-4.

Carter, Donald and Gragey, John. A Japanese management technique applied to local policing. *FBI Law Enforcement Bulletin,* 1985, 54(5), 20-24.

Depue, Roger L. High-risk lifestyle: The police family. *FBI Law Enforcement Bulletin,* 1981, 49(8), 7-13.

Eisenberg, Terry. Labor-management relations and psychological stress- View from the bottom. *Police Chief,* 1975, 42(11), 54-58.

Ellison, Katherine W., and Genz, John L. *Stress and the Police Officer,* Springfield, IL: Charles C. Thomas, 1983.

Hageman, Mary J., Kennedy, Robert B., and Price, Norman. Coping with stress. *Police Chief,* 1979, 46(2), 27-28 and 70.

Kroes, William H., and Gould, Sam. Job stress in policemen: An empirical study. *Police Stress,* 1979, 1(2), 9-10, 44.

Kroes, William H., Margolis, Bruce L., and Hurrell, Joseph J. Job stress in policemen. *Journal of Police Science and Administration,* 1974, 2(2), 145-55.

————. Job stress in police administrators. *Journal of Police Science and Administration,* 1974, 2(4), 381-387.

LeDoux, John C., and McCaslin, Henry H. Designing a training response to stress. *FBI Law Enforcement Bulletin,* 1981, 50(10), 11-15.

Moore, Larry and Donohue, John T. The patrol officer: Special problems/special cures. *Police Chief,* 1978, 45(11), 41-3.

Morrison, David E. Psychiatric consultation to management. *Psychiatric Annals,* 1978, 8(12).

Murphy, J.G. *Punishment and Rehabilitation.* Belmont, CA: Wadsworth Publishing Company, 1973.

Reese, James T. Family therapy in law enforcement: A new approach to an old problem. *FBI Law Enforcement Bulletin*, 1983, *51*(9), 7-11.

Sandy, Joan Philips, and Devine, Donald A. Four stress factors unique to rural patrol. *Police Chief*, 1978, *45*(9), 42-4.

Scott, Susan. Stress and the female cop. *Police Stress*, 1979, *1*(3), 31-4.

Sewell, James D. The development of a critical life events scale for law enforcement. *Journal of Police Science and Administration*, 1983, *11*(1), 109-116.

———. Police stress. *FBI Law Enforcement Bulletin*, 1981, *50*(4), 7-11.

———. Stress in university law enforcement. *The Journal of Higher Education*, 1984, *55*(4), 515-523.

Sewell, James D., and Crew, Linda. The forgotten victim: Stress and the police dispatcher. *FBI Law Enforcement Bulletin, 1984, 53(3),* 7-11.

Spiegal, Claire and Welkos, Robert. Malingerers-Dark side of the force. *Los Angeles Times*, 1985, Special Reprint of February 3-6 series 21-6.

Stratton, John. Police stress: An overview. *Police Chief*, 1978, *45*(4), 58-62.

———. Police stress: Considerations and suggestions. *Police Chief*, 1978, *45*(5), 73-78.

———. Police stress and the criminal investigator. *Police Chief*, 1979, *46*(11), 44-47.

———. Pressures in law enforcement marriages: Some considerations. *Police Chief*, 1975, *42*(11), 44-47.

———. Psychological services for Police. *Journal of Police Science and Administration*, 1980, *3*(1), 31-39.

———. The law enforcement family: Programs for spouses. FBI Law Enforcement Bulletin, 1976, 45(3), 1-7.

——— and Stratton, Barbara Tracy. Law enforcement marital relationships: A positive approach. *FBI Law Enforcement Bulletin*, 1982, *51*(5), 6-11.

Teten, Howard, and Minderman, John. Police personnel problems-Practical considerations for administrators. *FBI Law Enforcement Bulletin*, 1977, *46*(1), 8-14.

Yablonsky, Joseph. Stress and the undercover operative. *Police Stress*, 1979, *1*(3), 18-19.

33

Reducing Stress: An Organization-Centered Approach

Peter Finn

People in all walks of life experience, and must find ways to cope with, some degree of stress. However, in the past 25 years, researchers and criminal justice officials have identified stress factors unique to, or more pronounced among, law enforcement officers. Today, law enforcement is widely considered to be among the most stressful occupations, associated with high rates of divorce, alcoholism, suicide, and other emotional and health problems.[1]

Despite the growing understanding of stress factors within the law enforcement profession and enhanced treatment for stress-related problems, many officers feel that law enforcement is more stressful now than ever before. This sentiment can now be traced to several factors, including the rise in violent crime during the 1980s and early 1990s; perceived increases in negative publicity, public scrutiny, and lawsuits; fiscal uncertainty; fear of airborne and bloodborne diseases, such as AIDS and tuberculosis; rising racial tensions; and the transition from reactive to problem-oriented policing.

Sources of stress for individual law enforcement officers can be placed into five general categories: issues in the officer's personal life, the pressures of law enforcement work, the attitude of the general public toward police work and officers, the operation of the criminal justice system, and the law enforcement organization itself. Many people perceive the danger

---

1. R. M. Ayres, *Preventing Law Enforcement Stress: The Organization's Role* (Washington, DC: Bureau of Justice Statistics, 1990), 1; C.A. Gruber, "The Relationship of Stress to the Practice of Police Work," *The Police Chief,* February 1980, 16–17; "A Comparative Look at Stress and Strain in Policemen." in *Job Stress and the Police Officer,* ed. W.H. Kroes and J.J. Hurrell (Washington, DC: U.S. Department of Health, Education, and Welfare, 1975), 60; C.D. Spielberger, *The Police Stress Survey: Sources of Stress in Law Enforcement,* Monograph Series Three (Tampa, Florida: Human Resources Institute, 1981), 43.

and tension of law enforcement work—as dramatized in books, movies, and television shows—to be the most serious sources of stress for officers. In fact, the most common sources of police officer stress involve the policies and procedures of law enforcement agencies themselves.[2]

This chapter examines the often-neglected effects that organizational stress has on agencies and officers. It then discusses why managers should change stress-inducing policies. Finally, it presents steps that several agencies have taken to reduce organizational stress and thus enhance the productivity and job satisfaction of officers.

Treating the Symptom, Not the Cause

As part of a large-scale study conducted by the National Institute of Justice (NIJ) of programs devoted to reducing police officer stress, researchers interviewed nearly 100 stress-management program directors, law enforcement administrators, mental health providers, union and association officials, officers and their families, and civilians.[3] The respondents agreed that the negative effects of stress on individual officers typically harm agencies as well as officers. As observed by the respondents, the cumulative effects of stress among officers in a department can lead to:

- Impaired officer performance and reduced productivity
- Reduced morale
- Public relations problems
- Labor-management friction
- Civil suits stemming from stress-related shortcomings in personnel performance

---

2. Ibid., Ayres; Ibid., W.H. Kroes and J.J. Hurrell; *see also* J.J. Hurrell, Jr., "Some Organizational Stressors in Police Work ad Means for Their Amelioration," in *Psychological Services for Law Enforcement,* ed. J.T. Reese and H.A. Goldstein (Washington, DC: U.S. Department of Justice, Federal Bureau of Investigation, 1986).

3. The principal interviews took place in San Bernardino, California: Erie County, New York; Washington, DC: and throughout the state of Michigan (June-August 1995). Additional telephone interviews were conducted with similar individuals from San Antonio, Texas; Tulsa, Oklahoma; Metro-Dade, Florida; Rochester, New York; and Coventry, Rhode Island (June–August 1995). This research project was supported by the U.S. Department of Justice, National Institute of Justice, Contract OJP-94-C-007. *See* Peter Finn and Julie Eselman Tomz, *Developing a Law Enforcement Stress Program for Officers and Their Families* (Washington, DC: U.S. Government Printing Office, 1997).

- Tardiness and absenteeism
- Increased turnover due to leaves of absence and early retirements because of stress-related problems and disabilities, and
- The added expenses of training and hiring new recruits, as well as paying overtime, when the agency is left short-staffed as a result of turnover.

Most police stress programs and consulting mental health practitioners focus primarily, if not exclusively, on preventing and treating stress among individual officers. However, the "person-centered" approach currently employed by most departments fails to address the underlying organizational problems that form the basis of much of the stress experienced by officers.

It stands to reason, then, as one expert in the field suggested, that "... an organization-centered approach...identifying the problems the officers have with their work, supervisors, and pay, and making appropriate changes—may well have a greater influence on improving morale."[4] According to the head of the Michigan State Police behavioral science section, the emphasis placed by psychologists and police administrators on person-centered programs has overshadowed the importance of addressing organizational sources of stress.[5]

Unfortunately, stress program staffs and independent practitioners often lack the time to work with management to eliminate the sources of organizational stress. Moreover, few clinicians feel qualified to suggest organizational changes to law enforcement administrators.

At the same time, police administrators might not accept what they perceive to be the intrusion of a mental health professional into department operations. Administrators also may believe that they do not have the time or resources to make the desired changes, or they might simply not agree that organizational changes will reduce officer stress.

Yet, a growing number of agencies have found that even modest modifications in organizational structure can lead to enhanced morale and productivity among line officers. Although some administrators might institute organizational changes simply because they believe it is the right thing to do, there are a host of reasons that should compel reluctant administrators to consider such changes.

---

4. Supra note 1, Ayres 9.

5. G. Kaufman, "Law Enforcement Organizational Health Consultation," (paper presented at the Consultation with Police: Problems and Considerations Symposium, American Psychological Association 93rd Annual Convention, Los Angeles, California, August 23–27, 1985).

Organizational Change Benefits

Enhance the Department's Image

Bad press, public criticism, and legislative scrutiny can be sources of stress for both law enforcement administrators and line officers. Organizational changes that reduce officer stress can improve the department's's image simultaneously. Negative publicity resulting from 8 officer suicides in 5 years—3 of them in 1994—prompted the Philadelphia, Pennsylvania, Police Department to create the agency's first stress manager position in 1995. Among other duties, the stress manager examines departmental policies and procedure and recommends ways to make them less stressful.[6]

A newly appointed police chief in a West Coast law enforcement agency decided to remedy years of bad press caused by what many community members considered to be the departments' overly paramilitary image. The chief hired an organizational consultant and eventually won new community support by implementing several recommended changes designed to make the department less autocratic.

Save Money

Some departments have documented substantial cost savings resulting from organizational changes. The Mercedez, Texas, Police Department fields 25 sworn officers and serves a city of 14,000 residents. In 1986, the department reorganized to provide an employee development program that included establishing high professional standards, a reward system to promote superior performance, foot patrol assignments, and an increase in the annual in-service training requirement. In the 24 months following these changes, the department's turnover rate fell from 38% to 7%. Administrators estimate that reduced turnover has saved the department at least $53,000.[7]

Police administrators understand all too well the costs associated with replacing officers who take early retirement or go on disability. The department not only must pay benefits to departing officers, but it also must pay to recruit, test, hire, train, and equip new officers. In smaller agencies, sudden turnover can result in serious staff shortages that require paying other officers overtime.

---

6. "Tired? Stressed? Burned Out? Panel Seeks Answers for Philadelphia Police Officers," *Law Enforcement News* 22, 1995, 1, 10.

7. J.L. Pape, "Employee Development Programs," *FBI Law Enforcement Bulletin*, September 1990, 20–25.

Improve Department Morale and Efficiency

Reducing organizational sources of stress should lead naturally to better morale, improved productivity, and, therefore, enhanced overall department efficiency. Even a well-publicized statement from the department's administration recognizing the stress officers experience and expressing support for measures to reduce sources of stress demonstrates management concern about officer well-being. Such pronouncements also help promote the good will necessary to implement change.

Implemented Changes

Administrators in agencies across the country have implemented significant organizational changes as a way of reducing officer stress. The changes generally affect supervisory style, field training officer programs, critical incident counseling, command support after critical incidents, shift work, and job assignments.

Supervisory Style

One police department has undertaken a comprehensive effort to reduce organizationally generated stress among its 100 sworn officers.[8] A series of stress-related disability retirements prompted the Palo Alto, California, Police Department to commission a study in 1979 to identify sources of stress and suggest options for reducing or eliminating them. The report concluded that the formal and informal organizational structures in the department inhibited effective communication and created strained relationships among ranks, divisions, and individuals.

As a result, the department hired a management consultant and a mental health clinician to design and implement an 18-month trial program to alleviate organizational stress. Through team building and other methods, the consultant taught department members how to communicate, listen, and solve problems in an orderly, effective manner.

---

8. E.F. Kirschman, "Organizational Development," in *Police Managerial Use of Psychology and Psychologists*, ed. H.W. More and P.C. Unsinger (Springfield, Illinois: Charles C. Thomas, 1987), 85–106; S.E. Walima, "Organizational Health in Law Enforcement," in *Psychological Services for Law Enforcement*, ed. J.T. Reese and H.A. Goldstein, (Washington, DC: U.S. Department of Justice, Federal Bureau of Investigation, 1986), 205–214.

The program proved so successful that it has been continued ever since. It follows a 14-point written plan that serves as a basis for administrators to reduce organizational stress.

First, administrators must identify sources of organizational stress and consult with work units and individual managers to resolve them. For example, the management consultant for the Palo Alto Police Department trained all sergeants in how to prepare for and conduct a performance appraisal and discussed the importance of providing employees with behavioral feedback in a constructive manner.

In addition, administrators should monitor management decisions with regard to their stress impact, search for implementation methods that minimize the stressful impact, and advise management staff. For example, when the Palo Alto Police Department began to use computer-aided crime analysis to direct patrol and investigative resources toward apprehending career criminals, the consultant designed ways for the department's sworn and civilian personnel to influence and shape the change process.

It is also important to instruct field training officers, supervisors, and managers in communication, problem solving, conflict resolution, and supervisory skills that can minimize stress for employees. At the chief's request, the consultant hired by Palo Alto surveyed each manager on how the chief may have been creating undue stress for them, reported the results to the chief, and recommended changes based on the findings.

Another important step in reducing organizational stress involves training individual managers on stress-inducing practices and events within their units. This training typically results from a manager's request for specific training in problem solving. On occasion, it can be delivered in response to a large number of complaints from line officers, which suggests a management problem.

FTO Programs

A number of departments in California have used a private counselor to train their field training officers (FTOs) in the most productive ways to interact with trainees. The counselor explains to the FTOs how people react when they are criticized and presents the best approaches for offering constructive criticism to recruits who perform poorly. The counselor also tests the FTOs on their supervisory style and presents them with the results so they can see which areas they need to improve. Field training officers who have received the instruction gain a new awareness of the tremendous impact that an FTO program has on the organizational health of a law enforcement agency.

The counselor also advises police executives that they can enhance their departments' FTO programs by designating only officers who volunteer for the program to become training officers. Officers selected to serve as FTOs who have no interest in the assignment often feel that they are being punished. By accepting only volunteers and providing them with supervisory training, departments recognize the tremendous role field training officers play in acculturating new officers. For better or worse, many rookies emulate their FTOs and later use the same helpful or harmful training techniques when they train new officers.

Critical Incident Counseling

The Michigan State Police Behavioral Science Section trains both experienced and new sergeants every year in techniques to manage critical incident stress among officers. The section director designed the training to help sergeants respond in a manner that avoids creating additional stress for officers and reduces the inevitable stress that officers experience from the actual incidents.

During the training, the section director brings in a trooper who has experienced a critical incident and has received counseling through the program. The trooper gives a personal account of what first-line supervisors should—and should not—do when addressing the needs of troopers who require post-incident counseling. The sergeants learn what to expect from an officer who has experienced a critical incident, and the section director explains the warning signs that should alert sergeants that counseling is necessary.

The director of the Behavioral Science Section and another counselor also conduct 2-hour seminars for the agency's executive and command staffs. During this training, the counselors focus on helping managers recognize how their own work styles can impact subordinates. The counselors then suggest ways that managers can motivate their personnel to be more productive.

Command Support After Critical Incidents

The chief executive officer and other commanders of a law enforcement agency should make it a matter of policy to pay hospital visits to every officer shot or involved in a serious accident. This easily implemented policy can have a profound effect not only on the injured officers but also on the department as a whole. According to a veteran police counselor, "The impact of a shooting on the officers involved depends more on the attitude of the department toward the officers than on the incident itself."

The commissioner of Buffalo, New York, Police Department, personally visits every police officer shot while on duty. If he cannot do so, he makes sure that his deputy or another command-level officer goes to provide support.

Command-level staff also can offer assurance and support to family members—including helping with paperwork, finding babysitters, providing telephone numbers for follow-up assistance, and simply spending time with them. Word of the command staff's concern typically spreads through the department grapevine to every officer on the force, instantly improving morale and alleviating stress.

Shift Schedules

Like many law enforcement agencies, the Michigan State Police used to rotate shifts every 7 days, causing considerable stress for many troopers and their families. As a result, the troopers association received a constant flow of grievances from members complaining of fatigue, eating disorders, and other problems. In an effort to encourage the department to change to a less stressful work schedule, the association asked the department's Behavioral Science Section for any available research that documented the harmful effects of rotating shifts on employee productivity.

The department allowed troopers to determine the frequency of their shift rotation and gave them the option of changing their rotation schedule at least annually. When additional research suggested that all rotating shift work might pose health and safety risks, the command staff included permanent shifts as an option. Today, staff members at each work site choose shifts by majority vote. Many have adopted fixed-shift schedules.

The troopers association succeeded in negotiating the changes, in part, due to the compelling evidence showing the negative effects of shift work on officer productivity. But the department's Behavioral Science Section also helped convince commanders by providing research findings. The president of the troopers association credits that successful resolution of this potentially divisive issue with the fact that the association did not enter into negotiations with the goal of simply winning concessions from the administration. Instead, the association demonstrated to commanders that the department would benefit from healthier, more productive employees. In other words, by changing the work schedule, the department as well as the troopers won.

Job Assignments

The psychologist for the San Antonio, California, Police Department worked with administrators to improve the agency's ability to match officers' capabilities to the needs of their jobs. In convincing administrators of the importance of such an effort, the psychologist argued that stress

Suggestions for Implementing Organizational Change

Consultants provide the following suggestions for implementing any major effort to change organizational policies and procedures in law enforcement agencies.

- The administration should involve a sizable cross-section of the agency's personnel in identifying organizational issues that require attention, designing a prototype program, and hiring program staff
- The chief should endorse and provide support to any initiative
- Commanders should plan for an 18-month or longer trial period
- Commanders should rely on the core start-up group for support and feedback during the initial stages of the program
- Administrators should guarantee program success to all agency levels and work units
- Counselors or outside consultants should expect and encourage the agency and its personnel to take risks and accept some discomfort in the service of growth and positive change

Adapted from S.E. Walima and E.F. Kirschman, "Health Resource Coordinators: Organizational Consultation Services," *The Police Chief*, October 1988, 78–81.

management should go beyond counseling, that careful selection of job candidates can reduce the stress that arises from a mismatch between the candidate and the job requirements.

The psychologist argued that by performing a "person-job fit analysis" before hiring and placing officers, the department could reduce the need for subsequent mental health treatment for officers ill-equipped to handle the job for which they were hired. Likewise, this preventive approach to mental health would help prospective officers avoid the deep feelings of frustration, disappointment, and self-blame that occur when individuals attempt to perform a job for which they are unsuited.

To determine which skills are necessary for a patrol officer, the psychologist conducted a functional job analysis of the position. He asked a number of officers to identify the skills required to perform their jobs effectively. The department now uses the skills outlined in the job analysis to select officers for patrol.

The psychologist eventually conducted a functional job analysis of every position in the agency. The department now bases hiring and promotions not only on civil service exams but also on matching individuals' current skill levels with the job requirements for which they are applying. The psychologist also revised the training academy's curriculum to include more blocks on problem solving, critical thinking, and other skills related to preventing and managing stress. The changes in the curriculum involved identifying areas where recruits need expanded training to improve their future on-the-job performance and thereby reduce their levels of stress.

Conclusion

Everyone experiences stress. As any stress counselor would explain, a certain degree of stress is essential to a healthy, productive life. However, when stress impairs an individual's ability to function properly, the sources of that stress must be eliminated or reduced.

Likewise, organizations work with a certain degree of naturally occurring stress, generated by the pressures of performing the tasks for which the people in the organization are responsible. However, when an organization's policies and procedures themselves become overwhelming sources of stress, those policies and procedures should be reviewed and changed.

With pressures on law enforcement agencies to perform increasingly complex functions with minimized funding levels, police administrators must examine ways to enable officers to perform their responsibilities as efficiently as possible. The steps that a number of law enforcement agencies have taken to reduce organizational sources of stress illustrate that departments can change their policies and procedures in ways that enhance—and certainly do not compromise—their public safety missions. Given the pressures experienced by today's police officers, law enforcement administrators should address the problem of organizational stress by identifying recurring grievances among officers and working to change the policies that cause them.

34

Controlling Police Use of Excessive Force: The Role of the Police Psychologist

Ellen M. Scrivner

Police departments have used the services of psychologists for more than two decades. In the 1980s, police psychology began to be recognized as a distinct field, with psychologists' activities expanding beyond screening job applicants to include a broader range of psychological support services. These included counseling to help officers cope with the unique stresses inherent in police work, training in human relations and general stress management, debriefing after traumatic incidents, and such operational interventions as forensic hypnosis and assistance in negotiations with hostage holders or barricaded persons. Psychological support services for officers who used lethal force were more prevalent than interventions for managing nonlethal, excessive force.

Control of excessive force by police officers is a major challenge for the departments they work for, and it will be increasingly important to the success of community policing initiatives. In two of the most recent examples, excessive force triggered riots in Los Angeles and has been associated with charges of police corruption in New York City. In controlling the problem, the police psychologist can play a key role. This chapter discusses that role and presents ways in which psychologists can identify officers at risk and create remedial interventions, both at the individual level and the department level, to prevent the use of excessive force.

This chapter summarizes one of the studies sponsored by the National Institute of Justice as part of a Justice Department effort to identify additional means to control police use of force. The beating of Rodney King that precipitated the Los Angeles riots was the event that prompted the Justice Department initiative. On the basis of input from psychologists working in police departments in the nation's largest cities, profiles of officers who abuse force were developed. The study also identified the functions of psychologists that had relevance to officers' mental health, specifically their use of excessive force, and presented their recommendations on how best to predict, remedy, and prevent excessive force.

The highly experienced police psychologists interviewed for the study had worked a long time either as salaried employees or as consultants to police departments. One out of four were on police command staffs, a measure of the extent to which police psychological services had become established in law enforcement agencies.

A Shift in Police Department Focus

Attention by researchers and psychologists to police use of nonlethal excessive force represented a change in emphasis. For the first two decades in which police departments employed psychologists, the use of lethal force was the prime concern. Shootings by police were traumatic incidents that created strong emotional reactions from the officers who did the shooting. The need to provide psychological support for these officers was clear. Departments gradually recognized the need to provide such services immediately following these incidents.

That same level of concern did not generally carry over to the use of nonlethal excessive force. Officers who used excessive force in making arrests or handling prisoners might be evaluated for their fitness for duty, but psychological support services were not widely available.

Over the past few years, however, greater attention has been given to the issue. Recent research has identified multiple determinants of the use of excessive force, raising questions about whether police departments should rely exclusively on preemployment screening to identify violence-prone candidates and predict future officer performance. In fact, two reports that followed the Rodney King beating—the 1991 report of the Independent Commission To Study the Los Angeles Police Department and the 1992 Los Angeles County Sheriff's Report by James G. Kolt and staff—questioned the effectiveness of existing psychological screening to predict propensity for violence.

Profiles of Violence-Prone Officers

Psycholgists interviewed in the NIJ survey were asked about the characteristics of officers who had been referred to them because of the use of excessive force. Their answers did not support the conventional view that a few "bad apples" are responsible for most excessive force complaints. Rather, their answers were used to construct five distinct profiles of different types of officers, only one of which resembled the "bad apple" characterization.

The data used to create the five profiles constitute human resource information that can be used to shape policy. Not only do the profiles offer an etiology of excessive force and provide insight into its complexity, but they also support the notion that excessive force is not just a problem of individuals but may also reflect organizational deficiencies. These profiles are presented in the following sections in ascending order of frequency, along with possible interventions.

Officers with personality disorders that place them at chronic risk These officers have pervasive and enduring personality traits (in contrast to characteristics acquired on the job) that are manifested in antisocial, narcissistic, paranoid, or abusive tendencies. These conditions interfere with judgment and interactions with others, particularly when officers perceive challenges or threats to their authority. Such officers generally lack empathy for others. The number who fit this profile is the smallest of all the high-risk groups.

These characteristics, which tend to persist through life but may be intensified by police work, may not be apparent at preemployment screening. Individuals who exhibit these personality patterns generally do not learn from their behavior, so they are at greater risk for repeated citizen complaints. As a consequence, they may appear to the be sole source of problems in police departments.

Officers whose previous job-related experience places them at risk. Traumatic situations such as justifiable police shootings put some officers at risk for abuse of force, but for reasons totally different from those of the first group. These officers are not unsocialized, egocentric, or violent. In fact, personality factors appear to have less to do with their vulnerability to excessive force than the emotional "baggage" they have accumulated from involvement in previous incidents. Typically, these officers verge on burnout and have become isolated from their squads. Because of their perceived need to conceal symptoms, some time elapses before their problems come to others' attention. When this happens, the event is often an excessive force situation in which the officer has lost control.

In contrast to the chronic at-risk group, officers in this group are amenable to critical-incident debriefing, but to be fully effective, the interventions need to be applied soon after involvement in the incident. Studies recommend training and psychological debriefings, with follow-up, to minimize the development of symptoms.

Officers who have problems at early stages in their police careers. The third group profiled consists of young and inexperienced officers, frequently seen as "hotdogs," "badge happy," "macho," or generally immature. In contrast to other inexperienced officers, individuals in this group are characterized as highly impressionable and impulsive, with low tolerance for frustration. They nonetheless bring positive attributes to their work and could outgrow these tendencies and learn with experience. Unfortunately, the positive qualities can deteriorate early in their careers if field training officers and first line supervisors do not work to provide them with a full range of responses to patrol encounters.

These inexperienced officers were described as needing strong supervision and highly structured field training, preferably under a field training officer with considerable street experience. Because they are strongly influenced by the police culture, such new recruits are more apt to change their behavior if their mentors show them how to maintain a professional demeanor in their dealings with citizens.

Officers who develop inappropriate patrol styles. Individuals who fit this profile combine a dominant command presence with a heavy-handed policing style; they are particularly sensitive to challenge and provocation. They use force to show they are in charge; as their beliefs about how police work is conducted become more rigid, this behavior becomes the norm.

In contrast to the chronic risk group, the behavior of officers in this group is acquired on the job and can be changed. The longer the patterns continue, however, the more difficult they are to change. As the officers become invested in police power and control, they see little reason to change. Officers in this group are often labeled "dinosaurs" in a changing police world marked by greater accountability to citizens and by adoption of the community policing model.

If these officers do not receive strong supervision and training early in their careers, or if they are detailed to a special unit with minimal supervision, their style may be reinforced. They may perceive that the organization sanctions their behavior. This group would be more responsive to peer programs or situation-based interventions in contrast to traditional individual counseling. Making them part of the solution, rather than part of the problem, may be central to changing their behavior.

Officers with personal problems. The final risk profile was made up of officers who have experienced serious personal problems, such as separation, divorce, or even perceived loss of status, that destabilized their job functioning. In general, officers with personal problems do not use excessive force, but those who do may have elected police work for all the wrong reasons. In contrast to their peers, they seem to have a more tenuous sense of self-worth and higher levels of anxiety that are well masked. Some may have functioned reasonably well until changes occurred in their personal situation. These changes undermine confidence and make it more difficult to deal with fear, animosity, and emotionally charged patrol situations.

Before they resort to excessive force, these officers usually exhibit patrol behavior that is erratic and that signals the possibility they will lose control in a confrontation. This group, the most frequently seen by psychologists because of excessive-force problems, can be identified by supervisors who have been properly trained to observe and respond to precursors of problem behavior. Their greater numbers should encourage departments to develop early warning systems to help supervisors detect "marker behaviors" signifying that problems are brewing. These officers benefit from individual counseling, but earlier referrals to psychologists can enhance the benefit and prevent their personal situations from spilling over into their jobs.

Steps in Prevention

Because the profiles reveal different reasons for the use of excessive force, police departments need to develop a system of interventions targeted to different groups of officers and at different phases of their careers. The types of profiles also reveal that individual personality characteristics are only one aspect of excessive force and that risk for this behavior is intensified by other experiences. Some of those experiences implicate the organizational practices of the police departments in which the officers work. To the extent this is true, it indicates the need for remedial intervention at the department level as well as the individual level.

Preemployment screening. The first step in prevention logically entails not hiring officers who would present a problem. Such deselection is the aim of preemployment screening, a function in which the police psychologist has a role. Of the psychologists who perform preemployment screening, almost all rely on fairly traditional assessment tools—psychological tests and clinical interviews. By contrast, they make limited use of more innovative approaches.

There are sound reasons for using the traditional screening tools. They are valid and reliable measurements, and because they are standardized they can serve as the foundation for data bases useful for further analysis. But because the tools are used to prevent problem behaviors, including use of excessive force, screening has become psychopathology-driven. It is focused on identifying the characteristics of "bad" officers, and as a result, less is known about the characteristics of "good" officers or about how career experiences mitigate or reinforce these characteristics.

Although information about potential psychopathology is essential to making employment decisions for highly sensitive jobs, this focus has dictated the use of a single model, one that screens out. Reliance on this model makes innovation more difficult. The psychologists interviewed made limited use of other screening approaches—risk assessment models, situational testing, or job simulations—even though these approaches could incorporate a wider range of information for making decisions about the best candidates for police officers.

Innovation on the horizon. Opportunities for developing new screening techniques that may be better able to predict violence are arising for reasons that have nothing to do with excessive force. In particular, recent developments related to the Americans With Disabilities Act will change screening procedures. According to EEOC enforcement guidance issued in May 1994, some tests administered before a position is offered are now allowable only *after* a conditional job offer has been made. Tests that might detect mental impairment or disorder are include in this category.

As a result of the ADA-driven changes, "preoffer" testing could undergo substantial change, from which will emerge new screening technologies and analytic methods. These will be used to measure how prospective police officers are likely to interact with people under stressful conditions, make decisions, and solve problems consistent with community policing practices. Automated assessment systems, interactive video testing, assessment centers, job simulations, and role playing exercises all hold promise for meeting these goals.

Testing incumbent officers. The psychologists were divided on the use of psychological tests to routinely evaluate incumbent officers for a propensity toward violence. Overall, they supported alternatives to testing because the evidence is still not conclusive that all officers at risk for excessive force could be identified. Although significant strides have been made in methods to predict behavior, psychologists are mindful that human behavior is complex; they are cautious in claiming the accuracy of scientific prediction.

Thus, recommended alternatives to testing need to be considered. At the level of the individual, these alternatives should include increased attention to the availability of counseling and support for it. At the level of the department, alternatives should include increased attention to management strategies to improve training, monitoring, and screening.

Training

Some of the training described by the psychologists interviewed represents innovations and promising trends. The models are based on principles of adult learning that require class participation, using such techniques as patrol simulations and role playing. They emphasize the development of nonphysical skills as well as physical ones in a community policing environment that assumes frequent interaction between citizens and police.

For a majority of the psychologists, the excessive force training they offered was in the context of stress management only. To be sure, stress

---

Innovations in Excessive Force Training

Some of the psychologists interviewed in the study have developed training models that take into account how people function under adverse conditions and in highly charged situations. Components of these models include:

- Cultural sensitivity and diversity.
- Intervention by fellow officers to stop the use of excess force.
- The interaction of human perception and threat assessment.
- Decisionmaking under highly charged conditions.
- Psychological methods of situation control.
- Patrol deescalation and defusing techniques that not only teach a tactical response but also respond to the fear stimulated by confrontations.
- Anger management programs that use self-assessment and self-management techniques for providing individual feedback to officers on how variable levels of legitimate anger influence judgment.
- Training in verbal control and communication, including conflict resolution.

---

management training is important; it would be difficult to argue that police work in general, and use-of-force confrontations in particular, are not stressful. However, framing excessive force as a stress issue raises several questions, among them whether the notion is supported by research and whether the approach encourages the perception that stress justifies the use of excessive force.

Stress management training in police department has not been evaluated systematically, and this raises an additional concern. Beyond anecdotal evidence and limited research data, there is little to indicate how stress consistently affects general police performance. A more viable training focus would reflect departmental policy statements that clarify the tolerance limits for use of force and perceive excessive force as a patrol risk that needs to be managed through a range of specialized skills.

First line supervisors received less instruction on excessive force than did recruits. Yet the psychologists indicated that first line supervisors have greater influence on officers prone to excessive force than other police personnel. Police departments may need to shift the emphasis in supervisor training to one that incorporates larger behavioral issues in order to improve the management of excessive force. This level of supervisory training could also incorporate instruction on early warning behavioral monitoring.

Monitoring

Monitoring of officers' behavior to detect precursors of excessive force was the function used least often by psychologists. Although a majority of the police departments represented in the study sample used some form of monitoring, 58% did not include the psychologists in these efforts. Computer tracking of complaints appeared to be the most prevalent form of early warning. However, while computer tracking may provide useful management information, it is not as helpful in changing behavior because the behavior is relatively well developed by the time it is flagged by the computer.

Monitoring of police behavior can serve other purposes in addition to early identification and intervention. It can involve a sustained level of contact between supervisor and officer to reinforce policy and training on excessive force. Because it involves supervisors, monitoring can provide valuable information to help police managers evaluate the effectiveness of their policies. Thus it can change the behavior of the organization overall in addition to that of the individual officer.

The evidence showing the current emphasis on referrals to counseling and on fitness evaluations provides further support for increasing the monitoring function. The need for earlier interventions, which monitoring would provide, parallels the metaphor of "broken windows," which in a community are signs of deterioration viewed as forerunners of more serious criminal problems. The metaphor could be applied to human behavior within the police organization. Police managers should pay attention to the signals of deterioration in officer behavior, the behavioral equivalent of "broken windows," *before* it results in excessive force complaints.

Rethinking the Role of Police Psychologists

The study findings indicate the lack of a coherent strategy to systematically integrate the functions performed by psychologists that are relevant to the use of excessive force. Police departments do not appear to use psychologists as a consistent resource; rather, they use them on an "as needed" basis and as protection against liability from charges of negligence. There should be a greater emphasis on involving the police psychologist in a proactive approach to managing human resources. Screening out potential violators, counseling problem officers, and evaluating them for fitness to perform their duties are critical activities, but there is a strong need for ongoing prevention activities that lead to early identification of problems and timely intervention.

Within this context, the prevalence of excessive force needs to be considered as symptomatic of a systemwide problem that implicates administrative policies as well as key elements of the human resource system: selection, training, and supervision. These services should be integrated into a structure that maximizes the impact on the individual officer and on the department overall.

Simply using a new screening test or trying a new training program will only continue the piecemeal approach. It will not achieve the balance needed in the structure between predicting excessive force and managing it. A more balanced approach encourages attending to the front end of the system (selection) while building in safeguards throughout (monitoring, training, and supervision).

35

Retirement:
A New Chapter,
Not the End of the Story

Bill Rehm

Recently, an officer whom I supervise told me that he had decided to resign from the department. I could hardly hide my surprise; the veteran officer had been an above-average employee throughout his career and was only 5 years away from retirement.

At the same time, though, I understood his restlessness. Some time before, I had left the department to work in the private sector. Five years later, I returned to the department.

A subsequent discussion with the officer revealed that he had few plans for his next career move. Through several long talks, I helped convince him to stay with the department. Today, although the officer is looking forward to retirement and exploring future career options, he continues to serve the department with distinction, and in fact, is one of my best employees.

Nearly all police managers can cite similar experiences with officers in their departments. What compels some officers nearing retirement to decide to leave early? Why do other officers continue to stay long after their commitment to service and dedication to duty have waned?

It has been my experience that three central factors—career challenges, finances, and the psychological effects of withdrawal—play a crucial role in determining an officer's relationship with the department as the prospect of retirement approaches. By understanding these factors, agency administrators will be more informed to help officers look ahead toward their retirement. Administrators also can help officers realize that with a little planning in these areas, retirement from a law enforcement agency is not merely the end of a familiar way of life but the beginning of a new life with new challenges.

Retirement Issues

Career Challenges

Maintaining career challenges encourages job satisfaction and prevents frustration. However, efforts to promote job satisfaction in law enforcement may have the unintended consequence of making the prospect of retirement seem unappealing by comparison. As one writer put it, "The more satisfying the career, the more difficult it is to shape a satisfactory retirement."[1]

Of course, this is not to say that law enforcement agencies should not strive continually to provide new challenges to their officers. However, as officers begin to approach retirement age, agencies should encourage them to pursue opportunities outside their departments.

Unfortunately, law enforcement abounds with examples of officers who remain with their departments beyond their effective years. Often, these officers become the focus of jokes among other members of the department. Such scenarios are not only tragic endings to otherwise fine careers, but they also threaten the morale of entire departments.

For these reasons, agencies should counsel officers nearing retirement age to explore challenges outside the confines of the department. This will help them appreciate the many opportunities open to them after retirement and help them see that there is life outside the police work.

Finances

The Bureau of Labor estimates that individuals require an income equal to approximately 70 to 80 percent of their working income to maintain the same standard of living after retirement.[2] Undoubtedly, retirees in any field experience some anxiety about maintaining their standard of living.

A study of retiring Canadian police officers found that their concerns about retiring revolved primarily around income rather than "changed social circumstance or inactivity."[3] However, some officers use money as an excuse to remain with their departments. The truth is that typical retirement packages provide ample income, especially when supplemented by income from a second career or a part-time job.

---

1. Leonard Harrison, "The More Satisfying the Career, the More Difficult It Is to Shape a Satisfactory Retirement," *Police Chief*, October 1981.

2. John G. Stratton, "Letting Go: Retirement," *Police Passages*, (Manhattan Beach, CA: Glennon Publishing, 1984), 277–285.

3. Dennis Forcese and Joseph Cooper, "Police Retirement: Career Succession or Obsolescence?" *Canadian Police Journal*, 1985.

Consider, for example, the retirement-versus-working income of a typical captain in my department. Under our retirement plan, the captain's eligibility options include 70 percent of salary with 20 years of service or 80 percent of salary with 22 years and 10 months of service. The exact amount of the pension is computed from the employee's 3 highest salaried years.

Suppose that this captain has reached the higher threshold of 22 years, 10 months, making him eligible to retire with 80 percent of his salary. Now he is working on the highest 3 years of pay. The captain's gross monthly salary is $4,324. Current deductions, including a monthly contribution to the retirement fund of $429, lower his take-home pay to $2,922 per month. If he retired at the conclusion of 2 years at captain's pay, he would receive $3,023 per month. Subtracting $512 in monthly deductions leaves a take-home pay of $2,511 per month. By remaining 1 more year with the department, he will increase his take-home pay by $300 per month.

However, if the captain remains past this point, he actually will be working for diminishing returns. An additional year paid into the retirement fund will increase his net pay by only $40 per month. This equates to less than minimum wage at a part-time job. An experienced police professional is worth far more than that in the open job market. Analysis of this type should demonstrate to officers that remaining with the department past their retirement eligibility often is a poor financial decision.

Psychology

Many officers who remain past retirement age are not as discouraged by the financial aspects of retirement as by the psychological aspects. As officers make the transition to retirement, they find themselves leaving a job in which they personified authority and responsibility; they were empowered to solve many of the community's problems and authorized by law to take a person's life if necessary.

The day of retirement means losing many years of identity and fraternity, as well as the right to hold the symbols of authority, including uniform, badge, and weapon. In one of life's little ironies, the officer is about to join the ranks of a population often derided by police officers—civilians.

A key psychological factor contributing to many officers' decision to stay on the job past their retirement eligibility revolves around unfulfilled needs described by Maslow's Theory of Self Actualization. As some officers look back on their careers, they cannot see any signs of lasting impact on the department and the community that they served for so long. The significant contributions of a career in public service seem washed away by the circular procedure of placing the same individuals in prison on multiple occasions for short periods of time.

Although this condition is not easily overcome, neither the affected officers nor their departments are served well by allowing officers to remain on the job while they attempt to resolve the need. Agencies should address the perils of self-actualization through counseling before officers reach retirement age.

Retiring officers face additional psychological pressure related to the loss of structure that their police careers gave their daily lives. Some officers leave their departments only to spend long days or months looking for another job. A few seclude themselves in their homes and turn to alcohol to fill the void left in their lives by their retirements. Such worse-case scenarios are not only tragic but avoidable.

Retiring officers often sell themselves and their abilities short. Supervisors hear such comments as, "What could I do? All I have ever been is a cop." Officers retiring in their late 40s or 50s have many quality years left. They have made split-second decisions on a daily basis throughout their careers. They have interacted with people from all walks of life and in almost every conceivable situation. They have calmly resolved highly charged and emotional confrontations, responded to natural disasters, and tended to people with serious injuries. Administrators should ensure that retiring officers appreciate how unique and marketable these skills are.

Helping Officers Prepare for Retirement

Clearly, pressure relating to retirement issues can affect the psychological well-being of employees. In fact, retirement ranks as the ninth leading cause of stress in the United States.[4] However, despite the many serious retirement issues, a 1988 survey revealed that fewer than 15 percent of law enforcement agencies in the country provided retirement counseling for their employees.[5]

Police agencies' strengths generally lie in mobilizing resources and developing contingency and operational plans for various situations. But, sadly, they often fall short at developing their most important resources — their own employees. However, agencies can take a number of fairly simple steps to alleviate their employees' concerns and assist them in preparing for an active and satisfying retirement.

---

4. James T. Chandler, Ph. D., "The Transition to Retirement," *Law Enforcement Technology,* March 1991.

5. R.P. Delprino and C. Bahn, "National Survey of the Extent and Nature of Psychological Services in Police Departments," *Professional Psychology: Research and Practice,* August 1988.

Career Planning and Counseling

Career planning and counseling should begin in the academy and play an important role in all evaluations throughout an officer's career. Supervisors should focus heavily on career counseling with officers during their last 5 years of employment. Counseling sessions should stress that an officer is engaged in a *career* in public safety rather than a *job* with a specific police organization. Likewise, command staffs should design training paths to guide officers toward a lifetime career. Officers should be shown the utility of their chosen specialty, not only in their current capacity but also in terms of enhancing their marketability after retirement from the agency.

Academy counseling sessions should include a form that guides officers in developing a written career path. The form should help the officers identify specialties that they would like to pursue. As the officers meet career challenges, supervisors should revise and update these forms during subsequent performance reviews.

As officers approach retirement, career planning counselors should encourage those who have not decided upon their next career moves to consider returning to school. Because the retiring officers probably have not attended school on a regular basis for many years, counselors should assist them by locating proper funding perhaps by making the initial contacts with the learning institutions. Everyone from displaced factory workers to former prison inmates takes advantage of the self-enhancement and increased marketability that continuing education provides. Retiring police officers should be no exception.

Financial Planning

Career counseling also should include an explanation of how lifestyle choices affect long-term comfort and opportunity. Young officers untrained in financial matters may not grasp the ramifications of their actions. A seemingly simple decision, such as establishing a personal savings program, could have important long-term consequences.

For example, an officer who invests $100 a month in a savings account at an interest rate of 3.9% would have $36,431 at the end of 20 years. If this officer chose to deposit the same amount of money over the same period of time but transferred the balance every 12 months to a certificate of deposit yielding 5.5%, the officer would have $45,624 at the end of 20 years.[6]

6. Ms. Colette Tyler, Customer Service Representative, Sunwest Bank in Albuquerque, New Mexico, interviewed by author, November 1995.

To help clarify the advantages and drawbacks of alternative savings programs, agencies could arrange to have financial planners discuss investment opportunities with officers. In fact, most investment services would offer to deliver such presentations free of charge. Likewise, agencies could arrange to have outside experts discuss how health and leisure choices also can affect long-term opportunities for officers.

When officers are 5 years from retirement, administrators should hold a special counseling session for them and their spouses. The administrators should explain projected monthly income and other retirement benefits and services. Administrators should also illustrate to the officers and their spouses that the characteristics required of a career law enforcement official are equally in demand and marketable outside the department. The rewards and disadvantages of the job should be reviewed and compared to what the world outside the department can offer.

Effective counseling will help officers face retirement with eager interest in the challenges that lay before them. Counseling will also help alleviate officers' concerns about their families' ability to cope with the financial aspects of retirement.

Psychological Support

The psychological aspects of retirement may affect officers in a wide range of ways. Agencies can help relieve some of the psychological pressures that officers nearing retirement face simply by fostering a supportive environment.

Administrators should support establishment of a retired officers association (ROA) within the umbrella of the agency's officers association. Once established, the ROA could help show officers the benefits of retirement, assist with networking for social and employment needs, and help officers fill their self-actualization needs by showing them some of the positive changes that have taken place in the community over time as a result of the department's efforts. Just as important, the ROA can lead the retired officers in a direction that ensures their contributions to the community do not come to an end.

Employment Assistance

The ROA or counselors made available by the department also should refer officers to federal, state, local, and private agencies or organizations that offer various forms of assistance to retirees. Organizations such as the American Association of Retired Persons can provide valuable information to retirees and may be able to assist them with job placement at no charge.

Police agencies can train retiring officers in skills they will need for the job search, such as preparing resumes, writing letters to prospective employers, and developing effective job interviewing techniques. In addition, the ROA could compile lists of companies looking for employees with specific skills and recommend retiring officers to firms with positions to fill.

Agencies should also consider rehiring a limited number of retired officers as civilian employees. By doing so, departments retain a valuable resource—employees with years of experience and in-depth training. At the same time, retired officers can enter a new phase of their careers within a familiar organizational structure.

Like all civilian employees, retired officers can perform a host of clerical functions. However, agencies can also use retired officers in various specialty operations, including community policing programs, special problem assignments, and internal affairs investigations. After all, who knows more about police work than a career service officer? This cost-effective placement approach also frees active duty officers for other assignments and offers a valuable training resource to officers assigned to work with the retirees.

Honoring Retirees

Finally, agencies should help retiring officers celebrate this important life transition. Acknowledging the officers' contributions and achievements before fellow officers, family, and friends can address many psychological needs and resolve some potential problems before they arise.

Commanders should ensure that an officer's gun and badge—important symbols of a long association with the department—are given as gifts to the retiree. It is only right that agencies take time to show their appreciation for the service rendered by retiring officers. It also is in the best interest of agencies that retiring officers leave happy, not unfulfilled to go home to torment their families and speak ill of their departments.

Conclusion

Retirement from a law enforment agency can be a bitter-sweet proposition. Although logic dictates that officers should look forward to enjoying the benefits of a much less stressful lifestyle, experience shows that many retiring officers look back on their careers and feel that their lives after retirement will be considerably less fulfilling. Agencies should take steps to make the transition to retirement as smooth and painless as possible.

After all, retirement is a natural phase of the career cycle that offers benefits both to departments and officers. Departments gain opportunities to promote, which helps morale. Retirement of command officers also allows departments to place individuals with new ideas into the management force.

Retired officers can explore new opportunities to use their experience and training. They are free to find new roles in different organizations, interact with those outside the law enforcement profession, and perhaps earn more money.

By developing a comprehensive program to prepare officers for the career, financial, and psychological challenges of retirement, agencies can help take some of the mystery out of what lies beyond. Retirement does not end the story; it merely begins a new chapter.